W9-AEI-683

IDEALISM, POLITICS AND HISTORY

Cambridge Studies in the History and Theory of Politics

IDEALISM, POLITICS
AND HISTORY

SOURCES OF HEGELIAN THOUGHT

BY

GEORGE ARMSTRONG KELLY

Associate Professor of Politics
Brandeis University

CAMBRIDGE
AT THE UNIVERSITY PRESS
1969

Published by the Syndics of the Cambridge University Press
Bently House, 200 Euston Road, London N.W.1.
American Branch: 32 East 57th Street, New York, N.Y. 10022
Library of Congress Catalogue Card Number: 73–85721
Standard Book Number: 521 07510 6

Printed in Great Britain by
Alden & Mowbray Ltd
at the Alden Press, Oxford

PRO OMNIBUS ANIMAE SPIRITUSQUE
MAGISTRIS

CONTENTS

Contents

Contents

PREFACE

Happily there is no need to compliment data processing centres and munificent foundations on their timely support. Generous friends and wise teachers have meant all. The setting of my own 'phenomenology' has been Harvard University; its masters were Louis Hartz, who first whetted my appetite for political philosophy, and Judith N. Shklar, who sustained and refined it. My debt to them both is profound. Need I say, in acknowledging their influence with more than gratitude, that the positions taken here must not be imputed to them? While a student I also benefited from the insights of John Rawls and Harvey C. Mansfield, Jr. on idealist political philosophy. A longtime friend Eugene C. Black, my present faculty colleague at Brandeis University, helped me with an earlier version of this manuscript. And Mrs. Shklar was an inspired source of suggestion as I laboured to reshape the essay.

Audrey Ball, Claire Murray, Patricia Fleming, and Sally Cox steadfastly saw the typing along; I could not wish for better collaborators. My wife and children knew when to console me and were sportsmanlike enough to tolerate the march of Abstract Nouns through the house.

Some of the arguments and analyses presented here made earlier and differently garbed appearances, notably: 'Notes on Hegel's "Lordship and Bondage"', *The Review of Metaphysics* (June 1966); 'Rousseau, Kant and History', *Journal of the History of Ideas* (July 1968); 'The Structure and Spirit of Legality in Kant', *The Journal of Politics* (May 1969); and my critical introduction to Johann Gottlieb Fichte, *Addresses to the German Nation* (New York; Harper Torchbooks, 1968). I thank these editors and publishers collectively for permission to repossess my wares. The Presses Universitaires Françaises have kindly allowed me to reproduce Jules Vuillemin's chart of Fichte's genesis of the consciousness on page 215.   G.A.K.

Cambridge, Massachusetts
October 1968

x

PART ONE

INTRODUCTION

INTRODUCTION

Between the Indian summer of the *ancien régime* and the evanescent 'restoration' of post-Revolutionary continental Europe perceptions of the upwardly mobile intellectual classes took a decisive turn from nostalgia to anticipation, from criticism to intimations of dynamism. When Boulanger wrote in the *Encyclopedia* that 'the mind of men living in civilized states has been more or less the same throughout the ages; the difference lies only in the way it is used',[1] he was reflecting the Enlightenment's confidence in fixed nature, man's place in the world, and the causal reliability of the universe. But not half a century later, beyond the Revolution, that natural posture of harmony is shattered; a Romantic like Novalis can write of recent events as the 'stirrings of a puberty crisis'.[2]

There are many ways of tracing this development. An obvious one is through the impact of the events themselves: the traditional province of the historian. Another way is to keep events on the margin while dwelling chiefly on their relation to what may be called the historical consciousness, and by determining how conceptions of world history govern the interpretation of these events. By 'historical consciousness' I mean a sequential explanation of human and natural purpose, oriented toward collective human need and design, and bridging with its implicit time-span the gap between cosmological and logical visions of man's destiny. The work that follows is an attempt of the latter sort. Because it is not itself intended as an essay in philosophical history, but rather as an empirical treatment of the range and development of a number of basic themes, the arguments and methods should be made as clear as possible at the outset. That is the task of this introduction, taken at the risk of assuming the results of some of the investigations that follow.

[1] Article 'Prodige', *Encyclopédie ou Dictionnaire raisonné des arts, des sciences et des métiers* (17 vols., Paris, 1751–65), XIII, 423.
[2] Novalis, *Blütenstaübe*, no. 105, in C. Seelig (ed.), *Gesammelte Werke* (5 vols., Herrliberg-Zurich, 1943), II, 36.

Introduction

In the first instance, we might ask how the pursuit of an idealist tradition centres upon our problem, and how that tradition should be designated. Idealism has a multitude of shifty meanings and some precise philosophical ones. In the course of this essay it will be evident that the question is not one of demolishing or establishing idealism as a philosophical position, but of relating the consequences of the position to political tensions at the turn of the nineteenth century. The interest here, most especially, is in the political consequences of idealist systems as they came to be manifested in this period in Germany. Three of the four figures I treat are, by accepted definition, philosophical idealists; the fourth, Rousseau, is not. Yet Rousseau is both a foil and a groundwork for subsequent idealist systems, both in the ethical and political spheres. He is, by common consent of intellectual historians and by virtue of his later resonances, a pathbreaker of idealism as well as of romanticism, though his connection with either of these positions is at best ambiguous.

The way in which Rousseau—as much by his pedagogical doctrines as by his political theory of the 'general will' and 'social contract'—challenged the ingenuity of German political thought is well known and need not be rehearsed at this point. Rousseau is the first great modern philosopher of 'will' and 'community'.

My use of the notion 'idealism' is fairly restrictive and is not to be confused with common terminology. I am not speaking of brave efforts to bring better worlds into being. I am concerned specifically with the following ideas: (1) the explicit belief that man experiences and is composed of material and spiritual natures and that his awareness of the latter *should*, *might* and *does* progressively fashion his experience in the world; (2) the philosophical notion that the proof of the reality of the world demands recognition of this fact; (3) the relation of man, thus conceived, to a state or political society predicated on the fact that the vocations of both relate to this higher urgency; (4) the character and role of anticipatory norms or 'ideas' that cannot simply be fashioned out of empirical concepts as the epistemological form of these proceedings; (5) the belief that the concepts of time and space which extend and bound man's image of his endeavours are supplied by the human consciousness and not by the objective reality of things; (6) the form of the political community that incorporates the truth of these notions. Other ramifications must await their place in the subsequent exposition.

This general, and, one can say in anticipation, most complex evolution, fascinating in itself, is useful also for tracing a predominant current in European culture. Idealism creates a tension not felt in other traditions of European thought. In oversimplified terms, if one imagines a magnet of the ideal and a magnetized object of the real, it is not difficult to see how both a tension and a history are possible. Realist theories confine historical propulsion to the natural tendencies of the object. In idealism, the theories to be explored set moral goals against present deficiency, constructing a motor of history, and incidentally a purposive pattern of political life, from this tension. Having conceived a deep division between nature, sense and impulse, and spirit, wisdom and moral aptitude, idealism regards the problem of harmony and its recovery with particular urgency. In this perspective, a history of mind or spirit is gradually developed to parallel, or, better, express the inner reality of events.[1] Realist theories, even evolutionary ones, do not meet this issue so frontally.

A second point concerns the relation of this examination to the traditional issues of political philosophy. There are libraries of books and monographs, many of them excellent, that deal systematically with the theories of the state of Rousseau, Kant, Fichte and Hegel, or with their particular views on obligation, consent, authority, legitimacy and so forth. Without in any way deprecating that kind of inquiry, I have conceived my task differently. The customary form of political analysis is not eschewed where it casts light on how notions of historical genesis and the analytical substance of political issues meet. But the reader should not expect an encyclopedia of political *explications de texte*. Rather, I am anxious to establish a contextual basis, partly indebted to surrounding event and partly to permanent philosophical issues, for the understanding of idealist political theory.

---

[1] This essay will not, however, contribute to the polemic waged over the word 'progress'; for career and ramifications, see W. Warren Wagar, 'Modern Views on the Origins of Progress', *Journal of the History of Ideas* (Jan.–Mar. 1967), pp. 55–70.

Introduction

The usefulness of such a context should not be in dispute. When the intellectual milieu of these thinkers is ignored, when alien situations are read back upon them, or when the political parts of their *Weltanschauungen* are abruptly extracted from the whole, interpretations arise that are in wilful discord with each other over issues that might have been settled by an appeal to the intellectual concerns and strategies of the period. My prejudice here is to see political philosophy as a point of convergence and not as a settled domain of its own. Thus I shall not hesitate to trespass in a wider field in the hope of furnishing more valid political readings. In serving this goal, I have tried consciously to keep the discourse midway between the unmanageable richness of particular fact and the abstract realm of timeless political problems.

This search for a context should not be confused with any claim to have furnished *the* context. Approaches to such an 'open' topic are numberless; some are highly valid. This study is neither *Ideengeschichte* in the grand manner nor an expression of the radical truth stripped of accident. However, I would not have chosen particular themes and methods if I did not believe in their capacity to illuminate that world cleaved temporally by the French Revolution and spatially by the Rhine.

Thirdly, then, we must comment on the political significance of the development of the historical consciousness. I do not personally believe in attaching progressive connotations to this nettlesome phrase. But my own philosophical views are not at issue here, except in the sense that they may unobtrusively clarify the issues raised. The critical question might be phrased differently: to what extent is politics carried away by history—not just by history as experienced, but by formulas of history? Now it is fairly evident that collective beliefs in human destiny—whether they are mystic, eschatological, or secular—and the structures and habits of political communities react on one another. How could we decisively say that political forms inspire historical visions, or vice-versa? Unhappily, even if the question is insoluble, the subject is unavoidable. On the anthropological level, we see forms and functions generating ideas. However, when we remove the issue to the level of philosophical speculation, we cannot be so sure that a sense of destiny does not

4

sometimes govern function, producing at the same time political change and expansion of consciousness. In other words, we may envisage models where truth draws life in its wake—for the purpose of either justifying, guiding, changing or repugning the latter. The modern philosophies of Europe are characteristically secular. This means they do not 'repugn' life, but that they adopt one of the three other strategies. If this is true, it means that they must grapple with life, implying, at the greatest circumference, the largest organized and self-aware sphere of life, which is the political community. We shall see how idealism grasps this problem in a particular way.

If we take history to mean some intelligible pattern of human achievement over time, we shall discern that as philosophy reflects on political existence it must also cultivate an attitude toward history.[1] In ancient philosophy, the notion of recurrent cycles was at least tacitly adopted (or some similar metaphor of flux and reflux); in Christian philosophy, the idea of Providence provided for both the instrumentalism and the transience of secular politics; in geometric and strict rationalism—if there ever was such a thing— the temporality of the historical dimension was generally foreclosed by the timeless clarity of deduction; in empiricism, the cumulative weight of conventional experience as a guide to politics was emphasized; and, finally, in modern idealism, the notion of history as an immanent teleology came to the fore with important consequences for the role of the political community as a special participant in the stream of time.

The last of these aspects of historical consciousness, its genesis and development, and its implications for the understanding of political life will be our special concern. Of course, the destiny of history no more rules life than does the foreknowledge of death rule the motions of the human body. Even in abstruse formulations of philosophy, as we shall see amply, there is prodigious feedback from actuality to the structures of logical truth. I should be prepared to say that the post-Enlightenment civilization of the West records,

---

[1] It may be, as Frank Manuel ingeniously argues, in *Shapes of Philosophical History* (Stanford, 1965), that all historical perceptions are more or less intricately related to those two basic spatial symbols of time, the straight line and the circle. However, this is not an adequate *point de départ* for our present subject.

for better or worse, a growing conquest of destiny by actuality, a sacrifice, as Pitirim Sorokin would put it, of the *aevum* to the *tempus*.[1]

Nevertheless, in the climate of idealist philosophy, which arose, as is well known, out of an extremely disembodied and unsatisfying political culture,[2] there is considerable justification for tracing the pattern of political thought from destiny toward life, for interpreting the theory of the political community in the light of a hypothetical development which the grasp of history must provide. As a result, the 'context' I am establishing contains this presumption, not as a dogmatic *a priori* but as a guide: by working out these implications I attempt to explain the political problems the philosophers themselves faced. To put it more simply: given such-and-such a vision of history (and there is the necessity of first showing how the vision was constructed), what are the political consequences that follow from this total picture of man-in-the-world?

I am not uncritical of the notion just proposed, and shall be questioning it as well as exploring it. I adopt this method because of its utility for this special set of problems, not because I am committed to it philosophically or necessarily regard it as fruitful for explaining intellectual history in general. There are no hidden assumptions about the meaning of history or the structure of knowledge in this essay. Although an empiricist by conviction, I have tried to give the idealist position a sympathetic presentation. Mainly I have tried to allow the philosophers to speak for themselves and criticize each other in terms of the world they experienced.

If it strikes one at first glance that my interpretation collides with the familiar 'ideological' (the notion that ideas are determined by social environment) explanation of bourgeois political philosophy, the conflict is in some ways more apparent than real.[3] It seems to me beyond dispute that each of my four subjects was determined by his 'situation', though not necessarily by his class—there are many gaps in our understanding of pre-industrial vocations or classes—as much

---

[1] Pitirim Sorokin, *Sociocultural Space, Time, Causality* (Durham, 1943), p. 215.

[2] See ahead, especially Part III, Chapter 1.

[3] It is quite conceivable to interpret a situation 'ideologically' and still to grant transcendence to major components or themes of the situation, thus avoiding extremes of 'historicism' and *sub specie aeternitatis* dogmatism.

as by temperament and profession (or lack of it). But a major constituent of that milieu was a tradition of ideas, an inheritance of higher forms of discourse and argument and the urge to deploy them systematically. On the whole, psychology may be the best matrix for reconciling these two positions. Perhaps when we understand much more about how to apply what psychological research in time-perception can show us concerning class and professional attitudes and the transmission of philosophical ideas in historical situations, this will be a feasible and illuminating undertaking. For the present, it remains chiefly in the realm of literature and folklore.

Fourthly, it should be clearly understood that I do not claim to have treated Hegel except in the context of the issues raised in the preceding parts of the essay. One cannot lay this kind of groundwork and still have space to do Hegel justice. Of course Hegel terminates this flowering of the idealist tradition, and gives rise to many problems outside my present scope. And so it is the 'near side' of Hegel, or Hegel in relation to his predecessors, that will occupy our attention. This study suggests that any reinterpretation of Hegel should take its perspectives into serious account; but that labour is not attempted here in depth. However, one need not make Hegel teleological to guarantee his importance and enduring fascination.

I shall now proceed to further clarifications of method and theme:

1. *The perspective.* I have attempted to develop my explanations from a perspective of the period covered. Of course, I have benefited from secondary source material, but I have made conscious efforts not to recharge idealist political thought for posterior purposes and have, in some instances, pointed out where this was done. The creative re-creation of political philosophy is undeniably an important undertaking, but it is outside the limits of this essay.

2. *The relation of metaphysics and politics.* Where a political theorist is also a complete philosopher (like Hobbes or Hume), his branches of inquiry energize each other, in many ways explain each other, and should not be abruptly lifted out of context. However, among realist philosophers in general, where a close connection between human nature and the proper organization of life in common is conceded from the outset, the extraction of political philosophy from the comprehensive thought structure need

not lead to grave distortion. In the case of the present study, the question is more serious. Here politics not only accords with the system, but has a strategic place in it. Without sound notions of Kant's epistemology or Hegel's ontology one may discover their political formulations to be impenetrable. Consequently, it is impossible to evade the major issues of being and knowledge when we approach idealist politics. I have also explored Rousseau, who quite properly denied being a philosopher, in these terms, in order to exhibit the continuities and discontinuities of the philosophical assumptions underlying his political speculation and to establish more precisely Rousseau's own tradition and what he brought to the development of idealism.

There are also two general relationships between metaphysics and politics that should be distinguished. The first is the notion of government (or law or political theory) as occupying a particular and necessary place in the idealist cathedral of knowledge (the systemic aspect). The second is the notion that within a historical teleology (however generated), the Idea of political forms or of a community develops according to a postulated (moral or practical) necessity. Hegel's general contribution was to assimilate these two patterns of discourse to each other.

3. *A lacuna: international relations.* The implications of the idealist tradition for international relations theory have attracted repeated and concentrated attention, especially in connection with the rise of modern European nationalism. While the subject is far too important to exclude from the present work, I have kept it on the periphery of the argument both for lack of space and because, generally, its structure can be derived from the problems of community that are analysed here. I am not entirely sanguine about this omission.

4. *The cultural variable.* Having raised transcultural problems by inaugurating a chiefly German study with an essay on Rousseau, I am obliged to state my attitude toward this tricky matter. First of all it is important to know that Rousseau was Swiss and not French, that Geneva, as Spink and others have shown,[1] informed his perception of political culture even if in a highly idealized and

[1] See especially, John Stephenson Spink, *Jean-Jacques Rousseau et Genève* (Paris, 1934).

distorted way, and that 'political' France interested Rousseau very marginally except on the occasions when it interfered with his life. Secondly, it is equally important that Rousseau was a rather complete child of French culture, in whose stream he was such a deviant and revitalizing influence; consequently, it is the French intellectual setting alone which gives meaning to Rousseau's quarrel with the world. Thirdly, there is the matter of the complicated German adoption of Rousseau—especially by the turbulent but apolitical *Sturm und Drang*—as an ally against courtliness, rococo, absolutism and the bare rationalism of the Enlightenment. Fourthly, and in a way difficult to separate from the third point, there is the assimilation by the idealist philosophers of certain aspects of Rousseau's political voluntarism and attack on 'dogmatism'. I shall try to explain these things in the proper place.

Here, we can say the following. The Germans perceived Rousseau as Swiss, not as French, i.e. as the citizen of a *Kleinstaat*. Paradoxically, the Germans appreciated Rousseau for his 'Gothic' values, rather than his 'classic' ones, which are a good deal more evident to the student of politics. Conversely, Rousseau cannot be understood *ex post facto* in the light of an idealist philosophy that he helped inspire, since his own frame of reference was quite different. Yet the German reaction to Franco-cosmopolitan value structure of the eighteenth century—in its manifold variations—was made in part under the standard of the man who had had the temerity to call the French 'eux'.[1] It is against this larger picture that Rousseau's contributions to German political philosophy must be measured.

The study of idealism as a phenomenon *per se* will not have to deal so much with the problem of cultural transmission across the Rhine as with the reaction of the German (especially literary) consciousness. Indeed, when we come to put the whole problem of historical teleology in perspective, we shall discern a striking and profound difference between Rousseau and the idealists. And this discrepancy is to be explained partly by a persisting German tradition with mystical and religious attachments, partly by the 'spirit of the time' itself.

[1] See L. Reynaud, *Histoire générale de l'influence française en Allemagne* (Paris, 1915), p. 401.

9

Introduction

5. *The choice of subjects.* This is an extraordinarily fertile period for speculation as well as event. Why then is the analysis limited to four persons: Rousseau, Kant, Fichte, Hegel? Why not Condorcet or Herder, Humboldt or Constant? Why no Englishman? The last question is answered simply: there is no desire to create a cultural potpourri, or to abstract ideas entirely from their cultural sources.[1] As regards the first question, there are three good answers. The figures chosen describe an idealist tradition as I have used the term. They are, however, probably the four most important political philosophers of their period (I suffer the raising of eyebrows, no doubt, when Fichte is given eminence over Burke; Bentham I would be inclined to concede, but he is chiefly extraneous to the problems I discuss). Finally, and most importantly, within the idealist mutation, these thinkers illustrate cardinal developments with regard to the problem of the historical consciousness and its entangled involvement with theories of the political community. In the remainder of the introduction, I shall specify the way this comes about.

The next task will be to state in brief the principal themes of the inquiry. Only then will it be possible to orchestrate them in the present overture.

I call the first theme the problem of time-consciousness. Time-consciousness is both a matter of psychological and philosophical perception: it regulates life and it helps to define reality. The connection between these two modes is not altogether clear, and

---

[1] During the period I analyse, the much-heralded unity of Enlightenment thought (recently reasserted for us with brilliance and exaggeration by Peter Gay, *The Enlightenment, an Interpretation: The Rise of Modern Paganism*, New York, 1966) was decomposing—subject first of all to the widening cleavage between what Michael Oakeshott has termed *nomocratic* and *telocratic* views of society, secondly to the literal polarization caused by the French Revolution, and thirdly to the related rise of modern nationalism. In their own ways, Bentham and Hegel both attempt to bestride these contradictions. By the time of Madame de Staël, to be an *Aufklärer* did not mean to make 'Europe' one's nation and move effortlessly from place to place without leaving home, but rather to have a superior and comprehending view of its differences. In part, Pitt was able to fight France as effectively as he did because of this schism; as Richard Cobb writes ('The English Jacobins and the French Revolution', in Peter Amann [ed.], *The Eighteenth Century Revolution: French or Western*, Boston, 1963, p. 23): 'The English Jacobins were essentially foreigners in their own country, isolated from the masses who loathed them as hard-driving bosses, and ineffective as a pressure group.'

has occupied thinkers of the first calibre from the Eleatics on. These strains contribute to both the intellectualization and the sense of history. The issue is central to this study, for it is highly important to grasp Rousseau's essential orientation toward the past, Kant's subtle and ambiguous futurism, Fichte's progress to a futuristic chiliasm, and Hegel's Apollonian justification of the eternal present, and to see these strains in interactions with each other and events.

Second is the problem of analogy. Idealism tends to exalt the model of mind (which it sometimes calls ego or intelligence, and which Rousseau, in a more hedonistic context, called the 'moi') as the paramount structure of the entire universe which mind can comprehend. Whether these procedures are mere analogies, metaphors of being, or true metaphysical extensions of reality is of course a question which one must answer from one's own philosophical standpoint. But in the following pages we shall see the state both as a surrogate for nature (Rousseau) and as a model of mind (Kant). More important, we shall see the problem in its generative aspect, where both mind and world are seen as having parallel odysseys, and we shall examine how and why such theories arose.

Third is the problem of the transcendent object. I do not intend to treat this question as a philosopher, but merely to note its appearance as a fairly substantial political symbol within a philosophical school that treated politics as a reflection of epistemology. The idealist tradition sought with ever-increasing rigour to promote the subject's power over the external world. Politically the attempt can be associated with the general modern philosophical attack against the 'transcendent' institutions of Church and Crown, the rise of individualism, and the construction of personal and immanent standards of morality and worship. But idealism, fed by a spirituality that fluctuated between pantheist and mystical poles, also saw dangers in all ontological objectification. Mind's goal was to shape its world rationally by dissolving natural resistance or 'otherness'.

Fourth is the problem of the 'second nature'. Greek political philosophy taught that it was man's nature to live in society. However, the intervening Christian centuries had instilled the belief that human nature was 'fallen' and that political institutions were a consequence of man's tendency toward lawlessness and his need for an earthly order with which he could identify. The Romans had, in the meantime, suggested that adherence to custom or habit furnished the 'second nature' of man. Both neo-classicism and Cartesian rationalism agreed that man has a 'nature' which is essentially good and harmonious. The problem was to recapture it by removing error, superstition and abuse. But nature could be known by reason: thus the natural state was a rational state, and one was permitted to speak of a 'state of nature' as a quasi-primitive, quasi-mythical ideal. Robbed of all systematic historical association, it was useful to political theory as a tablet on which original rights could be inscribed. But where it acquired historical connotations—under the impact of the classics and voyages of discovery—it induced nostalgia and utopian melancholy. Modern idealism exalted the 'second nature', not as 'custom', as antiquity would have it, but as the capacities of the moral person abstracted from his fleshly desires. It became, by that token, a spur to future utopias and increasingly concrete definitions of the historical process of fulfilment.

Fifth is the problem of legality and morality, central to all that is today disparagingly called 'normative' political theory. To obey the laws and to obey one's conscience may be in critical conflict; yet the one may be necessary to the coherence of the social order and the other to one's dignity as a person. Can moral teachings be used to fashion legal imperatives? Or, conversely, how is it possible for the positive legal system to be moral at all, if one subscribes to an ethics of intention and treats external coercion as phenomenal? Can justice create external conditions for the moral life? Can one deduce a moral politics? These are some of the questions treated in our study. But beyond them there is a growing historical awareness suggesting that, over time, legality might be employed (by the consent of persons? by the judgment of the wise?) to create the discipline and harmony of a moral community.

Sixth is what I call the problem of politics and philosophical pedagogy. It is a continuing problem today, though in new formulations and disguises, and is apt to be important in any culture that speaks of 'political development' and 'modernization' in tones of either inevitability or approval. Professor Michael Walzer has

Introduction

written of the 'role of symbolism in political thought' with special reference to the transition between the medieval and modern world views.[1] The School became a powerful symbol of politics in the era I am treating, just as the Special Tutorial ('the education of princes') had been in an earlier period. The eighteenth century was an epoch of educational awareness, in which the 'classics' of modern pedagogy were written and broadcast, and works like the *Encyclopedia* spread knowledge to thousands. Idealism took over this enthusiasm from the Enlightenment, but in a necessarily peculiar fashion. Its epistemological structure and ethical teleology immediately suggested that history, as the learning process of mankind, and the education of the individual were analogous, that there was an educational imperative not just to promote individual self-fulfilment but to work toward the collective destiny of the human 'second nature'. This ideal was reflected back upon the philosophical vision of the state and political theory in general. The curiously ambivalent attitude toward Rousseau's *Emile* and the fact that the German theorists were professors are straws in the wind. Especially in Hegel, the educational problem is made parallel to the critical historical problem of mastery and slavery, and an escape is sought from the infinite demands of 'ethico-teleology', as Kant expressed it.

Seventh and last, I refer to the problem of 'life' and 'philosophy'. Here we are getting close to the core of the question of 'rational' and 'animal', the question of why man's presumably unremitting access to standards of reason cannot produce a pure will that creates a rational world. From a different angle, we confront the difficulty of the mind's apprehension of natural necessity. Hume showed, inconveniently, the cleavage between reason and existence ('matters of fact'). In Germany, Wolffian rationalism accepted a division between 'truths of reason' and 'truths of fact', the authoritarian order of the political world being of the latter sort. Rousseau held that philosophy was a *libido cognoscendi*, destructive to the balanced life of men in general. One of the critical problems of idealism was to join these pieces again. But only the upright mind, not the shattered world, could do this. Thus there is more a mood of struggle and

---

[1] Michael Walzer, 'On the Role of Symbolism in Political Thought', *Political Science Quarterly* (June 1967), pp. 191–204.

strife in idealism than one of complacency. Moreover, the relevant pattern of history, developed not from simplistic optimism but as an accompaniment to the disparity between the way men act and the way they ought to act, exacerbated by the fragility of German society and the cross-pressures of the Revolution, created an impetus for an elitism of teacher-rulers. The question was raised: with what kind of political society should men be endowed if they cannot yet conceive their proper moral destiny? But then one had further to ask: how are harmony and community possible in these terms?

These are the keynotes of the present inquiry. It remains to trace a summary of the argument which the following sections are intended to trace, clarify and establish.

One of the chief paradoxes of *Rousseau* is that, although he was an inspirer and in some ways a prognosticator of the future, his sensitive consciousness was directed toward norms of an absolute past, which commentators have not hesitated to associate with the womb, the innocence of an infra-morality, or an Eden. Moreover, Rousseau declared that his personal conviction of innocence at birth could be transferred to the whole of humanity, and he implied that the 'sense' of history must be constructed on this basis. Since, from such a point of departure, the 'sense' of history could only be bad, and since independent and unentangled man was not bad—contrary to Christian orthodoxy but not necessarily to the Pelagianizing views of eighteenth-century Christians—history was metaphysically contingent, if unstoppable. This latter fact accounts for Rousseau's despair as well as what has been called his 'conservatism', his desire to moderate, to limit the damage.

Against the whole corrupt procedures of phenomenological man in history Rousseau could oppose only exceptional and vanished ideals. Though they did not, or did not fundamentally, aim at restoring 'nature' in the primitive sense, as has sometimes been crudely charged, they did seek to provide nature-surrogates, patterns of order hurled with vain hope against the complexity, mobility, immorality and *pain* of life (ironically called 'perfectibility'). Rousseau himself called these visions of order 'chimeras', and he contrasted them absolutely with the 'prejudices' of the modern Europe he knew.

Introduction

The term 'chimera' furnishes the essential metaphor for this study. Rousseau gives us the clue that a 'chimera' is not identical with the ideal state (such as the *Social Contract* proposes) but that it signifies any conceivable situation where man can feel intact, harmonious, a valid part of the world—whether in withdrawal or in an intense and constraining social order. Rousseau was far more interested in the condition than the mechanics of the condition. But this raises an immediate problem for the study of politics. If the human ideal of a state of satisfaction is to be conceived politically in certain images, and in others not, can we easily make an artificial separation of the problem? Unfortunately we cannot. We can attempt only to give it system and synthesis, which was to be a major task of German idealism (not just its political part). This is why our investigation of Rousseau and the other figures must consider non-political writings, and must, to some extent, regard such texts as crucial. If we treat Rousseau only from the perspective of the *Social Contract* (and its antecedent tradition), we lose a great deal of Rousseau and distort his message. For he had a great variety of proposals, images and even fantasies for the possibility of order that need to be considered.

Rousseau had no historical method and little optimism for the passage from 'prejudice' to 'chimera', unless it was the prudent preservation of small, relatively primitive societies or the rebirth of the socio-political cycle of a people, a doctrine which later influenced the Robespierrist Left of the Revolution. Consequently, his most eloquent statements about liberty, morality and dignity are 'anti-histories' challenging the collective human experiment. The most comprehensive and significant one is the *Emile*, his 'best book'.

Rousseau's philosophical sense proceeded from a combination of the rationalist and empiricist traditions—not uncommon in his period and culture. Merging the latter with his pessimism, he obtained a 'phenomenology of despair', most explicit in the *Second Discourse*. From the former he derived penetrating analytical interpretations of man's moral freedom and of the legal anatomy of the just state. However, the latter two analyses are reconciled only within the phenomenological 'chimera' of Emile's education, again

15

to be questioned when the real world is thrust back upon Emile. *Emile* is against and not with history. The controlled education it recommends is not only impracticable in the world but is undertaken in a 'natural' order which history defies. *Emile* is also a paean to extreme intellectual self-limitation, to simplicity, and to a maximum of personal autonomy. Rousseau is at the antipodes of the type of politico-pedagogical orientation which, paradoxically inspired by his own work, develops in German idealism. Even though Rousseau wanted to make men citizens, he did not regard history as a cosmic tutor, and he hated inequality too much to imagine a long pedagogical ascent to as yet ungrasped values of culture and spirit. His 'second nature' involved retrenchment, if not return. Moreover, he drew an absolute distinction between gifts and works of the intellect and the average man's moral possibilities.

Kant saw Rousseau in a manner that would fit his own vision. No doubt they are close, especially in the areas of moral voluntarism, the revolt against dogma, and the attack on empirical politics; but there are two differences that balance the similarities. The first is Kant's championing of curiosity, formal inquiry and intellectual goals. Kant, in contrast to Rousseau, never drew an anti-intellectual breath, despite his desire to establish the possibility of a common ethics for all people. In his formidable epistemology Kant established a deep division between moral activity ('practical reason') and science ('theoretical reason'); but he also renewed the hope that systematic philosophy could show the way, if not to the primordial structure of the world, at least to the entire range of human possibility. His doctrine of Ideas is the cornerstone of this procedure.

In the second place Kant constructed a historical teleology as early as 1784, based on the premise that moral man needs to see progress in history, and he formally incorporated the theory into his *Critique of Judgment* in 1790. There is a large question as to whether Kant thought historically: the *Critique of Pure Reason* would seem to deny what some of the minor writings assert. However, Kant evidently found it morally necessary to propose that there is a history proceeding from worse to better (enriched also by intellectual achievement and culture), and to attempt to trace its pattern within the terms of phenomenal nature (a literal chaos which human reason

necessarily orders). If Kant never 'objectifies' history (inasmuch as
he regards the Idea of history itself as a free personal task), he at
least inaugurates the stimulus to do so, and, in some cases, suggests
the palpability of certain outcomes. In distinguishing between an
'end of nature', which is ambiguously phenomenal, and an 'end of
man', which is in the strictest sense regulative, he rejects chiliastic
premises, but at the same time gives substance to the notion of
an ideal legal community of the future. In so far as this notion is
concerned with the public possibilities for the exercise of private
freedom *via* the critical concept of legal respect, Kant's vision of
the mechanics of the state is 'liberal'.

But there are other implications to be drawn from this procedure.
In the first place, Kant, freely interpreting the *Emile* and also under
the influence of a climate of opinion that produced works like
Lessing's *Education of the Human Race*, saw the actual world in its
teleological continuity as a sphere of culture-building. He consciously equated the tasks of education with his 'end of nature' and
suggested that pedagogy was a 'discipline for freedom'. Rousseau
had made the latter point, too, but his method had been very different
from Kantian discipline. At the same time, there was an observable
correlation between the 'just tutelage' of education and the 'spirit'
of a teleological legal system working toward the Idea of the perfect
civil constitution. The question was: when did men cease to be
minors; in what sense did the moral personality of each one relate
to his participation in a political system of ends? How and in what
sense could 'discipline' be applied for the furthering of an Idea
subjectively proposed by philosophy for the sake of morality? There
is in Kant a conflict between the mechanics of republicanism and the
dynamism of a regulative Idea whose content can only be fulfilled
when all men are truly made worthy of self-government.

With his bifurcated analysis of freedom and necessity, timeless-
ness and time, spirit and letter, Kant also inaugurated an analytic
separation of morality and legality, which earlier Enlightenment
tradition had joined. Tactically a progressive move, this had certain
authoritarian implications for the future, especially in the hands of
Fichte. If the legal system, which is external and graspable, is made
not merely an analytic but a historico-teleological presupposition

of the moral community, it receives authoritative justification which Enlightenment philosophy had denied, especially to the claims of the Church.

All in all, Kant's politico-historical philosophy was a matter of subtle balances and counterweights, such as one might expect from this great watershed figure. Kant consciously sought a middle ground between revolution and reaction, with sympathies for both reform and the 'guiding thread' of continuity. Perceiving not a 'natural order' but a dialectic of 'unsocial sociability', he placed, like Rousseau, great emphasis on the internal value of order, but he also exalted the value of the intellect, as the Enlightenment had done. In wrestling with the characteristic problem of 'philosophy' and 'life', he therefore contributed obliquely to a new politics of elitism, now no longer arbitrary and hereditary but guided by philosophical qualification. He 'rationalized' Rousseau's 'chimera' by associating integrity with goals, not with origins, and he substituted a complex notion of historical justification for the idea of *bonté naturelle*.

Fichte carried some of the strains of Kantian philosophy into deep water. More 'Kantian' than Kant and more 'revolutionary' than other German intellectuals, he withdrew from the object (or 'nature') all ontological status that Kant had permitted it and he equated the first form of his philosophy, the *Wissenschaftslehre*, with the spirit of the Revolution in France. Fichte's moral and political doctrines developed from the tandem influences of his idealist epistemology and the onrush of events. An abstruse thinker, he nevertheless preached the primacy of 'act' over 'fact' and the involvement of philosophy in the 'spirit of the time'.

Unlike Kant's *Critique of Pure Reason*, which was an analysis of the powers and pitfalls of the human mind, the *Wissenschaftslehre* was a phenomenology of consciousness, a 'pragmatic history of the human mind' from its first infraconscious production of the external world, through its awakening to reality, toward its practical goals in the world. Eventually, Fichte came to construct a world history on a parallel basis, concerned with clarifying the great idealistically constructed categories of human development, culminating in 'life according to reason as art'. The processes of mind and history, both still subjectively generated by 'intellectual' or philosophical intuition in accord with moral goals, were made correlative. However, in both instances, the notion of philosophical guidance was critical: the common consciousness lagged one stage behind its intellectual preceptor until both finally reached a point where reason was shared. This history of the intelligence was set in parallel with a world history in whose 'final epoch' all would become rational and coercive institutions would vanish. The basic pattern of Fichte's pheno-menology transmitted an inevitable coercive flavour to his political system.

In the background of Fichte's attempt to superimpose the logic of the mind's expansion on history was the total separation of legality and morality in the deduction of the practical parts of the *Wissenschaftslehre*. Here, in his writings of 1796–8, Fichte proposed a preliminary legal formulation of the community of persons, an objective justice, prior to the clarification of moral relationships. His system of ethics reflected back on the largely rationalistic and atemporal system of rights a teleological setting of legal compulsion (*Notstaat*) in view of the ultimate moral community. This concept was thoroughly historicized in the *Grundzüge* lectures of 1804–5 and further sharply defined in the justification of pre-ethical state power that permeated his later writings.

Amid this development, Fichte had encountered obstacles and polemics, the loss of his chair at Jena, and the tortured vision of a Revolution aborting. Impelled by his own circumstances and the current of ideas around him in Berlin, he began a retrenchment from his earlier, Kantian cosmopolitanism toward a position of 'patriot-ism' in which the ideal Germany of the future, entering fresh and pure into the stream of history, was imagined as the 'phenomenon' of what was best and true in humanity. In the partly propagandizing, partly synoptic *Addresses to the German Nation* of 1808, he presented this position at length, contributing a cardinal document to national-ist literature. At the same time, he framed his conception of Germany in terms of the *idées forces* of his philosophical evolution.

The tension between radicalism and elitism is much greater in Fichte than in Kant. Not only is the political motivation much stronger, but one now concedes nothing to the reality of 'nature': one strives against its appearances. Fichte is in some ways radical like Rousseau, and is often called a 'Jacobin'. His ideas of social justice and social control are indeed rigorous. But his elitism is a measure of the distance between them. Unlike Rousseau, Fichte perceived a historical sequence tending toward, not away from, equality. But for the ambiguous 'meantime' he proposed, more and more stridently, a coercive leadership of the wise, of those who understood the Idea of human destiny. And since, despite the primacy of action in his philosophy, he was a professor and recondite intellectual, he preached a moralistic and pedagogical politics, indeed against Rousseau and with much greater vigour and elaboration than can be found in Kant. The German nation was to become a school with a powerful faculty, from whose number a sovereign *Zwingherr* would be chosen.

In terms of the Idea it was uncertain whether Fichte's ethical commonwealth was a realistic goal or a norm. In his later writings the Kantian distinction between the 'end of nature' and 'end of man' was blotted out. Utopia and chiliasm entered the Fichtean conception. And one is left with this either/or: if there is no eschaton, tutelary discipline must be perpetual; if there is one, all the restraints of Kantianism are gone. Neither case would seem to furnish the context for a 'tolerable politics'. Thus Fichte dogmatized the 'chimera' that Rousseau had set against 'prejudice'.

This is the tradition of philosophical politics into which *Hegel* entered. No doubt his mature career overlapped Fichte's, and he does not seem to have given much attention to Fichte's later doctrines and writings. Nevertheless, he studied both Kant and the early Fichte carefully and subscribed to some of the criticism presented above. An argument of this study, which does not claim to cover Hegel elaborately, is that Hegel must be seen not simply as the ultimate master of idealist thought but as a philosopher in profound reaction to some of the conclusions of his forerunners. This work is of course not a justification of Hegel, and the reader will observe that Hegel's views differ somewhat from the author's on Kant and Fichte. But Hegel was especially sensitive to the points raised here.

As a systematic idealist, Hegel's metaphysical structure contains the implications of his historical and political thought, just as Fichte's did. As is well known, Hegel developed a 'logic of the actual' by which thought itself was presumed to contain the patterns of reality, as the 'transcendental logic' (non-contradiction) of Kant and Fichte allegedly did not. This development was itself associated with the truth of actuality, Hegel's particular notion, derived from the metaphor of Christ in history, or present eternality. Hegel's time-concept and time-consciousness rejected the 'infinite task' or 'bad infinity' of the transcendental idealists for an objectively proposed course of the world.

Hegel's political and ethical notions are consistent with this revision. If they are 'conservative', they are so within this framework. His emphasis on the value of the present entailed, first of all, the definition of a human community, called the state, in which legal and moral relationships are reunited in an ethical whole. Influenced by his appreciation of the harmony of the classical *polis* and persuaded that the civic history of Christendom had produced an 'unhappy consciousness', Hegel was also reacting against the separation that Kant and Fichte had made. To Kant in particular Hegel attributed the exquisite moral technique of self-coercion; in Fichte he saw the stern outlines of the police state. His ambition was to gather the whole sphere of 'practical reason' into the living organic community.

It goes without saying that Hegel's type of solution, historically as well as philosophically inspired, denigrated the Enlightenment ideal of *cosmopolis* and exalted the notion of *Volksgeist* or homogeneous cultural whole, now, however, not simply as predicated (Fichte), but as realized.

Hegel wrestled also with the pedagogical problem. In his philosophical structure of *Vernunft* (a polemical word used by the idealists to mean 'reason' as against the mere *Verstand* of the adversary), it was necessary to pass from *phenomenology* (which is tutelary and disciplinary) into *system* (which is objective and self-perpetuating). Fichte's *Wissenschaftslehre* was, for Hegel, a phenomenology of constant coercion; his own is intended to show not that all men ought to be free, but that it is possible for them to be free *now* from an infinite pedagogical apparatus. Where this course is run, there are no longer 'masters and slaves'. That is Hegel's transformation of one of our basic political images.

Introduction

Undoubtedly, Hegel's conception was ideocentric. The state, however, is intended to accomplish in its sphere of *wirkliches Leben* what the phenomenological process achieves for the consciousness. The state 'knows' that all are free, and treats them accordingly. Hegel set the value of liberty against that of equality. He believed that one could have freedom *now* if the coercive teleology of equality were overridden. Although a much shrewder political empiricist than his forerunners (a quality aided by his grasp of time), Hegel reached conclusions that are at once too abstrusely spiritual and aesthetic for political analysis to sustain easily. His insights also go much deeper than I have been able to suggest here. As is well known, Hegelian problems and categories of argument have had an elaborate, creative career. But the image here is of the *reconciliateur manqué*. Hegel is both an end and a beginning; the ideal of the just state would not rest with his solution, and its real counterpart was nowhere in sight.

The essays that follow repeat these arguments in much greater descriptive, analytic and historical depth. Since each philosopher has his own particular centre of gravity, personality and flavour, I have thought it most truthful not to compress them into manipulable but deceptive categories, but rather to unfold their visions in a more native manner. Hopefully, these introductory remarks have clarified basic themes and procedures and can serve as a point of reference for the work as a whole.

J.-J. ROUSSEAU: THE LAND OF CHIMERAS AND THE LAND OF PREJUDICES

PART TWO

J.-J. ROUSSEAU: THE LAND OF CHIMERAS AND THE LAND OF PREJUDICES

HISTORY, ANTI-HISTORY AND THE MORAL EGO

A. THE UNREDEEMED FUTURE AND THE POLEMIC AGAINST KNOWLEDGE

In tracing the genesis of the modern historical consciousness and its subtle connections with idealist thought, Rousseau must be understood both as a point of departure and as a deliberate foil. He is neither an idealist—in so far as we can ascribe any consistent philosophical position to him—nor a metaphysician of the historical process. Yet it is with him that this discussion must begin. Since our focus is on political theory, only Rousseau can clarify our procedures; Leibniz or Hume might serve if our attention were elsewhere. There is no pretence, however, of making a full critical survey of Rousseau's unique and complex contributions to moral and political thought in this brief treatment.

For Rousseau, nature is a wise guide, man is an open question, and history is a tale of horror. These three elements form, at the outset, a chemistry of ambiguous potential. Since man is free because he commands his own will, exclusive of his intelligence or station in life,[1] and since each child born into the world or each act must be regarded as a perpetual beginning,[2] the possibility of salvation—in the act, in the individual, or in the community—cannot be cosmically foreclosed. If history is woeful, it is not authoritative. 'Man,' exhorts the Savoyard vicar, 'look no further for the author of evil; that author is you. No evil exists but that which you make or suffer; both are your works.'[3] 'By new associations', urges the first draft

---

[1] Not by his natural forces; cf. *Discours sur l'Inégalité*, *O.C.* III, 135–6. Citations from Rousseau are identified as follows: *O.C.* = *Œuvres complètes* (ed. Bernard Gagnebin and Marcel Raymond, 3 vols., Paris, 1959–64); Vaughan = *Jean-Jacques Rousseau: The Political Writings* (ed. C. E. Vaughan, 2 vols., New York, 1962); Didier = *Œuvres de Jean-Jacques Rousseau* (17 vols., ed. Didier, Paris, 1834); *C.G.* = *Correspondance générale de Jean-Jacques Rousseau* (ed. Théophile Dufour, 21 vols., Paris, 1924–32); *Emile* = *Emile ou de l'éducation* (ed. François and Pierre Richard, Paris, 1961).

[2] Cf. *Les Solitaires*, Didier, IV, 286: 'I told myself that everything is really only a beginning, and that there is no other connection in our existence but a succession of present moments, of which the first is always the one transpiring.' Also, *Rousseau juge de Jean-Jacques*, III, *O.C.* I, 972.   [3] *Emile*, IV, 342.

of the *Social Contract*, 'let us correct, if we can, the shortcomings of
the general association.'[1] The *Social Contract* carries us still more
pressingly, it would seem, away from defeatism: '. . .while a people
is forced to obey and obeys, it does well; once it can shake off the
yoke, and shakes it off, it does still better'.[2] Rousseau is, in this
sense, a philosopher of hope, a prophet of action. As such he contributed his share to the ideals of the French Revolution, to the
optimism of the Romantic movement, and to a whole school of
interpretation, which can be summarized in the following words of
Gustave Lanson: 'The idea of progress, the great idea of the century,
inspires all the work of Jean-Jacques: he seems to deny its reality
only so as to announce its possibility more loudly, its necessity
more demandingly.'[3]

Yet, setting aside all anticipations, Rousseau is much more a
philosopher of despair: 'Nature has made everything in the best way
possible; but we want to do better still, and we spoil everything.'[4]
Precisely for the same reasons that hope remains, salvation is most
unlikely: '. . .the vices that make our social institutions necessary
are the same that make their abuses inevitable'.[5] Moreover, man
hastens the deterioration of everything he sets his mark on, except in
the rarest of cases.[6] Rousseau is fundamentally the philosopher of
the note in the bottle thrown out to sea. 'I like to flatter myself', he
jotted among his papers, 'that some day there will be a statesman
who is [also] a citizen. . .that by some lucky chance he will cast his
eyes on this book [i.e. the *Social Contract*], that my loose ideas will
inspire in him more useful ones, that he will devote himself to making men better or happier. . .My writing has been guided by this
fantasy. . .'[7] The citizen of Geneva knew the odds. But better, as

---

[1] *Contrat social* (*Première version*), II, ii, *O.C.* III, 288. The 'general association' refers
to the 'natural sociability' theorized by Diderot in his article 'Droit naturel'.

[2] *Contrat social*, I, i, *O.C.* III, 352.

[3] Gustave Lanson, *Histoire de la littérature française* (Paris, 1895), p. 770. For a modified
version of the argument, see Ernst Cassirer, *The Question of Jean-Jacques Rousseau*
(trans. Peter Gay, Bloomington, 1963), p. 105: 'We cannot resist "progress" but, on
the other hand, we must not simply surrender to it. . .'

[4] *La Nouvelle Héloïse*, V, vii, *O.C.* II, 610.

[5] *Inégalité*, *O.C.* III, 187.

[6] 'Lettre à Philopolis', *O.C.* III, 232. Cf. 'Lettre à Vernet', 29 Nov. 1760, *C.G.* V,
271–2: 'Nothing can slow down the progress of evil. . .Luxury advances: there is
general decline; there is the pit where sooner or later everything perishes.'

[7] 'Fragments politiques', *O.C.* III, 474; cf. *Rêveries d'un Promeneur Solitaire*, III, *O.C.*

he wrote in the *Emile*, his 'land of chimeras' than the 'land of prejudices' of his readers.[1] Rousseau conceived models. There is a huge
gap between a model and a method. Whatever redemption Rousseau
held out for the individual, the domestic unit, or the society of
sovereign equality he hemmed in with insuperable provisos or felt
atavistically compelled to dynamite.[2]

It is indeed possible to regard Rousseau's writings as a fundamental attack on man as a history-making animal. The poignant
truth of the matter is that 'man is good and men are wicked'.[3]
History is a dangerous striving to be avoided. You may not shine
among the annals of the nations, he told the Corsicans, but you will
win a greater prize: you will be happy.[4] And yet man *is* that history-
making animal, willing himself above and beyond nature, the
coherent universal order where 'everything is renewed and nothing
degenerates'.[5] Man's fate is partly a result of his mortality, but in
the species (contrary to Kant) it is due to his corruption. Rousseau,
passionately concerned with the puzzle of man, viewed this perplexity against the background of time, the moral and physical
destroyer. In this regard (inspired by his reading and experience)
Rousseau has a deeply classical and anti-Christian time-sense.
Nature is complete and does not aspire toward a vindication.
Like most of the intellectual tradition in which he worked and unlike

---

[1] *Emile*, IV, 304.
[2] Rousseau's most finished and deliberate writings end or are tinctured with a note of
despair: cf. *N.H.* VI, xii, *O.C.* II, 740–1, for Julie's unresolved problem of love and
society, ending in death; *Solitaires*, Didier, IV, 296, for Emile's defeat and attempt to
reconcile liberty and submission ('...he who knows best how to will all that [harsh
necessity] commands is the freest, because he is never forced to act against his will'.);
and, for our purposes, most significantly in *Contrat Social, Première version*, II,
iii, *O.C.* III, 318–26; *Contrat social*, II, x, *ibid*. pp. 389–91, where he finds the just
society swiftly sabotaged by the remarkable set of conditions that must preside at the
establishment of a national civil community, satisfied alone for Corsica, and goes so
far as to speak of 'the impossibility of finding the simplicity of nature joined to the
needs of society'.
[3] Cf. *Inégalité*, note ix, *O.C.* III, 202; *Rousseau juge de Jean-Jacques*, I, *O.C.* I, 687.
[4] *Projet pour la constitution de la Corse*, *O.C.* III, 947.
[5] 'Lettre à M. de Franquières', *C.G.* XIX, 56.

I, 1018. Rousseau picked up and adapted the notion of the first citation from a paradoxical source (Hobbes, *Leviathan*, xxxi): 'I recover some hope, that one time or
other, this writing of mine may fall into the hands of a sovereign, who will consider it
himself (for it is short, and I think clear) without the help of any interested or envious
interpreter...'

the later Germans whom he partly inspired, he is profoundly anti-teleological. 'I judge the order of the world,' the Savoyard vicar says, 'although I am ignorant of its end.'[1] If the image of the clock and the master clockmaker appealed to this *horloger apprenti*, it is the ordered competence of the machine and not its ability to tick away the time of life toward a more perfect future that he appreciated. For Rousseau, the human clock, the clock of peoples, the universal clock all run down; we service them for better or worse. The main thing is to obey the inner clock of nature, and to discard our modern European time-pieces.[2] In a score of passages he seconded the sentiment of Montaigne: 'We are never at home; we are always beyond it. Fear, desire or hope drive us toward the future and deprive us of the feeling and contemplation of what is.'[3]

Rousseau undertakes the puzzle of history from the most anti-theoretical of angles: moral self-certainty.[4] Thus he inaugurates a new tendency to moralize history, not merely as a thesaurus of examples—though the Plutarchian strain is prominent—but also as a sequence of states of the human system of faculties, depicted as a kind of challenge–response pattern between sense and sensibility over time. Much of Rousseau's historical equipment is derivative; however, his combinations and emphases have much to do with his peculiar social and existential position, of whose 'uniqueness' he was so intolerably well aware.[5] It is scarcely too much to say that Rousseau attempted the first methodical liaison between the sense of world process and individual psychological tensions, a sort of

---

[1] *Emile*, IV, 332.

[2] Cf. *ibid*. II, 215; *Confessions*, VIII, *O.C.* I, 363. Also, Cassirer, *Question*, p. 41.

[3] Michel de Montaigne, 'Our Feelings Continue Beyond This Life', in *Essays* (trans. E. J. Trechmann, New York, 1946), p. 9. Cf. *Emile*, II, 67.

[4] This is what the Savoyard vicar means when he says: 'Sometimes I have good sense, and I have always loved truth...all I need do is expose what I think in the simplicity of my heart.' *Emile*, IV, 320. On Rousseau's concept of truth as equivalent to sincerity, see Judith N. Shklar, 'Rousseau's Two Models: Sparta and the Age of Gold', *Political Science Quarterly* (March 1966), p. 25. For the universality of the moral standard, see 'Lettres morales', V, *C.G.* III, 365–6; *Emile*, IV, 351.

[5] Cf., *inter alia*: *Rêveries*, I, *O.C.* I, 1017: 'the most ardent and sincere inquiries perhaps ever made by any mortal'; *Rousseau juge de Jean-Jacques*, I, *ibid*. p. 765: 'Such a singular position is unique in human existence'; *Confessions*, I. *ibid*. p. 5: 'I am not made like any I have ever seen.' In *ibid*. p. 418, the 'complot' directed against him by Grimm, Diderot, and Mme d'Epinay is 'the terrible and fatal epoch of a destiny without example among mankind'.

'phenomenology'. This is not to link him explicitly with Hegel, whose own *Phenomenology* analysed a consciousness that achieves concrete social content and passes beyond society in order to judge it, or with the modern neo-Freudians, whose concern with civilization and its neuroses is etched with the data of the industrial epoch and a different picture of man. Nevertheless, these and others can be regarded as Rousseau's successors. His own effort may be viewed as the despairing quest for unity by a man who accepted neither the Christian correlation of individual and historical destiny in the Last Judgment nor the secularist assurances of natural harmony so much in vogue about him.[1]

Rousseau connected the historical growth of knowledge with the corruption of wisdom. On the opening page of his first published work this treatment is, to all intents, clarified: 'It is not knowledge that I am flaying (*que je maltraite*)...it is virtue I am defending.'[2] For our purpose we shall pass over the fact that virtue meant a number of contradictory things to Rousseau.[3] What we should notice is that in establishing this priority Rousseau will reject all knowledge that gets in the way of virtue; he will extol and claim to teach 'useful' wisdom.[4] Now, this tradition, which can be traced in post-classical intellectual history from the *Idiota* of Nicholas of Cusa, is far from novel;[5] it is in fact an aspect of that very Enlightenment from which Rousseau takes his leave. But heretofore it had been used chiefly as a rhetorical weapon against Church dogmatism and intolerance—the metaphysics of priestly authority and public obedience—and not to attack the new structures of secular thought.

---

[1] Cf. 'Lettre à M. de Mirabeau,' in Vaughan, II, 160.

[2] *Discours sur les sciences et les arts, O.C.* I, 6.

[3] Virtue means essentially conscientious action against one's inclinations. It can encompass everything from taking care of one's parents ('Lettre à un jeune homme', Winter, 1758, *C.G.* III, 329) to slaughtering one's children for the good of the state (*Dernière réponse, O.C.* III, 88). Cf. *Rêveries*, VI, *O.C.* I, 1053; *Emile*, V, 567.

[4] Cf. *Emile*, III, 184: 'The point is not in knowing what is, but what is useful...' Regarding Rousseau's own learning (cf. *Confessions*, VI, *O.C.* I, 234–45, and 'Le Verger de Madame de Warens', *ibid.* II, 1124–9), I would agree with Jean Fabre, 'Réalité et utopie dans la pensée politique de Rousseau', *Annales*, XXXV (1959–62), 220: 'I think that Rousseau had rather good learning but not up to...the level of erudition of his age.'

[5] Cf. Henri Gouhier, 'Ce que le vicaire doit à Descartes', *Annales*, XXXV, 141. Also Bertrand de Jouvenel, 'Essai sur la politique de Rousseau', introduction to *Du Contrat social* (Geneva, 1947), citing Seneca, p. 35.

Rousseau's reaction (here we cannot help but be reminded of Book III of *Gulliver's Travels*) is to put both in the same boat. Both, in their instigation of pride and fear, were at war with virtue; both, as Rousseau would later conclude, were even capable of uniting in a single fanaticism bent on capturing the inner citadel of the conscience.[1]

Thus Rousseau announced his characteristically sharp separation of *science* and *sagesse*; *science*, at best, is for the few who can 'bring together great talents and great virtues'.[2] Let the rest leave well enough alone; half-educated people are both slaves to their illusions and promoters of the modern European personality split. Standards of public morality and human values cannot be set to accommodate genius. But it is conceivable that men might be 'wise'. Rousseau will refer *sagesse* to the seat of virtue, the conscience, which creates no 'lumières' but rather activates man's cosmic sense of proportion. He will put moral truth ahead of all speculative fact; or, rather, it will be made the unifying fact, the test and core of all reality. All method in Rousseau flows from this principle. And though his writings are charged with defeatism, he was convinced that he had recovered the way of wisdom: in an age when philosophy had destroyed, he was the single writer who had built solidly.[3]

'Sophisticated' knowledge was to Rousseau a compendium of conceited feints, of false lights, of 'ideologies', not of course in the modern Mannheimian sense, but with regard to his belief that the fashionable doctrines of his age were simple elaborate projections of *amour-propre*, rooted in the vain wishes of their proponents to be exalted in the esteem of others,[4] above all natural affinities,[5] and to seek unmerited laurels from posterity.[6] Philosophy would sell

---

[1] *Confessions*, XI, *O.C.* I, 567.

[2] *Observations*, *O.C.* III, 39. Rousseau is not far from Hobbes in this; cf. *Leviathan*, V: 'yet they that have no *science* are in better and nobler condition with their natural prudence than men that by misreasoning, or by trusting that reason wrong, fall upon false and absurd general rules'. However, Rousseau is thinking of conscience, not prudence.

[3] *Rousseau juge de Jean-Jacques*, I, *O.C.* I, 728; 'Lettre à Moultou', 25 Apr. 1762, *C.G.* VII, 191.

[4] 'Lettre à Franquières', *C.G.* XIX, 61: 'The philosopher needs to be exalted in the eyes of man, but in the eyes of God the just man prevails.'

[5] 'Préface à Narcisse', *O.C.* II, 967.

[6] Rousseau hit a nerve of his contemporaries; cf. Diderot, 'Lettres à Falconet', in

out mankind for a drop of honour.[1] By contrast, Rousseau believed himself to be the least ideological of men. He was the expounder of 'facts'—the pure facts of interior certitude—and not of 'systems'.[2] 'Readers', he exclaims in a characteristic vein, 'never forget that he who is speaking is neither a scholar nor a philosopher, but a simple man, a friend of the truth, unprejudiced, without a system...'[3] As such, he was the self-appointed mediator between those carnivorous extremes, the Church and the free-thinking intelligentsia, 'mad wolves ready to tear each other to pieces in their rage'.[4] His brain teemed with religious peace plans.[5] If he entered the intellectual fracas at all, it was to fly to the aid of virtue, though under compulsion to use the weapons of his adversaries. This is explained at some length in one of the polemics resulting from the *First Discourse*. Here Rousseau compares his reluctant immersion in controversy to the role of St Justin Martyr and other early Christian apologists: 'They had to take up the pen in self-defence.'[6]

Effusive and hypersincere, the pose is surely irritating. Rousseau annoyed his acquaintances by staking out a claim in the Parisian world of high culture while roaring at its shallowness and affecting strange habits. Like most other literary *fauves*, this 'simple man' employed levels of discourse that were far from homely even while he was conceding nothing to the epigones of modern learning beyond an occasional Bacon or Newton that could be afforded.[7]

---

[1] *Emile*, IV, 323. [2] *Ibid.* II, 107; III, 192, 203; IV, 285, 305.

[3] *Ibid.* II, 107; also 'Lettre à Duchesne', 24 May 1760, *C.G.* V, 109.

[4] *Confessions*, IX, *O.C.* I, 435. Cf. *Emile*, IV, 386: 'Dare to confess God among the philosophers; dare to preach humanity to the intolerants'; 'Lettre à Vernes', 1761, *C.G.* VI, 158: 'The devout Julie is a lesson for the philosophers and so is the atheist Wolmar for the intolerants.'

[5] Cf. 'Lettre à Beaumont', Didier, IV, 204 f.; 'Lettre à Usteri', *C.G.* IX, 234: 'How taken I am with this plan of a catholic, a really catholic religion.'

[6] *Observations*, *O.C.* III, 46.

[7] Leo Strauss, in *Natural Right and History* (Chicago, 1953), pp. 260–1, is mistaken in claiming that Rousseau preached intellectual elitism behind the back of his democracy. He simply gave genius its due without drawing political conclusions. Judith N. Shklar's interpretation of Rousseau's authoritarian streak is more profound: 'Rousseau's Images of Authority', *American Political Science Review* (December 1964), pp. 919–32.

Œuvres complètes (20 vols., ed. J. Assézat and M. Tourneux, Paris, 1875–7), XVIII, 179–80: 'O sages of Greece and Rome...how blissful to my mind it would be if I could raise my statue in the midst of yours and imagine that those one day stopping before it would feel the delicious transports that you inspire in me.'

But if he had committed any fault, it was not by joining in the over-bearing pursuit of the *libido sciendi*, but rather by carrying his own self-conscious citizen-virtue to absurdities that deepened his misery and abused his personality.[1]

History, never a point of departure for Rousseau (except as the projection of souvenir and chagrin), becomes the problematic means of extending the experience of personal tension to the race as a whole. It is a plot. The 'plot' cannot be halted, because 'individuals die, but collective groups know no death. The same passions live on, and their burning hatred, as immortal as the Demon who inspires them, acts always in the same way.'[2]

Thus we will not find Rousseau embarked on any effort to systematize the known facts of human social experience for any detached purposes of comparison and conclusion. He will not collect data and ask their meaning. Rather, his procedure will be the opposite: to use conjectural or probable data to verify his own sensitive convictions. 'To discover the connections between things,' he writes, 'I studied the relation of each thing to myself: from the two known terms I learned to find the third; to know the universe through all that might interest me, I had only to know myself.'[3] This is, in fact, the singular method of the *Second Discourse*: '...it is history's job, when there is a history, to give the facts linking [two known points]; it is philosophy's job, where history is wanting, to determine apparent facts which can link them'.[4] Rousseau's 'age of gold' is thus arrived at by 'philosophy', which for him is the logic that the heart knows to be true. Regarding the 'heuristic' and 'naturalistic' aspects of the *Second Discourse* I shall comment ahead. Here it is sufficient to note that his most extended research into human development is bounded by 'facts' joined by a deductively 'necessary' sequence of phenomena.

In *Emile*, Rousseau goes as far as to attack the recording of history

---

[1] See *Confessions*, VIII, *O.C.* I, 362; IX, 416–17. At Rousseau's first success as a writer, he became 'intoxicated' with a 'blaze of virtue...which for forty years had not emitted the smallest spark'. Finally, 'special circumstances...restored [him] to nature, above which [he] had tried to raise [himself]'. Also, *Rêveries*, VIII, *ibid.* p. 1079.
[2] *Rêveries*, I, *ibid.* p. 998.
[3] *Solitaires*, Didier, IV, 259.
[4] *Inégalité*, *O.C.* III, 163.

itself and to defend the notion that our impressions of the past should be used to further sound education, not to cultivate our theoretical knowledge.[1] Here he departs from the more neutral position of a *philosophe* like d'Alembert, who regarded history as a laboratory and wished it to regale posterity with a dispassionate spectacle of virtues and vices.[2] The virtues alone would be best. Though he had earlier argued with regard to the Spartans that virtue is its own reward,[3] he now sees the possibility that history might be used as a Trojan horse to carry virtue within the walls of the enemy. Our conception of the past might be used to challenge its bitter unfolding. Rousseau gives these views quite straightforwardly: '...we have no idea how to draw the truth out of history...as if it mattered much whether a fact was true, so long as it could furnish useful instruction. Sensible men should look on history as a tissue of fables with very appropriate moral lessons for the human heart'.[4] It is another case, another vain hope, of drawing the remedy from the source of evil. And yet Rousseau, almost against his will, has a view of history to propose.

B. A PHENOMENOLOGY OF DESPAIR

Rousseau's philosophical substructure commands our attention. His point of departure, as is well known, is the empiricist theory of knowledge, the impingement of sense data on latent faculties and the awakening of the human psychological mechanism to these external bombardments. Empiricism, as opposed to rationalism, has the implicit tendency to develop the historical viewpoint.[5] The logic

---

[1] *Emile*, IV, 282 ff. One should not overlook the classicism of this conception. Cf. Xenophon, *Anabasis*, V, *in fine*: 'it is noble, as well as just and pious, and more pleasant to remember the good things rather than the bad ones'.

[2] Cf. D'Alembert, article 'Elémens des sciences', *Encyclopédie*, V, 495–6; *Preliminary Discourse to the Encyclopedia* (trans. R. N. Schwab, New York, 1963), pp. 34–5.

[3] *Observations*, O.C. III, 83–6.

[4] *Emile*, II, 172 n.; cf. 'Fragment: Histoire de Lacédémone', O.C. III, 545; *Rêveries*, IV, O.C. I, 1029.

[5] On this point, cf. R. G. Collingwood, *The Idea of History* (Oxford, 1946), pp. 59–76; L. Lévy-Bruhl, 'The Cartesian Spirit and History', in *Philosophy and History: The Ernst Cassirer Festschrift* (ed. R. Klibansky and H. J. Paton, New York, 1963), pp. 191–6, emphasizes the anti-historical spirit of rationalism. These are of course only general tendencies.

of the mind is not prefigured. Sense experience gives not a simultaneous manifold of insight but a temporal sequence of indiscriminate events, leading to the combination of simple ideas and the laboured ascent from particular to abstract thought. Locke and Condillac were of course not concerned with the question of historical genesis but with the problem of how we know and how far we can know.[1] The Lockean *tabula rasa* is swiftly written on; the Condillacian statue is activated with dispatch. But Rousseau, whose interests were quite different, very properly asked the question: what happens if, because of literal human isolation, the complex ideas of reason are very long in forming? Since he had already decided that the source of evil was in man's social communication and that a core of goodness or innocence lay behind that, he inevitably historicized the problem beyond the requirements of a theory of knowledge.

The symbols used with such dexterity by Rousseau had also been invoked by Locke in his attack on innate ideas. What is the essence of man? Locke had asked; and he had cited reports of savages with tails, women with beards, etc., to show that there were no easy assumptions, that we could know only 'nominal' essences.[2] Rousseau, too, was searching for that essence, and he became convinced that one must go far behind anything the philosophers had imagined to judge it.[3] There were two possibilities: a hypothetical brute-man, living in a state that had 'perhaps never existed', or a child unexposed to society. Look at a young child, Locke had challenged; where will you possibly discover those famous 'innate ideas', especially practical-moral ones?[4] I shall take a child, Rousseau contended; I will discover there no ideas of God, or of duty, or of complex reason, but I will show you freedom from the stain of corruption. Here the concern of *Emile* joins that of the *Discourse*, forming commensurate fields of speculation—similes might be the proper word.

Rousseau, the methodological individualist, uses the human

---

[1] Cf. J. Starobinski, introd. to *Inégalité*, *O.C.* III, liii, lv: 'They hardly cared to project their hypothesis into the temporal depths of human history.'

[2] John Locke, *An Essay Concerning Human Understanding* (ed. A. Campbell Fraser, 2 vols., New York, 1959), II, Bk. III, vi, 22, pp. 73 ff.

[3] *Inégalité*, *O.C.* III, 132.

[4] Locke, *Essay*, I, Bk. I, iii, 1–5, pp. 92–4.

physical unit as his centre of reference and extends the analogy to his interpretation of corporate bodies.[1] He writes: 'Whoever knew perfectly the inclinations of each individual could foresee all their combined effects in the collective body (*corps du peuple*).'[2] Using a child who stands for all men,[3] Rousseau will be able to re-run a controlled experiment of the *Second Discourse* to prove that salvation is conceivable if society does not close in.

Rousseau accepted the pain–pleasure principle as the instinctual foundation of moral analysis.[4] Indeed, pain and evil are often one for Rousseau. He continued to the end to wonder whether avoidance of all contact that had the chance of being painful (i.e. human contact) was not the best way of settling the question: how shall I act?[5] But for one who believed as he did in the positive and indwelling presence of corruption in the human heart, a simple hedonism could not suffice. For one thing, it could not sustain that sometimes gruesome heroism in which he periodically set so much store. This dilemma runs throughout his writings and adds much to their ambiguity. Where, as in the growth of a child or in the development of the species, there is the preliminary mechanism of moral formation but, as yet, no completed activation of reason and personality, hence no full-fledged imputability, the empiricist procedures are useful: they furnish the original standard of innocence and establish the *why* of evil. But they do not really expose the character of evil itself. Evil may be brought on by external modifications wrought upon the *amour de soi* and the subsequent growth of cancerous

---

[1] Cf. *Emile*, I, 41; IV, 312 and n. For the corporate extension, 'Lettre à d'Alembert sur les spectacles', Didier, I, 285: 'Mankind is one, I confess; but men modified by religions, governments, laws, customs, prejudices, climates become so different from each other that we must no longer seek among us for what is good for men in general, but what is good for them in a given time or country.' The inspiration is of course from Montesquieu; cf. *Lettres persanes*, xxiv.

[2] *Ibid.* IV, 286. This 'psychologism' is a typical feature of liberal thought; cf. J. S. Mill, *System of Logic*, VI, vii, para. 1: 'Human beings in society have no properties but those which are derived from, and may be resolved into, the laws of the nature of individual man.'

[3] *Ibid.* I, 12: 'We must generalize our views, and consider in our pupil the abstract man, the man exposed to all the accidents of human life.'

[4] Cf. *inter alia, ibid.* III, 200: 'The happiness of natural man consists in not suffering'; V, 565: '...pain and vice are inseparable, and man becomes wicked only when he is unhappy'.

[5] *Rousseau juge de Jean-Jacques*, II, *O.C.* I, 855.

passions,[1] but 'it is the abuse of our faculties which makes us unhappy and wicked...Moral evil is incontestably of our doing, and physical evil [pain] would be nothing without our vices, which have made us sensitive to it.'[2] Here, a much more traditional and 'rationalist' formulation of the problem of evil comes into play, one which depends no longer on the description of the 'lente succession des choses' but rather on a stationary analysis of the moral equipment of rational man. Shorn of an earlier metaphysics, shorn of the Christian mechanism of sin and grace, shorn especially of the intellectualist disposition to relate virtue to knowledge, Rousseau's position rescues the soul (and the will) from physics in order to make evil and virtue plausible.[3]

Beginning the second volume of the *Confessions* with many gaps in his notes, letters and literal recollection of events, Rousseau comments: 'I have only one faithful guide upon which I can depend: the chain of feelings which have marked the development of my being...'[4] The journey of 'being' measured by the souvenirs of 'feeling': this is Rousseau's central notion of historical process. Feeling is 'fact', and it reaches over wide distances where *science* cannot follow. If 'feeling is existence' and means not the mere activity of the five senses but the inward capacity to judge the truth lying outside, 'the distinctive faculty of being able to give meaning to the word *is*',[5] then presumably no other method is more certain.

Rousseau is not against reason. But reason is highly corruptible; the passions distort it into self-serving 'raisonnements'.[6] Though reason enables us to know the truth, only conscience can make us *love* it, i.e. regard it as an end in itself.[7] But though conscience is indestructible, it flickers feebly in the souls of the mass of modern men, 'Europeans' and 'bourgeois', 'masters' and 'slaves', where it is 'smothered by [overbearing passions]' and remains only 'a word

[1] *Emile*, IV, 247.
[2] *Ibid.* IV, 341. The problem of the nature of evil in Rousseau is closely connected with his conception of education and his refusal to base his political theory on the notion of harmoniously legislated self-interest. In these respects, his most direct antagonist is Helvétius. For a brilliant discussion, see D. W. Smith, *Helvétius: A Study in Persecution* (Oxford, 1965), pp. 172–84, esp. pp. 175–9.
[3] *Rousseau juge de Jean-Jacques*, II, *O.C.* I, 805; also, *Inégalité*, *O.C.* III, 141–2.
[4] *Op. cit.* VII, 278.   [5] *Emile*, IV, 326.
[6] 'Lettres morales', II, *C.G.* III, 352.   [7] *Emile*, I, 48.

used for mutual deception'.[1] Man has forsaken the 'errorless' order of nature, and conscience 'speaks the language of nature which everything has caused us to forget'.[2]

Rousseau believed that he had been spared from these baleful consequences. He stood removed from the whole human spectacle, from brute to philosopher, so that he could take it all in and declare: *I have understood.*[3] Never had premeditated evil approached his heart;[4] always, even if he sustained the demands of virtue less well than others, he had known how to 'return to the order of nature'.[5] He had preserved his earliest integrity:[6] his education had modified him but little.[7] He was therefore qualified to speak.

He 'historicized' empiricism; but once he had descriptively brought the system to completion and man had, so to speak, become 'man' in the imputable-rational sense, he adopted the severer techniques of seventeenth-century moralism, minus, of course, its visionary theologies. But it is now conscience, and not reason, that sustains truth-seeking action.[8] 'Take away the *sentiment intérieur*,' he declared, 'and I defy all the modern philosophers together to prove to Berkley [*sic*] the existence of [physical] bodies.'[9] In a thoroughly 'rationalist' manner, the inner certitude establishes the outer fact; but the judgment is now moral (what Rousseau often calls 'useful'), not *more geometrico* and theoretical. The *je qui pense* is no longer the philosophical construction of an impersonal and universal reason, but the sensitive *moi qui existe*, the man in whom nature still speaks, in the instance Rousseau himself, by extension the Romantic artist. Truth remains externally grounded, but the

---

[1] 'Lettre à Beaumont,' Didier, IV, 362–3.
[2] *Emile*, IV, 355; 'Lettres morales', VI, *C.G.* III, 369.
[3] Cf. *Confessions*, I, *O.C.* I, 5: 'I feel my heart and I know men.'
[4] *Rêveries*, IV, *O.C.* I, 1028.
[5] *Ibid.* VIII, 1075–9.
[6] *Ibid.* IV, 1025.
[7] *Rousseau juge de Jean-Jacques*, II, *O.C.* I, 799. This, of course, does not mean that Rousseau was without self-doubt. Cf. *Confessions*, I, *ibid.* p. 31.
[8] Cf. *Emile*, IV, 348: 'Too often reason deceives us...but the conscience never deceives; it is man's true guide.' See Iring Fetscher, 'Rousseau's Concept of Freedom in the Light of his Philosophy of History', *Nomos IV* (New York, 1962), p. 42; and cf. Montaigne, 'Apology for Raimond Sebond', *Essays*, p. 412: 'We have indeed strangely overrated this precious reason we so much glory in...if we have bought it at the price of that infinite number of passions to which we are continually a prey.'
[9] 'Lettre à Franquières', *C.G.* XIX, 54.

subject must 'love' it, which is precisely what the philosophers, with their *furor systemicus*, do not do: they aspire to instruct others, not themselves.[1] Even one's own mistake, sincerely arrived at, is worth more than the truth of another's authority.[2] Thus, the personal history of a man of unspoiled feeling, fusing with his sensibility honest observations and the impeccable disclosures of men of the stripe of Plutarch and Fénelon, becomes, in some profound sense, a revelation of the millenial shocks of the human condition.

A fragment from the time of the *Second Discourse* discloses: 'I studied man in himself, and saw or thought I saw finally within his constitution [Rousseau's customary word for the 'changeable' aspect of humanity][3] the true system of nature, which people have not failed to call my own, even though to establish it I simply removed from man what, according to my demonstration, he had acquired for himself.'[4] Finally, at about the time of the writing of *Emile*, the citizen of Geneva makes his view more explicit: 'I conceive of a new kind of service to man: to offer them the faithful image of one of them so that they may learn to know themselves.'[5] If man is the 'dernière étude du sage',[6] Rousseau never doubted that he was the one to undertake it. And he spent much of his last years retracing, dissecting and transfiguring his own existence, seeking to justify man through his labyrinth of tribulation and neurotic anguish. Compulsively he asked: 'Am I alone good and wise among mortals?'[7] This was the 'error most to be feared' against which he had warned in *Emile*.[8] But through his life Rousseau shuttled between the extremes of feeling archetypically human and wholly unique, an oscillation reflected in his divided loyalty to the common man and the sublime hero, the solidaristic *cité* and the solitary wanderer, Emile and his tutor.

To ignore the subjectivist foundation—and incentive—of Rousseau's research and to attribute to him any 'scientific' experimentalism obviously passes wide of the mark. But there is also an opposite error to be avoided: that of taking his positions as simply

---

[1] *Emile*, IV, 285.   [2] *Ibid.* p. 323.   [3] Cf. notes to *Inégalité, O.C.* III, 1294.
[4] 'Fragment biographique', *O.C.* I, 1115.   [5] 'Mon portrait', *O.C.* I, 1120.
[6] *Emile*, II, 219.   [7] *Rêveries*, III, *O.C.* I, 1020.   [8] *Emile*, IV, 292.

'meta-historical'.[1] According to this view, 'history' becomes a metaphor for moral judgment, a figurative embellishment lightly gowning a diatribe against the gathered evils of contemporary man. Not all aspects of this problem can be treated here. But there are compelling reasons against the notion that the 'facts' of the *Second Discourse* are simply *écartés*.[2] To be sure, 'one must not take [these] inquiries...for historical truths, but only for hypothetical and conditional lines of reasoning'.[3] Conjecture is conjecture, and the reach of the Church is long. Moreover, Rousseau's intellectual milieu had two conflicting tendencies with regard to history, nowhere more sharply defined than in his own writings. In the first place, 'nature' was often absolutely opposed to 'history' for the purpose of establishing civil liberties based on 'natural right' as against prescriptive tyrannies. But, in the second place, 'history' was thrown against 'revelation' or religious authority in order to loosen the chains of ecclesiastical obedience.[4] The Pelagianizing Rousseau was no less concerned with the latter than the former problem and he needed history as a tool to deal with it. History, not primordial guilt, was the clue to corruption. It was the immense continuum stretching between man's anthropological innocence and his social misery. Seen in this light, it is improbable that Rousseau intended a relinquishment of fact to fancy. His materials are characteristic of the literary social science of the epoch. Even today (cf. Lewis Mumford), where artifacts are lacking, the interpreter scruples to imagine, or resorts to the evidence of myth and poetry. Kant, a distinguished anthropo-moralist himself and a tendentious examiner of Rousseau's arguments, was not incorrect in writing: 'The experimental moralist will be fair-minded enough not to classify M. Rousseau's propositions as merely fine fancies before having tested them out.'[5]

Rousseau saw historical process both as a deformation which man,

---

[1] Cf. Henri Gouhier, 'Nature et histoire dans la pensée de Jean-Jacques Rousseau', *Annales*, XXIII (1953–5), p. 11.

[2] See J. Starobinski's introduction, *O.C.* III, pp. liii–liv, and notes, p. 1302 and *passim*.

[3] *Inégalité, O.C.* III, 133.

[4] See especially, René Hubert, *Les sciences sociales dans l'Encyclopédie* (Paris, 1923), pp. 23–6.

[5] 'Note on the Wanderer Jan Kommarnicki', in *Gesammelte Schriften* (Akademieausgabe, 24 vols., Berlin, 1902–64), II, 489.

first victimized by excessive contact and competition for scarce goods and reciprocal approval, gradually imposed on himself, and as a nexus of socio-political growth cycles analogous to the human experience of youth, maturity and decrepitude. There is at least some ambiguity between these two interpretations, encouraging the hesitation between cosmopolitan and particularistic values so pronounced in his works. It is perhaps convenient to see the first image (forcefully expressed in the *Second Discourse* and in texts like the 'Lettre à Philopolis') as a refutation of the most optimistic and 'progressivist' strains of the Enlightenment—ideas found especially in the writings of St.-Pierre, Grimm, Turgot and, somewhat more guardedly, d'Alembert. Unlike these men, Rousseau feared the future. He inveighed often against the sacrifice of the present for uncertain gains.[1] 'In the long run all men become similar, but the order of their progress is different', he writes;[2] this is not meant as an encouragement. Perhaps the Russians will overrun Europe, to be followed by the Tartars.[3] Above all, he is concerned to show that *science* is destructive to *sagesse*. In his *Reply to the King of Poland*, he argues thus at considerable length over the field of post-classical European history.[4] The polemic is aimed chiefly at the Church, but Rousseau makes it amply clear that the free-thinking philosophers come under the same rubric. Indeed, he regarded the two camps as even capable of uniting in a single fanaticism, as had happened in China.[5] It is difficult to comprehend why certain historians still persist in claiming Rousseau as 'progressivist'. *Perfectibilité* is a bitter irony, and 'progress' is surely what history *is not* or, better, an expression of the human condition run amok.[6]

The problem of man is thus the problem of evil, not sin, and evil is fundamentally psychic pain. Evil is to be sought for in history, among men, not in the mysterious designs of the creation. Theology, among its other abuses, begs the question by making corruption its own cause. Thus Rousseau challenges Archbishop Cristophe de Beaumont: '...I concluded that it was not necessary to imagine

---

[1] Cf. *Solitaires*, Didier, IV, 289.   [2] *Essai sur l'origine des langues*, Didier, II, 362.
[3] *Contrat social*, II, viii, *O.C.* III, 386.   [4] *Observations*, *O.C.* III, 43–56.
[5] *Confessions*, IX, *O.C.* I, 435; XI, *ibid.* p. 567.
[6] Cf. *Rousseau juge de Jean-Jacques*, I, *O.C.* I, 687; also *Emile*, IV, 342: 'Take away our evil progress...and all is well.'

man wicked because of his nature, when one could assign the origin and progress of his wickedness.'[1] The defence of *Emile* continually verges toward a vindication of the *Discourse on Inequality* because Rousseau saw the two works as complementary explorations of the same issue.

Of course, the *Second Discourse* was not intended as a philosophical disquisition on the development and function of the faculties of the will and understanding. Rousseau shuddered at being called a philosopher. He had a burning message of grievance addressed, as he well knew, not to an academy but to dissolute Parisians and (as he then fancied) respectable Genevans. Thus, when an able scholar of the sources of the work writes: 'Rousseau sought to provide the experimental history of societies',[2] the definition sounds a little cool. Rousseau had a personal heartache. Yet we may agree that Rousseau regarded his research as 'conjecturale mais vraisemblable...'[3] No other sequence of argument, he felt, could bridge the lacuna between natural goodness and social corruption: '...upon the principles I have just established, it would be impossible to form any other system that would give the same results or from which I could draw the same conclusions'.[4] Somehow the composite of brute flesh and corrupted spirit which he perceived in humanity had not just appeared ready-made, as the legal philosophers seemed to argue. As the child is father to the man, so are the instincts to the moral and rational equipment of a later age. Hereupon, Rousseau created one of the most fruitful but least tempting visions of humanity ever put forward. For he said straight out that anthropological man was good but that historical man had become perverse, that the development which made virtue possible had also given rise to supreme viciousness, and that a history attributable somehow to human volition had become a decisive blockade to human fulfilment. This denial of the efficacity of civilization profoundly challenged the later adepts of history who fell under Rousseau's influence.

Conceivably, this is the first moment in European thought when, without theological contrivance or scholastic obfuscation, the

---

[1] 'Lettre à Beaumont', Didier, IV, 393–4.
[2] Jean Morel, 'Recherches sur les sources du Discours sur l'Inégalité', *Annales*, V, 131.
[3] *Ibid.* 132. [4] *Inégalité, O.C.* III, 162.

enormous contradiction of man as moral *and* as historical agent is posed without diluting either of the two terms to suit the other. Henceforward, theodicies and natural orders (style of the Physiocrats) will not suffice. Man is, as Rousseau believed, both responsible and victimized. The tragic irony is that he has truly become a victim before becoming responsible. The tormented hope is that his responsibility could conceivably provide a method of escaping his victimization.

To understand the first point—which is no doubt inseparable from Rousseau's early-developed feelings about his own destiny[1]— it is convenient to go back to the *Second Discourse*. Here, the problem of the generation of evil is most ambiguous. Ideas of morality, we are told, arise only when habitual and regular contact among human beings is established.[2] Long before this, however, a sequence of events and modifications is established that foreshadows society, morality and corruption. Man is, to begin with, created with potential capacities of will and perfectibility.[3] Thus he is presumably, even in nature, a creature that begins to reason from acorn to oak in order to subserve his hunger. But, according to Rousseau, despite his innate proclivities, he might never have used his will for more than animal satisfaction, might never have 'perfected himself' one iota, might never have groped his way toward reason and reflection.[4] On the other hand, nature, 'ever the same order...[with] ever the same revolutions',[5] cannot be brought to account for engendering progress. Consequently, there is need for a *tertium quid*, chance, represented generally by Rousseau as 'unnatural' modifications in nature.[6] Chance forces man beyond himself to obtain what he

---

[1] Notably his adolescent experience of returning too late to Geneva to be admitted through the gates (*Confessions*, I, 42: 'Il était trop tard'), which launched him on the world; re-echoed in the closing of the monastery gates at Turin (*ibid.* II, 60). See also his experience with the manuscript of the *Dialogues*, when he was barred from the high altar of Notre Dame, where he wished to entrust it to Providence ('Histoire du précédent écrit', *O.C.* I, 978–80); and the final detemporalization of this theme, indicating submission, in *Rêveries*, I, 998: 'il est trop tard.'

[2] *Inégalité*, *O.C.* III, 170; cf. 'Fragments,' *ibid.* pp. 404–5; 'It is certain that from this [human] commerce are born their vices and virtues and generally their whole moral being.'

[3] *Inégalité*, *O.C.* III, 141–2.   [4] *Ibid.* p. 162.   [5] *Ibid.* p. 144.

[6] *Ibid.* pp. 162, 171; *Langues*, IX, Didier, II, 357: 'The associations of men are in large part the work of accidents of nature.'

needs, to become imaginative and *prévoyant*. It makes him enter into competition with other animals and finally into conflict and co-operation with his own kind; it drives him into unfavourable geo-graphical milieux; it deflects him into specialized ways of life, in which he loses a part of his integrity for the sake of necessity or advantage. Rousseau's recourse to the notion of chance as the instigator or trigger for human development is not only a serious departure from his conviction of the plenitude and 'goodness' of nature, but also underscores the profoundly anti-teleological implications of this particular work.[1]

Later, when Rousseau comes to lavish his enthusiasm on that point in evolution, that 'age of gold', where man has allegedly achieved a happy balance of need and want, a psychological notch equidistant from reason and instinct, it is again some 'funeste hasard' which launches the species on its further course.[2]

Spangled throughout this speculative narrative are the minor nodes of varied significance. Man early learns to fear death.[3] He raises himself above the other animals by slaying them and wearing their pelts.[4] Finally, he begins to commingle with his fellows, to compare and judge, and to desire preference and approval.[5] It seems that vision itself ('of all the senses the least separable from the judg-ments of the mind')[6] conspired to betray man into the snares of pride.[7] Starobinski brilliantly interprets the supreme irony with which Rousseau treats the primary form of social contact. That very primitive feast, described with such loving detail in the *Essai sur les origines des langues* and echoed in the *Second Discourse*, which con-secrates the birth of love and community, also unleashes the demon

---

[1] Whether or not men were destined to live in society according to Rousseau depends very much on what meaning one gives to destiny. In *Inégalité* chance is the culprit, but see 'Lettres morales', V, *C.G.* III, 367; *Emile*, IV, 354; 'Fragments', *O.C.* III, 504–5.

[2] *Inégalité, O.C.* III, 171.

[3] *Ibid.* p. 143; cf. 'Lettres morales', V, *C.G.* III, 367.

[4] *Inégalité, O.C.* III, 140. Rousseau sees prefigured in man's assertion of primacy among the animals the inequality within his own species (p. 166). This is very different from Kant's opinion of the 'fourth and final step which reason took'. Cf. 'Conjectural Beginning of Human History', in L. W. Beck (ed.), *Kant on History*, p. 58.

[5] *Inégalité, O.C.* III, 170.

[6] *Emile*, III, 153.

[7] *Inégalité, O.C.* III, 169: 'Each began to look at the others, and to want to be looked at himself...'

of *amour-propre*.[1] Equality is effectively lost when independence is lost: the syllables 'aimez-moi' and 'aidez-moi' are the first verbal links in man's perennial chains.[2]

The foregoing is not intended to serve as an adequate summary of the *Second Discourse*, even up to the point where 'all our faculties [are] developed, memory and imagination [set] in play, vanity stimulated, reason made active, and mind evolved practically to the limit of its possible perfection', that is to say, where 'rationalism' can be called into being to redress the inadequacy of 'empiricism'.[3] We are only concerned to ask: is man imputable for any part of this course of events? And the answer is, of course, that he is not; no more than a child is responsible for bad handling. What has been described is 'pre-evil'. Man has entered the clutches of development unknowingly; like the gates of Geneva and of the monastery at Turin, the barriers of his retreat have been fatally closed. Against infernal novelty, order is helpless. Human history is the record of the abolition of patterns of order; morality and legality will be the conceivable tools for the recovery of order. But man becomes responsible only after he has been victimized, corrupted in his help-less minority.

Let us repeat: for Rousseau the riddle of life was essentially a question of the journey of 'being' interpreted by the instrument of 'feeling'. The corollary questions that most preoccupied him were: Am I not, as my whole inner being tells me but as the slanders of others deny, spared from evil? How is it that such gross wickedness thrives around me, seemingly perpetuated by the process of social communication itself? From this fundamental *point de départ* we pass to such propositions as: 'If, as I feel, I am good, then man must be good.' *Evil takes time.* The extrapolation of personal experience into the social world is, of necessity, a historical problem. Man has been corrupted in history and is trapped in the consequences of this fact. He has fought free from God and nature and constructed

---

[1] Starobinski stresses the irony: '. . . thus is aroused the overbearing desire to be preferred, the comparison that makes us attentive to others only if we can surpass or displant them. Unanimity is lost in the same ceremony that seems to celebrate it.' Notes to *Inégalité, O.C.* III, 1344.

[2] *Langues*, X, Didier, II, 363.

[3] *Inégalité, O.C.* III, 174.

the world from his own (mostly deplorable) desires. What can he then do? There is a customary answer. In the words of one analysis: 'salvation must be immanent in history'.[1] This logically follows upon what has been said, and yet is curiously mis-stated in terms of Rousseau's vision and beliefs. A fair correction might be put this way: salvation, if salvation there be (and so as not to give up all human dignity, we must never renounce its possibility), will be a human act against history or, as I put it earlier, an attempt to substitute for the historical pattern of corruption the natural pattern of birth, growth and decline, which is also the rhythm of the human heart. To say that salvation must be immanent in history comes perilously close to arguing that history (driven by spirit, nature, providence, or whatever) unfolds toward salvation. But by no stretch of the imagination can Rousseau be made to entertain such a notion. The 'pre-Kantian' version of Rousseau founders precisely on this most critical of issues: the sense of the world and the destiny of the human race. 'Man is very strong when he is content to be what he is.'[2] That simple statement, almost tautological, is the foundation for the only kind of 'salvation' Rousseau really believed in.

[1] Lionel Gossman, 'Time and History in Rousseau', *Studies on Voltaire and the Eighteenth Century*, xxx (1964), esp. pp. 338–45.
[2] *Emile*, II, 65.

IMAGES OF INTEGRATION

A. 'EMILE': THE ENCYCLOPEDIC IMAGE

If we do not accept either the view which commits Rousseau to a total unconcern with history or that which attributes to him a belief in the goal of historical salvation, we are obliged to locate some middle ground that can illustrate the historical tension of his thought and, if possible, relate his intellectual constructions to a historical context. There are three sequences of examination that I would propose. These could be called, respectively, the 'juridical' perspective of the *Social Contract*; the 'customary-defensive' solution of *Corsica* and some of the other writings; and the 'comprehensive' demonstration of *Emile*. These sequences are neither discrete nor correlative.

Emile, which Rousseau rightly thought his masterwork, sets what I shall call the pattern of 'triplicity' against the 'dualism' or 'bipolarity' so frequently noted in Rousseau's moral and social doctrines.[1] *Emile*, as we have seen, is correlative to the general problem of human development in time. Controlled education and rampantly uncontrolled history are set against each other to show what Everyman might have been; 'chimera' is posed against 'prejudice'. In Rousseau's case, however, we have both correlation and inversion: 'good' education against 'bad' history. That is enough to set the Genevan off very clearly from prophets of progress like Lessing, who spoke of the 'education of mankind' as if, despite travails, history had proved the good handmaiden of human evolution.

In developing the idea of 'triplicity' I shall recall the earlier distinction made between Rousseau's genetic-historical treatments of the human condition and his purposively rationalist-analytical ones. In the first category fall the *Second Discourse* and *Emile*, although it is important to note that each contains passages of the

---

[1] See the brilliant essay by Jean Wahl, 'La bipolarité de Rousseau', *Annales*, XXXIII (1953–5), pp. 49–55.

latter sort. The second category would comprise the first part, generally, of the *Second Discourse*, the *Social Contract*, and parts of the *Emile*, most notably the *Profession de foi*. It is not hard to establish the distinction. The first sort of writing is temporally grounded and displays the triple pattern *instinct–morality–law*; passages of the second type, interludes which 'interrupt' the development of man, depend on dual analytical contrasts, respectively those between the real man of nature and the 'natural man' of the philosophers, between law and lawlessness, and between the moral and physical sense apparatus. As for the temporal exemption of the latter group, it is obviously not entirely pristine: not only are human concepts riveted to time, but the 'chimera' of social harmony seems to be pitted against time's very relentlessness.

In the 'dual' sections Rousseau's emphasis is on contrast and analytic exploration; in the 'triple' ones it is on the 'lente succession des choses'. Of course, except in the case of the *Social Contract*, the divisions I have made are not thoroughly obvious. But it is significant that Rousseau has provided three analytical set-pieces which probe the nature of the three major stages of human development. Each man possesses, after all, three interwoven systems of action, the sensual-physical, the moral-spiritual, and the legal-political, depending on the primacy of three stabilizers, the senses and natural instincts, the moral conscience, and the general will. Chronologically developed, each has its role to play in the completed individual. Thus, it is no less interesting that each 'systems' description—one directly inserted, the others in précis—is found incorporated in the structure of *Emile*, a work which is itself keyed on evolution.[1] If the previous suppositions are useful in understanding Rousseau's doctrinal centre of gravity, one might conclude that *Emile* is the capstone or 'encyclopedia' of Rousseau and that his other writings must be interpreted in the light of this relationship. This is, to be sure, not a magic formula for resolving contradictions that stubbornly resist all academic ingenuity. It may at least be a means of weighing them against each other.

'Make man whole and you will make him as happy as he can

[1] Aside from the 'Profession de foi', *Emile*, II, 137–74, on the senses, and V, 585–96, the précis of the *Social Contract*.

be. Give him entirely to the state, or leave him entirely to himself.'[1] Rousseau sounded that trumpet call more than once. After all, he preferred being a 'man of paradox' to a 'man of prejudice'. But he did not intend simply to rest with the impossible. His own preference was for some intermediate solution, as is evident in his dedication of the *Second Discourse* to the magistrates of Geneva, and in passages like the following: 'Our sweetest [form of] existence is relative and collective, and our true self (*moi*) is not entirely inside us.'[2] The word *relative* here seems to be a kind of rehabilitation of the 'moi relatif', damned in the *Emile* as the agent of *amour-propre*.[3] In any case it sometimes passes unnoticed that *Emile* is not simply a forceful exposition of the individualist side of Rousseau's paradox: rather, it is an experimental resolution of both terms. The passage where this is asserted deserves to be exhumed:

...what will a man brought up uniquely for himself become for others? If perhaps the double object proposed could be combined in a single one, a great obstacle to man's happiness would be removed with the removal of man's contradictions.[4]

The Rousseauian ideal is, in fact, a man who is both for himself and for others, and *Emile* is intended to show whether such a supposition is possible. Emile will be neither a solitary hedonist fleeing social pain nor a 'denatured' Gaius or Lucius, but will somehow bestride both positions. Unlike the unhappy universal victims of the *Second Discourse* (who had no 'gouverneur' to ward off the 'funestes hasards' of history), he will presumably run the race right. But he will not be natural in the sense that a primitive is 'natural': he will be a savage trained to live in cities, because he has learned to *think*.[5] If, lacking a *patrie*, he cannot be a citizen (and it is doubtful that modern Europe would make him a statesman), he will at least be a law-abiding spectator.[6] *Emile*, then, is Rousseau's vision of how nature might be projected into society without the awful wrench that most men suffer.

There are, as I have suggested, three divisions to this work. The first part, containing the education of sense experience and a long analysis of the senses (including the 'sixth' *sensus communis*

[1] 'Fragments', *O.C.* III, 510; cf. *Emile*, I, 9–10.
[2] *Rousseau juge de Jean-Jacques*, II, *O.C.* I, 813.
[3] *Emile*, IV, 290.　　[4] *Ibid.* I, 11.　　[5] *Ibid.* III, 240; IV, 306.　　[6] *Ibid.* III, 227; V, 606.

or simple reason) culminates in the third book, where sense experience creates the basis for the pre-moral judgments that form the substructure of all knowledge. There the methodology of the relations of the self to the sheerly physical objects of existence is set forth: the symbol is Robinson Crusoe, the motto is *il faut que je vive*.[1] Rousseau never allowed his moral preoccupations to disguise his primary concern over the maldistribution of the physical necessities of life. With the fourth book, 'we finally enter the moral order... man's second step';[2] the *grande leçon* is the *Profession de foi*. In the fifth book, Emile is initiated to domestic life as well as the consequences of living in a civil community; he will be a parent and a citizen: '...after having considered himself in his physical relations with other beings and moral relations with other men, he has still to consider himself in his civic relations with his fellow citizens'.[3]

Man would be defective without his 'triplicity', which he develops as he ages but, once grown up, generally employs chaotically, with psychological and physical damage to himself and others. Emile is the 'chimera' set against this pessimism: as his styles of order change with increased age, responsibility and 'connaissances', he will pass smoothly between levels of existence without the cruel contradictions of logic or the millenial disorder which history has spread in its wake. He will be able to suffer the knowledge of evil and remain good. In him the psychological, moral and political faculties will be perfectly joined. He will be man and citizen without division or mutilation. He will be the person sufficient unto himself, farmer, husband, father, companion, bearer of the general will—the 'citizen who decides only according to his own judgment'[4]—even *Weltbürger*. Man's true destiny was to be all these things.

The *Emile*, however, is not history, but literature. If not a fiction, it is a fancy; and Rousseau was well aware of this. Although he was undeniably pleased to gain disciples for his precepts, he had no expectation that a world of 'natural men' would ever be brought into being. 'You can teach the people [all you like],' he replied to a

---

[1] *Ibid.* III, 200, 211, 224.   [2] *Ibid.* IV, 278.

[3] *Ibid.* V, 581. Rousseau makes elsewhere (III, 185) the more conventional distinctions of the necessary, the useful, the good; the triad—sensuous, intellectual, moral—informs the interpretation of Paul Duproix, *Kant et Fichte et le problème de l'éducation* (Geneva, 1895), p. 74.   [4] *Contrat social*, II, iii, *O.C.* III, 372.

correspondent, 'but you will make them neither better nor happier.'[1]
Rousseau, after all, was not writing a treatise on education, but a
curious, original document about 'le bonheur ou le malheur du
genre humain',[2] an anti-history, as well as a proof that evil is neither
supernatural nor hereditary.

The child Emile represents the way man might have been if
God had brought him out of nature into society instead of abandon-
ing him before the portals of his human vocation. The freedom and
responsibility that were to become the cornerstone of Kantian ethics
are measured by Rousseau against a deism of despair in which man
alone among phenomenal beings has been torn from the natural
order. That is why we must, beyond the equality of respect that the
conscience enjoins, beyond the mathematical equations of the just
polis, have tutors, legislators, Wolmars, 'devins du Village,' Claude
Anets, God-surrogates for the precariousness of this earthly life,
ordainers, symbols of order.[3] That is why we must also have the
cement of custom, levels of autarky, 'noble lies', civil religions, and,
indeed, the fictional but forceful personality of the state. Above all,
we must have, to the extent of the possible, self-control, whether
it is the virtue that comes by force or the less demanding routine of
the natural, unspoiled inclination.

Emile, the hothouse plant, is thus really a completed perspective,
not a reconstructed humanity. He is mankind only until he comes
among men. Personalized at last when he is thrust into the world,
he then encounters that society of the *Second Discourse* to which
his entire education had been a challenge. It proves immediately to
be an unequal combat. For all this, Emile does not join the villainous
tormentors. Instead, he retreats to the last outpost of psychological
endurance, already prefigured in his training,[4] a stoical reduction
of voluntary evil to physical law: 'Was I not born slave of necessity?
What new yoke can men place upon me?'[5] Emile's final answer was

---

[1] 'Lettre à H. Tscharner', 29 Apr. 1762, *C.G.* VII, 202.
[2] Preface to *Emile*, pp. 2–3; cf. 'Lettre à Philibert Cramer', 13 Oct. 1764, *C.G.* XV, 339.
[3] Fully covered in J. N. Shklar, 'Rousseau's Images of Authority', *op. cit.*
[4] Especially in the long 'dialogue' of *Emile*, V, 603–7.
[5] *Solitaires*, Didier, IV, 295. Interestingly, Emile, who leaves his country and is cast
adrift on the world (p. 290), has virtually the same feelings as those of Schiller in 1784:
'I have lost my country and exchanged it for the vast universe.' Quoted by Maurice
Boucher, *La révolution de 1789 vue par les écrivains allemands* (Paris, 1954), p. 34.

evidently also Rousseau's. 'The man of nature', he writes, 'learns in every affair to bear the yoke of necessity and submit to it.'[1] *Emile* is thus Rousseau's essay on truth and failure, man against man, education against history, ending in a freedom that becomes elliptical and repressive. The completed vision is a vision of impasse. A man has been made for a community of equals, but has not found it. Can we imagine a community that is made for men?

B. THE 'SOCIAL CONTRACT': THE IMAGE OF LEGAL MORALITY

In the 'triple' scheme of *Emile*, 'natural man' is, as we have suggested, an appropriate and balanced system of instinct, morality and legality. Each element is in its place, and none is precisely paramount because each is indispensable and, alone, each is insufficient. In the whole man these aspects are built upon each other and interwoven in the personality. Nevertheless, both in individual growth and in the psychological act of volition, the moral conscience would appear to have an intermediary role. Developing out of the primary instincts, in which it is evidently latent or 'innate', and often described by Rousseau as the 'voice of nature', it is also the 'love of order' or of 'virtue', the prelude to a rational and just system of social relationships.[2] The conscience (assisted by reason) is in some sense the link between nature and spirit. However, this faculty, most precious and important to the human condition, is also the feeblest and most precarious: as the 'voice of nature' it is choked off by the unremitting interplay of desire and need; as the 'love of order' it is faulted by man's insatiable penchant to have himself preferred above others, to vaunt his glory and his commodities, to tyrannize. In history, nature has been mortgaged by the time morality appears. Conscience was not given to man to ward off expected trials, but rather developed with, and as a result of, those experiences.

---

[1] *Rousseau juge de Jean-Jacques*, II, *O.C.* I, 864. Cf. *Rêveries*, VIII, *ibid.* p. 1077.
[2] Cf. *Emile*, IV, 320. Conscience 'stubbornly follows the order of nature against all the laws of men'.

Images of integration

Conscience conveys the 'natural law' to the rare individual who has *sagesse*.

For Emile, educated to be *sage*, the concern of the conscience is central. 'The eternal laws of nature and order do exist,' he is told. 'For the wise man they take the place of positive law; they are written in the depths of his heart by the conscience and by reason: to them he should hearken if he is to be free.'[1] But even Emile, as he acquires the responsibilities of parenthood and citizenship, will pass from the tutelary (or meditative) condition of contemplating the love of man to the close-quarters relationship of a community. Here is echoed the tension between Rousseau's highly personal defence of solitude ('When one lives alone, one loves men better; we are attached to them by a tender interest, our imagination develops the charms of society...')[2] against Diderot's barb ('Only the wicked man lives alone')[3] and his idealization of the small republic of his birth ('where all the members [should] know each other').[4] Emile must now learn, despite his *sagesse*, to owe, not to nature, but to his country 'the morality of his actions and the love of virtue'.[5] The paradox is that in an order without evil (a *siècle d'or*), conscience would not be necessary (indeed could scarcely have developed), while in the actual order of men, conscience is ineffective in keeping the peace. In fact, if taken as the rule of general order, it will simply lead to the discomfiture and injury of good men.[6] Instead of the 'divine instinct', it is the laws of the land, even the 'simulacrum of laws', that 'give [a man] the courage to be just, even among the wicked' and 'teach him to rule himself'. Evidently, this 'legal' morality is quite opposed to the earlier 'moral' morality whereby, through the agency of conscience, '[man] discovers his real interest in being good, in doing good far from the gaze of men, and *without being forced to by the laws* [my italics], in being just in the sight of God, in doing his duty even if it should cost him his life...'[7] We might, however, explain the paradox in the form of an aphorism: natural law without sanctions is social impotence; positive law without morality is social injustice. Legal morality is designed to

---

[1] *Emile*, v, 605.　　　　　　　　　　　　[2] 'Lettres morales', VI, *C.G.* III, 370.
[3] Cf. *Confessions*, IX, *O.C.* I, 455.　　　　　[4] Dedication to *Inégalité*, *O.C.* III, 112.
[5] *Emile*, v, 605.　　　[6] *Contrat social*, II, vi, *O.C.* III, 378.　　　[7] *Emile*, IV, 389.

supervene upon the arbitrary combat of restraint and self-interest, virtue and *amour-propre*, which is the actual result of free will, by furnishing the sanctions provided for by the artificial, though general, will of a community.

The triple action of *Emile* is thereupon compressed into the dual analytical mechanism of the *Social Contract*, law and lawlessness, state and statelessness. Morality (as analysed in the *Profession de foi*) does not disappear in this perspective, but it is dispersed between the 'order of nature' for which the state attempts to provide a surrogate and the 'legal order' by which the popular state, through a 'general will', attempts to condition itself to virtue. For the characteristic 'double man' of Christian moralism, the man of instinct and rational morality, Rousseau had already, in the *Emile*, suggested the substitution of a 'triple man', the man of instinct, morality and law. 'Triple man' would succeed if he lived in a world of respectful 'triple men', but even Emile is made to bear the woe that no such world exists, no world social and natural at the same time, no 'heureuse Salente', no 'general society of mankind'.

Consequently, Rousseau returns to a juridical 'duality', in which, however, the postulates of morality have been subsumed, collectivized and turned into a 'general will'[1] whose superiority over the personal conscience as a guarantor of order is established both by its physical power to coerce through the consensus of the community and through its psychological power to divert man's outer-directedness away from the mirror of preference and vanity and toward the common task.[2] Here Rousseau suppresses the ideal of personal morality, not because it is formal, as in Hegel's general critique of Kant's 'Moralität', but because it is feeble.

The sense of Rousseau's juridical analysis is expressed particularly

---

[1] On Rousseau's conception of the 'general will' and the origin of the term, see Paul-L. Léon, 'Rousseau et l'idée de la volonté générale', *Archives du droit public et de la science politique*, Nos. 3–4 (1936), pp. 148–200; Iring Fetscher, *Rousseaus politische Philosophie* (Neuwied, 1962), pp. 111 f.; B. de Jouvenel, 'Essai', *op. cit.* pp. 105–14; Georges Gurvitch, 'Kant und Fichte als Rousseau-Interpreten', *Kant-Studien*, XXVII (1922), pp. 151–3. No less than the Rousseauian state itself, the 'general will' is conventionalistic.

[2] Cf. *Emile*, IV, 303: 'Let us extend *amour-propre* to others, thereby transforming it into virtue.' This is what a 'general will' routinizes. Cf. in this connection Rousseau's stress on opinion (*Contrat social*, II, xii, 394) and on public surveillance (*Montagne*, VIII, 845), important ideas among the Paris sections in years II and III of the Revolution.

by two well-known passages from the *Social Contract*. In the first of these the duality is dramatically presented:

This passage from the state of nature to the civil state produces in man a very remarkable change, substituting justice for instinct in his conduct, and giving his actions the morality that they previously lacked. Only then, with the voice of duty replacing physical impulse and law replacing appetite, is man, who up to that time had been only self-regarding, forced to act on different principles and to consult his reason before listening to his inclinations.[1]

In the second passage, the reason for that compression is made clear:

That which is good and in conformity with order is so by the nature of things and independent of human convention. All justice comes from God, he alone is its source; but if we could receive it from so high up, we would need neither government nor laws...for want of natural sanction the laws of justice lack force (*sont vaines*) among men...[2]

One may very easily put Rousseau in contradiction here by inquiring how, if divine justice (natural law) is not merely empty speculation, the transfer from instinct to morality could result solely from the political act. And of course the answer must be that the genetic and analytical strains of his thought are pitted against each other at this point. Some legal analysts have exploited this confusion to insist that the Rousseauian pact of association is null and meaningless if it represents a common undertaking of pre-moral beings.[3] But it must be recognized that Rousseau has said elsewhere that a (pre-political) 'société commencée' possesses a 'moralité commençante',[4] and that moral relationships begin, in effect, with the act of visual comparison: 'As soon as a man compares himself to others he necessarily becomes their enemy...There is the primitive and radical contradiction...'[5]

---

[1] *Contrat social*, I, viii, *O.C.* III, 364.

[2] *Ibid.* II, vi, 378. God's effective justice relates to the *post mortem*; cf. 'Lettre à l'abbé de Carondelet', Mar. 4, 1764, *C.G.* x, 341: 'Take away eternal justice and the prolongation of my being after this life, and I would see in virtue nothing but madness masked by a fine name.'

[3] Cf. Raymond Carré de Malberg, *Contribution à la théorie générale de l'Etat* (2 vols., Paris, 1920–2), I, 61 ff.; and Franz Haymann, 'La loi naturelle dans la philosophie politique de J.-J. Rousseau', *Annales*, xxx, 65–109.

[4] *Inégalité*, *O.C.* III, 170.

[5] 'Fragments', *O.C.* III, 478.

The 'Social Contract': the image of legal morality

We can ease the confusion somewhat by presuming that Rousseau intended not to place the origins of moral life within the state by mere rhetoric, but to insist that only the bonds of political association could create the structural guarantee for a 'moralité bonne'. We should remember, too, that he was concerned to prove, against Diderot, that political society was a pure convention, not a natural development.

The *Social Contract* is not history but logic. Indeed, it denies all explanations of social conditions, being rather an explanation of how the maximum of juridical and moral integrity (of individuals) could be preserved in the light of those conditions. Still, it has some peculiar connections with the historical perspective. Like *Emile*, it is an anti-history, flinging not only the standard of political right but the accusation of delinquent development against virtually all governments, despite its pragmatic passages and protective overtones of abstract discourse. It implies that if there is no public virtue, this is a direct consequence of the way men have formed their political associations. It is a gloomier anti-history than *Emile* because, far from assuming the image of uncorrupted man, it takes as its point of departure the pre-civil (or, by extrapolation, 'pre-legitimate'), 'war of all against all' described in the *Second Discourse* and, by implication, transfers this war to the level of political communities rather than that of the mere strivings of individuals to be preferred.[1] That leads, paradoxically, to both greater abstraction and greater realism. The entire marathon of humanity is not to be problematically rerun, only its darker half.

Even this 'squaring of the circle' does not escape from the burden of history. The remarkable I, ii of the *Geneva Manuscript* ('De la société générale du genre humain') attempts to phase out the 'philosophical' history of the *Second Discourse*, which had suggested pre-rational and pre-political nodes of order and had invoked accident to account for their demolition. Now man, clearly destined for civil society by a virtually Hobbesian necessity, suffers only enough of a break with isolated brutishness as is required to define a life-or-death choice. Gone is the cherished 'age of gold', '... always a condition foreign to the human race, either for our having

[1] *Contrat social*, I, vi, *O.C.* III, 360.

55

failed to recognize it when it was possible to enjoy it, or for having lost it even when it has been possible to know it'.[1] This delight forsworn, man is now compelled to choose the civic order which can alone inspire him to conscientious virtue, 'the most delicious feeling of the soul'. No doubt there is a wrench here, elaborated more finely in *Rousseau juge de Jean-Jacques*, between ideals of logic and emotion, duty and innocence. But, as Emile is told by his tutor, 'lawfulness (*le droit*) does not bend before human passions';[2] and it is 'droit politique' that Rousseau is intent on establishing. It is not so much that Rousseau has arbitrarily demolished the *siècle d'or* (whose legacy he will continue to discover in the solid independence of small peasant communities), but that he has recognized the gap of awareness between the natural *per se* and the reflective yearning for the natural.[3] The simple soul, absorbed in his routine, cannot step back from it to measure his felicity. Memory and imagination, those sources of our hopes, fears and woes, also secure what pleasures are to be had from life. And, as Rousseau writes with reference to Emile's 'sensibilité naissante' (adolescence), which is clearly to be related to the 'société naissante' of the happy paleolithics: 'There are ages in human life which are made so as never to be forgotten.'[4] The adolescents of the world had never acquired a consciousness of their fortunate years, but we can stand on the high ground of experience and regret in order to commemorate such blessedness, which we still sense in 'fertile fields', 'festivals' and 'country games': 'People treat the golden age as a chimera, and so it will be always for the man whose heart and taste are spoiled...What then must be done to bring it back to life? A single, but impossible thing: to love it.'[5]

---

[1] *Contrat social* (*P.V.*), I, ii, *O.C.* III, 283.

[2] *Emile*, V, 597.

[3] Rousseau's wishful image of the *siécle d'or*, which permeates most of his writings, even the 'Spartan' ones (cf. *Sciences et arts*, p. 22), expresses an alchemization of psychology into history. See especially his rendition of this theme in the air 'Les consolation des misères de ma vie', *O.C.* II, 1169–70: 'Mais qui nous eut transmis l'histoire/De ces tems de simplicité?'

[4] *Emile*, IV, 398. Cf. V, 550, clearly an idealization of childhood: 'If you would extend the effect of a fortunate education over a whole lifetime, prolong the habits of childhood into early manhood; when your pupil is what he ought to be, keep him the same from then on.' Also V, 565.

[5] *Ibid.* V, 606.

It has been suggested that Rousseau failed to include *Geneva Manuscript* I, ii in his final version of the *Social Contract* because, as a personal polemic waged with Diderot over the universality of reason and the rational accessibility of a standard of natural right, it seemed out of place in a deductive essay on 'droit politique'. In any case, by the time we reach *Social Contract* II, vii–x (also included in the *Geneva Manuscript* in a single large chapter called 'Du peuple à instituer'), we are resolutely back in the realm of history and all too aware of the catalogue of limitations that the 'succession des choses' imposes on the ideal of civic order. Now it would seem that just communities are not simply vaulted out of a crumbling world of nature in which dependence has caused men to pool their strength; they require a deliberate pause between socialization and legislation, no longer represented as a 'wrench' between instinct and duty, brutishness and reason, but as a transformation of natural simplicity into the rational-legal order. Hereupon, Rousseau cites two cases: the Russians, who have been 'civilized' ineptly and too early;[1] and the Corsicans, who, alone among the peoples of Europe, are ripe for institutions of freedom. With these examples, the shadow of history once again crosses the monochrome landscape of 'droit politique'. We are thus prepared by the most corruscating sort of anti-history for the historical limitations of political justice as Rousseau conceived it.

C. CORSICA: THE CUSTOMARY-DEFENSIVE IMAGE

This third pattern of possibility, which I have labelled 'customary-defensive', is Rousseau's most consistent effort to come to grips with the historical problem of a 'good' political development. It is his most tangible. The 'customary-defensive' solution is prefigured by the historical intrusions upon the *Social Contract*. The key is to be found in a displacement of emphasis from virtue to habit and from

---

[1] Rousseau's dislike of Peter the Great was proportional to the adulation heaped on that monarch by Voltaire and the Encyclopedists. Cf. Damilaville, article 'Vingtième', *Encyclopédie*, XVII, 856; 'The Russians were a people before the reign of Tsar Peter. The prodigious changes wrought by the genius of this great man make them a more civilized but not a new people.'

ethics to natural morality, indeed from institutions to custom. This shift of emphasis is, in itself, a source of prime Rousseauian confusion, because we are given variously to understand that custom has unquestionable attachments with nature[1] and yet that, no less than the work of formal legislation, it must be the concern and challenge of that superior and misty figure who forms a people and, in Rousseau's term, 'denatures' it.[2] We are left uncertain as to whether, like the austere, political virtue described elsewhere by Rousseau, it is a socialized transformation. Probably it was vaguely intended to have connections with both, in a manner that Rousseau never made very clear. We see, for example, in one passage that it has appeared as a substitute for moral conscience: 'The law acts only externally, governing the actions; custom (*les mœurs*) alone penetrates within and directs the operations of will.'[3] Custom, according to the *Social Contract*, is the fourth and most important sort of law;[4] by extrapolation, it may even underlie that so-called 'voix céleste' which teaches each citizen 'to act according to the maxims of his own judgment and to avoid being in contradiction with himself'.[5] 'When philosophy has once taught a people to despise its customs,' we are told, 'it soon discovers the secret of bypassing its laws.'[6] But custom is apparently, in the perspective of the *Social Contract*, as artificial an acquisition as positive legislation itself: that sort of people fit for legislation is 'one which has neither customs nor superstitions deeply rooted'.[7] It is Lycurgus who made the Spartans and Moses who created the Jews.

Nonetheless, we get a quite different picture from Rousseau's treatment of the *Project for Corsica*. Here the anteriority of custom to law and the connection between nature and custom is emphasized, and the trick is apparently to bring a 'natural' people unmutilated

[1] Cf. *Emile*, I, 8.
[2] *Contrat social*, II, xii, *O.C.* III, 394.
[3] 'Fragments', *O.C.* III, 555. Cf. Montaigne, 'Of Custom', *Essays*, p. 96: 'The laws of conscience, whose origin we attribute to nature, are born rather from custom.' This is, of course, implicit in the linguistic parallels: *ethos-ethika* (Gr.) and *mos-moralis* (Lat.). Rousseau's distance from a later liberal tradition is underlined by this position; cf. J. S. Mill, *On Liberty*, in *The Philosophy of John Stuart Mill* (ed. Marshall Cohen, New York, 1961), p. 192: '...the magical influence of custom, which is not only, as the proverb says, a second nature, but is continually mistaken for the first.'
[4] *Contrat social*, II, xii, *O.C.* III, 394.
[5] *Economie politique*, *O.C.* III, 248.
[6] 'Préface à Narcisse', *O.C.* II, 971.
[7] *Contrat social*, II, x, *O.C.* III, 390.

into the political world. It is very much as if a colony of *sièclatoriens*, threatened not by 'funeste hasard' but by the proximity of civilization, were enjoined to freeze its patterns of social behaviour in defence against outside contamination.

In hypothesizing this historical liaison between the natural and the political *via* the bridge of socialization (a people 'already bound by some tie of origin, interest or convention'),[1] Rousseau permits himself a reminiscence about the destiny of the early Swiss. In the *Lettre à d'Alembert* he had first painted their idyllic portrait: 'In [his] youth, on the outskirts of Neufchatel...' he had seen: '...a mountain entirely covered with dwellings, each in the midst of its land, so that those houses, as equally spaced as the fortunes of their owners, at once gave the numerous inhabitants of that mountain the inner contemplation of withdrawal and the charms of society.'[2] The *Corsica* manuscript further explains that 'this people...had no virtues because, having no vices to conquer, it acted well at no cost; it was good and just without even knowing what justice and virtue were'.[3] This is the model for the Corsicans. There are lessons for them, too, because whereas once 'the uniformity of [Swiss] life took the place of law', it later happened that contact with other peoples 'made them admire what they should have despised', inaugurating *amour-propre*, inequality and corruption. In Rousseau's judgment, 'the Corsicans are still almost in the sound and natural state'.[4] Before the fate of the Haut-Valaisians catches them, they must cross the frail bridge to organized political life, because, in words written for another context, 'there is no longer time to draw us outside of ourselves, when once the *moi humain* concentrated in our hearts takes on that contemptible activity that absorbs every virtue...'[5]

Whether or not Rousseau really imagined himself as a legislator for Corsica is a moot point. He had both misgivings and temptations: after all, he was the man who could find his own traits in both the patient and the healer, in Saint-Preux and in the mentor of Emile.[6] He seems to have hedged the issue in his own mind:

[1] *Ibid.*   [2] *Lettre à d'Alembert*, Didier, I, 329.   [3] *Corse*, O.C. III, 914–15.
[4] *Ibid.* p. 950.   [5] *Economie politique*, O.C. III, 259.
[6] *Rousseau juge de Jean-Jacques*, II, O.C. I, 778.

Images of integration

...in order to live quietly there, I made up my mind to abandon, *at least to all appearances* [my italics], the work of legislation, and in order to repay my hosts in some measure for their hospitality, to confine myself to writing their history on the spot, with the reservation of quietly acquiring the information necessary to make me of greater use to them, if I saw any prospect of success.[1]

Nonetheless, the fragments of his *Project* resound with the hope of taking advantage of the opportune historical moment to thrust this people outside of European history and into a 'natural' history all its own. And despite frequent references to republican Rome (especially where economic policy is discussed), the grave and spectral virtues of antiquity will not be the pole star for the Corsicans:

I will not preach morality to them, I will not prescribe virtues for them; but I shall put them in such a position that they will have virtues without knowing the word, and that they will be good and just, scarcely knowing what justice and goodness are.[2]

In short, the Corsicans, in their isolation from the wickedness of Europe, are to be much like Rousseau himself in his flight from 'intolerance and fanaticism', children of an order in which nature is not so much supplanted but strengthened by political institutions: 'Noble people, I have no wish to give you artificial and systematic laws of man's invention, but to bring you back beneath the laws of nature and order which alone command the heart and do not tyrannize the will.'[3] To 'have virtues without knowing the word' is to surrender the boon of virtue for the sake of immunity to vice and thus to surrender conscience; to be 'beneath the laws of nature and order' is somehow to recapture that symmetrical distance between instinct and reason which verified man's orderly place in the cycles of nature and yet already bespoke his privileged position

[1] *Confessions*, XII, *O.C.* I, 651. Also, 'Lettre à Buttafuoco', 22 Sept. 1764, in Vaughan, II, 356: 'The very idea [of legislating] rouses my soul and transports me...But...zeal does not supply the means, and the desire is not the power.'
[2] *Corse*, *O.C.* III, 948; cf. *Emile*, III, 223. Rousseau's own expectation was undoubtedly more complex. In *Confessions*, XII, 648, he speaks of the Corsicans' 'naissantes vertus' which might some day equal those of Sparta and Rome.
[3] *Ibid.* p. 950.

in the creation. Custom now becomes the spring of the will, and the will is so conditioned that it ceases to aspire beyond the rectitude of custom. Like de Tocqueville, Rousseau saw societies essentially regulated 'by the feelings, the beliefs, the ideas, the habits of heart and mind of the men who compose them',[1] not by the documentary passion of recurrent constitutional assemblies. 'There will never be a good and solid constitution unless the law rules over the hearts of the citizens', he reminded the Poles.[2] The passion for order had to come first, and that conviction was essentially rooted in a series of attitudes related to the will and sometimes called custom, a core of communal being, 'which should be tampered with only with extreme circumspection'.[3]

But the problem is more complicated than this. Rousseau stood half-way between believing that customs, developed in a 'nuit des temps', were a primitive substrate for positive law and order, and that there was a genuine necessity for legislators, 'gods on earth', who from mysterious depths of skill dispensed law and custom at prime historical moments, miraculously forming 'peuples' from mere 'peuplades'. The one feeling derived from Rousseau's own historical perception of 'rustic feasts', 'village games' and 'joyful harvests'; the other from his indebtedness to Machiavelli, Montesquieu and, above all, Plutarch and the classics. He attempted to join both visions by seeing in the patriotic festival and other exhibitions of civic solidarity the emotional remnant—or should one say, equivalent?—of a primal and spontaneous community, and by formulating a theory of 'droit politique' that would reassert men's independence *vis-à-vis* each other while binding them equally beneath laws of general adoption and application. The essay on Poland, particularly, is full of the first preoccupation.

Rousseau was torn between a conviction of the need for order and authority in the light of the fundamental weakness of man and an overpowering sense of the corrupt inclinations of authority measured against the fundamental goodness of man. The solution then was to imagine a type of alien authority that disinterestedly created order

---

[1] De Tocqueville to Corcelle, 17 Sept. 1853. Cited in Richard Herr, *Tocqueville and the Old Regime* (Princeton, 1962), p. 35.
[2] *Pologne, O.C.* III, 955.   [3] *Ibid.*

under which a still uncorrupted man could then be placed and could, within limits of natural devolution, prosper. Such is the situation of the legislator and the inchoate 'peuplade'. Unquestionably, the parallel with the tutor and the child, reinforced by the classical correlation of education and laws and by Rousseau's own wishful reflections on his early years, affected this portrait. Nor should we fail to notice that, like the eighteenth-century *deus absconditus*, legislator and tutor withdraw from their creation once it has been completed, leaving behind a human product of custom, law and education which it is now man's responsibility to guide and preserve.

Rousseau's demigods are, in one sense, creators but, in another, interpreters and intermediaries. Despite the mathematical clarity with which Rousseau presented his either/or images of 'man and citizen', we have seen that his real preference was for a combination of the social and personal that would avoid contradiction, a 'moi relatif' untinged with *amour-propre*. This required the assimilation of the independence of nature to the mutuality of communal life. In effect, his demigods of authority redirect nature into new patterns of order rather than abolishing it completely. To speak of the antithesis of nature and political society in Rousseau is to recognize the deep dilemma between independence and community which underlay his thoughts. But to coronate this antithesis as his last word is to misconstrue him. In this regard, the term 'denature' is unfortunate, because it suggests dehumanization rather than the humanizing redirection of a corruptible impulse. The more accurate slogan, also used by Rousseau, is that art makes reparation of the evils consequent to the breakdown of the natural order.[1] This is the task of the mysterious figure of authority: to assure the continuity of nature in a new perspective, to create, if one pleases, a 'second nature', but not one which is a substitution for that older and more fundamental principle, rather one which saves it from its own cumulative and destructive defects. The old Adam is not forsworn, for it comes again to birth at every moment of human time, the carrier at first of helplessness and soon thereafter, if unchecked, of vanity and licence, but also of those imperishable assets which bad society stifles, independence and innocence.

[1] *Contrat social* (*P.V.*), I, ii, *O.C.* III, 288.

Conscience is an individual affair upon which one might construct a society of the wise or a republic of the just. Custom, on the other hand, achieves—or might achieve—the bond of a people who share an 'origin, interest or convention'. Made formal in the state, it is nevertheless also a link with nature, drawing, as Rousseau thought he perceived among the Corsicans, the 'simplicity of nature' into the system of 'needs' inaugurated by society. If it be argued that Rousseau vaunted ethnic particularism as against the ideal of 'natural' cosmopolitanism, the 'general society' proclaimed by the intellectual republic of Europe of his day, it should be remembered that he admired the particularisms of rural Switzerland, of Corsica, and later, of Poland, because he believed them close to the spirit of the popular and 'natural', to feasts, rites and occurrences of millennial origin, not because he rejected the criterion of 'humanity' so abundantly acknowledged in the *Emile*. Politics, for Rousseau, meant making a tradition out of nature by giving civic foundations to a once spontaneous enterprise. The wise legislator shapes his materials as he can. But where intolerable inequality presides over the political act, the state will be similarly misshapen and thus no happy meeting of art and nature.

Unlike later theories which owe much to Rousseau's moral-juridical analysis, this presupposes no purposeful unfolding of the state toward goals of justice and freedom, no explicit destiny for socialized man to develop his culture and intellect, no meeting of the nations in a cosmopolitan world order. Rather, there is an insistent correlation between origins and ideals, isolation and innocence, wisdom and immobility, and politics and the natural life cycle. Far from 'standing on the shoulders of the ancients' or striving for a perfectibility in the species, men and peoples run the same race over and over, mostly for the bad; and if they transmit any accumulated knowledge to descendants, compatriots or foreigners, it is almost inevitably corrupt. Though each life is a fresh start, the bad currency tends to drive out the good. Circumstances might save Corsica from this horror of history; she might meet her 'salvation in time'. But it will involve putting her in a museum.

Having with some care explored three approaches of Rousseau to the question of evil in history, of which the first probably represents his most personal and comprehensive treatment, we are better able to savour his pessimism and to disown critical attributions of 'progressivism'. He composed lengthy anti-historical treatises with flourish and genius in order to demonstrate that human development was, for the most part, a comfortless anomaly. What, then, could one do? Remake humanity or human institutions? Substitute a 'good history' for a bad? *Recommencer à zéro?* Scarcely, in view of the prevailing forces. In the present state of morality, anarchy was more to be feared than injustice. In the end, there is no answer but perseverance and counterpressure against the vortex. The 'moi' must move within the sphere of its competence. If no wider field of expansion can be imagined, it becomes a task to place oneself 'in order', 'adding no other chains to those which nature and the laws impose'.[1] In effect, the only barrier to history was order itself.

D. ORDER AND DISORDER

'What sweeter felicity,' asks the Savoyard vicar, 'than to feel ordered in a system where everything is good?'[2] Although the vicar's remark commends the divine order, which is, for Rousseau, effectively the order of nature, here is a motto for all the researches of this brilliant and disturbed man into the requirements for human peace and well-being. Order, however, did not have the fundamental meaning of authority, but of justice.[3] Rousseau indeed extolled superhuman symbols of authority that could create order or cure disorder, but he was far from cherishing human authority as such, except when, as 'love of virtue', it redressed violations. Justice, on the other hand, carried overtones of equality and cohesiveness, of harmony and integrity within a given sphere of operation, as well as the fear of problematic extension in time or space. For Rousseau, there were essentially concentric circles of order, most valid at the greatest circumference, most intense and reliable at the narrowest.

---

[1] *Emile*, v, 567, 603.   [2] *Ibid*. IV, 357.
[3] Cf. *ibid*. IV, 342: '...the love of order which preserves [order] is called justice'. Also, *Confessions*, IX, *O.C.* I, 327: 'The justice and uselessness of my complaints left in my mind the seeds of indignation against our foolish civil institutions, whereby the real welfare and true justice are always sacrificed to an apparent order, which is really subversive of all order...' In a more theoretical vein, *Emile*, IV, 344.

Order and disorder

If history is the record of *perfectibilité* and, more especially, of *'la prévoyance*...which bears us ceaselessly beyond ourselves... the true source of all our wretchedness',[1] order is the idea that reasserts 'nature' or attempts to reorient history to a natural rhythm. Order is that style of human affairs in which reason becomes possible, because reason's determinations are essentially directed toward a static field of analysis in which the components tend to remain as given. Where order prevails, life can be encompassed, worked out, and savoured.[2] In this sense, Rousseau is surely a rationalist.

Once more, Rousseau's anxiety for order mounts from the depths of his personality and experience. Throughout his life, but acutely in his later years, Rousseau was tortured both by the sense of time, which played on his memory and imagination, and of space, which both affronted his ego with limits and drew it out to unsafe distances.[3] To these issues was intimately related his groping for unity or a centre of order, akin to Paradise, where, as he put it, '...I shall be me without contradiction, without division',[4] and to his notion of psychological balance, defined as 'the perfect equalization of power and will'.[5]

Rousseau's final position, 'less a morality of action than of abstinence',[6] was less a solipsism than an infinite retreat. Projecting his own consciousness upon the world, he did not aspire to draw the entire world back into the ego. He still found time to praise virtue, even if he could not rise to it, or the solidarity of games and feasts, even if he felt alone.[7] In *Emile* he had written: 'Everywhere that there is feeling and intelligence there is some moral order. The

---

[1] *Emile*, II, 67.
[2] Cf. 'Lettres morales', II, *C.G.* III, 350: '...for want of knowing how we ought to live we all die without having lived'. Cf. *Confessions*, IX, *O.C.* I, 426: 'I saw myself reaching the gates of old age, and dying without having lived.'
[3] These observations are much indebted to two brilliant studies by Georges Poulet: *Etudes sur le temps humain* (Paris, 1949), pp. 158–93; and *Les métamorphoses du cercle* (Paris, 1961), pp. 102–32. Also of interest is Mark J. Temmer, *Time in Rousseau and Kant* (Geneva and Paris, 1958).
[4] *Emile*, IV, 358.
[5] *Ibid*. II, 64.
[6] *Rousseau juge de Jean-Jacques*, II, *O.C.* I, 855.
[7] E.g. *Rêveries*, IX, *O.C.* I, 1085: 'Is there sweeter satisfaction than to see a whole people joyful on a festival day...?'

65

difference is that the good man orders himself in relation to the whole, and that the wicked man orders the whole in relation to himself. The one makes himself the centre of all things; the other measures his radius and holds himself at the circumference.'[1] Rousseau's own radius had finally shrunk to a point where centre and circumference were congruent, where memory and imagination had fallen in upon the undifferentiated moment; the man himself had become the god of a miniscule cosmos.[2] By his earlier definition, Rousseau had passed beyond good and evil.

But his literary career had been a frantic groping for other solutions of order: the private and eternal order of God 'who can because he so wills';[3] the order of nature 'whose first motions are always right'; the hypothetical order of primal, instinctive man; the order of the *siècle d'or*, equidistant between reason and instinct; the societal order of being 'just and virtuous without knowing the meaning of justice and virtue'; the 'denatured' order of the patriotic *polis*; the domestic order of the Wolmars at Clarens; the juridical order of 'laws above men'; the precarious moral order of the very wise; and the wistful order of the 'homme nouveau', *pret à tout*, even slavery in Algiers; even that facetious but meaningful 'hobbisme le plus parfait';[4] not to mention those particularistic solutions for societies at mid-drift in their political life. For every kind of order there was a price to be paid—ignorance, self-limitation, psychological sublimation, arrested development, inaction, the chains of society or the forfeit of reason—but there was the consolation of feeling intact, sustained at a point of balance and not driven in two directions.

This does not mean, however, that order was a pick-and-choose proposition. One did not, could not, go back to superannuated solutions.[5] Nor could one wish to sacrifice the hazards of moral life for a sub-human security. History and consciousness denied that

---

[1] *Emile*, IV, 356.
[2] *Ibid.* IV, 347: '...the goodness of man is love of his fellows and the goodness of God is love of order'. Cf. *Rêveries*, I, *O.C.* I, 999: 'Everything outside me is henceforth foreign to me.' In *Emile*, IV, 344, he writes, 'I know that the identity of the ego is given continuity only by the memory.'
[3] *Emile*, III, 347.
[4] Cf. 'Lettre à Mirabeau', 26 July 1767, *C.G.*, XVII, 157.
[5] Cf. *Inégalité*, *O.C.* III, 193.

alternative.[1] The destructive liberty of the savage or of the child is curtailed by his weakness; but our only hope is to curtail it with a reason that is too often fatally corrupted. In view of this situation, and since man is now just as destined to live in a community as if his instincts had commanded it, Rousseau found himself hesitating between logical and psychological answers to the problem of order. The logical answer, prefiguring Kant and his successors, is in the alchemical transformation of the law of freedom into a law of necessity:

If the laws of nations, like those of nature, could have an inflexibility which no human force could ever defeat, man would then return to a dependence on things; in the republic there would be combined all the advantages of the natural and civil conditions; to the liberty that keeps man from vice would be added the morality that raises him to virtue.[2]

This is what Rousseau called 'squaring the circle'. He had no more confidence in its achievement than would a geometer. Nor is the logic of the proposition really very evident once one plunges beneath its brittle 'metaphysical' veneer. The cruel metaphorical play on the triple meaning of the word 'law' (physical, moral, juridical), unhappily a temptation in the major European languages and undoubtedly an important clue to the Western mind, has encouraged both noble and evil ideological consequences that need not be spelled out here. In effect, one is trying to correlate forms of order that are, respectively, natural and coercive (necessary), natural and non-coercive (injunctive), and artificial and coercive (admonitory and punitive). It is difficult to see how a 'dependence on things' can be moral or how 'the liberty that keeps man from vice' (self-sufficiency) can be combined with 'the morality that raises him to virtue' (society, implying the eternal possibility of vice).

Rousseau would seem to be saying that we escape moral harm by escaping moral relations. But we must remember that Rousseau's natural order is more an animism than a mechanism (as indeed was Diderot's). 'Mortals,' he could exclaim, 'you are not abandoned; nature lives on.'[3] This 'vast ocean of nature'[4] in which we draw

---

[1] Original nature contains the seeds of its own destruction, because 'the first law of nature is the concern of self-preservation'. *Emile*, II, 223.
[2] *Ibid.* II, 71.　　　　[3] *Emile*, IV, 432.　　　　[4] *Rêveries*, VII, *O.C.* I, 1066.

breath adds beauty, tranquillity and innocence to the diurnal course of the Newtonian cosmos; 'douce félicité' softens the acute angles of the geometer's exercise. Above all, Rousseau postulates kinds of order in which there is some vitalizing principle, not merely an automatic conjugation of the 'private vices–social virtues' variety. They have no 'laws of motion' but are the antithesis of that relentless, if self-contained, mobility. 'The great maxim of Madame de Wolmar', we read, 'is to favour no changes in condition, but to contribute to the happiness of each one in his own.'[1] In *Emile* he comes down hard on the same point.[2] 'Because of my attachment for [your constitution], I would have wished that nothing could change it,' he tells the Genevans.[3] His ornate catalogue of exaggerative compliments in the Dedication to the *Second Discourse*—freedom, longevity, staticity, virtue, modesty, piety, friendship, gentleness of climate—come probably as close to his psychological centre of gravity as any passage written before his final embitterment.[4] Here, time is domesticated but not assassinated, space is restricted but not driven within the ego, custom and will, law and liberty are harmonized. 'Puisse durer toujours...!' he could exclaim. But the search in the crevasses of history had turned up only a chimera.

'[Man] realizes form', wrote Schiller, 'when he creates time, and contrasts the changeable with the permanent, the manifoldness of the world with the eternal unity of his ego; he gives a form to matter when again he abolishes time, maintains permanency in change, and subjects the manifoldness of the world to the unity of his ego.'[5] Despite Rousseau's acknowledged role as midwife to the Romantic movement, he had never believed that man could do so much. Should man's strength ever carry him to the brink of mastering historical time, nature would not then accept the imprint of the ego's new-found unity; rather, the ego, historically torn between capacity and desire, would be healed by glimpsing the true shape of nature. Man might conceivably become just and wise—an artist— by submitting to his reintegration, but not by assembling nature in forms to satisfy his expansive will. Rousseau and Schiller agree on

---

[1] *N.H.* V, ii, *O.C.* ii, 536. [2] *Emile*, I, 12.
[3] *Montagne*, VI, *O.C.* iii, 809. [4] *Inégalité*, *O.C.* iii, 112 ff.
[5] F. Schiller, *Letters on the Aesthetic Education of Mankind*, 11th letter, in J. Weiss (tr.), *The Aesthetic Letters, Essays, and the Philosophical Letters* (Boston, 1845), p. 51.

the necessity for a recaptured harmony of art and nature. Where they differ—and it is the whole distinction between a future open to man's wilful designs and one foreclosed by the accumulated travesties of *perfectibilité*—is in the plausibility of the attempt. Yet Rousseau's very doctrines would prove a dynamite to force the future, while Schiller later attempted to cover his ears from that explosion.

Rousseau came in his turn to be possessed by history and modern factionalism. Split away from their precarious private core, his doctrines led in oblique directions and, in the opinion of some post-Marxian critics, led nowhere—except to an intangible 'petty bourgeois' or pre-industrial solution already denied in advance by forces of change embedded in the Old Regime.[1] On the other hand, Rousseau's radical protest lodged deeply in the febrile sensitivities of a whole younger generation of intellectuals and *roturiers*, aspirants for the discordant acquisitions of respect, autonomy, power and order—for mastery over a history which, they thought, had cheated them blind.

Daniel Mornet writes of the *collèges* toward 1770: 'Public exercises testify that history is becoming more than a chronology or a pretext for moral sermons. One discovers a real curiosity about customs and a taste for thinking about the life of nations and governments.'[2] He is speaking roughly of the graduating class of the Brissots and the Robespierres. According to the testimony of these men and many others, it was Rousseau who laid the groundwork for this will to action. Rousseau stepped beyond the Enlightenment—beyond reason into feeling. Shortly after his death he began his conquest of the France that spurned and persecuted him. Robespierre received the living word from his lips in 1778;[3] but the Jean-Jacques mania was no respecter of causes, and Marie Antoinette and her children accomplished the pilgrimage to Ermenonville in their turn.[4] Rousseau taught men that they were 'good' apart from social station and intellect, paradoxically good in both their independence and solidarity.[5] These lessons come, of course, from *Emile* and the

---

[1] E.g. E. J. Hobsbawm, *The Age of Revolution, 1789–1848* (New York, 1964), p. 293.
[2] Daniel Mornet, *Les Origines intellectuelles de la Révolution française* (5th ed., Paris, 1954), p. 329.
[3] *Ibid.* p. 416.   [4] *Ibid.* p. 227.   [5] Cf. R. Hubert, *Sciences sociales*, p. 364.

discourses; Mornet 'has not managed to collect ten pieces of evidence concerning readers who, before 1789, received a strong impression from [the *Social Contract*]'.[1] It is only after the first shock of liberty that the political Rousseau is 'discovered', via Sieyès, Marat and others.

According to Rousseau, history blocked justice because it carried man expansively away from nature in a fatal reciprocity of moral and physical demand and satisfaction, spreading mastery and slavery in its wake. This corruption was itself superimposed upon a natural life cycle of peoples, measured by political criteria and modelled on the biological career of the individual. Somehow, Rousseau believed, the viciousness of man could be overcome only in the youth of his undertakings and then only through extraordinary tutelage. He had, however, severely questioned the legality of all political relationships, and had remarked that peoples were sometimes granted a 'seconde naissance': Sparta and Rome among them.

That is the script by which the most fervent Montagnard ideologists understood the Revolution that they had to make. They would return France to 'nature' and to a 'seconde naissance'. 'If nature created man good,' declared Robespierre, 'he must be brought back to nature.'[2] It is not simply a juridical demand. Saint-Just, though his political ideals varied considerably between 1791 and 1794, played unceasingly with similar notions: '...an enslaved people which suddenly emerges from tyranny will not return to it for a long time, because freedom has found new, uncultured, violent souls...'[3] In short, where Rousseau had seen masters and slaves, the leaders of the Terror proclaimed the hidden 'natural' of a French people ready to burst from ancient bondage. Though 'despotism corrupts...the most intimate feelings of the oppressed', and though 'a people is critically situated when it passes suddenly from slavery to freedom, when there is contradiction between its customs and habits and the principles of its new government', 'the [French] *peuple*, that large, industrious class...is

---

[1] Mornet, *Origines*, p. 96.
[2] Maximillien Robespierre, *Œuvres complètes* (10 vols., Nancy, 1910–67), *Lettres à ses commetans*, 2nd series, no. 2 (10 Jan. 1793), V, 207.
[3] Louis Antoine Léon de Saint-Just, *Œuvres* (ed. Jean Gratien, Paris, 1946), pp. 91–2.

untouched by the causes of depravation which has doomed...those
of a superior condition...It is closer to nature..."[1] In Robespierre's
rhetoric, it is as if Rousseau's legendary Corsicans had been transplanted to Picardy and the Ile de France. And as Rousseau never
failed to enjoin isolation upon the peoples of his choice—for the
sake of solidarity and justice—so Robespierre put forward a similar
barrage of arguments against the Girondin appetite for war and
cosmopolitan fraternity in 1792.[2] To use a Thucydidean metaphor,
the Robespierristes remind us of Sparta after the Persian wars;
by contrast, the Brissotins are Alcibiadean. Or, taking a modern
parallel, they were respectively the Stalinists and Trotskyites of their
own revolution.

Granting this link with Jacobin and *sans-culotte* lyricism, there is
definitely something about Rousseau's concatenation of moods that
evades the equation. In the end, he stands alone. There is a vast
distance, not to be measured by decades or kilometres, between the
Isle of Poplars and the Panthéon, between Arcadia and the Hôtel de
Ville. That something is pathos, passivity and regret. It is a matter of
non-expectation. Rousseau's adieu to his century was not in favour
of the next, but in favour of a *temps mort* or a *nulle part*, a place of
childhood denied by history, denied by the fate of growing old.
'Will', writes the philosopher Louis Lavelle, 'converts the future into
a sensuous present, while memory converts the past into a spiritual
present.' Further, 'will is, in a certain sense, the reverse of memory;
it makes a perception out of the image, just as memory makes an
image out of the perception'.[3] Despite his defence of the will,
Rousseau is fundamentally an apostle of the memory: his perceptions become images. Still, he is at a point of tension, trying to
resolve the contradictory triads of *past–memory–regret* and *future–
will–desire* into a perfect present, where, as he puts it, 'each moment
is a perpetual beginning'. Sociologically, this attitude has a good
deal of resemblance to what Georges Gurvitch has labelled the

---

[1] Robespierre, *Défenseur de la Constitution*, no. 4, *O.C.* IV, 113–15; also *Lettres*, no. 4, V, 20.
[2] See H. A. Goetz-Bernstein, *La politique extérieure de Brissot et des Girondins* (Paris, 1912), *passim*, and Georges Michon, *Robespierre et la guerre révolutionnaire, 1791–1792* (Paris, 1937). Also, Albert Mathiez, *La Révolution française et les étrangers* (Paris, 1918), pp. 158 ff.
[3] Louis Lavelle, *Du temps et de l'éternité* (Paris, 1945), p. 283.

sense of 'erratic time': '...a time of uncertainty par excellence where contingency is accentuated...the present appears to prevail over the past and the future, with which it sometimes finds it difficult to enter into relations'.[1] Rousseau's political disciples of the Montagne will take the decisive step of transforming 'memory' into 'will' across the atemporal *kairos* of the 'recommencement' (whose aptest symbol is the Revolutionary calendar). And this will mean, once the deed is accomplished, a future; with that future a past; and with the past a history, a new 'nuit des temps', new heroes, a new *cité*. In a matter of time that history can join the 'old' history which has never ceased. Progress can achieve a double boon. But Rousseau himself did not cut this Gordian knot; he did much to call attention to it.

[1] Georges Gurvitch, *The Spectrum of Social Time* (Dordrecht, 1964), pp. 31 f.

PART THREE

IMMANUEL KANT:
THE RATIONALIZATION OF THE CHIMERA

I

INTRODUCTION: THE GERMAN
POLITICAL CONSCIOUSNESS

A. ROUSSEAU AND THE GERMAN REACTION
TO THE ENLIGHTENMENT

'Comment arriver aux cœurs?' the *Gouvernement de Pologne* had lamented.[1] Rousseau touched many across the Rhine. Goethe remembered it this way: '...Rousseau had really touched our sympathies. Yet we found, on considering his life and fate, that he was nevertheless compelled to find his highest reward in the fact that he was allowed to live unacknowledged and forgotten in Paris.'[2] That was the characteristic reaction of the literary *Sturm und Drang*, motivated to escape from burdensome reality and to long for purpose and purity of conscience—what Hegel would later describe as 'the good heart'. The political Rousseau would be discovered no earlier in Germany than in France. Only in the wake of the Revolution would it seem to Goethe that he, with Diderot, '[had] unobtrusively paved the way for those monstrous world-wide changes in which all that had hitherto existed seemed to be swallowed up'.[3] For the meantime, the Sturmers exclaimed with the character from Leisewitz's *Julius von Tarent*: 'And must the whole human race, in order to be happy, be locked up in states— where each man is a slave of the others, and no one is free—where each is riveted to the other end of the chain by which he holds his slave fast?'[4] Herder, in the eighth book of his *Ideen*, wrote bitterly of 'those state machines for which one must pay so dearly'.[5] This was Rousseau's problem of the social contract—unsolved; the German pre-Romantics could not even accept 'chains garlanded with flowers'.[6]

[1] *Gouvernement de Pologne, O.C.* III, 955.
[2] J. W. Goethe, *Poetry and Truth* (tr. Minna Steele Smith, 2 vols., London, 1908), II, 36.
[3] *Ibid.*
[4] Quoted from Roy Pascal, *The German Sturm und Drang* (Manchester, 1953), p. 48.
[5] J. G. Herder, *Ideen zur Philosophie der Geschichte der Menschheit* (2 vols., Leipzig, 1828), Bk. VIII, v. I, 334.
[6] *Sciences et arts, O.C.* III, 7.

Introduction: the German political consciousness

Rousseau's first apostles—with the significant exception of Kant —were individualists and theoretical anarchists. However, Karl Moor of Schiller's *Die Räuber*, the *locus classicus* of protest heroes, moves not only in an ideal situation where the individual must take it upon himself to right cosmic wrongs, but in a suffocating real world of brusque materialism and archaic princely *Kleinstaaterei*. The just political order is simply unimaginable; heroes and artists are the resources.

This reaction was waged against the German Enlightenment, felt as an alien force. It must be remembered that the country was the hollow shell of a Holy Roman Empire, divided into some three hundred and sixty kingdoms, duchies, free cities, prince-bishoprics and more obscure political forms—only a handful much above manorial status. Petty sovereigns—especially in the south—flattered their vanity and increased their subjects' misery by constructing miniature replicas of Versailles, maintaining brilliantly cockaded and ineffectual standing armies while selling their own peasants into foreign wars, and continually importing troupes of French or Italian singers and actors. Most of the states were miserably run, some rather intelligently (like the Saxe-Weimer of Karl-August and Goethe), others severely (like Frederician Prussia). But the sway of French manners and culture, if debased, was general. As Gérard de Rayneval wrote in 1787: 'This part of Europe is France's boulevard...the Treaty of Westphalia has always been considered one of the finest gems of the crown.'[1]

None of this sounds very *aufklärerisch*; but the *Aufklärung*, too, was a French boulevard. While in France philosophy and despotism lived in a state of armed truce, the German Enlightenment was paternalistic, authoritarian and cosmopolitan to the detriment of Germans. Here, Prussia was the outstanding case: 'by 1740... about one-quarter of the subjects of Frederick the Great are said to have consisted of immigrants or their descendants. In Berlin they were particularly to the fore...'[2] Berlin was a city of Huguenots and soldiers. The *émigré* base was then strengthened by

[1] Quoted from Marcel Dunan, *L'Allemagne de la Révolutionet de del' Empire* (Cours de Sorbonne, Paris, n.d.), I, 3.
[2] W. H. Bruford, *Germany in the Eighteenth Century: The Social Background of the Literary Revival* (Cambridge, 1965), p. 173.

76

Frederick's importation of French scholars and functionaries, headed by the formidable Voltaire. The nobility read French when it read at all. The poet Klopstock, honoured by Denmark and Austria, received no favour from German sovereigns. Although, thinking better of the matter, Herder scratched the passage out before publication, he had still written for the *Ideen*: 'My voice is too weak to address one of the rulers of the world, who, in majority, even on German thrones, are Frenchmen and neither read nor understand the barbarous language in which I write.'[1] Thus, in spite of its connection with reform, education, religious toleration and intellectual liberty, many felt the Franco-cosmopolitan *Aufklärung* to be alien and menacing to the German genius. 'A Frenchman is a thing no German man can stand,' Goethe wrote in *Faust I*, 'and yet we like to drink their wine.'[2] That was about the size of it.

Still, it was not difficult in the Europe of the time to regard Frederician Prussia as a progressive, if severely governed, state. Kant called his epoch the 'century of Frederick' with entire sincerity. Because it was not 'enlightened' but 'becoming enlightened', Kant held that 'a lower degree of civil freedom ... provides the mind with room for each man to extend himself to his full capacity'.[3] Frederick was a *philosophe*; the 'first servant of the state' brooked no nonsense about divine right, though his own notion of obedience may have amounted to something very like it. Thus, even wistful Girondins would look to Prussia as a potential ally before the blow of war fell in 1792.[4] When the Peace of Basel was signed in 1795, progressives hoped for a constitutional pacification of Europe by those two master-architects Kant and Sieyès.[5]

[1] Third draft, cited in Max Rouché, *La philosophie de l'histoire de Herder* (Paris, 1940), p. 297 n.

[2] *Faust*, Part I, ll. 2272–3.

[3] 'What is Enlightenment?' in L. W. Beck (ed.), *Kant on History* (New York, 1962), p. 11.

[4] See H. A. Goetz-Bernstein, *Politique extérieure*, pp. 108–11 and especially p. 95. The Girondin Isnard declared to the National Assembly on 5 January 1792: 'Ah, if Frederick [the Great] were alive, that philosopher-king would surely have greeted the French Revolution as a means for consolidating the balance of power in the North.'

[5] Cf. Jacques Droz, *L'Allemagne et la Révolution française* (Paris, 1949), pp. 160–1. Parts of Kant's 'Perpetual Peace' were reproduced approvingly in the *Moniteur*. Sieyès was highly popular among the enlightened in Prussia. Karl Engelbert Oelsner translated his writings; see Droz, pp. 74–5. Also, Paul Schrecker, 'Kant et la Révolution française', in *La Révolution de 1789 et la pensée moderne* (Paris, 1940), pp. 266 ff.

Introduction : the German political consciousness

We see here the collision between pre-Revolutionary liberalism and the tortuous revelation of the national cultural consciousness. There was always an air of the formula: *Aufklärung* = Rococo = France = Cultural Subordination. In such an atmosphere, caught between the despotism of dry reason and the brutality of feudal manners, an artist like Schiller could write: 'The poet must live in an ideal world... must find refuge in the realm of ideals from the wretchedness of reality.'[1] A German refrain—or requiem—whose orchestrator was Rousseau, whose theme was the intellectual destitution of the educated bourgeoisie, and whose melody was a preformed tradition of Reformation spirituality.

Rousseau was a kind of linking trait. The 'literary' Rousseau became also a chief expositor to the Germans of the French 'political' Revolution. His glorification of sentiment and human goodness, animated descriptions of nature, solitude, *Innerlichkeit*, haunted convictions of the evil of the age, and paradoxical particularism and humanitarianism appealed to the German soul. 'How from heaven you have fallen, morning star!' lamented Herder at the news of his death.[2] Klopstock, Hölderlin and Schiller wrote sonorous odes to his genius. If, as one historian has put it, the more turbulent and sentimental works of Rousseau and Diderot opposed a 'new France' to a straitjacketed classicism, this struggle was perceived across the Rhine as one of German against French civilization.[3] We shall presently see how Kant was touched by these currents.

B. THE GODS OF GREECE

The rise of German classicism is marked by renewed involvement in the problem of community as opposed to the abstract question of rebellion raised by the *Sturm und Drang*. After 1775 Goethe and Herder migrate to Weimar to take up state offices, and there is a more plausible marriage of ideals with concrete forms of life. Still, there is airy and sublime regret. The German classicism is *sui generis*, and also a distillation of the processes earlier described.

---

[1] *Schillers Persönlichkeit* (ed. Hecker and Petersen, 3 vols., Weimar, 1904–8), II, 39–40.
[2] J. G. Herder, *Sämmtliche Werke* (ed. Suphan, Berlin, 1877–1913), IV, 413.
[3] L. Reynaud, *Influence française en Allemagne*, p. 401.

The gods of Greece

The successive 'classicisms' of Italy, France and Germany were not just reverences for antiquity but also assertions of national cultural primacy in new kinds of world order. If the French used the arguments of nature and antiquity to challenge both Christianity and the feudal past, to assert themselves as 'the culture', Germany used its passionate Hellenism to confront Rome, Latinity, France, the Enlightenment, pre-Romantic Gothicism, Christianity and eventually—at a distance—the disturbing features of the French Revolution. Since it exalted the culture of the *polis* but had no political nation of its own, it was well accommodated by philosophical idealism—especially the balanced Apollonian variety produced by Hegel. German classicism must also be understood as a 'romanticism', one of the 'sun' and not of the 'night', especially because of its questioning of the rational-legal-religious heritage of Latinity. Thus, German culture could be, simultaneously, or at least interchangeably, Northern and Hellenic without any great wrench.

The problem of Rome and Greece in German culture is inseparable from the political and intellectual fortunes of Germany in Europe. Just as the intelligentsia of the eighteenth century feels culturally depreciated, so the 'nation' is seen as having no prerogatives but its culture. Decades of controversialists argue over whether political fragmentation promotes spiritual depth or whether the nation must be made whole to be civilized. These nuances are not lacking in complexity, because the models of the Greek city-states and of the Roman Empire (*qua* absolutist and, later, Napoleonic France) are at hand. Herder, for example, straddles the question, appearing to find in the division of Greece the cause of its greatness,[1] but arguing in many other places for the cultural unity and common destiny of the German race. The first line of reasoning is shared by Justus Möser, Johannes von Müller and other empirical 'localists': behind it is not only Greece, but the example of happy Switzerland and the writings of Rousseau.[2]

Goethe, on the other hand, whose tastes and *Bildung* are cosmo-

[1] Herder, *Ideen*, Bk. XIII, ii, II, 108. The notion was not just a German fantasy; Hume endorses it in his essay on 'The Origin and Progress of the Arts and Sciences'.
[2] Cf. E. Sieben, *Die Idee des Kleinstaats bei den Denkern des XVIII. Jahrhunderts* (Basel, 1920).

politan but whose soul is integrally German, bewails the vitiating effects of localism. In his famous essay, *Literarischer Sansculottismus* (1795), he openly declares that to have outstanding national authors a nation is required. And to the end of his days he laments: 'Everyone is content with the views of his province, his town or his own mind, and we may have to wait a long time before we achieve a creditable standard of cultivation.'[1]

Germany = Greece: the politically plural land of noble art, harmonious nature and generous hearts;[2] France = Rome: the belligerent voluptuary and thief of culture. The Germans of the eighteenth century knew it was not so, but they groped subconsciously for this equation. This is not a Goethean thought, of course; it is more in Herder's line. But with copious argument and illustration it will fuel the Fichtean fires against Napoleon and become a credo of the Romantics. Herder begins to justify this position with a theory of ethnic relativity, much in the same way that the French had earlier set out to prove their excellence by invoking the immutability of human nature. As for Romanism and Latinity, Herder could hardly be more deprecatory: its single virtue is as a conveyor belt, 'a bridge thrust by Providence across the abyss of the centuries so that a few remnants of [Greek] antiquity could be carried to us'.[3] Few Germans will have much good to say about Rome until Mommsen.

It is curiously in French historical polemic that we see the germs of the Aegean-Nordic coalition first sprouting;[4] Montesquieu exports these implications across the Rhine in his praise of 'our fathers, the *Germains*'. Montesquieu was of course interested in the 'Frankish' theory of French history, which placed the weight of authority behind mixed government and the role of the *parlements* and nobility, as against the 'Gallo-Roman' thesis, which, depending

---

[1] J. P. Eckermann, *Gespräche mit Goethe* (Wiesbaden, 1955), Conversation of 3 May 1827, p. 566.
[2] It has been truly remarked that for most Germans Greece was simply one big Periclean Athens tempered by a certain amount of Homeric great-heartedness. In Herder, especially, these two ideals seek to join. But there is a great distance between Winckelmannian calm and Heinsean fury.
[3] Herder, *Ideen*, Bk. XIV, vi, II, 214–15.
[4] On the subject of French eighteenth-century 'Gothicism', see Auguste Le Flamanc, *Les utopies prérévolutionnaires du XVIIIe siècle* (Paris, 1934), *passim*.

on its application, could support absolutism or popular sovereignty. To the Germans, however, this recalled the idea that both the Greeks and they were 'mother races', the respective creators of ancient and modern civilization. The *stürmisch* idea of liberty could also feel vindicated in passages from Montesquieu such as the following: 'The Goth Jordanes called Northern Europe the factory for the tools that break the chains forged in the South. There are formed those valiant nations that leave their lands to destroy tyrants and slaves.'[1] This notion was a commonplace of the 'theory of climates' dating back to Aristotle and Pliny: de Jaucourt repeats the passage almost word for word in his article 'Fief'.[2] Charmingly enough, the rabid cosmopolitan Clootz, a Westphalian, seriously proposed to the French revolutionary Convention on 26 April 1793, that with the abolition of countries all should become 'Germains', citizens of a 'République des hommes, des germains, des universels'.[3]

By exposing foreign layers of accumulated artificiality, the Germans, too, went in search of the 'natural man', not for purposes of establishing political right, like Rousseau, but in order to lay bare an ethnic model which, noble and harmonious like the Greeks, could serve as a microcosm of everything best in humanity. Of the Western European peoples that had arisen from the anarchy of the *Völkerwanderung*, the Germans were the least mixed and defiled, the purest of speech—with a perfect correspondence of sounds and notions—and the most profound and moral; in these qualities they resembled the immortal Hellenes. Thus the myth of the *Urvolk* gradually took shape, a pattern which, with nuance and deviation, can be traced from Herder to its full explosion in Fichte's *Reden*.[4]

More poignantly and sensitively, the problem was recreated at

---

[1] *Esprit des lois*, XVII, v. Cf. also Rousseau's sarcasm (perhaps directed toward Voltaire), *Inégalité*, note i, *O.C.* III, 206–7: 'Will someone have the goodness to tell us what produced the swarms of barbarians which, for so many centuries, flooded Europe, Asia and Africa...how could these wretches have had the presumption to test themselves against such clever people as we were?'

[2] *Encyclopédie*, VI, 68.

[3] Buchez and Roux (eds.), *Histoire parlementaire de la Révolution française* (Paris, 1834–8), XXVI, 156–7.

[4] Cf. J. G. Fichte, *Addresses to the German Nation* (ed. G. A. Kelly, New York, 1968), pp. 47 ff., 115. Fichte's linguistic theory is indebted to the 101st of Herder's *Briefe zur Beförderung der Humanität*. Cf. Alexis Philonenko, *La liberté humaine dans la philosophie de Fichte* (Paris, 1966), pp. 36–7.

the personal level of the artist. Goethe and Schiller shared no easy delusions about *Urvolk* or the alleged Hellenic prowess of their compatriots, but they strove for the harmonization of their own life and work. This, too, led to some extraordinary bifurcations of the real and ideal. As Schiller wrote to Goethe on 23 August 1794: 'Since you were born a German, since your Greek spirit was hurled into this Northern world, you had no other choice than either to become a Northern artist yourself or by substituting in your imagination, through the power of thought, the element of which reality had deprived it; and thus intellectually, as it were, giving birth to a Greece of your own from within.'[1] *'The power of thought'* ...such *aperçus* make Hegel's dilemma seem much clearer.

Even without the Kantian *Zweiweltentheorie* or any explicit philosophical separation of ideality and reality, the German intellectual had little choice but to lay culture against politics, seeing in the one the unity of the spirit and race which the other denied. The numerous literary reviews—which individually, however, never gathered in more than two thousand subscribers—were the lonely ambassadors between fragments of a nation.[2] Consequently, it is not surprising that the Schlegels, Hegel and others welcomed the advent of Napoleon, and that Goethe had an admiration for him which the French intelligentsia could not share. In his poem *Pandora* Goethe gives the Germans the only national mission that seems feasible, that of dominating the ideal world, while the French are left to conquer and govern in the real one.

Finally, just at the moment when the ancient Reich is crumbling, Schiller will give full expression to the German mission and vision:

Sundered from politics, the German has founded a value of his own, and even if the Empire should perish, this German dignity will abide unchallenged. It is an ethical greatness, it dwells in the culture and character of the nation, which are independent of any political destiny... The German is chosen by the world spirit to work, amid the struggles of time, on the eternal building of man's education [*Menschenbildung*]; not to glitter for a moment and play out his role, but to make a conquest

---

[1] Quoted from Henry Hatfield, *Aesthetic Paganism in German Literature* (Cambridge, Mass., 1964), p. 108. The discussion of the Greece–Germany problem in Droz, *Allemagne et Révolution*, pp. 482–8, is excellent.

[2] Cf. Bruford, *Germany in the Eighteenth Century*, pp. 281–2.

of the great process of time. Each people has its day in history, but the day of the German is the harvest of time as a whole [*der ganzen Zeit*].[1]

C. THE FRENCH REVOLUTION ENTERS GERMAN THOUGHT AND HISTORY

Classicism and idealism are the forward positions of German thought by the early 1790s; the romantic movement follows within a decade. All are woven around the French Revolution, whose cumulative impact on Germany is no simple matter to describe. Let us begin with the philosophical connection.

The habit of joining the 'Copernican' and 'bourgeois' revolutions is an old affair. The analytical mind can sense a *rapprochement* between the subjective grounding of consciousness and experience and the great uprising against arbitrary power and unnatural privilege. *I think, I feel, I am, I order my experience* means, in some way, that nothing outside of me performs these operations on my behalf legitimately. Nobody, of course, summoned the Estates or stormed the Bastille in the name of Kant or even pure reason; but the feedback from the Revolution to transcendental philosophy was immediate. Kant became prophetically fascinated by the events in Paris and devoted much of the decade to writing on law and politics. And in 1795 Fichte wrote to the Danish poet Jens Baggesen: 'While I was doing a work on the Revolution [the *Beiträge* of 1793], the first signs, the first hints of my [philosophical] system welled up inside me.'[2] A whole generation of philosophers-to-be, among them Hegel and Schelling at Tübingen, became passionately excited;[3] a few years later, after they had separated, Hegel penned off these revolutionary words to his friend: 'Philosophers will demonstrate the dignity of man; the peoples will learn to feel it, and they will not be content to demand their rights that had been cast in the dust, but will seize them back and put them to use.'[4]

---

[1] F. Schiller, sketches for 'Deutsche Grösse', an unfinished poem of 1797, not discovered until 1871, *Sämmtliche Werke* (22 vols., Munich and Leipzig, n.d.), XIII, 278–9.

[2] H. Schulz (ed.), *Fichtes Briefwechsel* (2 vols., Leipzig, 1925), I, 449–51.

[3] Karl Rosenkranz, *Georg Wilhelm Friedrich Hegels Leben* (Berlin, 1844), p. 29.

[4] Johannes Hoffmeister (ed.), *Briefe von und an Hegel* (4 vols., Hamburg, 1952), 4 Feb. 1795, I, 24.

Introduction: the German political consciousness

Marx and Lorenz von Stein both connected Kantian legal doctrine with the legislative acquisitions of the French revolutionary bourgeoisie. Both also theorized that backward social conditions in atomized Germany had caused an ideal replication of those forms which the French had been able to translate into reality.[1] While it is true that material conditions for a political revolution were conclusively absent in the Germany of this time,[2] few souls could be found to preach one. It was easier to be an expansive *Weltbürger* in Paris than a lonely subversive at home. Kant himself observed that the Germans were 'the most easily and constantly governable people... inimical to novelty and to resisting the established order'.[3] This in no way contradicts Madame de Staël's almost contemporaneous judgment.[4] Modern history has encouraged us to forget that the Germans were then noted for their jugular instinct in academic debate, rather than for any special martial qualities. The jurist Karl von Moser put it nicely: 'We will think our "Ça ira", but not sing it.'[5]

Still, the outbreak of the Revolution had thrilled intellectual and upper middle-class Germany. The hated Capets had been taught a lesson. Klopstock, dean of the poets, burst into song, recanting his previous glorification of old Germany and extolling the French in 'They and Not We', an ode written for the first anniversary of the storming of the Bastille. Wieland, Schiller, even Friedrich Gentz, later the translator of Burke, hailed the dawn of a new age of reason. Herder himself, quartered at Aix-la-Chapelle while his prince and his friend Goethe marched to the front with the coalition armies in 1792, wished for the success of the revolutionary forces.[6] On 26 August 1792, Schiller, Klopstock, Washington,

---

[1] See Karl Marx, 'Zur Kritik der Hegelschen Rechtsphilosophie', in Marx-Engels, *Werke* (39 vols., Berlin, 1957–67), I, 379–80; Lorenz von Stein, *History of the Social Movement in France* (trans. K. Mengelberg, Totowa, 1964) p. 281.

[2] See Reinhold Aris, *History of Political Thought in Germany, from 1789 to 1815* (London, 1936), pp. 39–44.

[3] *Anthropologie*, in *Gesammelte Schriften* (Akademieausgabe, 24 vols., Berlin, 1902–64), VII, 317–18. All Kant citations from German according to this edition.

[4] Germaine de Staël (-Holstein), *De l'Allemagne* (Paris, 1871), I, ii, 23–5.

[5] *Neues patriotisches Archiv* (Mannheim and Leipzig, 1794), quoted by J. Droz, *Allemagne et Révolution*, pp. 119–20.

[6] Maurice Boucher, *Révolution vue par les écrivains*, p. 77.

The French Revolution enters German thought and history

Thomas Paine and a handful of other foreigners were voted citizens of the French Republic by the Legislative Assembly.

It is difficult to compose in one statement all the things the French Revolution meant to German intellectuals. Here, however, are a few: the birth of idealism in politics, the levelling of a haughty and supercilious absolutism, the triumph of reason, the poetry of a united people, the blood of ancient Gaul rising, the resurrection of the heroism of Thermopylae and Marathon. Joachim Campe, best known as the tutor of Wilhelm von Humboldt, reported breathlessly from Paris on 4 August 1789: 'Is it really true that I am in Paris? that the new Greeks and Romans whom I see around me were really still Frenchmen a few weeks ago?'[1] Karl Friedrich Reinhard, journeying coincidentally from Bordeaux to Paris in 1791 in the company of Vergniaud and other deputies of the Gironde, found his coachmates charming but politically naive(!);[2] he had written to Schiller the year before in the following terms: 'I have seen in the French Revolution not just something happening to a nation with which I will probably never be in complete sympathy, but a giant step in the course of the human spirit and a happy occasion for dignifying the human condition.'[3] In brief, the Germans admired the Revolution because they thought it 'human' and universal, not because it was French.

For this reason, most of the enthusiastic German émigrés in Paris attached themselves to Girondin circles, after having followed approvingly the acts of the Constituent Assembly. Even though the Girondins were the war party, they were also the cosmopolitans, the cultured republicans, the believers in an 'Athenian ideal' and an aristocracy of merit. The war itself, as Brissot and Condorcet had made amply clear, was being fought in defence of freedom and in the name of humanity ('Guerre aux palais, paix aux chaumières'). The shrill obligato of the fanatic Clootz added a German accent to the war hysteria. 'I love the French Revolution,' wrote Archenholz. 'I honour the French constitution...I esteem the National As-

---

[1] Quoted by Alfred Stern, *Die Einfluss der französischen Revolution auf das deutsche Geistesleben* (Stuttgart and Berlin, 1928), p. 20.
[2] Cf. A. Aulard, *L'éloquence parlementaire pendant la Révolution française: Les orateurs de la Législative et de la Convention* (2 vols., Paris, 1885), I, 307.
[3] Quoted by Droz, *Allemagne et Révolution*, p. 55.

sembly...I despise the Jacobin chiefs [i.e., the later Montagnards] ...since they are leading the fickle masses astray. I lament the King ...I tolerate the aristocrats still dwelling in the kingdom...however, I detest the aristocrats who fled abroad...'[1] A fairly average set of reactions for the progressive German colony of Paris.

With the fall of the Gironde at the beginning of June 1793, the sky rushed down on these worthies. Robespierre's alliance with the *sans-culotte* commune demanded, among other things, the sacrifice of some foreign heads to appease popular xenophobia.[2] 'Paradise', writes Droz, 'turned quickly to hell';[3] and the choice was generally to hide or flee. Even the genial and noble Forster, who died not long after of broken ideals and domestic misery, was moved to write from Paris on 7 July 1793: 'I have no more place to call home, no more country, no more friends...'[4] Together with the Gironde, 'the Republic would seem to have gone to its grave', he commented in a letter of 20 November to his wife.[5] Karl Oelsner, intimate of Condorcet and Brissot, and a perceptive reporter of day-to-day events, wrote a damning indictment of Robespierre and the Montagne ('convulsionaries of fanaticism') scarcely rivalled by any propaganda out of London.[6] With the onset of the Terror the Germans gloomily noted the demise of ordered meritocracy and of the majesty of the law.

Back across the Rhine, where many French events reached the enlightened public by way of lengthy dispatches from these same sources, the evolution was similar, or more abrupt. Appalled by the trial and execution of the King, Klopstock did penance in 'Mein Fehler': 'My golden dream is no more...' Wieland saw reason overcome by fanaticism, fell back, *aufklärerisch*, on Pope's maxim: 'For forms of government let Fools contest;/What e'er is best administer'd is best'; in a sequence of lucid essays he predicted a dictator for France, and, in 1798, named him Bonaparte.[7] The

---

[1] Quoted by Stern, *Einfluss*, p. 32.
[2] Cf. A. Soboul, *Les sans-culottes parisiens en l'an II* (Paris, 1962), pp. 208–9.
[3] Droz, *Allemagne et Révolution*, p. 49.
[4] Quoted by Henry Brunschwig, *La crise de l'Etat prussien à la fin du XVIIIᵉ siècle* (Paris, 1947), p. 208.
[5] Quoted by Stern, *Einfluss*, p. 27.
[6] See Alfred Stern (ed.), *Charles Engelbert Oelsner : Notice biographique, accompagnée de fragments de ses mémoires rélatifs à l'histoire de la Révolution française* (Paris, 1905).
[7] Cf. M. Boucher, *Révolution vue par les écrivains*, pp. 56, 70.

execution of the king was too much for Herder. Even Kant, who continued to defend *the* Revolution (if not revolution) on higher ground, was repelled: 'It is the formal execution of a monarch that fills the soul, conscious of the ideas (*Ideen*) of human justice, with horror...How can this feeling be explained? It is...a moral feeling arising from the complete subversion of every concept of justice. It is regarded as a crime that remains eternally and cannot be expiated...'[1] Schiller saw the human race set back a century and unworthy of self-government. 'When in March 1798 he finally received his diploma of French citizenship, he noted...that all the signatories were dead and that he seemed to be getting a message from beyond the grave.'[2]

By 1791 the *Reflections* of Burke had reached Germany in Gentz's translation, and the pamphlet commenced to enjoy wide influence.[3] The leading German Burkeans—Ernst Brandes and August-Wilhelm Rehberg—came, significantly, from Hanover, the hereditary fief of the English monarch. Both were admirers of the British constitution. Their polemical works, less exalted but more sensible than Burke's classic, breathed a respect of tradition and political experience and a penchant for responsible aristocracy and mixed government. 'No state', Rehberg wrote, 'has ever been founded on the universal rights of man; in fact it is thoroughly impossible for any state to be so founded.'[4] They accepted little or nothing of the Revolution beyond the decrees of 4 August 1790, except the civil constitution of the clergy. The doctrines of these conservative constitutionalists, for whom the arch-fiends were the republican Girondins, the fallen heroes of the German colony of Paris, had wide influence over the German reaction, especially as it became tinctured with the cosmopolitan disillusionment of the idealists. Prime antagonists of Fichte, they later affected, albeit distortedly,

---

[1] Immanuel Kant, *The Metaphysical Elements of Justice* (trans. John Ladd, New York, 1965), p. 87 n. This is an abridged version of the 'Rechtslehre' from the *Metaphysik der Sitten*.
[2] M. Boucher, *Révolution vue par les écrivains*, p. 104.
[3] On this phase of German political thought, see F. Braune, *Edmund Burke in Deutschland* (Heidelberg, 1917); Jacques Godechot, *La Contre-Révolution, 1789–1804* (Paris, 1961), pp. 113–30.
[4] A. W. Rehberg, *Untersuchungen über die französische Revolution* (Hanover and Osnabrück, 1793), I, 44.

the reactionary 'historical' school of Stahl and Savigny, and probably moderated Hegel's views.

It was Hegel himself who described the tottering structure of the legendary German polity shortly before its collapse: '...just as fallen fruit is recognized as having belonged to its tree by the fact that it lies under the tree top, but neither its position below the tree nor the tree's shadow which falls on it can save it'.[1] Inadequacy in the war with the French Republic, cession of the trans-Rhenan lands, and the separate peace of 1795 have proved that the states are rotting apples beneath the German tree. 'It is not what is that makes us irascible and resentful,' says Hegel, in the earliest expression of a characteristic thought, 'but it is the fact that it is not as it ought to be. But if we recognize that it is as it must be, i.e. that it is not arbitrariness and chance that make it what it is, then we also recognize that it is as it ought to be.'[2] This excursion into the ills of the realm concludes that 'a human work of justice and dreams fulfilled' cannot be secure against 'the higher justice of nature and truth', thus foreshadowing the main theme of Hegel's entire philosophy.[3]

But before that systematic criticism of 'dreams fulfilled' can be made comprehensible, we have the course of the idealist tradition to consider. The point of departure is a closer look at Kant's relation to Rousseau.

[1] G. W. F. Hegel, 'The German Constitution', in T. M. Knox (ed.), with an introductory essay by Z. A. Pelczynski, *Hegel's Political Writings* (Oxford, 1964), p. 143.
[2] *Ibid.* p. 145.
[3] *Ibid.* p. 199.

2

MORALITY, KNOWLEDGE AND
HISTORICAL VISION

A. KANT AND ROUSSEAU

Committing neither the errors of certain *Aufklärer* who leaped upon Rousseau's idea of *perfectibilité* without regard for its content, nor those of the soulful Sturm und Drangers who saw in his life and works a *beau geste* against authority and order, Kant was well aware that Rousseau's major message centred upon the contradictions between nature and civilization, civilization and morality. For all that, it would be misleading to represent Kant as a disciple or successor of the Genevan. The gist of the difference is this: Kant tended to see civilization as a mediating term between the ideas of nature and morality, which Rousseau, against the general thrust of the Enlightenment, had set asunder. What Rousseau desired with respect to 'nature' and 'morality' (in their positive sense) was not so much a mediation but a reciprocal subsumption. For him, it was precisely 'civilization' that stood in the way. From the outset, Kant's outlook bespoke the idea of a laboured historical continuity as opposed to Rousseau's indictment of history and drift toward fatalism. Thus, from the special angle of this study Kant was, preeminently, an indebted but problematic critic of Rousseau.

The point, however, requires further investigation. Substantial Rousseauian building blocks including that keystone (expanded into a concept of 'transcendental freedom'), the liberty which is self-enacted law rather than mere wilful resistance to external and arbitrary coercion, spangle Kant's architectonic rampart against 'dogmatism and fatalism'.[1] Moreover, the 'dialectic' of the *Critique of Practical Reason* seems almost to be a philosophical grounding of the Savoyard vicar's rejection of theological metaphysics and his postulation of God, freedom and immortality as the *idées forces* of

---

[1] Cf. 'Preface to the Second Edition', *Critique of Pure Reason* (hereafter, *C.P.R.*), trans. Norman Kemp Smith (New York, 1963), pp. 32–3.

the moral life.[1] It is also possible, especially if the contextual pre-occupations of both thinkers are thrust aside, to discover a fundamental equivalence between Rousseau's model of political legitimacy and the ideal *societas sociorum* of Kant in which the actions of communal life would be made reciprocally co-restrictive by the 'laws of freedom' of a juridical commonwealth or republic.[2] Plausibly, these resemblances alone are decisive enough to justify the frequent academic generalization that brings Rousseau and Kant together. We seem to find a correlative appreciation of how men *ought to live* in their moral relationships and in an organized society where the obligation of personal respect, expressed outwardly by common adherence to laws that satisfy both criteria of justice and autonomous consent, has been made the source of order.

Paradoxically, if inevitably, both Kant and Rousseau brought upon the intellectual horizon doctrines which were to stimulate ideologies and fuel factions. For both the Genevan 'historian of the human heart' who 'alone had built solidly' and the Koenigsberg professor who made such extravagant claims toward establishing the conditions and possibilities of knowledge saw themselves as reconcilers.[3] Rousseau, we know, conceived of a mission to arbitrate between the extremes of ecclesiastical and intellectual intolerance by revealing the common source of their pretensions. Both of them, he thought, distorted human nature through the sin of pride,

[1] *Emile*, IV, 343–5, 385. For a general examination of the Kant–Rousseau correlation, especially with regard to the notion of self-legislative autonomy and the question of 'sentiment', see Arturo Deregibus, *Il problema morale in Jean-Jacques Rousseau e la validità dell'interpretazione kantiana* (Turin, 1957). Deregibus considers and evaluates the explanations of Cassirer, Schinz, Derathé, Delbos, Sacheli and others. Even C. A. Sacheli, *Rousseau* (Messina, 1942), whose interpretation is perhaps more 'rationalist' than Cassirer's, says that it is 'dangerous to see Rousseau by way of Kant', p. 16.
[2] See, in general, Kant, *The Metaphysical Elements of Justice* (hereafter, *Justice*), 'Introduction to the Elements of Justice: Division of the Metaphysics of Morals in General', pp. 45–7.
[3] Cf. *C.P.R.* A xii (hereafter, A = first edition, B = second edition), p. 10: 'I venture to assert that there is not a single metaphysical problem which has not been solved or for the solution of which the key has not been supplied'; also, *Justice*, p. 6: 'When the critical philosophy announces that it is a philosophy prior to which there was absolutely no philosophy, it is not doing anything different from what anyone who constructs a philosophy according to his own plan has done, will do, and indeed, must do.' Obviously, such a position is a direct denial of Hegel's famous equation of philosophy and the history of philosophy.

engendering moral injustice and 'disorder'. This preoccupation led indirectly to such consequences as a 'civil religion' which would extend the juridical equality of the ideal political society to the public ethic while borrowing for civil order the force of religious commitment, and to a scarcely qualified derogation of any cognitive knowledge that repressed or hindered the 'natural' moral life, an opposition of *sagesse* to *science*, wisdom to intellect. 'Rentrons en nous-mêmes' meant more than a psychological precaution against social injury: it was an injunction to correlate desire and power toward the vanishing point of perfect justice and order.

Though Rousseau's tortured problems are hardly marginal to his culture, he expressed them in an elliptical way. His creed was personal and cantankerous, integrally inaccessible to the developing European philosophical vision, which encompassed both political cleavage and cultural continuity. Seen in this light, Kant is probably the more consequential reconciler, not so much because of his systematic erudition but because, while weighing Rousseau's dilemmas seriously and sympathetically, he shunned the impasse of despair.

What issues, then, critically affect Kant's ambiguous connection with Rousseau? It is fortunately possible to trace these concerns from their genesis. As one of Rousseau's earliest and most ardent readers and exponents in Germany (a famous 'snapshot' provided many years later by Herder of his former professor establishes this),[1] Kant allows us to discover in his marginal notes accompanying the composition of the essay on *The Sublime and the Beautiful* (the so-called 'Bemerkungen', posthumously edited and published) how forcefully 'the singular and paradoxical opinions of the author' struck him.[2] The 'servant of Frederick' found himself seduced by 'this rare depth of spirit...noble force of genius...soul burning with sensitivity'. Kant studded these jottings with appeals to liberty and justice palpably inspired by the *Social Contract*. In a frequently cited passage, he draws a distinction which will loom large in the career of 'transcendental idealism', creating problems for its adepts, ammunition for its critics, and matter for the post-Marxian study

---

[1] J. G. Herder, *Briefe zur Beförderung der Humanität*, *S.W.* XVIII, 324–5.
[2] Kant, *Gesammelte Schriften* (hereafter, *G.S.*), XX, 44.

of 'ideology'. 'My taste is that of a scholar,' he writes. 'I feel the thirst, plainly and simply to know, the restless desire to extend my knowledge...' This had led him to a contempt for ignorance and the ignorant. However, Kant continues, 'Rousseau straightened me out...I learned to honour mankind.'[1] Henceforth, Kant is seized with the will to use his erudition on behalf of humanity by establishing the rights of man philosophically. In the same notes, Kant makes his well-known reference to Rousseau as the 'Newton of the moral world';[2] and it is fatally under the impact of *Emile* that he begins to offer courses in the theory of education at Koenigsberg in 1765–6.[3]

Was this the proclamation of an uncritical discipleship? Rather, we shall find that Rousseau's were a set of insights to be absorbed in the enormously complex and prudent structure of a 'critical' philosophy that was not even in germ at this moment of first contact. 'The restless desire to extend knowledge' and the exhortation 'let us return to ourselves' were fundamentally incompatible. *Science* and *sagesse* would strive for a renewed alliance; the basic Kantian condition for realizing the human vocation would be an acknowledgment of purpose in history rather than counsels of withdrawal or evasion. In turn, this conclusion, filtered through Kant's subtle separation of faith and science, would place the intermediary 'human' disciplines of moral anthropology, political right, and history itself in peculiar positions, suspended, as it were, between the sensible and intelligible worlds.

Kant's cogitations led him swiftly to at least three significant and related areas of disagreement with the Genevan. In the first place, he felt compelled to dissipate the ambiguous connection between nature and origins that Rousseau's anti-teleology suggested. To be sure, he could for the moment agree that 'nature never created man for civic life' and could repeat the exhortation of *Emile* for some solution whereby 'one might, within civilization, remain a man of nature'.[4] However, this was a kind of *élan* to be abandoned with the full development of the Kantian system. Already he was

---

[1] Kant, *G.S.* xx, 44.   [2] *Ibid.* pp. 58–9.   [3] See Paul Duproix, *Kant et Fichte*, p. 49.
[4] 'Bemerkungen', *G.S.* xx, 31, 15. Actually Kant continued to hold this view in the sense that the state is not intended as a matrix for happiness, which is better obtained in nature.

contrasting his methodology with Rousseau's: 'Rousseau proceeds synthetically and starts from man in the state of nature; I proceed analytically and I start with civilized man.'[1] By this somewhat sybilline remark, Kant implies, among other things, that he will make the 'state of nature' a purely heuristic device, essentially for measuring criteria of legality, and that he will regard civilization (which is, after all, the content and motor of history) as a purposive given in the demonstration of a plan whereby man's vocation is to be developed. He will reinterpret the 'social contract' or 'pact of association' not as the quasi-historical juridical ingredient by which civil society becomes possible but as the Idea (*Idee*)[2] toward which the legal-political order, progressively civilized, should, and in a moral universe does, tend: 'The social contract is the rule [i.e. regulative principle] and not the origin of the constitution of the state.'[3] Thus, in Kant's vision norms of order become ambiguously transferred to a future in the same fashion that Rousseau's had been nebulously assigned to a past, to a beginning, or conceivably to a *recommencement*. For Kant the course of history will be seen as irreversible and unbroken in so far as being a sequence of phenomenal event, and, by necessity, it will involve the entire race.

In the second place, Kant transmutes Rousseau's *Emile* into a codex for universal civilized advance, which is indeed a common interpretation of that work. Rousseau's treatise is raised to the status of a rational Idea: 'The Idea is a universal rule *in abstracto*, the ideal is a particular case which I subsume beneath this rule. Thus, for example, with Rousseau's *Emile*, the education to be given Emile is a true Idea of reason.'[4] Relying on textual and psychological evidence, I have already argued that Rousseau presented *Emile* both as an 'anti-history' and as a proof of man's irrefutable but poignantly ineffective anthropological goodness. But if Rousseau set little store

---

[1] *Ibid.* p. 4

[2] On 'Ideas' (*Ideen*), see ahead, pp. 128–134.

[3] *Reflexionen zur Rechtsphilosophie*, No. 7956, *G.S.* XIX, 564. Cf. *Justice*, p. 79; 'On the Common Saying: That What Holds Good in Theory is Worthless in Practice', in C. J. Friedrich (ed.), *The Philosophy of Kant* (New York, 1949), p. 422: '[the social contract] is a mere Idea of reason, but an Idea that has an unchallengeable practical reality.' See also the remarks by Eric Weil, *Problèmes kantiens* (Paris, 1963), p. 117.

[4] *Vorlesungen über die philosophische Religionslehre* (ed. K. H. L. Pölitz, Leipzig, 1832), p. 3. Quoted by A. Deregibus, *Problema morale*, p. 77.

in the power of his moral-legal 'chimeras' to challenge a history which, though metaphysically contingent, was phenomenally all too real, Kant strove to see how the 'chimera' might be plausible. With enthusiasm he wrote: 'The education of Rousseau is the only way to make society flourish again... Thanks to it governments will be better ordered and wars will become rarer.'[1] Here we get an *aperçu* of the importance of the tutelary ideal in Kant's subsequent political doctrines, a component of his thought closely wedded to both his historical and legal perceptions.

Kant's practical pedagogical interest, which cannot be dissociated from his professional and class optic or from the political situation of the German states in his time, will differ sharply from Rousseau's, despite a common ethical emphasis. Where Rousseau (inspired by his Genevan ideal and its amorphous extension in both 'Spartan' and 'Corsican' directions) had in view a closed society of the 'moyen ordre', frank, self-reliant, uncomplicated by *science*, and, in straits, taught to 'bear the yoke of necessity', Kant envisaged a triple education that would equip rulers, scholars, and public alike to play appropriate roles in the temporal unfolding of the rational state and the achievement of cosmopolitan order, an education to 'give humanity its whole deployment and make it possible for us to reach our destination'.[2] Kant was already reaching toward a refurbished theory of the 'education of princes', the acknowledged precondition for a liberal 'Revolution von oben', especially against surviving feudal privilege, the kind of reform whose usefulness to the 'children of Adam' Rousseau had once deprecated in his letter to Mirabeau.[3] Here, divergent perceptions of history, as well as local conditions, cut across pedagogical ideals that start with rather similar materials.

Thirdly, there is the large question of the value of knowledge itself and of the role of the man of learning. However much Rousseau might teach him to revere the common man, Kant, as a professional philosopher and speculator in the theoretical faubourgs of natural science, could scarcely be expected to follow the naysayer of the *First Discourse* to his redoubt of entrenched anti-

---

[1] 'Bemerkungen', *G.S.* xx, 175.
[2] 'Introduction' to *Pädagogik*, *G.S.* IX, 444.
[3] See Kant's remarks, *ibid.* p. 448.

intellectualism. 'Science', Kant will later say, 'is the narrow gate that leads to the doctrine of wisdom.'[1] Somehow, man's *ought* could not be restrictively applied to an unsophisticated model of human relationships where power and desire were in low-keyed equilibrium, but had to be extended to the mind's full potential of development. To be sure, the imperative of self-development must be seen from a moral (practical) point of view, unsolicited by selfish impulses of advantage. Nevertheless, the cultivation of the powers of reason is a duty:

Man owes it to himself (as a rational being) not to leave idle and, as it were, rusting away the natural dispositions and powers that his reason can in any way use. Even supposing that the native scope of his powers is *sufficient* for his natural needs, his reason must first show him, by principles, that this meagre scope of his powers is sufficient; for, as a being who is able to set ends (to make objects into his ends), he is indebted for the use of his powers not merely to natural instinct but rather to the freedom by which he determines his scope.[2]

Moreover, 'theoretical philosophy [*science*] can help to promote the ends of wisdom [*sagesse*]'.[3] Kant saw very clearly that mankind possesses a primal curiosity, awakened by the first stirrings of reason, which demands expansion and will not be inhibited: 'Reason has this peculiarity that, aided by the imagination, it can create artificial desires which are not only unsupported by natural instinct but actually contrary to it.'[4] Rousseau, too, had seen this insatiable propensity as a source of the possibility of morality (virtue and vice). But Rousseau wanted it heavily curtailed: 'The real world is bounded, while the imaginary world is without limit. Being unable to extend the one, let us retract the other.'[5] Kant's tone is different. While endorsing Rousseau's attack on luxury and vanity, he commends curiosity, 'man's attempt to become conscious of his reason as a power which can extend itself beyond the limits

[1] *Critique of Practical Reason* (ed. and trans. L. W. Beck, New York, 1956), pp. 167–8. Hereafter, *C. Prac. R.*
[2] *The Doctrine of Virtue* (ed. and trans. Mary J. Gregor, New York, 1964), p. 111. This is the second part (*Tugendlehre*) of the *Metaphysik der Sitten*. Hereafter, *Virtue*.
[3] *Ibid.*
[4] 'Conjectural Beginning of Human History', in L. W. Beck (ed.), *Kant on History*, pp. 55–6.
[5] *Emile*, II, 64. Cf. *Observations*, *O.C.* III, 41.

to which all animals are confined', and, in a following paragraph, *prévoyance*.[1] Does imagination carry man beyond his depth, making him wretched and evil? Unquestionably; but it is also an indispensable and glorious faculty: 'The imagination (as a productive faculty of cognition) is very powerful in creating another nature, as it were, out of the material that actual nature gives it.'[2] This is the realm of the Idea. Once the methodology of its practical side has been explored in the *Grundlegung* and the second *Critique*, the mission of the critical philosophy will be precisely to assert the proper uses of imagination and curiosity in the service of freedom, which is to say the duty of the ascent toward a moral 'second nature'.

Instead of confirming the historical blockade of Rousseau, where will (*libre arbitre = freie Willkür*) is enjoined to set limits to the morally destructive, passional imbalance between *désir* and *pouvoir* unleashed by the demon of *perfectibilité*, Kant will erect a paradox according to which the entire field of history receives the widening clash of these elements in the interest of an education and civilization that are not moral in themselves but are the evidently indispensable foundation (*Bildung*) for moral progress. But we should notice that Kant's dualist epistemology (based on the 'critical' distinctions between sense experience and moral, i.e. good action, understanding and reason) will be able to support a quasi-deductive theory of history that is 'progressive' and 'optimistic' even though no consistent pattern of moral event appears. On the other hand, Rousseau's empirico-realist formulation of knowledge, though unorthodox in some respects, presupposes the judging of history by appearance, making material evil the warrant of spiritual deformity, hence the more desperate and intolerable to its critic.

These discrepancies (doubled by Rousseau's rejection of *telos* for the model of natural growth cycles) affect the question of knowledge as a value and intellectuals as purveyors of values. If, as Rousseau would have it, *science* unconnected to virtue and reason unrelated to a minimization of wants and needs are snares for moral man,

---

[1] Kant, *loc. cit.* Cf. *Anthropologie, G.S.* VII, 250: 'luxury is a superfluous expense that makes one poor'.

[2] *Critique of Judgment* (trans. J. H. Bernard, London, 1931), 'Aesthetic', para. 49, p. 198. Hereafter, *Judgment* ('Aesthetic' or 'Teleological'). Cf. *C.P.R.* A474 = B502, p. 429: 'Human reason is by nature architectonic.'

Kant equates the drive for knowledge with reason itself and makes it obliquely a moral necessity. In accord with the teleological principle that 'nature does nothing in vain', the *homo scientificus*—who is a part of nature's purpose—has focused his cognitive apparatus on his surroundings with increasing refinement, even at the peril of wilful abuse or 'dialectical' misuse in his thirst to understand the cosmic order.[1] Abuses are a consequence of evil, coexistent with freedom; misuses relate to the impropriety of certain forms of intellectual operation. However, 'true' scientific knowledge (within the proper limits of reason) and moral activity have in common the fact that they are ultimately 'reasonable', and that ultimately (although we cannot prove it) reason is one.

Kant, on his part, created in the first two Critiques a deep epistemological cleavage between science and conduct, at equal distance from Rousseau's pessimistic conjugation of the two and from the classical Greek harmony of truth and goodness. On the other hand, he learned from Rousseau (and it was a fundamental discovery) that cognitive or theoretical reason is powerless to teach men how to act or to prescribe ends. After years of fermentation, in which many other influences must be acknowledged, this had the consequence of leading Kant to undertake an exclusive 'metaphysics of morals' on synthetic *a priori* grounds, analogous in method to the cognitive 'critical' structure but discrete because of its independent deduction and imperative formulation. The problematic division of reason, which, according to the 'critical' analysis, reason had itself imposed, was to raise a wide field of problems with regard to man as a creature in history, torn between will and world.

When Rousseau made his initial impact on Kant, neither the 'critical' categories nor the primacy of the practical Ideas nor the apparatus of the teleological judgment had been worked out. They would follow at an interval of about fifteen years. Kant's intellectual formation, if not precisely in the bosom of the *Aufklärung*, had been progressively shaped by the recondite quarrels of the schools,

---

[1] Cf. Karl Jaspers, *Kant* (New York, 1962), p. 98: 'Finite but rational beings can never be wholly content with their whole existence, for that would suppose a consciousness of self-sufficiency.'

especially between Wolffianism and Newtonianism and between the conflicting claims of mathematics and inductive science to furnish the model for the systematic philosophical pursuit of knowledge. It is sometimes held that Kant, whose early interests and writings lie astride these controversies, brought the arid biases of science to the study of ethics, or, conversely, that early pietistic influences of family and school sustained a lively faith that went far beyond scientific detachment.[1] The truth is probably more simple. Kant always took the method of science (predominantly Newtonian, as he understood it) for the working model of intellectual endeavour.[2] At the same time he had a commanding appreciation of questions into which this method could not reach satisfactorily or, as he came quickly to see, reached only at its own peril. He regarded such matters as ineluctable consequences of the use of reason. As he later put it: 'it is an essential *principle* of reason, however employed [i.e. theoretically or practically], to push its knowledge to a consciousness of its *necessity*'; since that necessity is an ever-receding goal, or, as he would later establish, unavailable as a constitutive principle to the discursive understanding, 'the satisfaction of reason is only further and further postponed'.[3] Only the extension of rational faith embodied in the Idea of freedom (which is also a concept 'whose incomprehensibility we can at least comprehend') will be capable of settling this issue, and only then on practical grounds. Finally, despite his long involvement with science, Kant seems never to have lost sight of the sphere of freedom, which meant to him not hazard or licence but the notion of an immanent and spontaneous rationale of external action.[4]

Faith never discovered for Kant what reason refused to condone. If freedom and science came into insoluble conflict, he declared in

[1] Cf. Karl Vorländer, *Immanuel Kants Leben* (2 vols., Berlin, 1911), I, 22 f.
[2] Herman-J. De Vleeschauwer, *The Development of Kantian Thought* (trans. A. R. C. Duncan, London, 1962), pp. 20–1.
[3] *Judgment*, para. 76 ('Teleological'), pp. 318–19; *Fundamental Principles of the Metaphysic of Morals* (trans. Thomas K. Abbott, New York, 1949), p. 80. Abbott's translation of *Grundlegung* is misleading; 'foundations' is much superior; the work is not a system of ethics, but, like the more extensive *C. Prac. R.*, a preliminary to one. Hereafter, *Foundations*.
[4] See De Vleeschauwer, *Development*, pp. 22–4. The coexistence of the causalities of science and freedom was already asserted by Kant in his *Principiorum Primorum Cognitionis Metaphysicae Nova Dilucidatio* (1755).

the first *Critique*, it is freedom that would be jeopardized.[1] Kant must also be defended against charges of excessive 'formalism' and the opposite stricture of fideism: most of his lasting work in the sphere of ethics was concerned with founding its possibility and methodology.[2] Only in his waning years did the long-announced bipartite 'metaphysics' (i.e. deduction of the content of rights and duties) appear, and the result has often been thought disappointing. However, in the final analysis, to Kant's manifest and dogged efforts to use reason only 'reasonably' in all branches of philosophy must be added his profound conviction of freedom's value and magnitude.

Thus, when his bookseller Kanter provided the *Social Contract* and *Emile* in 1762, Kant's emotions went all the deeper for his reason's having been implicated. But even while the appeal of Rousseau was most irresistible, Kant took his distances. Agreeing with Rousseau that the development of the sciences was inseparable from the progress of luxury and corruption, he insisted (in an elliptical turn very reminiscent of Rousseau's justification of civil society in *Geneva Manuscript* I, ii) that it was now the expanding activity of these forces that promised remedy for human ills.[3] 'The intellectuals,' he concedes, 'are clearly the most useless class in the state of natural simplicity,' but 'they are the most indispensable class in the state where men are oppressed by prejudice and force'.[4] The twin standards of 'publicity' and academic freedom begin to assert their claims; there is to be no burning of membership cards in the *Gelehrtenrepublik*. Voltaire, one might say, takes his revenge on Jean-Jacques: not only is learning therapeutic but it is valorous in the age of princely and ecclesiastical *Willkür*. Kant, speaking through the oracle of Enlightenment, withdraws from the full bombardment of Rousseau's moralism while accepting his insights on freedom. *Sagesse* will be mediated by *science*; and, in the perspective of a

---

[1] *C.P.R.*, 'Preface to Second Edition', p. 29.
[2] A. R. Duncan, *Practical Reason and Morality* (Edinburgh, 1957), argues convincingly that the *Foundations* is an examination of the requisite universal conditions for a morality. See, in this light, the 'categorical imperative' is much less the ethical directive for a contentless morality than the basis of a valid ethics which can proceed to employ an *a priori* rule apodictically. Concerning the connection between the *Foundations* and the second *Critique*, see Beck's remarks in his introduction to *C. Prac. R.*, pp. vii–viii.
[3] *G.S.* xx, 39–43, 130. [4] *Ibid.* p. 10.

history opening to this view, the weapons of corruption will be beaten into the ploughshares of a culture that elevates and—as our duty is to believe—improves human conduct.

Deeply engaged in Rousseau's dilemmas, Kant absorbed a Rousseau to his liking, made for his own sense of history. This is shown in his curious little essay on 'The Conjectural Beginning of the Human Race', evidently intended to challenge Herder's theo-bio-naturalistic portrait of man's ascent but also possible to interpret as a rejoinder to the *Second Discourse*:

> In his *On the Influence of the Sciences* and his *On the Inequality of Man* [Rousseau] shows quite correctly that there is an inevitable conflict between culture and the human species, considered as a natural species of which every member ought wholly to attain his natural end. But in his *Emile*, his *Social Contract*, and other writings he tries to solve this much harder problem: how culture was to move forward, in order to bring about such a development of the disposition of mankind, considered as a *moral* species, as to end the conflict between the natural and the moral species.[1]

That Kant retained the same version of Rousseau's diffuse indictment of modernity up to the end of his active career is shown by an almost identical passage in the *Anthropology*.[2] He is, in effect, attributing to Rousseau both a 'criticism' and a 'metaphysics'. Rousseau, in fact, had neither the faith nor the epistemology to reach Kantian conclusions, especially no earnest vision of a future fluctuating between impalpability and fulfilment. But if Rousseau blocked out the future to condemn most of the past, Kant's subtle analytic of progress would now paradoxically redeem that past by means of the 'guiding thread' that carries man's hope into the future. 'Rousseau', writes Kant, 'was right to criticize historical institutions. But they are the germ of the good ones to come.'[3] Thus Kant stands Rousseau on his head, remarries him to the Enlightenment.

B. 'CRITICAL' AMBIVALENCE

'Kant's thinking', Karl Jaspers asserts, 'never ends in compromise ...What he conceives as the middle term of his philosophical

---

[1] 'Conjectural Beginning', pp. 60–1.   [2] *Anthropologie, G.S.* VII, 326–7.   [3] *G.S.* XX, 14.

dualism is an insight that does not flatten out the oppositions but elucidates their origin.'[1] However, not just the origin is involved here; it is also the end. If, at the origin of human experience, there is a break between a theoretical will desiring its grasp of unity and the limitations of reason, or between what might be called moral ends and natural inclinations in the 'practical' sphere, there is also a tension between motives and ends themselves, between 'concept' and 'Idea'. This latter problem has strongly historical overtones, because the projective act of framing purely motivated ends must transpire through time, change and the social milieu. The terminal Ideas—God, the Sovereign Good, the contemplation of the beautiful, peace, the ethical commonwealth, etc.—are, to be sure, rational norms or, as Kant would say, rules. But they are also to be grasped as a consequence of reason's examination of its own finite limitations.

Those limitations are the consequence of the mundane weight of that peculiar concoction of flesh and spirit called humanity. Where the Ideas acquire a content (God as the supersensible ground of all reality, the Sovereign Good as the accommodation of happiness to duty, peace as the formal resolution of man's 'unsocially social' combativeness beneath the law of respect, etc.), that content presupposes experience as well as reason. Thus the Idea communicates between fundamental *is* and final *ought*, traversing a world of mortal men set in time and space which is not *rationale* but merely *rationabile*.

The phenomenal–moral dialectic in Kant, established by the 'critical' procedures, gives a first impression of setting apart what philosophy had always traditionally attempted to join. But Kant's temper was not that of Hume. He sought to outflank the sceptical rocks on to which he saw the philosophy of his time being driven. This involved an elaborate interlocking of the 'critical' and 'systematic' functions of the rational experience.

Kant's mediations implicate the whole structure and method of knowledge. In the first place, the 'critical' method involved the rigorous, though discerning, demolition of previous metaphysics (directly, the Wolffian, but by proxy all the great mathematical

[1] Jaspers, *Kant*, p. 132.

thought-systems of the seventeenth century).[1] At the same time, the systematic reconstruction he undertook called not only for salvaging the higher truths from sceptical erosion, but for a revaluation of the position of all the intellectual and moral disciplines within the 'critical' architecture. Consequently, Kant was very much concerned in the first *Critique* to reorder the philosophical 'curriculum'.[2] He rebuilt so considerably, even while demolishing, that the very notion of 'criticism' became confused, even in the philosopher's mind. 'Our age', he once declared, 'is, in especial degree, the age of criticism, and to criticism everything must submit.'[3] But did this mean criticism of previous philosophies,[4] criticism of reason by its own procedures, the elaboration of a 'propaedeutic' for valid philosophical inquiry, or did it directly create that 'future metaphysics' for which the first *Critique* and the *Prolegomena* would seem to furnish, respectively, the synthetic and analytic prologues?[5]

Probably the second and third notions, close to each other, are closest to the general drift of this elusive word which the English language is forced, for clarity, to emphasize or paraphrase. However, such a 'metaphysics of metaphysics' does not seem a particularly promising point of departure for an investigation of man, that time-bound 'creature of the middle span'. Nonetheless, Kant maintained, like the empiricists, that we can know nothing properly if we do not first know how to *know* properly. And contrary to that school, which he assimilated, refuted and went beyond, he asserted that reason cannot rest with knowing; it in fact knows nothing except by way of the concepts furnished it by the understanding (the faculty that orders the chaos of sensible appearance). Reason, however, *thinks*;

---

[1] Cf. De Vleeschauwer, *Development*, pp. 33–4.
[2] *C.P.R.*, 'The Architectonic of Pure Reason', pp. 653–65.
[3] *Ibid*, xvii, p. 9 n.
[4] *Ibid*. 'I do not mean by this a criticism of books and systems, but of the faculty of reason in general...' But cf. Preface to *C. Prac. R.*, p. 10 n: 'It will be noticed throughout the critiques of both the theoretical and the practical reason that there are many opportunities for supplying inadequacies and correcting errors in the old dogmatic [i.e. realist] procedure of philosophy...'
[5] After Kant had completed the second edition of the *C.P.R.* in 1787, it became clearer to him that the 'critical' philosophy was a great deal more than 'propaedeutic' to a future system. In the polished but unpublished *Welche sind die wirklichen Fortschritte?* (*c.* 1790), the *C.P.R.* is made introductory to an integral metaphysics. The *Critique of Judgment* and the later *Opus Postumum* develop the same tendency. See De Vleeschauwer, *Development*, pp. 152–67.

it adds thought to knowing and thereby forms Ideas, which may be practically dogmatic but theoretically only regulative.[1] Ideas, in short, may function either as goals of action or as scientific guidelines, never as objects of knowledge. If Kant had merely discussed the function of Ideas within the conceptual framework of reason, giving detached illustrations of what they might be, relevant only to logic, the central 'critical' structure might then seem to be a methodological 'propaedeutic'. However, the concept of freedom, implicit in the moral law, is the primary ingredient of the rational structure itself and develops from its own apodictic nature a sequence of applications that immediately involves the whole of human existence.

To know *what* we know and *how* we know is therefore fundamentally inseparable from our work in the world as morally conscious agents of reason and truth. Although the ethical law, according to Kant, 'borrows nothing from experience' and is construed as affecting not man but 'all rational beings',[2] it will found the right judgment of particular questions that men are called on to solve. A single illustration should suffice. As is well known, Kant deduces from the *a priori* concept of freedom a so-called universal principle of justice, which is as follows: 'Act externally in such a way that the free use of your will is compatible with the freedom of everyone according to a universal law.'[3] In a passage from his essay *On the Presumed Right of Lying*, he continues down the scale toward the particular: 'To proceed from a metaphysics of right...to the principle of politics...the philosopher must offer these three things: (1) an axiom, that is an apodictic and certain proposition, resulting directly from the definition of external right...(2) a postulate of external public law, as the collective will of all according to the principle of equality...(3) a *problem* of determining the means of preserving harmony in a society...'[4] Here, the input of freedom

---

[1] Cf. the discussion by Weil, *Problèmes*, p. 112. Also, *Foundations*, p. 75: 'When practical reason thinks itself into a world of understanding, it does not thereby transcend its own limits, as it would if it tried to enter it by *intuition* or *sensation*.'

[2] *Foundations*, p. 26; cf. *C. Prac. R.* p. 17 and p. 9: 'a critique of practical reason... gives an account of the principles of the possibility of duty, of its extent and limits, without particular reference to human nature'.

[3] *Justice*, p. 35.

[4] 'Über ein vermeintes Recht aus Menschenliebe zu lügen', *G.S.* VIII, 429.

Morality, knowledge and historical vision

has furnished the notion of strict justice, which in turn has found application *via* the Idea (not necessarily the actuality) of the 'republican' form of government to a specific legislative decision. By such descending procedures, the epistemological core of Kantianism reaches toward the raw content of political society and enters the world that the understanding knows and shapes. The decisive act of human reason, here illustrated, is called the *judgment*.

Thus the abstract and concrete, methodology, system and application, are met in Kant in a way that allows us to consider his post-1781 occasional writings as applied essays in the 'critical' method and not simply as mere expressions of opinion by a philosopher. Of course, Kant was not a totally efficient logic machine—the word 'deduction' covers a variety of intellectual operations, sometimes specified, sometimes not; it would be totally unrealistic to expect his topical positions to be derivations of 'pure reason'. However, we must assume that the variety of contradictions that Kant seeks to mediate have a plausible coherence within 'criticism' itself.

3

HUMANITY, TIME AND FREEDOM

Our chief task is to examine the extremely subtle ambivalence between normative and historical uses of reason in Kant's philosophical structure. There is little in either the *Critique of Pure Reason* or the *Critique of Practical Reason* to mark Kant as a philosopher of history. Indeed, in view of the extraordinary philosophical importance of the first of these works and the great interest still attached to its examination, it is at least as controversial to assign a 'historical' position to Kant as it is to Rousseau. If we place great emphasis on the logical structure of 'criticism', history vanishes in the mechanics of the 'transcendental ego'. On the other hand, if close attention is paid to the 'Critique of Teleological Judgment' and the minor historical writings, another impression will be received. No doubt there is a considerable tension between the two aspects. But we are obviously moving away from the realm of the *Discours de la Méthode* toward the historical consciousness of the nineteenth century, and discovering some of its themes. In a sense, Rousseau's 'lente succession des choses' has prepared us for this line of attack.

There is a second question, of greater interest to compilers of anthologies of political thought than to us. Does Kant, like Rousseau, have any real political theory? Unquestionably, he does have a legal theory, the traditional prelude to systematic political thought in the era which his work may be said to close. He has also an ethical theory and an anthropological theory. The consistent core of Kant's political thought can best be discovered in the areas where these other theories overlap. Central to the following analysis are the questions of freedom, which is timeless, and time, which accompanies each appearance of freedom.

Kant's work is rife with plausible and fruitful dichotomies, related to a handful of propositions, among which are the following: (1) man, by contrast with a hypothetical Supreme Being, has a limited or 'discursive' understanding which is inept at synthesizing or 'knowing' those supersensible categories in which his reason at the same time encourages him to believe; (2) man, as a finite, temporal and phenomenally situated creature, has a will (*Willkür*) equally susceptible to the legislation of inner freedom and to determinations of the external world and the impulses it stimulates; (3) man is distinct from all other living products of nature in that he is unable, as an individual, to realize his full development, perfection or *telos*; (4) man, on the contrary, shares with all possible rational beings the quality of being an end-in-himself, but he inevitably fails to treat this as a universal and obligatory proposition, to make it his own maxim; (5) the end of creation is the perfection of man, collectively organized, but this must be regarded as a task and never as a foregone conclusion; (6) for the sake of man's undoubted moral career, history needs to be seen as a plan whereby certain obvious and disagreeable facets of human nature can be regarded as paradoxically contributing to the goals of pure practical reason. Within these parameters are traced a progress of society, a formal valuation of political institutions, and a rhythm of human development, from barbarism to legalism *via* the self-fulfilling Idea of the State.

A. FREE WILL

Kant's view of necessity and freedom is both a reconciliation and a rupture. It is a reconciliation because Kant undertook to preserve the validity of knowledge by causes, which Hume and philosophers of lesser stature had jeopardized, and at the same time to liberate the notion of free will from both the destructive fideism implicit in Hume's critique and the 'dialectical' blockade of dogmatic metaphysics. To show how these apparent opposites could be freed from their antinomic relationship, or at least to show how this is rationally possible (the demonstration of the first *Critique*) must be regarded as a mediation.[1] On the other hand, this coexistence (conceding Kant's solution) is at first mysterious and impalpable. It is all very well to say that 'the concept of freedom as little disturbs the legislation of nature as the natural concept influences the legislation through the former',[2] or to distinguish the provinces of theoretical and practical reason by means of the following perplexing chiasmus: 'in the former, the objects must be the causes of the

---

[1] *C.P.R.* A558 = B586, p. 479.   [2] *Judgment*, 'Introduction', p. 11.

conceptions which determine the will, and in the latter, the will is the cause of the objects'.[1] But one does not yet exactly see how this two-sided vision can be applied to the only existentially known creature of reason, man himself.

In pursuing Kant's vision of man, we consider the acts of a being who wills and is morally responsible for the orientations of his will. Will is the faculty (philosophical 'faculties' are, in effect, metaphors for elucidating the transactions that take place formally within that 'black box' of spontaneity and receptivity that scholasticism had divided into body and soul) in which the higher and lower natures of man are met.[2] By a division familiar, in one or another form, to Western philosophy, the Kantian will (*Willkür*) possesses a lower determination of brutishness and a higher self-determination according to duty (*Wille*), the former based on instinct and interest, the latter grounded in the moral law and hence identical with pure practical reason itself.[3] The *Willkür* is free in the potential sense, because it is endowed with the capacity to choose its maxims of action in accord with interest, i.e. heteronomously (externally grounded), or with duty, i.e. autonomously. Thus the notion of will as *Willkür* bestrides the whole perplexity of the human condition, serving as the link between the spiritual and sensuous aspects of man,[4] and could therefore be taken as a microcosmic representation of the problem of history itself. This is not to say that, with Kant, will makes history in the sense that could be imputed to later German philosophy: it is to say that man cannot fulfil his destiny if he cannot will it.[5]

[1] *C. Prac. R.* p. 46.
[2] For a superior discussion of the problem of will and freedom in Kant, see L. W. Beck, *A Commentary on Kant's Critique of Practical Reason* (Chicago, 1963), pp. 37-42. Also, by the same author, 'Deux concepts kantiens du vouloir', *Archives de philosophie politique*, IV (1962), pp. 119-37; and the analysis by John R. Silber, 'The Ethical Significance of Kant's *Religion*', introduction to Theodore M. Greene and Hoyt H. Hudson (eds.), *Kant's Religion Within the Limits of Reason Alone* (New York, 1960), pp. xcix-cvi. Hereafter, *Religion*.
[3] Cf. *C. Prac. R.* p. 109.
[4] This is simply and well stated by a modern Kantian, Eric Weil (*Philosophie politique*, Paris, 1956), p. 27: 'This *I*, whose task is to transform the empirical ego, without itself being empirical, is manifested only in the empirical ego and has no other activity.'
[5] The Kantian use of the term 'practical reason' needs clarification. He generally takes it to mean 'pure practical reason', i.e. morality (philosophy of action) from an *a priori* concept. The distinction between theoretical or speculative and practical

Just as we found the notion of a universal ethic to be implied in the question of knowledge, we might suppose an extension of the mechanism of theoretical reason into the sphere of human action, where its presence is inappropriate, if we imagined a man totally determined by the maxims of his lower will.[1] In such an extreme, a man would become a thing or a beast, totally ordered by impulse or outward circumstance, possessed at best of an *arbitrium brutum*, thus by definition unfree. In actual fact, man is never reduced to a 'thing of science' in theory predictable and lacking in all spontaneity: he has an *arbitrium liberum*.[2] But man progressively reduces himself toward such a state in the measure that he allows his free moral choice to be determined by impulse or advantage. Such activity is a facet of what Kant calls 'radical evil'. In the Kantian sense, man is 'evil' to the degree that he permits his own reification, placing himself under the causality of nature. In so doing, 'he reverses the moral order of the incentives when he adopts them into his maxim'.[3] However, there is a limit to this dissolute regression: 'Man (even the most wicked) does not, under any maxim whatsoever, repudiate the moral law in the manner of a rebel', because '. . . the injunction that we *ought* to become better men resounds unabatedly in our souls'.[4] On the other hand, man's constitution forbids him to become a creature of pure reason, a disembodied 'holy will', for this would imply from the practical standpoint that the moral law

---

[1] This extension of 'theoretical' reason into ethics corresponds with what Kant calls 'technically practical' as opposed by 'morally practical' reason, i.e. the grounding of action in natural concepts. Cf. *Judgment*, 'Introduction', pp. 8–11.

[2] Cf. *C.P.R.* A534 = B562, p. 465; also, *Justice*, p. 13: 'Human will. . .is affected but not determined by impulses.'

[3] *Religion*, p. 31.

[4] *Ibid.* pp. 31, 40. Notice how the modern philosophical idea of 'rebellion' (e.g. Camus) is, historically, a rejection of the Kantian *a priori*.

---

reason is traditional in Western philosophy, dating back to Aristotle. What Kant did was to accept the empiricist basing of theoretical reason on science, and then to 'purify' practical reason of both speculative and empirical contingencies, thus re-defining the dichotomy between the intellectual and the moral. When, for example Rousseau writes (*Rousseau juge de Jean-Jacques*, II, *O.C.* I, 818): '. . .what is practical reason, if it is not the sacrifice of a present and fleeting good for the means of one day obtaining greater or more solid ones, and what is interest, if not the increase and continual extension of these same means?' this is not what Kant ordinarily means by the term, but is rather an example of 'impure' practical reason or the exercise of skill ('hypothetical reason').

had become for him analogous to a physical law, in short, he would possess the attributes of God.[1] Nevertheless, failing this, the Idea of membership in a supersensible 'kingdom of ends' where each would govern himself according to the laws of freedom (i.e. in pure autonomy but still through effort) is set as a task or intelligible maximum for moral conduct, needless to say in disregard of all subjective maxims of happiness.[2]

One might say that there are two conceptions of necessity in Kant. The one, an effect of the physical laws of nature, applies to objects and brutes in the natural world. The other, relative and uncertain, concerns man's appearance as a phenomenon.[3] Kant never maintained that man could *know* himself; he said simply that man can know *how* and *what* he knows, and that he needs to know *why*. Analytically separable, the natural and supersensible spheres of human participation cannot be grasped as a unity; yet one knows that they are united in every deliberative act through the medium of the *Willkür*. We do not understand the causality of freedom; we understand only why it is necessary. But we know that where rational beings are found (other men), there too are found beings who can act under the Idea of freedom.[4] Thus we come to recognize other persons who, like ourselves, may be qualified as belonging to two systems of causation but who act, in unpredictable ways, under the laws of both throughout their mortal and finite existences.

We can distinguish three ideas of freedom in transcendental idealism. I have already referred to the notion of free choice which consists in the *Willkür*'s capacity to choose between the maxims of interest and of duty in consideration of an action. In this sense, one is free because of the potential to choose for good or ill. This is what is often called independence or 'negative liberty', and it is

---

[1] A 'holy will' has no obligation, i.e. is not bound by an imperative. Cf. *Foundations*, p. 31.
[2] Kant does not deny happiness as a value; he merely denies it as a moral goal. Virtue should produce happiness; the thought of happiness should not be the determinant of virtuous acts. Cf. *Virtue*, p. 35: '...the pleasure that must precede our obedience to the law in order for us to act in conformity with the law is pathological, and our conduct then follows from the *order of nature*'.
[3] Cf. *G.S.* xx, 66–7: 'The movements of matter are subject to a rule that is sure... Man's sensations are freed of all rules.'
[4] *Foundations*, p. 64.

essentially the description of freedom offered by the Enlightenment. Although Kant himself designated the *Willkür* as free in this sense, he attached very little value to it.[1] What Kant called 'negative liberty' is substantially different: 'The sole principle of morality consists in independence from all material of the law [i.e. heteronomous influence]...that independence, however, is freedom in the negative sense...' 'Positive liberty' is contained in the very notion of *Wille*: '[the] intrinsic legislation of pure and thus practical reason is freedom in the positive sense'.[2] The moral law effects the autonomy which is the formal condition of the maxims determining true acts of freedom. Thus freedom, too, is a task, a postulate as well as a power. However, the *Wille* (pure practical reason) does not choose or enjoin a specific type of conduct; rather, it prescribes the motive of duty in the form of the categorical imperative to the *Willkür*. One should not pass from this point without noticing the analogical application of Kant's view of freedom and the operations of the will to his later separation of legislative, executive and judicial powers in elucidating the 'republican' form of civil constitution, as well as to the formal logic of the syllogism.[3] There is throughout Kant's 'critical' structure a subjacent unity of method whereby rational constructs or Ideas tend to be treated as extensions of the pure patterns of reason itself.

Filtered through the *Willkür*, the spheres of natural causation and of freedom are seen to coexist in the human being but to be analytically separated into science and ethics. At the same time, the notion of freedom is propounded in a new way, becoming not only a capacity to resist external impulse but also an immanent sort of causality derived from the moral law. Moreover, Kant specifically informs us that this free causality is not simply restricted to a neverland of *ought* or of motive which cannot appear, but that it makes itself the source of new sequences of phenomenal causality.[4] In other words, man forms his world spontaneously and, in so far

[1] See, for example, *Justice*, Introduction to the 'Metaphysics of Morals', p. 10.

[2] *C. Prac. R.* p. 33. Cf. *Justice*, pp. 21-2.

[3] Cf. *Justice*, p. 78; 'Perpetual Peace', in *Kant on History*, p. 96: 'The legislator can unite in one and the same person his function as legislative and as executor of his will just as little as the major premise in a syllogism can also be the subsumption of the particular under the universal in the minor.'

[4] *C.P.R.* A550-2 = B578-80, pp. 474-6.

as he intends that world to transpire in the image of his moral ideas, autonomously and, in the highest sense, freely. On the other hand, when we look at the world as a *factum*, as a concatenation of objects and effects, we are bound to regard it, within the limits of our understanding, as a nexus of physico-mechanical causes. It is a question of perspectives.[1]

If man is at the same time a creature of both the natural and intelligible spheres, this does not mean he is a noumenon who appears to himself as a phenomenon; the indication is, rather, that he possesses two principles of causality which make it possible for him to regard himself in two ways in theory, and to treat himself and be treated in two ways in practice. But both aspects in their pure form are limiting concepts. The human reality is more complex.

I have already shown how the *Willkür* is the pivot on which man's two worlds turn. Now it is reasonable to inquire by what means this is possible. Here I am much struck by the suggestion of Havet that the notion of 'radical evil' (which was earlier compared with man's reduction of himself toward a thing or a brute) is the 'representative of the sensible world in the intelligible world' and that 'respect' performs the liaison in the opposite sense.[2] This is plausible because, as we have already seen, evil is 'radical', that is, born with the capacity of freedom, itself the content of a timeless and intelligible sphere that, nevertheless, acts upon man's world. Respect, 'the feeling of our incapacity to attain to an Idea *which is a law* for us', is, consequently, 'the esteem which a rational being must have for [the law]'.[3] In other words, it is our effective sensuous contact with the sphere of freedom. Thus there is also considerable merit to the insight of Vlachos, if not carried too far, that respect bears heavy legal as well as moral connotations, representing a kind of not-too-

---

[1] Although it is not precisely a Kantian position, the philosophical derivation is clear: cf. Tolstoi, *War and Peace* (New York, n.d.), p. 1129: 'Thus our conception of free will and necessity is gradually diminished or increased according to the degree of connection with the external world, the degree of remoteness in time, and the degree of dependence on causes we see in the phenomenon of man's life that we examine.'

[2] Jacques Havet, *Kant et le temps* (Paris, 1946), p. 180.

[3] *Judgment* ('Aesthetic'), para. 27, p. 119; *Foundations*, pp. 52–3; *C. Prac. R.* pp. 79–81. 'Respect' seems to me to be a hypostasis of the Biblical category of the covenant between God and Israel. Cf. Exodus ii. 24–5: 'And God heard their groaning, and God remembered his covenant with Abraham, with Isaac, and with Jacob. And God looked upon the children of Israel, and God had respect unto them.'

far-not-too-near relationship that persons must maintain with each other if they are to treat each other externally (*in actu*) as ends in a 'republic', a kind of resolution of the dialectic of 'unsocial sociability'.[1] We find in Kant, even more than in Rousseau, that transparent analogical fluctuation between the meanings of the word 'law'. Whereas Rousseau's final position seems to have been a psychological effort to 'naturalize' moral obligation and legal constraint *via* habit as a way of evading the inevitability of social pain, Kant opts for the legal or juridical mean. Just as human history is the meeting ground of strict and free causality along a linear time-sequence, the notion of right seeks to relieve the tension between man's physical *is* and spiritual *ought*.

We are now in a somewhat better position to understand how the Kantian dualism applies to the life and works of man. Life, which Kant regards as a mystery and further subtly dualizes in his dialectic of the individual and the species, is where 'determining' and 'being determined' clash.[2] 'The faculty of desire [here regarded as both the higher capacity related to the *Wille* and the lower related to objects or interests]', he writes, 'is the capacity to be the cause of the objects of one's representations by means of these representations. The capacity that a being has of acting in accordance with its representations is *life*.'[3] Only in the perspective of life do we begin to grasp the function of the moral law. Its effectiveness is real only in time, where ideally 'it determines our will (*Willkür*) to impart to the sensuous world the form of a system of rational beings'; as pure reason it would 'bring forth the highest good were it accompanied by sufficient physical capacities'.[4] In the world, then, two things are lacking: the continual triumph of reason over inclination, and the physical power to remove obstacles in freedom's path. As for the latter, the moral law cannot obligate us to any action not within our power (that is the meaning of 'you ought to, therefore you can'—

---

[1] Georges Vlachos, *La pensée politique de Kant* (Paris, 1962), p. 255. Cf. 'Conjectural Beginning', pp. 58–9; *Virtue*, pp. 116–17.

[2] *Judgment* ('Teleological'), para. 77, p. 326: 'No finite reason can ever hope to understand the production of even a blade of grass by mere mechanical causes.' As an ultimate value, life can be understood only by reference to the moral law.

[3] *Justice*, Introduction to the 'Metaphysics of Morals', p. 10.

[4] *C. Prac. R.* p. 45.

ultra posse nemo obligatur).[1] As for the former, which Kant calls the achievement of a 'good will' and qualifies as the only thing absolutely good, it is possible and therefore a moral task, even though it may never have been or may never be accomplished in any given instance.[2] The world is a nexus of natural causes and free acts. Man is their locus because he can choose to be determined or to determine himself, in which latter case his acts have a truly 'free' repercussion on nature. Significantly, for each term of the dualism there is a mediating substance or faculty which represents, one could say, the point of view of the world: between pure practical reason (*Wille*) and inclination, there is *Willkür*; between understanding and reason, there is the role of judgment; between animality and personality there is humanity; between the natural order and the moral order there is the legal order; between mechanism and pure autonomy there is teleology. However, 'the concept of freedom is meant to actualize in the world of sense the purpose proposed by its laws'.[3] This is why teleology is transformed finally into a confirmation of the immanent and dogmatic primacy of moral goals, an 'ethico-teleology' corroborated, perhaps, but never supplanted by physical manifestations of design.[4]

B. THE DIALECTIC OF TIME AND FREEDOM

Aside from the popular use of the word *idealism* (a disclaimer of 'reality' in favour of what is thought to be desirable or fitting), which has only the most tenuous connection with Kant's thought, the 'critical' philosophy may be called an 'idealism' in three respects: (1) it places uncommon emphasis on the productive power of 'Ideas' which are not given through the media of sense; (2) it alleges the reality of a noumenal or 'ideal' world that is unknowable; (3) it subscribes to the central doctrine of the 'ideality' of time and space.

---

[1] Cf. John R. Silber, 'Kant's Conception of the Highest Good as Immanent and Transcendent', *Philosophical Review* (Oct. 1959), p. 479: 'By restricting man's obligation to the actual limits of his capacity...Kant succeeds in making the highest good immanent in the life of man...'
[2] *Foundations*, p. 24.
[3] *Judgment*, 'Introduction', p. 13.
[4] *Ibid.* ('Teleological'), para. 86, pp. 370–6.

Kant sometimes calls his method 'transcendental idealism', and he understood the term generally on the basis of our third definition. This definition is, in fact, almost the reverse of the second one, since time and space are 'ideal' precisely because they do not have noumenal existence but only 'empirical reality'.[1] In taking this position, Kant adhered in the large to the philosophical position of Leibniz as against Newton and the realists, who held that time and space were qualities of objects and that the objects given in representation were 'things-in-themselves'.

Kant begins with reason as a *prius*. Its manner of operating has not been investigated, but the 'I think' is axiomatic. As the fundamental property of the transcendental ego, it is above all cosmic concern, above the forms of apperception (time and space), and above the understanding (which receives intuitions and forms concepts of sensuous experience): '...since reason is not itself an appearance, and is not subject to any conditions of sensibility, it follows that even as regards its causality there is in it no time-sequence...'[2] The causality of reason is thus a causality of freedom, and the idea of freedom is not limited by the restrictions of time and space. On the other hand, as logically prior to the activity of the understanding, 'time is the formal *a priori* condition of all appearances whatsoever'.[3] And since we 'know' ourselves only phenomenally, although we can 'think' ourselves as members of an intelligible sphere, time is also 'the form of inner sense, that is, of the intuition of ourselves and of our inner state'.[4] 'Knowing' is thus a historical operation, a sequential formation of concepts, symbolized spatially by 'a line progressing to infinity'. Our conception of ourselves in time is, *stricto sensu*, a matter of the understanding.[5]

One effect of Kant's doctrine is to prohibit to speculative philo-

---

[1] Of course, Kant did not deny the reality of appearances, but he presented a purely epistemological view of being. On the 'ideality' of time and space, see *C.P.R.* A35 = B52, p. 78.

[2] *Ibid.* A553 = B581, p. 476.

[3] *Ibid.* A34 = B50, p. 77.

[4] *Ibid.* A33 = B49, p. 77.

[5] Regarding the implications of the ideality of time for freedom, see *Justice*, 'Introduction', p. 45; also, *C. Prac. R.* pp. 105–6, where Kant argues that if time is not 'merely a sensuous mode of presentation belonging to thinking beings in the world', Spinozism is the logical outcome.

sophy any interest in creation or eschatology, 'times' before and after time. With a half-profound, half-witty style he takes this stance in his 'Conjectural Beginning' and in the remarkable 'End of All Things', which angered the severe ministers of Frederick William II in 1794. Reason takes the place of a beginning; the moral Ideas provide the ulterior limit. Kant intended his theory of knowledge to undermine, on the one hand, all chiliasm, all utopia and, on the other, all recourse to despotism in the name of a crude, literal authoritarian finalism. 'Since', as he argues, 'the idea of an end of all things does not originate from reasoning about physical [i.e. temporal] things but from reasoning about the moral course of the world and nothing else, the moral [i.e. atemporal] course of events can be applied only to the supersensible (which is comprehensible only in relation to the moral). The same is true of the idea of eternity.'[1] Moral ends are reprieved from the will of authority—and, it might be said, from the physical goals of revolution as well—and consigned to 'the judgment of one's own conscience'.[2]

The really critical problem is with regard to history, where all literal event is absolutely time-rooted, causal and sequential, but where the entire field of rational action is apparently determined by supra-temporal human inputs. Here the French scholar Victor Delbos speaks knowingly of the 'two tendencies that struggle to unite but are both accompanied by a train of rather different ideas, the ethico-juridical tendency and the ethico-religious tendency'.[3]

Legality, or justice, although it is a part of 'practical philosophy', that is, grounded in the concept of freedom, is the framework of a system of external coercion which is, by definition, phenomenal. On the other hand, religion, which, in the Kantian sense, does not exceed, unless symbolically, a pure rational ethic, is perfectly timeless, except in impure manifestations of ecclesiastical history.[4] The idea of the state is the notion of external law by which rights are asserted among a given body of individuals; and right, in turn, is the negative correlate of duty, i.e. one's assertion of a right

---

[1] 'The End of All Things', in *Kant on History*, p. 71.
[2] *Ibid.* p. 73.
[3] Victor Delbos, *La philosophie pratique de Kant* (Paris, 1905), pp. 297–8.
[4] Cf. *Religion*, p. 115 f.

compels others to a duty.[1] On the other hand, the ethico-religious ideal is the internal legislation of a 'kingdom of ends', which is self-organizing and dependent purely on free acts according to duty. Put more simply, the concept of freedom is at the origin of (juridical) law, whereas ethical religion sets as its goal the pure Idea of freedom. But the ethico-juridical and ethico-religious strains are correlative as well as opposed. Both announce the task of achieving a society or commonwealth; and Kant makes it clear in his work on religion that the legal society is both the precondition and model for what he calls in various places an 'ethico-civil' state, or by extension a 'kingdom of ends'.[2] We are challenged immediately by the paradox that man's penetration to the timeless sphere of freedom, an attribute of personal striving by the rational 'personality', is somehow conditioned by his efforts in organizing the temporal political sphere toward that goal.[3] In the *Religion*, we are told that only an 'association with others' (a spiritual liaison or Church) can maintain the single individual (who is always, by the premises of Kantian individualism, the locus of the moral struggle) from falling back under the 'sovereignty of evil'.[4]

Now it is a commonplace to say that the possibility of a moral life requires a social situation and social rules. By extension, it is not more difficult to argue that 'good morality' might presuppose the idea of a free community of individuals living according to precepts of respect and reason. But it is not entirely clear how or why this must proceed by way of the political analogy or somehow presuppose political progress, unless one is prepared to argue that the habituation or 'discipline' provided by juridical constraint teaches men to obtain their maxims of action from the moral law. Indeed, Kant plays around the margin of that supposition. In that case, however, a false juncture would be made between the realms of autonomous and heteronomous causation, one which the Kantian knowledge

---

[1] *Justice*, 'Introduction to the Elements of Justice', p. 45.

[2] Kant's first allusion to the notion of an ethical republic occurs in his *Träume eines Geistersehers*, *G.S.* II, 336 n., where he introduces the regulative notion of a *geistige Republik*.

[3] In *Religion*, p. 86, Kant says of the heuristic 'ethico-civil society' that 'unless it is based upon such a ['juridico-civil'] commonwealth it can never be brought into existence by men'.

[4] *Ibid.* pp. 85–6.

structure would seem to forbid. In effect, it should be impossible for citizenship or public law-abidingness to make men moral. As Kant goes to pains to emphasize, the social inculcation of custom or any form of automatic behaviour is an insufficient, and clearly heteronomous, basis for virtue or truly moral action. 'Virtue', he states succinctly, 'is...the moral force in the accomplishment of duty, a force which should never become habit, but should always proceed anew and originally from the way of thinking...In principle, all mechanical habituation should be proscribed.'[1] Nevertheless, as man grows up to reason and truth, he also grows toward the life of virtue and liberty under law. He substitutes his own 'master' for the precautionary restraints of the social milieu. Custom and time, freedom and duty, instrument and value, are joined in the training of the will.

This helps to account for the fact that moral and legal issues are often confusingly related in Kant's analysis. Evil is timeless but *appears* only in temporal social relations,[2] rendered effective by the uniquely human instinct of 'unsocial sociability', the urge that drives men into contact but under conditions of envy and competition, even repugnance. On the other hand, the human societies thus developed through time have gradually thrust forth civil or political forms that not only permit the expansion of order but, in at least one case, the 'republican' ('law and liberty under coercion'),[3] contain in germ the Idea of external freedom, a fourth derivative of the categorical imperative. However, a close examination of Kant's model of the perfect civil constitution shows that, if it can be understood as the phenomenal matrix for morality, it has no formal resemblance with a 'kingdom of ends'. Essentially, it is a way of translating moral statesmanship into technically valid prescriptions.

C. THE INDIVIDUAL AND THE SOCIAL

As a consequence of the above, the relation between the individual and the social is intricate in Kant. In this philosophy, the individual

---

[1] *Anthropologie, G.S.* VII, 147.
[2] Cf. *Religion*, p. 28: 'the multitude of crying examples which experience *of the actions* of men puts before our eyes'.   [3] Cf. *Anthropologie, G.S.* VII, pp. 330–1.

is strikingly finite, as Jaspers puts it, 'always dependent on something other and...in no respect absolutely perfectible'.[1] Yet the moral part of the individual, his personality, is priceless beyond all value. At the same time, the civil society, seen not as a *Gemeinschaft* but as a legal rampart against barbarism, has no ethical 'oversoul', although it would appear to have a conditioning and disciplining role. Finally, the race (a continuous *cosmopolis*) assumes the qualities of both the clash of culture and historical ascent and the potential but imaginable form of the final moral commonwealth. The end is freedom, the moral law triggers the quest, the formed societies are, in a sense, tools, and the 'great society', whose historical limits are dim, is the vehicle of moral sociability, furnishing 'enough time' within time for the hope that our moral obligations might be fulfilled. Imbedded in man is his capacity for conversion, his 'hope'; imbedded within the race is the great collective enterprise of reason fulfilling itself.

So far as the rational act is concerned, the 'critical philosophy' begins with an abstract mind-model that is of no historical consequence and is common to all (rational) individuals, a logical self presupposed in the act of knowing which Kant calls the 'transcendental unity of apperception'. The possibility and fundamental character of morality (pure practical reason or *Wille*) is similarly grounded and is furthermore common to 'all rational beings'. Both are aspects of that reason which is above time and space and prior to the understanding. Thus Kant can say: 'Reason is present in all the actions of men at all times and under all circumstances, and is always the same; but it is not itself in time, and does not fall into any new state in which it was not before.'[2]

But the world of appearances must furnish a content to knowing and, ultimately, to thinking a destiny that conforms to the precepts of reason. In the sphere of sense, of time and space, reason, by its descent, becomes impure but also engaged to purify itself, to assimilate the obstacles it has encountered to the sphere of freedom. This is also the sphere of evil and the overcoming of evil. It is, by extension, the historical, phenomenal sphere of man and society.

[1] Jaspers, *Kant*, p. 98. [2] *C.P.R.* A556 = B584, p. 478.

There is, as we know, a peculiarity about the transcendental ego that began its epistemological search from its own *a priori*. From the theoretical point of view, it is not reason-in-itself because it is capable only of 'knowing' discursively, i.e. under the conditions of time and space; if intuition were not supplied, it would know nothing. Thus it can never 'know' the world as a unity; it remains a human, and not a divine, consciousness.[1] Its access to divinity or, let us say, to final purpose is by way of its practical employment. Here, it shares with 'all rational beings' the possibility of establishing its maxims autonomously, of being an end-in-itself and, in so far as this is done, an end of creation. This capacity is assured by the apodicticity of the moral law. This penetration beyond the forms of the discursive understanding establishes the 'primacy of practical reason'. But practical reason, too, is human, not divine, because it involves obligation, which is why we say that 'the practical rule...is a rule characterized by an "ought"'.[2] The *is-ought* dichotomy is not only a logical tension between the direct use of reason in the moral sphere and its mediated use (*via* the forms and categories of the understanding) in the sphere of science, but a personal and human tension between the imperfect present and the world that reason desires.

The conceptual extremes of the whole intermediary sphere of 'life' are the 'person' and the 'race'. If, in its analytical structure, the transcendental ego stands for a mind, it stands also for mind in common, for what mind is and can do. If, under its practical aspect, reason stands for a morally responsible individual, it stands also for the moral responsibility that all have in common, for the ideal membership of the spiritual commonwealth or 'kingdom of ends'. The individually rational is the perfectly cosmopolitan. 'Objective morality' is private and immanent; the 'Copernican revolution' in moral philosophy means precisely that, while remaining universal, reason has abolished transcendent authority in favour of the inner voice. It is the fact of having a personality, defined as the ability to say 'I', to have an ego,[3] that asserts man's closest identity with his fellows and rejects those vagaries of 'negative liberty' that produce

---

[1] As Kant puts it in *Judgment*, 'Introduction', p. 20, nature is 'a unity not indeed to be fathomed by us, yet thinkable...'

[2] *C. Prac. R.* p. 18.   [3] *Anthropologie, G.S.* VII, 127.

discord and injury. Personality is 'the capacity for respect for the moral law as *in itself a sufficient incentive of the will* (*Willkür*)'.[1] However, 'mankind (rational earthly existence in general) *in its complete moral perfection* is that which alone can render a world the object of a divine decree and the end of creation'.[2]

In the vast conceptual distance between the individual who, as agent of reason and personality, is of unique moral worth and the ensemble of persons freely gathered in a moral commonwealth lies the whole tangible and historical sphere of phenomenal man, the creature of *Willkür*, subdivided into communities, abusive of the moral law, externally constrained, often evil or feeble but, by nature, *rationabile*. This is what Kant generally calls *humanity*, which, higher than *animality*, furnishes the matrix of history.[3] Here, pure instinct is subordinated to manipulations of reason, which, however, is as yet 'impure', employed only for the purpose of realizing material incentives. Reason is not yet 'practical of itself'. This is the very sphere of society and politics itself, and of what Kant terms 'pragmatic anthropology'.[4] It does not create the social impulse, but it uses it in a way that we may safely call historical. There is a perfect correspondence between this range of existence and Rousseau's world of *amour-propre* and *perfectibilité*, for *humanity* implies 'a self-love which is physical and yet compares', wherefrom 'springs the inclination *to acquire worth in the opinion of others*'.[5] But Kant uses his tableau for an entirely different purpose than Rousseau. Whereas the latter has equated the evil of history with this inclination and despaired of its domestication, Kant, though acknowledging the 'diabolical' nature of the attendant vices, regards such moral Hobbism as inevitable, justifiable 'as a spur to culture', and conciliable (historically) with the 'predisposition toward good (i.e. observance of the law)'. Even if 'Rousseau was not far wrong in preferring the state of savages' to this,[6] even if it is all at best 'bustling

---

[1] *Religion*, pp. 22–3. [2] *Ibid.* p. 54.
[3] *Ibid.* pp. 22–3. Kant intends 'animality' as an analytical term in the sense that it may be applied to human behaviour.
[4] 'Pragmatic anthropology' may be defined as empirical practical philosophy, i.e. without *a priori* moral grounding: how men *do* act.
[5] *Religion*, p. 22.
[6] 'Idea for a Universal History from a Cosmopolitan Point of View' (hereafter, 'Idea'), in *Kant on History*, p. 21.

The individual and the social

folly',[1] it is still the lesson of philosophy to justify 'contentment with Providence, and with the course of human affairs, considered as a whole'.[2] 'We must still', says Kant, 'give credence to a concurrence of divine wisdom with the course of nature in a practical sense, if we do not prefer to relinquish our ultimate purpose altogether.'[3] Thus, in a well-known passage replete with the best of Kantian sarcasm: 'Thanks be to Nature, then, for the incompatibility, for the heartless competitive vanity, for the insatiable desire to possess and to rule!'[4]

All societies grounded in history, all situations of human inter-relatedness, viewed phenomenally, reflect this predisposition of *humanity* (Kant may very well have used the term not only as a paradoxical counter-weight to Rousseau's *perfectibilité* but as a barb against Herder, for whom the word carried the most noble connotations). Its essence is the notion of 'unsocial sociability', fully developed by Kant in the fourth thesis of the 'Idea for a Universal History'. If morally lamentable, humanity's vicissitudes, even up to and including war, must be regarded as rungs on the ladder from barbarism to culture: 'thence gradually develop all talents, and taste is refined; through continued enlightenment the beginnings are laid for a way of thought which can in time convert the coarse, natural disposition for moral discrimination into definite practical principles, and thereby change a society of men driven together by their natural feelings into a moral whole'.[5]

That is a particularly remarkable sentence. Is Kant simply repeating 'partial evil, universal good'? Evidently not, or not in the fashion of a theodicy; nothing evil can be good in its time. The source of evil, in fact, like freedom, is not in time at all, according to the premises of transcendental idealism.[6] In a real sense, then, the historical past is a *factum*, not to be interpreted by any moral calculus but to be regarded, in so far as it is 'known', i.e. documented,

---

[1] 'An Old Question Raised Again: Is the Human Race Constantly Progressing?' in *ibid.* p. 140.   [2] 'Conjectural Beginning', p. 68.
[3] 'End of All Things', p. 81.   [4] 'Idea', p. 16.   [5] *Ibid.* p. 15.
[6] Cf. *Religion*, p. 36: 'In the search for the rational origin of evil actions, every such action must be regarded as though the individual had fallen into it from a state of innocence...it can and must always be judged as an *original* use of his will.' Repentance is not connected with time, but with the 'possession of an act'; cf. *C. Prac. R.* p. 102.

observed, remembered, as causal and phenomenal.[1] Kant is not interested in examining consciences of dead men; he is exclusively concerned with what 'humanity', taken as a part of the order of nature, has done. None of this is the sphere of freedom. But the sphere of freedom is not only the timeless and impalpable 'whenever'; it is also the impending 'from now on'. As Havet ingeniously puts it: 'the whole sense of the Kantian ethic is that the evil is *done*, while the good is *to be done*'.[2] That means that the future is open. Practical reason enjoins the actualization of virtue; theoretical reason, tied to physico-mechanical causality, can extend its actuarial notions into the future but it cannot predict moral outcomes.

The 'Idea' is not an ethical treatise but a prescriptive work for phenomenal development in accord with the primacy of practical Ideas. In so far as these are not yet made actual (here one should recall Kant's judgments that Europe was not 'enlightened' but 'becoming enlightened' and that it might be 'cultured' or 'civilized' but not 'moral'),[3] they are a task. But the finalist perspective (of which more, below) frames a method whereby the tasks, which as solutions to the problem of freedom are morally binding, dictate the interpretation of the data. The vector of these forces, temporal in possibility because prefigured by the appearance of political societies and the historical evidence of their refinement, but fulfilling the external conditions of the law of freedom, is the Idea of the perfect civil constitution. A practical Idea, it is also the phenomenal limit, the limit of *humanity*. Its difference from the 'kingdom of ends' is striking: for one thing, it is not a democracy, which is the only imaginable form of a moral commonwealth.[4]

Personality, individual and conscientious in its source, is also the warrant of perfect cosmopolitan fraternity because it enjoins the

---

[1] Cf. *C.P.R.* A495 = B523, p. 442: '...the real things of past time...are objects for me and real in past time only in so far as I represent to myself (either by the light of history or by the guiding chain of causes and effects) that a regressive series of possible perceptions in accordance with empirical laws, in a word, that the course of the world conducts us to a past-time series as condition of the present time...'

[2] Havet, *Kant et le temps*, p. 198.

[3] Cf. 'What is Enlightenment?' in *Kant on History*, pp. 8–9; 'Idea', p. 21.

[4] Interestingly, the formal phenomenal potential of the democratic 'kingdom of ends' is established at the dawn of history, when man, by setting himself above the beasts as an 'end in himself', asserts the Idea of his own juridical equality as a human participant in nature. Cf. 'Conjectural Beginning', p. 58.

universal and reciprocal treatment of men as ends-in-themselves. The task of each man, guided by the moral law, is to use his will in the world to bring about in nature what is true in logic, to institute a real universality. Phenomenality supplies the content to this obligation, the material to be mastered. But phenomenality also introduces all the restraints of man's physical nature, subjecting him to impulse, to the limits set by his circumscribed horizon and the agonizing brevity of his life. The human skin cannot be shed.

The vast distance between the creature of reason and the goal of reason or personality is historical because time is the condition for our knowing everything, with the single exception of the moral law. It is also the condition in which we extend our knowledge and, in so far as this knowledge creates a receptivity for moral Ideas, become better men. Time exists so that good may be done, so that man may come into his kingdom. However, no man fulfills his destiny in a life span; the practical postulate of immortality is necessary to compensate the individual for this difficulty. Yet the world of nature (cosmos) must also be regarded as fulfilling itself by design if that world is to be reasonable. Thus this task must be assigned to the species, which, unlike the individual, has an indefinitely prolonged career. The species is, moreover, in potential that real universality implied in the logical identity of the reason of all men. At the hypothetical moral end-points individual and species are joined by dignity and respect.

If historical fulfilment is a function of time, it also involves a natural history of reason. Although reason is eternal and dwells above the cosmos or deep within the soul of man, reason's apprehension of itself can be acknowledged only historically. This notion is akin to freedom's dual role as an *a priori* concept and as a mission. There are, in effect, two kinds of reason in Kant, explored according to the point of view: a reason that *is* and a reason that *becomes*. The latter is an appearance, the former a thing-in-itself. The reason that *is* is available to us practically as a determinant; it shows us what *ought* to be. The reason that *becomes* is the plan by which history or phenomenal succession must be viewed if the viewer is reasonable (i.e. moral).

But a phenomenal sequence can have only a historical destiny, even if that goal is ordered by the moral Ideas. It can concern only the species, which has 'time enough' for its accomplishment. But it must be a paradigmatic ordering of 'humanity' in history along lines which a moral commonwealth would bring to pass autonomously. In short it must be (allowance made for the political weakness and temporal-spatial unwieldiness of a universal state) a federation of *reipublicae phaenomena*. Justice is regarded as the phenomenal shadow of autonomy. Peace, Kant tells us, is the ticket of passage between these legal and moral worlds.[1] With the practical Ideas of the perfect civil constitution and eternal peace we are poised ambiguously between *ecclesia* and *cosmopolis*, but still perhaps on the border of time and phenomenality. The conditions of respect appear, though its free generation is a matter that exceeds the understanding.

Thus, both individual and species have natural and moral definitions. Only 'anthroponomy', never 'anthropology', can guarantee the sphere of freedom and virtue. But in history 'anthropology' strives toward 'anthroponomy', its infinite goal being the perfect commonwealth. Amid his many sharp perceptions, Vlachos has thereby been led to speak of the 'individual, accident of the species', regarding Kant's goal as a *telos* of the legal order, a domestication of humanity at the pinnacle of culture and respect, but scarcely 'autonomous' in the self-legislative sense.[2] On the other hand, Kant is emphatic that man is an end-in-himself, as a person due the respect of all others. Conscience is the only high court before which a man judges himself.[3]

Which notion then has the priority? Perhaps that question is badly put. Eric Weil's excellent analysis unhesitatingly develops the side of morality. 'Historical teleology,' he maintains, 'no matter how basic to ethics, was never at the centre of Kant's reflection.' The historical world remains, in effect, for Kant a world of nature, a cosmos. Weil goes on: '...the connection is between God and the moral individual, not between God and the subjects of history, societies, peoples, individual states which remain, in relation to

---

[1] *Löse Blätter*, *G.S.* XXIII, 353–4.
[2] Vlachos, *Pensée politique*, pp. 193 f.
[3] See *Virtue*, pp. 60–1.

ethics, means, tools, objects, but not subjects...'[1] Weil is right about the subjects. Yet Kant was very much a philosopher of this world, who, for reasons of systematic method, was obliged to construct an exotic form of interpreting it. Paradoxically, his rigidly abstract propositions for a universal ethic of freedom tend not toward the religious image of a person before God but toward a conformity of reason in which human variety is muted by collectivist overtones.

By its internal necessity, the human consciousness has created time in order to represent its objects and, though itself dominating time in a way they do not, must live in and through time to the extent that its goals are not fulfilled. Our historicity is a consequence of the way we know ourselves. Liberty is an interiorized fact in the historical world that draws us toward a future for which we will be responsible.

---

[1] Weil, *Problèmes*, pp. 139-40.

4

THE AMBIVALENCE OF PROGRESS

A. KANT'S DOCTRINE OF IDEAS

The Idea, as Kant puts it, promotes the goal of history 'from afar'. It is the vehicle, available to reason and a product of the irrepressible will of the understanding to advance its knowledge, which mediates the distance between the *is* of hazardous appearance and the *ought* of system or unity. No analysis of Kant's view of history, no assessment of his positioning of morality against time or of his appraisal of culture, enlightenment and the legal order as phenomenal supports of ethical life can dispense with a close examination of the way the consciousness constructs and uses Ideas.[1]

'Ideas', Kant writes, 'are rational concepts, for which there can be no adequate object in experience. They are neither apperceptions (like space and time), nor feelings (as the eudaemonistic doctrine would hold...), but concepts of a perfection that one can ever approach in reality without, however, being able to reach it completely.'[2] Unlike the 'apperceptions' and categories of the understanding, by which the consciousness combines sense data, the Ideas lie beyond any concrete empirical correspondence[3]. Lacking this measure of empirical reality, they can be said to approximate, though not reach, the perfection of universals. As Richard Kroner puts it: 'they are rules (like the categories) only for the possibility of knowledge, for the subject, but not for actuality [*Wirklichkeit*], for nature'.[4] As 'concepts of reason' they reply to the necessity that reason establishes for the systematic ordering of its world. As opposed to 'concepts of the understanding', they concern an awareness

---

[1] For much of the following analysis I am indebted to G. Vlachos, *Pensée politique*, 111–19, and to Richard Kroner, *Von Kant bis Hegel* (2 vols. in one, Tübingen, 1961), I, 119–30, 381–92.

[2] *Anthropologie, G.S.* VII, 199–200. In *Judgment* ('Aesthetic'), para. 15, p. 78 n., Kant distinguishes 'transcendental' or material perfection from 'teleological' or formal perfection, 'the agreement of the characteristics of a thing with a purpose'.

[3] See *Prolegomena to any Future Metaphysics* (trans. P. Carus, Chicago, 1909), para. 56, pp. 118–19; *C.P.R.* A567–58 = B596–7, pp. 485–6.

[4] Kroner, *Von Kant bis Hegel*, I, 124. Cf. Beck, *Commentary*, p. 183: 'A category freed from the limitations to possible experience and handed over to reason for a complete synthesis of all experience is called an "Idea".'

of which actual experience is only a part.[1] Consequently, Ideas
are goals or *maxima*, conceived of as possible but not constitutive of
experience. Their transcendental employment by theoretical reason
enables the formation of higher concepts from 'notions' (i.e. pure
abstractions from experience alone). Thus the unity of the understanding is extended from particular operations toward a grasp of
the unconditioned or universal.[2] The Ideas systematize or rigorize
the data of the understanding. Conversely, the objects of experience
may be viewed as the result of limitations set phenomenally on their
Ideas.

Especially important for Kant are the notion and use of practical
Ideas: 'Reason has a presentiment of objects which possess a great
interest for it. But when it follows the path of pure speculation,
in order to approach them, they fly before it. Presumably it may
look for better fortune in the only other path which still remains
open to it, that of its practical employment.'[3] If, he argues, we
allow ourselves to suppose that theoretical reason can project its
concepts beyond the barriers of empirical understanding, thereby
revealing an intelligible world of things-in-themselves, we are im-
properly creating transcendent ideas subject to dialectical contradiction. This occurs whenever we speculatively 'prove' God,
immortality, or the entire range of the supersensible. Our only certain
knowledge of anything non-empirical, according to Kant, is of the
moral law itself. But when it is a question of objects formally transcending the consciousness, the practical use of reason (i.e. that
reason based on our certainty of freedom), being subjective and
immanent in derivation, is in a position to furnish us with an order
of Ideas 'which tell us what ought to happen' or, better, 'what I
ought to do'.[4] In this case, 'reason can at least attain so far as to determine the will, and, in so far as it is a question of volition only,
reason does always have objective reality'.[5] Ideas may be constitutive of practical experience; on the other hand, they can establish
maxima that permit theoretical reason to undertake its causal investigations according to a meaningful unity, i.e. they can be used
'regulatively'. Kroner explains this well when he writes of the Idea

[1] Cf. *C.P.R.* A310-11 = B367, p. 308.   [2] *Ibid.* A323 = B380, p. 316.
[3] *Ibid.* A796 = B824, p. 629.   [4] *Ibid.* A802 = B830, p. 634.   [5] *C. Prac. R.* p. 15.

as 'a maxim of the theoretical volition, an imperative for scientific, especially experientially scientific thought'. 'The Idea,' he continues, 'extends the understanding not as understanding, but as will [*Wille*]; it extends it in a practical, not a theoretical manner...'[1]

The operation just alluded to is performed by the judgment, 'the faculty of thinking the particular as contained under the universal'.[2] 'Nature', Kant explains, 'is represented by means of this concept as if an understanding contained the ground of the unity of the variety of its empirical laws.'[3] Reason disposes us toward this means of grasping the world, and 'we more gladly listen to one who offers hope that the more we know nature... the more simple we shall find it in its principles'.[4] According to the regulative use of the Ideas, although 'nothing justifies us in deriving an existence from a condition outside the empirical [i.e. mechanico-causal] series...[it] does not in any way disbar us from recognizing that the whole series may rest upon some intelligible being that is free from all empirical conditions...'[5]

The *Critique of Pure Reason* is merely permissive of the realm of freedom, even though it concludes with a 'canon of pure reason' that is practical in use. The second *Critique*, however, asserts the primacy of practical reason and establishes the methodology whereby the moral law obliges us to pursue the fulfilment of the practical Ideas by opposing our autonomy to the whole range of choice conditioned by impulse and directed toward goals of presumptive happiness. The *Critique of Judgment* is intended to suggest the way in which a reason, ultimately moral in force, directs the employment of the understanding without dialectical pitfalls of transcendent illusion. In that reconciliation of the two orders, world history necessarily assumes great importance as the field in which knowledge is extended, a position already implied in Kant's earlier historical essay and reiterated by paragraph 83 of the 'Critique of Teleological Judgment'. In short: 'Ideas carry into history the unity of meaning expressed by the word "culture", just as the natural laws carry to

---

[1] Kroner, *Von Kant bis Hegel*, I, 122.　　　　　[2] *Judgment*, 'Introduction', p. 17.
[3] *Ibid*. p. 19. Regarding the possible congruence of causalities, cf. *C.P.R.* A544 = B572, p. 471.
[4] *Judgment*, 'Introduction', p. 30.
[5] *C.P.R.* A561–2 = B589–90, p. 481; cf. A509 = B537, p. 450.

the world of apperception the conceptual unity covered by the word "nature".[1]

Thus, despite the historical intangibility of *maxima* of perfection in the transcendental philosophy, the Idea takes on logically posterior, axiologically superior, and temporally future implications.

In a logical sense, the transcendental ego, the preliminary and formal 'I think', masters time and rules the architecture of reason, but the Ideas of reason nonetheless depend on the possibility and content of sense experience, on the 'knowing' which demands extension. This ambiguity is most clearly demonstrated in the historical progress of philosophy itself. 'It is a very notable fact,' Kant writes, 'although it could not have been otherwise, that in the infancy of philosophy men began where we should incline to end, namely with the knowledge of God, occupying themselves with the hope, or rather indeed with the specific nature, of another world.'[2] If Kant does not go so far as to imply (at least to the extent of his contemporaries Lessing and Herder) that God is rational cosmic genesis,[3] he tentatively suggests a history of philosophy (or of reason) displaying the progressively more perfect production of the Idea of God. But there are 'hierarchies' of Ideas short of God, leading not directly to the intelligible destiny of man but to a destiny of man 'in nature' quivering on the margin of time. One such Idea is the rational state, whose achievement is undeniably a practical goal but whose construction may be seen as phenomenal and technical. It is therefore justifiable to maintain that Kant, through the medium of the Ideas pertinent to 'ends of nature', performs a 'historicization' of the ancient corpus of natural rights doctrine.[4] Although he dissolves the past (the 'historical contract') in heuristic abstraction, he establishes contact with a future rendered tangible through evolution and enlightenment.

---

[1] Fritz Münch, 'Erlebnis und Geltung: eine systematische Untersuchung zur Transzendentalphilosophie als Weltanschauung', *Kant-Studien*, Ergänzungsheft No. 30 (Berlin, 1913), p. 132.

[2] *C.P.R.* A852 = B880, p. 666.

[3] For the tendencies of Lessing and Herder, see the discussion by Martial Gueroult, *L'évolution et la structure de la Doctrine de la Science chez Fichte* (2 vols., Paris, 1930), I, 11–12.

[4] Cf. Bruno Bauch, 'Das Rechtsproblem in der Kantischen Philosophie', *Zeitschrift für Rechtsphilosophie*, III (1920), 13 f.

However, the Kantian Idea is intended to repel epistemological attack since it is a guiding principle and never a plan of perfection, never, we might say, a utopia. 'We can always have a thing in our thoughts although it is [really] nothing, or we can represent a thing as given, although we have no concept of it,' he declares.[1] From the perspective of 'criticism', this 'thing' is not an Idea but an 'ideal', an imagined and fleshed out essence, useful perhaps to our moral improvement but never, despite its pictorialization, to be regarded as an object of knowledge.[2] Here Kant explains himself by reference to Plato. The discriminations are of considerable interest.

'For Plato,' Kant says, 'ideas are archetypes of things themselves', ontologically superior even to the categories of the understanding. As such, they are constitutive principles, directly accessible to philosophical wisdom, strictly speaking 'ideals' and not Ideas.[3] An ideal, however, is really even more distant from objective reality than an Idea (Kantian) because it presumes to represent the Idea as a thing, in concrete individuality. This is to say that ideals are imaginatively visible constructs and not merely regulative guides. Ideas give rules, while ideals serve as archetypes for the determination of the phenomenal copy.[4] To illustrate: the Stakhanovite is an ideal, whereas the precept, 'Work as hard as you can without damage to others or injury to yourself', might be an Idea. Kantian practical Ideas are, in fact, formulations of some aspect of the law of freedom (e.g. the basis of the perfect civil constitution is: 'Every action that in itself or in its maxim is such that the freedom of the will of each can coexist together with the freedom of everyone in accordance with a universal law';[5] this is transformed into an imperative by the addition of the preamble 'So act that...').

Even though, following Kant, ideals supply reason with indispensable standards,

...to attempt to realize the ideal in an example, that is, in the field of appearance, as, for instance, to depict the [character of the perfectly] wise man in a romance, is impracticable...Natural limitations, which are

---

[1] *Judgment* ('Teleological'), para. 76, p. 315.
[2] *Ibid.* ('Aesthetic'), para. 17, p. 85; '*Idea* properly means a rational concept, and *ideal* the representation of an individual being, regarded as adequate to an Idea.'
[3] *C.P.R.* A313 = B370, p. 310.   [4] *Ibid.* A568–9 = B596–7, pp. 485–6.   [5] *Justice*, p. 35.

constantly doing violence to the completeness of the Idea, make the illusion that is aimed at altogether impossible, and so cast suspicion on the good itself...[1]

The Kantian position is clear: Ideas 'help', as he once remarked, but ideals are chimerical. Kant's bias, unlike Plato's, is both progressivist and anti-utopian. A characteristic statement: '...nothing else remains for [practical] reason except to visualize a variation that proceeds into the infinite (in time) within the perpetual progression toward the ultimate purpose in connection with which its disposition endures...'[2] However, against this pure routine of infinite progression must be set the aggregate of remarks which speak of a 'perspective assured to the human race in the centuries to come, a felicity which will not collapse',[3] and his criticism of Moses Mendelssohn's 'historical abderitism' in the second part of the *Conflict of the Faculties*.[4] Most emphatically, Kant denied cyclical history or human regression.

In his anxiousness to 'repudiate the audacious assertions of *materialism*, *naturalism* and *fatalism* that narrowly restrict the field of reason' and to 'procure a place for moral Ideas outside the sphere of [mere] speculations', Kant still attaches great interest to the Platonic method, relieved of its 'extravagances'.[5] 'The Platonic ideas', he writes, though lacking creative power, as Plato believed, 'have *practical* power (as regulative principles), and form the basis of the possible perfection of certain *actions*.'[6] Even though the 'fiction in which we combine and realize the manifold of our Idea', that is, the 'ideal', cannot be correlated with phenomenal reality, '[Plato's] spiritual flight from the ectypal [i.e. impure] mode of reflecting upon the physical world-order to the architectonic ordering of it according to ends, that is, according to Ideas, is an enterprise which calls for respect and imitation.'[7] Kant rarely comes closer than this to counselling the fabricating of political life *de novo*.

[1] *C.P.R.* A570 = B598, pp. 486–7.
[2] 'End of All Things', p. 77.
[3] *Anthropologie, G.S.* VII, 277.
[4] 'Old Question', pp. 140–1; cf. also, 'Idea', p. 22: '...it seems that our own intelligent action may hasten this happy time for our posterity'.
[5] *Prolegomena*, para. 60, p. 137.   [6] *C.P.R.* A569 = B597, p. 486.
[7] *Ibid.* A318 = B375, p. 313.

Perhaps bad states are not an unavoidable consequence of human nature but are due rather 'to a quite remediable cause, the neglect of pure Ideas in the making of the laws'.[1] This mood is rather far from the hard-bitten phenomenal dialectic of 'unsocial sociability' and the trial-and-error of reason so forcefully described in the 'Idea for a Universal History'. Ultimately, however, he says, we must pursue the principle and the task, and cannot translate the model. And the reason for this is freedom: 'How great a gulf may still have to be left between the Idea and its realization...no one can, or ought to, answer. For the issue depends on freedom; and it is in the power of freedom to pass beyond any and every specified limit.'[2]

Kant's 'two worlds' are hypothetically combined in the infinitely receding Idea of God. On the other hand, all moral action starts from the rational will and all knowing from the transcendental ego. We do not assume God behind either of these operations because this would be an explicit denial of *our* freedom.[3] Teleology is the *purely theoretical* principle which 'proves that, according to the constitution of our cognitive faculties and in the consequent combination of experience with the highest principles of reason, we can form absolutely no concept of the possibility of such a world [as this one] save by thinking a designedly working supreme cause thereof'.[4] Ideas or ends, however, belong to the realms of both teleology and ethics, their character being determined by their form and use. Teleology frames hypotheses for the clarification of scientific (causal) knowledge. Ethics can 'be defined as the system of the ends of pure practical reason'.[5] Their connection is explained in a note from the *Grundlegung*:

Teleology considers nature as a kingdom of ends; ethics regards a possible kingdom of ends as a kingdom of nature. In the first case, the kingdom of ends is a theoretical Idea, adopted to explain what actually is. In the latter it is a practical Idea, adopted to bring about that which is not yet, but which can be realized by our conduct, namely, if it conforms to this Idea.[6]

---

[1] *Ibid.* A316 = B373, p. 312.   [2] *Ibid.* A317 = B374, p. 312.
[3] Cf. *C. Prac. R.* p. 130: 'It is...not to be understood that the assumption of the existence of God is necessary as a ground of all obligation in general...'
[4] *Judgment* ('Teleological'), para. 75, p. 311.
[5] *Virtue*, p. 39.   [6] *Foundations*, p. 53 n.

The anthropological substrate

Of the Ideas prominently featured in Kant's historico-political writings, two (the perfect civil constitution and the eternal peace assured by a league of nations) are practical because they relate to an obligation derived from the notion of external freedom or respect, and one, the presumptive unity of nature, *vide* the human race, is theoretical because it is a hypothesis for scientific anthropology.[1] Now it will be noticed that these views are, to some degree, interchangeable, because 'natural' cosmopolitan unity can certainly be seen from a moral angle, while both the rational state and peace are notions that have mechanical, legal and coercive overtones.[2] This connection is clarified by one of the corollaries of the categorical imperative: 'Act as if the maxim of thy action were to become by thy will a universal law of nature.' But one must also 'so act as to treat humanity, whether in thine own person or in that of any other, in every case as an end withal, never as a means only'.[3]

For Kant the final resolution of this theoretical-practical parallelism is found, as we know, in ethical finalism. The so-called physico-teleological proof of cosmic unity, however suggestive, cannot be intellectually decisive, 'but it mingles itself unnoticed with that moral ground of proof, which dwells in every man and influences him secretly...' The physico-teleological proof 'has only the merit of leading the mind'.[4] Nowhere in Kant, however, do we encounter any doubt that the mind should be thus led, or that the theoretical use of Ideas is not important as a clue for moral behaviour.

B. THE ANTHROPOLOGICAL SUBSTRATE

There is an astringent empirical substrate to Kant's view of the human condition, already noted in his discussion of *humanity* in the work on religion, which he refuses to the doctrine of ethics but emphasizes in his historical dialectic. In this perspective, it is not only man's social antagonism but his skills as a culture builder that are set off against the pure obligations of freedom and respect. This peculiar duality of Kant's philosophy of history—what might

---

[1] See L. W. Beck's introduction to *Kant on History*, p. xxi.
[2] Cf. 'Perpetual Peace', p. 112.   [3] *Foundations*, pp. 38, 46.
[4] *Judgment* ('Teleological'), para. 91, p. 418.

be called his Platonic and Hobbesian sides—carried an impact into the historiographical theory of the nineteenth century. Recently, an Italian scholar has described Kant's scattered historical writings as a 'fourth critique'.[1] A fourth critique they are not, evidently, because Kant, no historian himself, explicitly discounted his 'Idea' as such an adventure.[2] For Kant the *a priori* of history is impure; it is in fact the empirical notion of man existing as an *animal rationabile* stated in the first part of the 'Conjectural Beginning', a 'something which human reason cannot derive from prior natural causes'.[3] History *a priori* is actually a self-fulfilling prophecy, sanctioned by the fact that Kant's particular prophecy is a vision of the moral law increasingly manifested on earth.[4]

This is why an anthropological discussion on the surface very much like that of Hobbes must lead to rather different results.[5] In fact, the phenomenal juggernaut of 'unsocial sociability' and culture building depends on an empirical view of human nature where the *bellum omnium contra omnes* and the social interdependence of Enlightenment theory are mediated, where desire and power do not create a wild crescendo. Kantian man is saved from the absolute outcome of the state of war by his ineradicable moral awareness, not by his craft or intelligence: once more the lesson of Rousseau. Finally, it is possible to say that in Kant's legal philosophy force may very well accompany justice but has no power to create it. Withal, however, the axiom that 'man needs a master' is much closer to Malmesbury than Geneva.

Thus, it would be imprudent to dismiss Kant's anthropological vision of history as irrelevant to his political ideas. We must rather set side by side the raw aspect of conflict and *amour propre* and the sacred moment of moral awareness, of 'changes in ways of thinking'. The motto which establishes this connection is man's ascent 'from

---

[1] Renato Composto, *La quarta critica kantiana* (Palermo, 1954).
[2] 'Idea', p. 12.
[3] 'Conjectural Beginning', pp. 54 f.; and 'Idea', p. 25. Cf. Emil L. Fackenheim, 'Kant's Concept of History', *Kant-Studien*, XLVIII (1956–7), 387.
[4] 'Old Question', p. 137.
[5] See, in general, on the Kant–Hobbes relationship: Vlachos, *Pensée politique*, pp. 300 ff.; also, Pierre Hassner, 'Les concepts de guerre et de paix chez Kant', *Revue française de science politique* (Sept. 1961), p. 647. The latter stresses the similarity too much.

bondage to instinct to rational control—in a word, from the tutelage of nature to the state of freedom'.[1]
Kant recognized three sorts of anthropology, straddled across the curriculum of philosophical inquiry. Two of them are evidently theoretical sciences: 'theoretical' anthropology, which involves the natural study of the races of man in their external character and development, and 'physiological' anthropology, or the investigation of man as a biological species. Additionally, there is 'pragmatic' anthropology, which studies 'what [man] as a creature possessing liberty of action makes of himself, or what he can and ought to make of himself'.[2] Obviously this latter division, as a *mélange* of norms and observations, has close connections with the Kantian treatment of history itself. Kant began to lecture on anthropology at Koenigsberg in 1772, and the substance of his lectures provided the last work published before his death. Partly because Kant's *Anthropology* is empirical, not transcendental, and partly because it amalgamates views on humanity drawn from the various branches of his philosophy, it repays close study by anyone interested in Kantian politics. It is also usefully supplemented by the hundreds of 'anthropological reflections' which were collated and published from Kant's notebooks long after his death.

Even if man is construed as having an ethical destiny and the Kantian ethics is not founded on human nature, Kant's view of the technics of culture has a frankly realist and anthropological foundation. At moments we feel we are back with Rousseau or Buffon: 'One should observe savages and children under all circumstances,' Kant writes. 'Thus one can see what that animal is that must be governed or disciplined by reason, and if its personal (moral and social) nature and its animal nature are in conflict or in harmony...'[3] 'Social' is a fluctuating term in Kant: as an instinct it arises in animal life;[4] as the formulation of cultural and, beyond that, moral goals it receives all the content of higher freedom. History advances us from the horde to the commonwealth. History is, *inter alia*, the record of the art of government, our government of ourselves and our government by vested authorities. 'Man', says Kant, 'is capable

---

[1] 'Conjectural Beginning', p. 60.   [2] *Anthropologie, G.S.* VII, 119.
[3] *Reflexionen zur Anthropologie, G.S.* XV, no. 1211, p. 532.   [4] *Religion*, p. 22.

135

of governing things by his *technical* dispositions...of governing others by his *pragmatic* dispositions...of acting on himself by his *moral* dispositions.'[1] The idea of discipline is emphatic. Morality can be only self-discipline, but in history we have not yet reached a moral world. 'The most important revolution [again, we notice Kant's preferred use of the word] within man is when he emerges from a necessary apprenticeship.'[2]

Behind 'pragmatic' anthropology are the sparse scientific outlines of the 'theoretical' anthropology. The natural unity of man is a theoretical Idea that subserves the Kantian vision of history. Despite the ultimate primacy of ethics over teleology there is joined in history an extensive parallelism of man's natural unfolding and his moral progress. In Kant's essay 'On the Different Races of Men' (1775) and in some of his other minor writings we get a close impression of how the human sciences support the ethical vision of evolution. In the essay on the 'Races' Kant begins with the proposition (echoed in the 'Conjectural Beginning') that the human race must have started from a single manner of reproduction; thus 'all men throughout the wide world belong to one and the same natural species'.[3] 'From this unity of the natural species,' he continues,

...one can derive another natural fact: namely, that all belong to a single branch, from which, notwithstanding, all differentiations have originated or at very least could have originated. In the first case, men belong not merely to one and the same species, but also to a single family.[4]

Elsewhere, Kant speaks of a 'mother race of which the known races would be nothing but pure and simple modifications'.[5]

Kant, as we know, attributed unexceptionable scientific causality to the world of phenomena. 'Theoretical anthropology' is no doubt a discipline to be conceived within these limits. But the actuality of freedom would have been jeopardized, as well as the realm of nature, were it not true that (1) the phenomenal unfolding of man was somehow preconditioned by the original generation, and (2) somehow man was able to develop outside of a strictly natural or environmental causation. This leads Kant to his theory of 'preformation',

---

[1] *Anthropologie, G.S.* VII, 322.   [2] *Ibid.* p. 229.   [3] *G.S.* II, 429.
[4] *Ibid.* pp. 429–30.   [5] 'Bestimmung einer Racen', *G.S.* VIII, 101.

which, on the one hand, thrusts back a 'predetermination' where freedom cannot enter, and, on the other, makes it possible to study humanity from the scientific point of view: 'Neither chance nor universal mechanical laws could have brought forth such congruous conditions (*Zusammenpassungen*). Thus we must envisage such occasional developments as preformed (*vorgebildet*).'[1]

Out of this process of 'preformation', according to Kant's account, have issued four major races (white, red, black, olive).[2] Their possibilities were contained in the original germ of human creation. Kant's anthropological investigation of their temperaments, physiques and habits, as well as his close examination of the principal sub-races of Europe and indeed of characteriology in general, leaves no doubt that this philosopher of the categorical imperative was deeply concerned with the diverse manifold of environment, custom and racial differentiation. He was quite as sensitive as Montesquieu or Hume concerning both the physiological and historical limitations on the unity of humanity. This is a side of Kant which is often lost to the student who confines himself to the major systematic writings.

But Kant evidently did not believe, with Herder, that the condition of variety and differentiated production was an ultimate sign of the glory and fecundity of creation.[3] Just as man has a moral obligation to place himself under the sovereignty of reason and, in so doing, to strive toward the formal condition of the 'kingdom of ends', so it is conceivable that in the scientific destiny of the species there will appear a tendency to return to the matrix of the original race. The idea intrudes in several places. In an essay on teleology,

---

[1] *G.S.* II, 435. [2] *Ibid.* p. 441.

[3] As opposed to the quantitatively 'cosmopolitan' ordering of man's phenomenal destiny, which is the anthropological complement to the transcendental ethics, German thought had a qualitative side (the general line of Herder, Goethe, the Romantics, and indeed Nietzsche) that speculated on the achievement of an 'ideal type' of humanity or *Menschentypus*. This question of whether there can be a synthesis of universal and 'best' (aristocratic) values, a meeting ground of humanity and genius, permeates *Faust* and *Wilhelm Meister*. Under the aegis of such problems and against the vivid background of the political events of the turn of the nineteenth century, the humane-aristocratic *Gemeinde* tended to be transvalued *via* the growing value of nationalism; we shall follow the process in the thought of Fichte. For some suggestive remarks, especially regarding Goethe, see H. A. Korff, *Humanismus und Romantik* (Leipzig, 1924), pp. 88 f.

he writes of the reduction of 'infinitely variable ends' and a 'diversi-
fication of races' tending toward 'more essential but less numerous
ends'.[1] And, more specifically, in one of his notes on anthropology,
he allows himself to imagine an eventual reassimilation of the races
and a recapturing in biological history of the primitive model
(*erstes Urbild*).[2]

It is evidently not permissible to infer from these scattered
evidences that Kant saw 'physiological anthropology' as guiding the
destiny of man. But we cannot discard the impression that Kant's
vision of human development implied a correspondence between
the literal career of the race and the ethical idea of achieving universal
recognition of each man as an end.

Seen from one angle, speculative anthropology suggests a confirmation of the *fictio heuristica* of the moral commonwealth. But
history is the barrier, the long, even infinite distance, the ponderous
'meanwhile'. Man remains 'an animal that requires a master'. He is
as yet untamed by others, untamed by himself, 'unenlightened'. Not
only do most men not yet know 'how to know', nor do they 'dare to
know', but there are still four races about whose inadequacies Kant
minces no words. The human race is young, and the trial promises
to be long. 'If', Kant says, 'one adds episodes from the national
histories of other peoples in so far as they are known from the history
of the enlightened nations, one will discover a regular process in the
constitution of states on our continent (which will probably give law,
eventually, to all the others).'[3] Whatever conclusions we draw from
the 'plan' of history that we make for ourselves, we cannot help
realizing that the mass of human beings have no notion of such a
plan. The great effort will be one of law and discipline, an effort just
beginning. Europe must first reform itself, then radiate its hard-won
lessons to the rest of the globe. Before all men are treated as ends,
they must be taught that they are ends. 'No one is a slave (or bonds-
man) but the man who wills to be one, and only so long as he wills.'[4]
In phenomenal life, this is not an instantaneous undertaking.

---

[1] 'Über den Gebrauch der teleologischen Prinzipien in der Philosophie', *G.S.* VIII,
167–8.
[2] *Reflex. Anthrop.* XV, no. 1453, pp. 634–5.
[3] 'Idea', p. 24. [4] *Religion*, p. 76.

History annuls the intelligible 'from now on', and makes the precondition of a 'revolution in one's cast of mind' the formal, pedagogical preparation of the mind itself.

C. FINALITY AND ULTIMACY

If history is to be construed as having design, the problem of corruption in history must be faced. For Kant, the question of morality, and hence of evil, poses itself timelessly and ever anew in the imputable part of the individual called the personality. But there is indeed corruption *in* history, a corruption of human responsibility denounced as ringingly as Rousseau had done: '[History] teaches [man] that he must not blame the evils which oppress him on Providence, nor attribute his own offence to an original sin...[He] must...thus blame only himself for the evils which spring from the abuse of reason.'[1] Were the evil cacophonies necessary? Apparently they were, because reason itself, no longer timelessly pure, becomes historical, requiring 'trial, practice and instruction in order gradually to progress from one level of insight to another'.[2] *Ars longa, vita brevis.* On the other hand, to say that *history is corrupt* is not only to forswear the possibility of divine wisdom but, more importantly, to transgress against the dignity befitting the human being. The timeless, of which man is a part and which is a part of man, makes him the end of history to the extent that he treats it as an ethical chronology.

A fair amount of nonsense has been written about Kant's 'ruse of nature', according to which nature wills, urges or grants this or that, leading men in ways they do not suspect and toward goals which, ultimately, will prove to be compatible with a voluntary moral destiny. Kant's own metaphors from the 'Idea for a Universal History' are surely at fault for this confusion. It is relevant to inquire at this point about the meaning of such phrases as 'the intention of Nature' and 'the secret wise guidance in Nature'.[3]

Nature means, in effect, two things for Kant. It means first the

---

[1] 'Conjectural Beginning', p. 68.
[2] 'Idea', p. 13.
[3] *Ibid.* pp. 19, 20. Cf. also 'Perpetual Peace', pp. 112–14.

external or sensible world, in so far as this is scientifically explicable, or, in his own words, 'the existence of things so far as determined by universal laws'.[1] At the same time, nature retains its classical meaning of the full development or actualization of a thing according to its *telos*.[2] Thus, regarding man as a creature of liberty, Kant can write: 'Whatever good man is able to do through his own efforts, under laws of freedom, in contrast to what he can do only with supernatural assistance, can be called *nature*, as distinguished from *grace*.'[3] The tension of man is contained between these two propositions, as an object of science and as a subject of freedom, the *maxima* of reification and spiritualization. Now the possibility of freedom is in human history, in the sphere of what has been called 'humanity'. Man as historical actor is, to be sure, physically endowed with certain drives and dispositions, with certain technical capacities which assuredly we cannot attribute to a self-creation. We do not in fact know where he got them, and, in this sense, it is appropriate to speak of nature as the supplier. But man recognizes nature only through his own rationality; his consciousness imposes the very frame of temporal and spatial reference in which nature can be understood at all. Thus reason is the intellectual or formal creator of nature.[4]

However, this is not all. Man can understand his place in nature only through the stimulus of the moral law and the productive power of reason to frame Ideas. Otherwise he would be in no position to write of 'nature's intentions'. Consequently, the teleological method of inquiry is placed at the service of reason so that knowledge may be extended, so that man may attempt to discover *to what end* his natural endowments have been provided. Eventually this line of inquiry leads to ethical conclusions (the practical Ideas) which oblige an action toward the ends in view. Teleological Ideas are not *a priori* concepts; they are immanently established schemes for investigation or action. Though 'objectively' useful, they are not

---

[1] *Prolegomena*, para. 14, p. 50.
[2] These two notions of nature are analysed in a somewhat different context by L. W. Beck, *Commentary*, pp. 159–60.
[3] *Religion*, p. 179.
[4] See the discussion in Gueroult, *Doctrine de la Science*, I, 42; also, Havet, *Kant et le temps*, p. 19.

transcendent, but rather 'transcendental'. Consequently they owe their entire origin to the rational subject. 'We bring in a teleological ground,' Kant writes, 'where we attribute causality in respect of an object to the concept of an object, as if it were to be found in nature (not in ourselves).'[1]

This should dissipate any animistic illusions about 'nature's purpose'. That purpose is the purpose which we, as rational agents, assign to it by means of the teleological perspective. Human history is, consequently, not a natural history, like that of the 'bees or beavers'. To discover a 'natural' purpose in history means simply to consider men, taken in the large (humanity), from a 'cosmopolitan point of view', that is, as a hypothetical ordainer. Nature, Kant wittily says, will have to produce the men capable of establishing the laws of such an inquiry, just as she produced Kepler and Newton in order to explain the performance of the planets.[2] However, in a real sense it is the freedom and reason (of Keplers, Newtons and Kants) that produce nature, and, in the case of man, transform it into history.

That is essentially why history is not corrupt despite its corruptions. The business of making sense out of it while preserving the Kantian ideal of dignity demands that its course be seen 'not as a decline from good to evil, but rather a gradual development from the worse to the better' and that nature be seen as having 'given the vocation to everyone to contribute as much to this progress as may be within his power'.[3] But that is not quite all. Evil, Kant insists, has no character.[4] It has, he writes elsewhere, 'the indiscerptible property of being opposed to and destructive of its own purposes (especially in the relationship between evil men); thus it gives place to the moral principle of the good, though only through a slow progress'.[5] What I think Kant means here is that evil, based on

---

[1] *Judgment* ('Teleological'), para. 61, p. 261. Cf. 'Perpetual Peace,' pp. 106–7: 'We do not observe or infer [historical] providence in the cunning contrivances of nature, but . . . we can and must supply it from our own minds in order to conceive of its possibility . . .' This is why Hassner's analysis, 'Concepts de guerre et de paix', pp. 663–4, misses the point. Kant is not sponsoring a natural theodicy, but is regarding it as a morally useful idea. Still, there is at moments a disturbingly independent flavour to Kant's 'nature'.
[2] 'Idea', p. 12. [3] 'Conjectural Beginning', p. 68. [4] *Anthropologie, G.S.* VII, 329.
[5] 'Perpetual Peace', p. 127.

interest and advantage, does not allow for the construction of large Ideas that bring humanity nearer any purpose; it is a demon on the fringes of freedom doing tenacious but hopeless battle with the moral law.[1] War, the worst evil, should ideally teach men the logic of peace. Unfortunately Kant was far from imagining those essays of evil which, in the guise of large Ideas, would later come to chisel at the foundations of his cherished enlightenment.

Kant harshly distinguishes between the human goal of 'finality' and the natural goal of 'ultimacy' in his historical dialectic. The first notion is related to virtue and is an intelligible maximum set for the person; the second is related to culture, or the pragmatic conquests of skill according to virtue, and applies to the destiny of the race. Regarding 'finality', Jaspers's assertion is correct: 'Its place is the actuality of the good will. We represent it in the image of the future, but this future has no objective reality.'[2] As for ultimacy, its temporal qualities are somewhat obscure.

Virtue or *moral behaviour* is the principle of the personality functioning as the hypothetical member of a kingdom of ends; *culture* is the maximal accomplishment of man's phenomenal or historical purpose viewed from the perspective of education and legal organization. The dichotomy is clarified by Kant in Paragraphs 83–4 of the *Critique of Judgment*, where he labels the latter an 'ultimate purpose of nature' and as 'the production of the aptitude of a rational being for arbitrary purposes in general (consequently in his freedom)' and the former as a 'final purpose of the existence of the world' or 'man as a moral being', which, however, is 'not a purpose which Nature would be competent to bring about and to produce in conformity with its Idea'.[3] As we have previously seen, *culture* abides on the margin of phenomenality and temporality, whereas *morality* lies beyond, yet the pure Idea of freedom draws toward it the 'guiding thread' of history. The question is that of the conjugation of *culture* and *morality*, which, as we know, is regarded as imperative but incomprehensible.

---

[1] Cf. 'Old Question', p. 145: '…genuine enthusiasm always moves only toward what is ideal and, indeed, to what is purely moral, such as the concept of right, and it cannot be grafted on to self-interest.'

[2] Jaspers, *Kant*, p. 109.

[3] *Judgment, loc. cit.* pp. 355, 360.

Finality and ultimacy

In Paragraph 83 of the third *Critique* Kant investigates the double nature of culture, its combination of perverseness and historical rationality whereby 'splendid misery is bound up with the natural capacities of the human race, and the purpose of nature itself, although not our purpose, is thus attained'.[1] This repeats the same scheme put forward in the 'Idea' and later reiterated in the essay on 'Eternal Peace', culminating in the achievement of lawful civil authority and world order. It is not a moral analysis, and it fully explores the (phenomenal) serviceability of vice as a spur to virtue.[2] There is a full-blown echo of the earlier *Bemerkung* in which Kant spoke of drawing the remedy out of the evil itself.

However, culture is not only (competitive) *skill*; it is *discipline*. In discipline, there is 'a purposive striving of nature to a cultivation which makes one receptive of higher purposes than nature itself can supply'.[3] Discipline is then the link between the disorder of phenomenal progress and the possibility of moral progress, just as peace is the link between legality and autonomy. Within this area we can identify education (the culture-builder), the state (the culture-preserver), and the arts and sciences (culture-carriers). With respect to these latter Kant writes:

The fine arts and the sciences, which, by their universally communicable pleasure, and by the polish and refinement of society, make man more civilized, if not morally better, win us in large measure from the tyranny of sense-propensions...and so make us feel an aptitude for higher purposes, which lies hidden in us.[4]

This is the point at which Kant 'straightens out' both a Rousseau who had denied the possibility that acculturation and polish could mediate between man's nature and his achievement of a moral community and an Enlightenment which had too lightly assumed that morality and knowledge were congruent and that nature was consistent with both terms.

---

[1] *Ibid.* p. 356.
[2] See the excellent description in Fackenheim, 'Kant's Concept of History', *op. cit.* pp. 381–98.
[3] *Judgment*, p. 358.
[4] *Ibid.* The aesthetic experience, it should be noted, is a cornerstone of Kantian inter-subjectivity.

It is important to grasp where Kant places his contemporary world in the history whose 'plan' he has sought to establish. Unlike the school of 'positivistic' progress inaugurated by Condorcet in France, Kant sees a humanity fundamentally just emerging from darkness, 'becoming enlightened'.[1] It is relevant to note here that Kant, a fine classicist himself, was, almost alone among contemporaries, immune to the fever of Greece and Rome. He found their governments despotic[2] and their cultures, if admirable, certainly not unsurpassable. His heroes were Frederick II, Newton and Rousseau, not Lycurgus and Socrates. Thus there is no question of a 'lost paradise' or of solving the dialectical riddle of 'barbarism and Christianity'. Little has been done, much remains in the human ascent.[3] 'To a high degree we are, through art and science, *cultured*. We are *civilized*—perhaps too much for our own good [a characteristic concession to Rousseau]—in all sorts of social grace and decorum. But to consider ourselves as having reached *morality*—for that, much is lacking.'[4] However, Kant continues, 'the ideal of morality belongs to culture...' This is as much as saying that the environmental demands for a real morality can be stimulated only by enlightenment, not, as Rousseau had thought, in the simple milieu of a 'société naissante' or 'système rustique'.

But enlightenment itself (or so Kant at least thought until he, like so many others, was roused by the events of 1789) is scarcely visible among men: '...culture, considered as the genuine education of man as man and citizen, has perhaps not even begun properly, much less been completed'.[5] Culture and nature are out of sorts, because culture turns instinct in vicious directions, while instinct interferes with culture 'until such time as finally art will be strong and perfect enough to become a second nature'.[6]

In the *Anthropology* Kant tells us that 'the internal perfection of man consists of his achieving power over the use of all his faculties and of his submitting them to his *Willkür*', under the rule

---

[1] 'What is Enlightenment?' p. 8.   [2] 'Perpetual Peace', p. 97.
[3] Cf. *Reflex. Anthrop. G.S.* xv, no. 1453, pp. 634–5.
[4] 'Idea', p. 21. Cf. 'Conjectural Beginning', p. 67: 'Only in a state of perfect culture would perpetual peace be of benefit to us, and only then would it be possible. But God alone knows when this will be achieved.'
[5] 'Conjectural Beginning', p. 62.   [6] *Ibid.* pp. 62–3.

of reason.[1] Self-mastery is the ultimate end of man.[2] But, in the great distance still to travel, 'natural impulse interferes with culture'. What is to be done? There are for Kant two principal answers or collaborative agencies. The one is education; the other is the state. 'Man must be trained, so as to be domesticated and become virtuous later on. The coercion of government and education make him supple, flexible and obedient to the laws; then reason will rule.'[3] As yet, of course, in keeping with the liberal view of the matter, state and school are merely parallel forces in the accomplishing of this *Bildung*. As for the arts and sciences, they soften the rough edges, they 'contribute to the lowering of [man's] resistance. Thus he becomes not better, but docile...'[4] Through his historical dialectic, Kant has arrived at the notion of a tutelary state and a moral-legal pedagogy rounded off by a Humean appreciation of the civilizing effects of art and science. The phenomenal world of Kantian politics will turn out to be a frankly disciplinary propaedeutic for a humanity of minors.[5]

---

[1] *Anthropologie, G.S.* VII, 144.
[2] *Virtue*, p. 70.
[3] *Reflex. Anthrop. G.S.* XV, no. 1184, pp. 522-3.
[4] *Erläuterung-Baumgarten, G.S.* XIX, no. 6583, p. 94.
[5] See *Reflexionen zur Rechtsphilosophie, G.S.* XIX, no. 7848, p. 534, where the tutelary metaphor is used to describe the relations of government and people.

5

PROBLEMS OF POLITICS

A. UTOPIA AND CHILIASM

Kant was a social and ethical philosopher of the extremes in conception and of the middle ground in practice. By the use of such terms as, on the one hand, 'kingdom of ends', 'republic', 'peace', and, on the other, 'radical evil', 'unsocial sociability', and 'animality', he drew harshly clashing portraits of the human *is* and *ought*, and yet claimed the possibility and, indeed, the necessity of their rapprochement. Obviously, a 'pure' ethics based on the precept of a trans-human (though humanly circumscribed) reason could sidestep the problem of man's natural goodness or wickedness (crucial for such moral philosophers as Hobbes and Butler), thereby permitting the coexistence and indeed the collaboration of a Mandevillian *humanity* and an almost saintly vision of the goals of *personality* subscribed to in a commonwealth.

In one of his later essays Kant identifies his personal centre of gravity, 'the *liberal* way of thinking—equidistant from both the sense of servitude and anarchy'.[1] Still, that centre of gravity is marked by the enormous tension of the extremes. This point can be well illustrated by a discussion of his concurrent attack on forms of utopia and on the whole range of *status quo* politics implied in such terms as 'historical right', prudence, technique, empirical statesmanship, and the like.

If ethically Kant is a rigorist, i.e. unwilling at any point to compromise the *a priori* foundation of his moral metaphysics, he is operational in the sphere of politics (taken in the large sense of the word). By this I mean that he is fundamentally concerned not only to show how a moral politics is possible but how it is to be implemented contextually. The context is the world of the German dynastic states, especially Frederician Prussia, of *Aufklärung*, of absolutism under law, and later the world of the French Revolution, its impact within the Empire, political reaction, and not least the

[1] 'End of All Things', p. 83.

146

Peace of Basel, signed in 1795 between Revolutionary France and northern Germany, which was the first important dynastic recognition of the French Republic. The Kantian problem is to describe a politics which fits this sequence of events in such a way that neither is the ethical foundation of civil order forsworn nor is the progress of that order (good in itself as containing the germ of the solution to the achievement of *culture*) under the inspiration of the moral Ideas merely seen as a chimerical substitution of the *ought* for the *is*.

Evidently the structure of the transcendental philosophy would forbid any appeal to custom or venerability in Kant's production of political principles. The legal order and the principle of justice are presumably derived from the law of freedom and have no connection with psychology, anthropology, or political precedent.[1] The *gute, alte Zeit* is totally alien to Kantian political theory. Even the historical slippage of earlier jusnaturalism (e.g. Grotius's defence of slavery, so bitterly criticized by Rousseau) is forbidden. The historical pretensions, in particular, of the Church and the hereditary nobility are attacked in Kant's *Rechtslehre* in a manner akin to the arguments of revolutionary France.[2] Although the constitutional solution of monarchy is defended at many points, the argument is made in terms of the problem of sovereignty and never as an appeasement to tradition.

There is one point at which history intrudes upon the logical clarity of Kant's constitutional deductions. This is indeed not a positive impingement, as might be the case if one argued that the test of time is the test of right. It is rather negatively connected with Kant's own vision of history as a 'plan' or a progress, uninterrupted in its grand lines as man raises himself *via* civic institutions toward the goal of culture. Man, according to this view, cannot wish to break his 'guiding thread'. This firm sense of continuity leads Kant to such declarations as: 'the Idea should be attempted and carried out through gradual reform according to fixed principles'.[3] The 'Idea of a political constitution' relates not only to the goal of perfect

---

[1] Cf. *Justice*, pp. 34–5; *Virtue*, p. 56.
[2] *Justice*, pp. 95–9, 134–8; *Religion*, pp. 140–1.
[3] *Justice*, p. 129.

justice but to the whole historical underpinnings of law and civil order. Thus, such an Idea is 'holy and irresistible, [for] it is an Idea that is an absolute command of practical reason judging in accordance with concepts of justice...'[1] By this means, while rejecting empirical history as a test of politics, Kant anchors his principles to teleological history, attempting to correlate tutelary authority with the stage of enlightenment and obedience with the Idea of the state. From this angle, it is not a mystery that such conservatives as Rehberg and Gentz could consider themselves Kantians.

Kant's attack on the empirical politics of prudence is chiefly contained in his essay 'Perpetual Peace', a work inseparable from the surrounding events of the Revolution and the Peace of Basel. The terms of this favourite piece among Kant's writings are well known. For our purposes, a number of points are made. Kant once more argues that the external establishment of republican civil laws (a technical problem) 'not only gives a moral veneer (*causae non causae*) to the whole [political society] but actually facilitates the development of the moral disposition to a direct respect for the law by placing a barrier against the outbreak of unlawful inclinations'.[2] He attempts to conjugate politics and morality, by emphasizing the simplicity of their connection so long as the ethical law is taken as the major premise in making political decisions: a 'moral politician' is perfectly conceivable, while a 'political moralist' is mere hypocrisy.[3] Politics uses ethics for its justification, while shunning all observance of the principles of right. But right binds politics to morality, or rather 'cuts the knot which politics could not untie when they were in conflict'. The 'transcendental' test of a moral politics is 'publicity'. Morality is simple, its guidance is universal; whereas a prudential politics of skill is complicated, subjective and unsystematic.[4]

If Kant's own solution to the problem of the civil constitution is itself 'technical', applicable even to a 'race of devils', we must remember that it is viewed as a part of culture, not of morality, but that it is deduced from and inspired by pure practical reason. This relates the state to the moral universe. Thus Kant's approach

[1] *Ibid.* p. 140. [2] 'Perpetual Peace', p. 123 n.
[3] *Ibid.* p. 119. [4] *Ibid.* pp. 134, 128, 134–5, 125.

suggests, but does not produce, a 'metaphysical state', not only because in the legal theory there is constant emphasis on the state as the guarantor of private rights otherwise insecure but also because the instrumentalism of the civil order is clearly defined. To say that 'justice ought to be' includes the notion that justice is secured only in the civil order, but it does not hypostatize that order as the source of justice. Justice remains a derivative of the moral law, which is the *a priori* of private personality.

Kant's charges against hypothetical statecraft and historical legitimacy acknowledged, one might then wonder if the alternative was not some transcendental air-castle. Kant himself thought not, and he made some very earnest onslaughts against utopian and chiliastic formulations of the political problem. The nature of his argument against 'utopia' will of course depend on what one means by that word. If one means a languorous 'golden age' or Arcadia fixed somewhere imaginatively on the boundaries of past time, then Kant is categorical: there is no going back, there should be no wish to go back, and it is wrong to yearn for a eudaemonistic paradise of reduced wants and activity. The whole course of history is an affirmation of the temporal irreversibility treated logically in the *Critique of Pure Reason*.[1] Most of Kant's observations on this score are contained in a passage at the end of his essay on the 'Conjectural Beginning of Human History'. Here he contrasts utopia ('an empty yearning') with what is presumably the transcendental Idea ('a genuine wish'). The passage is worth giving in full:

The existence of such yearning proves that thoughtful persons weary of civilized life, if they seek its value in pleasure alone, and if, reminded by reason that they might give value to life by actions, fall back on laziness, to counteract this reminder. But this wish for a return to an age of simplicity and innocence is futile. The foregoing presentation of man's original state teaches us that, because he could not be satisfied with it, man could not remain in this state, much less be inclined ever to return to it; that therefore he must, after all, ascribe his present troublesome condition to himself and his own choice.[2]

It is easy to see that this argument implicates, in a wide sweep,

---

[1] *C.P.R.* A198–9 = B243–4, pp. 224–5.   [2] 'Conjectural Beginning', pp. 67–8.

the nature utopias of the eighteenth century, certain aspects of Rousseau's 'chimerical' struggle with the incompatibility of civilization and morality, and, especially, the one-sided interpretation of Rousseau by the German *Sturm und Drang*. Kant was aware that Rousseau had also pronounced against a 'return to nature', but he took exception to Rousseau's 'Arcadia of the human heart' and to the tendency of his political visions to trail off into fantasy. Corsica would not have been Kant's choice for the inauguration of the *respublica phaenomenon*. Rather, he was convinced of the historical improvement of legal-constitutional forms. On similar grounds, Rousseau's defence of solitude is objectionable to Kant. Man is humanized in society; the whole pivot of human history has been the invention of the civil order.[1] Moreover, man has the right to compel all lawless individuals to enter that order (the social compact being an Idea, not a quasi-historical fact). 'The highest moral good', Kant emphasizes, 'cannot be achieved merely by the exertions of the single individual...'[2] If 'Rousseau was not far wrong in preferring the state of savages' to civil injustice and international anarchy, he was wrong enough.[3]

Kantian history, epistemology, ethics and anthropology make no concession to idylls of the past. But they do engage a future, comprising the Idea of a fully developed culture. Is not this in its way a utopia, now future-oriented, with the 'empty yearning' of the past replaced by the pregnant possibility of a time yet to come which we draw toward us by our free acts upon the material content of nature?

Utopia is, above all, a matter of stipulation. Sometimes it is a map of action; sometimes a pattern of regret. Etymologically, a utopia is a 'nowhere', and it may also be a 'uchronia' or an 'at no time'.[4] In pure form, it is, as Judith Shklar says, a standard for judging.[5]

---

[1] Cf. *Anthropologie*, G.S. VII, pp. 186–7, praising foresight and civilized calculation (*contra* Rousseau); also, *Reflex. Anthrop.* G.S. XV, no. 1501, p. 789: 'Men are destined to live in society.'   [2] *Religion*, p. 89.   [3] 'Idea', p. 21.
[4] See Alfred Doren, *Wünschräume und Wünschzeiten* (Leipzig, 1924–5), on this problem. Here, 'Wünschraum' is associated with utopia and 'Wünschzeit' with eschatology. Historically, utopia begins to be future-oriented just prior to the French Revolution in such works as Sebastien Mercier's *L'an deux mille*; cf., in connection with this study, J. G. Fichte's *Die Republik der Deutschen zu Anfang des 22. Jahrhunderts unter ihrem 5. Reichsvogte*, ahead, p. 267.
[5] See Judith N. Shklar, 'The Political Theory of Utopia: From Melancholy to Nostalgia' in *Daedalus* (Spring 1965), special number on utopia, pp. 367–81.

Utopias may be regarded as supreme fictions or intended as tangible, phenomenal blueprints. There is a dynamic play to this problem which it is important to keep open. On the one hand, we know that there has been both utopian theory and practice. On the other hand, we know that utopia is a connotative word used both for imaginative concepts of perfection and for literal political failure. All normative political theory shares with utopia the notion of raising a standard for judgment. However, we can exonerate theory from 'utopianism' either on the grounds of its 'rule-mindedness' (ideality) or by the argument of Hegel's 'owl of Minerva', that it constitutes the abstract summary of a sum of concrete conditions already existing ('ideological' explanations of classical political theory are based on this proposition, by way of the Marxian notion of the 'superstructure').[1]

Against this background of ideas we may appreciate Kant's position. Since his future-orientedness is controlled by the moral possibility of free acts, it may be asserted that he is not utopian in the sense of heralding a rationally soluble future. He propounds moral Ideas, not transcendent 'ideals' that would be their concrete conceptualizations, as spurs to action. He settles the conditions for justice and morality; he does not tell us what the just society or the moral commonwealth would look like. As Sorel once put it, we are confronted by 'a description of will rather than a description of things'.

Nevertheless, Kant himself touches on utopia in some ways, since he regards these goals as obligations. Bare as it may be of detail and indeed divorced from the psychological underpinnings that utopias usually receive, the Idea of perpetual peace has both that 'hope but do not expect' quality that Mrs Shklar emphasizes, as well as some of the restless overtones of utopian activism. There is extreme tension between the possibility of the infinite journey (which Mannheim identifies with the very notion of 'liberal-democratic'

---

[1] If the type of political theory popularly called normative is really, as Hegel and Marx suggest, *a posteriori* to the concrete conditions of political life, then it can scarcely be called utopian. However, in fact, political theories of this sort are rather like Kantian 'Ideas'; they are *Nachbilder* of certain concrete representations of society as well as *Vorbilder* of conceivable social organization. It may also be argued that certain normative theories escape any charge of utopianism through 'rule-mindedness' or by describing the patterns of a 'tolerable politics' rather than a 'best politics', allowing for flexibility of value and technique in the middle range of political construction.

utopia)[1] and the moral necessity of perfection or arrival; and Kant is ambiguous where it is most difficult to become explicit.

On the other hand, the goal of nature, as distinguished from the goal of man, appears to assimilate but not abolish those 'unsocially sociable' traits of *humanity* which Kant set forth so vigorously in his 'Idea for a Universal History'. Nature, or nature as we conceive it for a moral purpose, never perfectly straightens the 'crooked wood' with which it has to deal. The 'society of greatest freedom' which Kant associates with the highest purpose of nature is, in appearance, simply the rationalization of liberalism, not a republic of angels: 'Such a society is one in which there is mutual opposition among the members, together with the most exact definition of freedom and fixing of its limits so that it may be consistent with the freedom of others.'[2]

Kant's historical model, like those of most German philosophers of history up to Nietzsche, has basic connections with the Christian tradition. But in Kant's case the connection with Stoicism is much closer. A measure of this is his resolute anti-chiliasm. Chiliasm in Kantian terms would mean the phenomenal liaison between the collective spheres of culture and of virtue. In fact, this problem is inseparable from the attack on utopianism, as Kant makes clear in the following passage: 'Everyone can see that philosophy can have her belief in a millennium, but her millennium is not Utopian, since the Idea can help, though only from afar, to bring the millennium to pass.'[3] The decisive argument against chiliasm (which is to say the refusal to give any temporal content to the moral commonwealth) is made in Kant's treatise on religion, where, in arguing that the notion of the moral commonwealth must be based on our conception of the political one and that man has an obligation to leave the 'ethical state of nature', he concludes: 'The Idea of such a [moral] state possesses a thoroughly well-grounded objective reality in human reason (in man's duty to join such a state), even though, subjectively, we can never hope that man's good will will lead mankind to decide to work with unanimity toward this goal.'[4] By 'objective', Kant means here the 'objective reality' of practical

---

[1] Karl Mannheim, *Ideology and Utopia* (New York, 1936), pp. 219 f.
[2] 'Idea', p. 16. [3] *Ibid.* p. 21. [4] *Religion*, p. 86.

reason based on the moral law. In the 'End of All Things' he uses similar arguments to repel the notion of spatio-temporal apocalypse. Reactionary providence and revolutionary consummation are rejected.

B. REVOLUTION AND CONTINUITY

Kant's political equilibrium was not only moderate but quite novel, dynamic but shunning all explosive excess, denying both the immobilist and radical conservatisms of his time, emphasizing continuity rather than rupture. It remains to examine this last notion in terms of Kant's position on revolution.

Unlike Rousseau, Kant lived long enough to weigh the portentous events of 1789 and their aftermath. In all his late political writings (most notably the *Doctrine of Right* and the essay on 'Eternal Peace') they are implicitly juxtaposed against the absolutism of his own German surroundings. However, the methods and standards of 'criticism' were firmly established before the epoch-making explosion in France.[1] The Revolution did not so much 'change' Kant's political views (with the possible exception of making him receptive to the principle of representative government) as compel him to make a large allowance for it within his doctrines of history, justice and legal evolution.

Kant is sometimes accused of talking about revolution out of both sides of his mouth. For some he is a discreet Jacobin; for others a liberal of the establishment. When Kant finally dealt with the question of the right to rebellion in his *Rechtslehre*, he was in the curious position of defending both the French Republic and the dynasties.[2]

We may feel sure that Kant would not have so strictly and elaborately rejected civil rebellion out of mere prudence, and we may reasonably infer that he felt his stance on revolution to be the logical result of his philosophical analysis of legality. C. J. Friedrich goes too far when he writes of Kant's 'sympathy for the *esprit révolution-*

---

[1] Although the *Critique of Judgment* was not published until 1790, its genesis belongs to the pre-Revolutionary period. Kant alludes to the Revolution in a note attached to para. 65 of the 'Critique of Teleological Judgment'.
[2] Clearly indicated in 'Perpetual Peace', p. 120.

naire' and his further notion that the only state against which rebellion is unlawful is 'synonymous with a constitutional order in the modern sense'.[1] Despite some ambiguity, Kant disapproved of *all* political revolutions. His rejection of this means of political change is compatible with both his notion of the development of culture in history and his high valuation of civic order in general as the spatio-temporal milieu for the unfolding of the rational Idea of the perfect constitution. Though revolutions are indeed a part of historical event and to be acknowledged as such, they ought not to be hailed as part of a morally guided 'plan' of history, since their ideal object is the destruction of the culture-bearing state.[2] We may visualize revolution as an extreme term to be discarded in Kant's mediation between empirical *status quo* legitimacy and sudden irruptions grasping at an 'ideal' rather than being sanely guided by an Idea. Put in simplest terms, Kant, like the great majority of the German intelligentsia of his time, watched the French experiment with awe and sympathy, but had no desire to see the principles of mass uprising or *monarchomachia* universalized.

In his 'Idea for a Universal History', Kant paradoxically anticipates that revolutions (like wars) may pave the way for international arbitration and the experiment of supranational federation. However, he clarifies at the end of the passage that the 'universal cosmopolitan condition' will come as a result of 'many reformative revolutions'.[3] It is 'enlightenment' which must 'step by step ascend the throne', not the leaders of public fury. The earlier essay 'What is Enlightenment?' expresses views which Kant will proclaim to the very end. 'The public', he writes, 'can only slowly attain enlightenment. Perhaps a fall of personal despotism or of avaricious and tyrannical oppression may be accomplished by revolution, but never a true reform in ways of thinking. Rather, new prejudices will

---

[1] C. J. Friedrich (ed.), *The Philosophy of Kant*, 'Introduction', pp. xliv–xlv.
[2] In 'Perpetual Peace', p. 119, Kant states: 'the disruption of the bonds of a civil society ...before a better constitution is ready to take its place is against all politics agreeing with morality'. Cf. Kurt Borries, *Kant als Politiker* (Leipzig, 1928), p. 180. Borries suggests that for Kant revolution, like war, is at most an aspect of the teleology of nature, never of right. This idea might, in turn, be related to the previously mentioned distinction in the realm of culture between 'skill' (meaning essentially competition) and 'discipline' (meaning restraint) in *Critique of Judgment*, para. 83.
[3] 'Idea', p. 23.

serve as well as old ones to harness the great unthinking masses.'[1]

It is surely true that Kant was stirred by the great acts of the Constituent in 1789–91. Vast amounts of contemporary evidence attest how paradisical this all seemed to the advanced bourgeoisie in Germany. Moreover, the powerful undercurrent of economic and juridical liberalism sweeping Western Europe created an inestimable cosmopolitan bond at this moment. However, when all is said and done, it is most difficult to discover in Kant any specific endorsement of revolutionary acts in France following the dethronement of Louis XVI. Kant simply refused to forswear his enthusiasm for the noble experiment, to deny the Republic validity as an example of the *respublica phaenomenon* and basis for international order, or to disown its legacy of moral penetration into the European mind.

The 'true reform in thinking' was what impressed Kant most. Intellectual Europe had so shivered with this tremor in 1789 that he thought he had at last found historical evidence of the intrusion of morality into the phenomenal sphere of culture. The famous passage from the *Conflict of the Faculties* bears repeating:

The revolution of a gifted people which we have seen unfolding in our day may succeed or miscarry; it may be filled with misery and atrocities to the point that a sensible man, were he boldly to hope to execute it successfully the second time, would never resolve to make the experiment at such cost—this revolution, I say, nonetheless finds in the hearts of all spectators (who are not engaged in this game themselves) a wishful participation that borders closely on enthusiasm, the very expression of which is fraught with danger; this sympathy, therefore, can have no other cause than a moral predisposition in the human race.[2]

It is indeed remarkable that this old man, who had led the most insular of lives, could have generated such fervour for a distant if preponderate event. However, there is an innuendo here of spectator solidarity with the advanced minds of Western Europe. Indeed, it is the sympathetic intellectuals who are the moral heroes of the Revolution; theirs is the admired 'mode of thinking', theirs the thrill of dangerous opinions, without responsibility for any 'misery and atrocities'. That is the really sublime accomplishment of this volcano: it has caused the appearance of 'a moral character of

[1] 'What is Enlightenment?' p. 144.   [2] 'Old Question', p. 144.

humanity, at least in its predisposition', 'a passionate participation in the good'. No-nonsense violence has often fed the cravings of intellectual comradeship. *Suave est mari magno turbantibus aequora ventis*...

Kant is pre-eminently gifted at taking back with one hand the dangerous doctrines extended in the other. In this same essay, he later comes upon the question: 'In what order alone can progress toward the better be expected?' The answer is this: 'not by the movement of things *from bottom to top*, but *from top to bottom*'.[1] A paean to education follows. 'It might well behoove the state likewise to reform itself from time to time and, attempting evolution instead of revolution, progress perpetually toward the better.'[2] The German sovereigns are warned; the French Revolution is vindicated, chastened and surpassed in this commendable display of rhetoric and argument. Kant defends himself similarly on both the right and the left in his essay 'On the Common Saying: This May be True in Theory but is Useless in Practice', where, after a stirring philosophical defence of the rights of man, he proceeds coolly to argue that 'all resistance against the supreme legislative power, all instigation to rebellion, is the worst and most punishable crime in a commonwealth'.[3] This latter injunction should not be regarded as applying only to a republic of perfect form, as Kant's subsequent debate against Achenwall makes clear. Of course, Kant is simply preferring the value of order to the threat of anarchy, not renouncing his preference for constitutional evolution.

In view of the fact that people in general are not 'enlightened' and that a people in mass characteristically makes revolutions on behalf of an imagined 'happiness', the philosophy of right is perfectly consequent in refusing them their undertaking. From the *Critique of Practical Reason* it will be recalled that happiness is a subjective maxim which cannot be universalized. But the state does not exist to make men happy; it is the matrix for their realization of higher purposes: '...the well-being of the state must not be confused with the welfare or happiness of the citizens of the state, for these can be attained more easily and satisfactorily in a state of

---

[1] 'Old Question', p. 152.
[2] *Ibid.* pp. 152–3.
[3] 'Theory–Practice', in Friedrich (ed.), *Kant*, p. 423.

nature (as Rousseau maintained) or even under a despotic government'.[1] Moreover, 'the purpose is not sensuous welfare, but rational welfare (*Verstandeswohl*); the preservation of the state constitution previously existing is the supreme law of civil society in general; the latter can only survive through the former'.[2] It is appropriate to recall that the state of which Kant speaks is not the organic matrix of a people possessed of certain vital moral or cultural attributes, *à la* Herder: 'The State is an automaton. It is a sacred duty...not to disturb that artificial creature.'[3] Kant does not disown revolution because it is a crime against the national continuity, genius and history; he does so because it threatens by its very nature to destroy the machinery of social life which man has so elaborately and miraculously prepared.

Consequently, Kant rejects any collective action against the source of authority which is based on eudaemonistic grounds. Even though he accords to the 'rights of man' a dignity distinct from interest, he refuses to grant the judgment of this motive to the conscience of a collectivity which, one may be certain, comprises men 'in need of a master', 'in need of education'.[4] A revolution is 'always unjust'. If we place these precepts within the context of Kant's historical teleology, where the hoped for and expected progress 'from worse to better' is transacted at a gradual rate under the aegis of enlightenment and where the torch of the Idea is set to guide us, the conclusion should elicit no surprise. Kant did not construct a philosophy of exceptions. One does not therefore come unprepared for Kant's considered judgment framed in the very decade of the Revolution:

If the people were to hold that they were justified in using violence against a constitution, however defective it might be, and against the supreme authority [which, by Kant's notion of sovereignty, is not subject to formal constraint], they would be supposing that they had a right to put violence as the supreme prescriptive act of legislation in the place of every right and Law.[5]

This position timelessly safeguards the political order from a logic of

---

[1] *Justice*, p. 83.
[3] *Reflex. Rechtsphil. G.S.* XIX, no. 7778, p. 513.
[5] *Justice*, p. 140.

[2] *Anthropologie, G.S.* VII, 331.
[4] Cf. 'Old Question', p. 150.

vicious regression. But it is also the fulfilment of the historico-teleological thought expressed years earlier, when Kant saw historical institutions as 'the germ of the good ones to come'.[1]

The only revolution that Kant really endorses is the moral one, as described in his work on religion:

...man is under the necessity of, and is therefore capable of, a revolution in his cast of mind, but only of a gradual reform in his sensuous nature (which places obstacles in the way of the former)...That is, he can hope ...to find himself upon the good (though strait) path of continual *progress* from bad to better.[2]

What Kant wished for, above all, was this revolution in thought on the part of rulers, so that their peoples might receive discipline, enlightenment and justice, and on the part of teachers, so that the cultural base of morality might be gradually expanded. There is a more than hypothetical connection between this 'revolution in the cast of mind', the 'true reform in ways of thinking' of the essay on Enlightenment, and the 'wishful participation in the hearts of all spectators' of the *Conflict of the Faculties*; moreover, a connection between these and the 'manner of governing' which ultimately supersedes the strict niceties of constitutional republican form in Kant's doctrine of politics.[3]

---

[1] See note 3. p. 100.   [2] *Religion*, p. 43.   [3] See ahead, pp. 169 f.

6

THE TELEOLOGY OF PRACTICAL REASON

A. THE STRUCTURE AND SPIRIT OF LEGALITY

Kant sets the moving vision of man's destiny against the most unyielding possible ideal of obligation. Somehow both terms must be accommodated if one is not to fall into a politics of prudence, on the one hand, or a politics of chimerical impossibility, on the other. The 'chimera' must inform the stream of time, serving man as a culture builder without any sacrifice of its *a priori* ethical ground. In general, this mediation is attempted through law. Law, in turn, receives both the transcendental attributes of the Idea of justice and the technical dispositions of the positive sociopolitical system of order. The latter obliges men to 'respect' through the imminence of coercion, insuring against a regress of collective development, and thus helps to actualize the Idea. In Kantian legal metaphysics one encounters complex tensions between ethics and positivity, functional and spiritual criteria, and rational and historical norms. Not the least of these tensions is the dialectic between the *a priori* of justice, a fourth form of the categorical imperative, and the phenomenal role of rulership or political authority.

These are complex problems. The locus of the civic order gathers in the same content of anthropology and inspiration of ethics that informed our historical diagnosis. History is spread out along its 'guiding thread'; the legal order is concentrated. Yet there is an essentially legal teleology that enters history to provide visible benchmarks for the 'end of nature'. We can pursue only a few issues in Kant's legal labyrinth. But it is already clear that these problems are inseparable from the destiny of the state as a historical unit.

A setting for these problems is necessary. Kant is variously described as a late, original jusnaturalist or as a systematic destroyer of that school. There is truth in both descriptions. If, in the words of Jouvenel,

When one speaks of natural right, one principally means that the foundation of positive law is found in ethics (which also sets the limits of positive law) and additionally that this ethics is 'natural', that is, inherent in man as such, independent of time and place,[1]

we might attempt to measure Kant against that definition. Kant did indeed hold that right was 'natural' in the sense that it was an attribute of pure reason: '..."right" (*Recht*) can never be an appearance; it is a concept in the understanding, and represents a property (the moral property) of actions, which belong to them in themselves'.[2] Right, thus, does not 'appear'—i.e. the discrimination between natural and positive right is retained; it morally informs phenomenal sets of legal rules.

But, in contrast to many earlier theories, ethics and right are not similarly 'natural' in character. Moral man does not appeal to 'right' for the motives or maxims of acts (the way things ought to be objectively); virtue, rather, is associated with the source of the intention: 'The agreement of an action with the law of duty is its *legality*, that of the maxim of the action with the law is its *morality*.'[3] Elsewhere, Kant describes virtue as 'the command, namely to bring all [one's] powers and inclinations under his (that is reason's) control—hence the command of self-mastery'.[4] On the other hand, '"right" [or "justice"] and "authorization to use coercion" mean the same thing'.[5] The concept of a right, derived from the law of freedom, is the capacity to obligate others to a duty.[6] Moral choices are exclusively self-coercive, whereas legal acts (assuming their rectitude) carry a notion of external compulsion.

Undoubtedly, legality, as coercion, belongs to the phenomenal world, and its transactions may be heteronomous. Republican legality, however, strives to equate the consequences of the act of justice with what the exercise of virtue would freely bring about. This might seem to verge on the notion of a pre-established harmony between moral possibility and legal technicality based on the intervening criterion of a 'general will' or moral grounding of the legal rule through 'respect' and the analogy of internal legislation. Yet, the Kantian notion of the 'republic' translates a civic 'mind' in

---

[1] Bertrand de Jouvenel, 'L'idée de droit naturel', *Archives de philosophie politique*, III (1959), p. 162.
[2] *C.P.R.* A44 = B61, p. 83.   [3] *Justice*, p. 27.   [4] *Virtue*, p. 70.
[5] *Justice*, p. 37.   [6] *Ibid.* p. 45.

which the functions are faculties, not the autonomous democracy of the ethical commonwealth. It provides no other guarantee of the congruousness of moral intention and legal result than that the 'Idea of the state as it ought to be...provides an internal guide and standard (*norma*) for every actual union of men in a commonwealth'.[1] But this conception is far from clear. By whom and how is the Idea of justice to be apprehended and enacted? How are moral dignity, the uses of power, and the 'end of nature' to be reconciled?

A brief historical excursion into the question of legality and morality will give some added perspective. 'Natural law' has always been (in theory) a double-edged weapon, and that in two senses. In the first place, it can refer (as traditionally) to the location within man's rational nature of a personal source of order, universal in its form, by which the judgment of the morality of actions is possible. In the eighteenth century, as one knows, this source of order came increasingly to be construed as a psychological *sensorium* reflecting man's 'natural' qualities as a sensuous and pleasure-seeking creature. Kant's separation of the phenomenal and noumenal spheres left phenomenal man with as fully utilitarian a disposition as the century had claimed, but reserved ethics and right as practical doctrines completely to the realm of freedom or 'law according to the concept'.[2] So far as Kant's theory of law is 'natural' it is rigorously rationalist, not only set against all hint of psychological input, but designedly in disregard of 'human nature'.

Secondly, there is a fluctuation of ethics and right within the 'natural law' framework. Where universal ethical authority is claimed for legal derivations, this can be, and has proved, a formidable siege weapon against any arbitrary or tradition-based authority.[3] It has been truly said that natural law arguments revive wherever libertarian acquisitions are jeopardized. On the other hand, where the fundamental appeal of politics must always be to a prevailing system of morality, this connection can become a tool of authoritarian power. Ethics can be incessantly invoked to stifle free political development. This is precisely what Kant means when he writes:

---

[1] *Ibid.* p. 77.
[2] Cf. *C. Prac. R.* p. 63: '...as far as our nature as sensible beings is concerned, our happiness is the only thing of importance'.
[3] Cf. De Jouvenel, 'Droit naturel', p. 164.

'Politics [or prudential statesmen or 'political moralists'] readily agrees with morality in its first branch (as ethics) in order to surrender the rights of men to their superiors.'[1] In the reigning school of Christian Wolff, there had developed a conception of natural law in which the inseparability of right and morality had become compatible with the absolutist and paternalist governments of the princely states and had, as needed, furnished their philosophical vindication.[2] This indeed seemed to Kant an unholy alliance. The rise of liberal individualism and the revolt against dictation to the conscience argued for a separation of themes which had been so craftily woven together. Thus, probably on the model of the Protestant separation of natural law (including obligations of political obedience) from divine law (or the individual relationship between God and man), it became strategically important to distinguish notions which, taken together, had had repressive consequences. Kant achieves this result with his dual (analytic and synthetic) deduction of the doctrines of right and virtue from the law of freedom.

On the other hand, there is always the danger that, by such means, right will slip from the grasp of an ethics now purified of its absolutist and transcendent connections. That would be a new form of Machiavellianism or *Staatsräson* which had passed through the purifying crucible of natural right and into a peculiarly modern shape. Kant neither intended nor achieved that result. He insisted that the law of freedom should be the major premise of every political judgment. But if right were divorced from ethics and presumed to precede it logically, it might appear to do so temporally, providing in the state a new matrix of legal, cultural and moral authority, terms which the Enlightenment had set apart.

Kant describes man as a creature of moral possibility in a world where morality has scarcely entered. However, it is not just the concrete conditions of the phenomenal 'now'—the *now* of the German princes, of the French Republic, or of the Revolutionary wars— that might disbar him from true freedom. It is also his very phenomenal existence and, beyond that, the entire sphere of 'culture',

---

[1] 'Perpetual Peace', p. 134.
[2] See the discussion by Vlachos, *Pensée politique*, pp. 262–3.

solely graspable within the historical process, where at best only
the external conditions of freedom may be won. Although 'a *person*
is subject to no laws other than those that he (either alone or at least
jointly with others) gives to himself',[1] a *man* is 'a creature who needs
a master. In that respect he is situated beneath all the animals which,
to keep their societies in order, have no need of a master'.[2] This
double image of *personality* and *animality*, inseparable antagonists
locked in combat throughout the whole chronological plenum of
humanity, contestants in history and in the *Willkür* (where freedom
enters time), informs Kant's view of the problem of political
relationships and is resolved only by the moral (obligatory) belief
that things are proceeding 'from worse to better'. How, then, is
a social ethic possible? History might produce no more than a
technical solution to the moral problem. Kant attempts to deal with
this difficulty in his essay on 'Eternal Peace', where he attributes a
priority and sureness to the solving of the *problema morale* that he
refuses to the employment of hypothetical skill.[3] This argument is,
in fact, an applied repetition of the thesis of paragraphs 83–4 of the
Critique of Judgment.

But if this appears a decisive vindication of a moral politics,
it still leaves some uneasiness regarding the phenomenal content of
civil order. On the one hand, the phenomenal goal of humanity
might appear to be nothing more than a reasonably foolproof system
of public legal constraint in which each member of the *respublica
phaenomenon* was leashed in from invasion of the rights of others,
thus either compelled or trained to treat his fellows, in act, as
ends-in-themselves. Although allegedly this situation would transpire from respect for the law, one might attribute the results to
simple prudence in the face of positive coercion. Kant indeed
admits that reason 'uses [incentives of prudence]...as counterweights to inducements to do the opposite of what is moral',
even though this does not implicate the 'authority' of the law.[4]

---

[1] *Justice*, p. 24. [2] *Reflex. Anthrop. G.S.* XV, no. 1500, p. 785.
[3] 'Perpetual Peace', pp. 124–5.
[4] *Justice*, 'Introduction to the Metaphysics of Morals', p. 16. Cf. 'Old Question', p. 151:
'Gradually violence on the part of the powers will diminish and obedience to the laws
will increase...without the moral foundation in man having to be enlarged in the
least...'

Moreover, the 'law' of reciprocal coercion consonant with the freedom of all 'exhibits this concept [of justice] in a pure *a priori* intuition on the analogy of the possibility of the free movement of bodies under the law of the equality of action and reaction'.[1] Fluctuating between the empirical requirements of an anthropo-historical order and the critical relation to man as an end in himself, right seeks to comprehend both the means of coercion or discipline (*Zwang*) and the ends of autonomy. In the later career of philosophical idealism it is therefore not surprising that Fichte defined the science of right as the 'theoretical part of practical philosophy' while Schelling construed it as purely theoretical in his treatment of the subject.[2]

But it is the legal-natural correlation in Kant that also bears the most striking analogical resemblance to the society of moral equals prefigured by the Idea of the 'kingdom of ends'. The theoretical problem is the calculus of legal equality. But, when viewed from the practical side, one sees not a juridical mathematics but a moral problem of how to get from worse to better. Analysis and teleology are in conflict.

Or, it might be better to say that the calculus of legality (*problema technicum*) requires not simply a solution but a long transition by which man, in society and under laws, works toward the system which is a total hindrance to hindrances of freedom.[3] In this sense, 'the civil union does not...constitute a society, but rather produces one'.[4] And this is why, if the resolution of the *problema technicum* is phenomenally uncertain, requiring 'so much knowledge of nature',[5] the *problema morale* raises all the difficulties of applying the rule of justice to the anthropological materials at hand. '...In the practical execution of this Idea we can count on nothing but force to establish the juridical condition, on the compulsion of which public law will later be established. We can scarcely hope', writes Kant, 'to find in the legislator a moral intention sufficient to induce him to commit to the general will [i.e. the 'universal' relationships of wills (*Willen*) in so far as they are free] the establishment of a legal constitution

---

[1] *Justice*, p. 37.
[2] Cf. M. Gueroult, *Doctrine de la Science*, I, 292; F. W. J. Schelling, *System des transzendentalen Idealismus*, S.W. III, 592–3.
[3] *Justice*, p. 35.　　　　[4] *Ibid.* p. 71.　　　　[5] 'Perpetual Peace', p. 125.

after he has formed the nation from a horde of savages...'[1] In metaphysics the external correspondence of justice to the law of freedom is *a priori* and unconditional. In history, however, one must conjure with the passage of a suddenly all-too-human nature to the control of justice in the form of political institutions.

Another tension, whose historical implications are not immediately evident, is reflected in Kant's bipartite separation of private and public law, derived from Roman jurisprudence.[2] Presumably, all legality (i.e. as system, not application) is derived from the universal principle of justice, 'act externally in such a way that the free use of your will is compatible with the freedom of everyone according to a universal law', which is, in turn, a form of the categorical imperative.[3] Hence comes the notion of 'strict justice', which involves the possibility of coercion in pursuit of the freedom described above. Private law, fundamentally concerned with the provisional validation of property, furnishes rights but no juridical relations; it describes a 'state of nature'. In contrast, 'a juridical state of affairs is a relationship among human beings that involves the conditions under which alone every man is able to enjoy his right'.[4] Only public law, a product of the civil society, can guarantee the *a priori* rights inherent in nature, which were deduced analytically from the law of freedom. Hereupon, Kant tells us that the postulate of public law is a consequence of the insecurity of the heuristic former state: one 'ought to...enter, with all others...a state of distributive legal justice'[5]. In one or another form, this is a familiar 'moment' of liberal contractualism. But Kant would appear to be deriving the Idea of public law from tacit empirical presumptions about human nature and not from pure reason at all. He quotes from the Latin: 'Everyone is presumed bad until he has provided assurance of the opposite.'[6] Now Kant has a quite ingenious way of saving himself

[1] *Ibid.* p. 118.
[2] See Huntington Cairns, *Legal Philosophy from Plato to Hegel* (Baltimore, 1949), p. 440.
[3] *Justice*, p. 35.   [4] *Ibid.* p. 69.   [5] *Ibid.* p. 71.
[6] *Ibid.* p. 72. This is scarcely a characteristic liberal proposition. It is, however, a liberal prelude to the construction of a system of public law, which the transcendental moralism of the categorical imperative is not. That is why so acute an analyst as Georges Burdeau (*Traité de la Science politique, V : L'Etat libéral et les techniques politiques de la démocratie gouvernée*, Paris, 1953) can write (p. 324): 'All justice is a protest against what is, a reaction of thought against fact: but society [i.e. the liberal deity] is by its very definition a consecration of fact.' Kant bestrides both positions

from transparent empiricism by maintaining that one 'can quite adequately observe within himself the inclination of mankind in general to play the master over others'.[1] But it is doubtful that this auto-psychologism suffices to keep his transition pure.

Thus there is an 'anthropologism' inherent in the whole Kantian conception of civil society that cannot be pristinely removed by the rationality of republicanism. All societies short of the noumenal commonwealth exist because 'man needs a master'. The mastery of laws, not men, is often sublime in Kant, but the whole project of civic order is tinged with a pessimism that is far from *a priori*. Here, history and time re-enter, for we have to do not simply with the analytical development of distributive justice but with the problem of 'getting from worse to better', of public domestication. This reopens the subject of enlightenment and the tutelary image.

Law would be seen then to mediate temporally between the 'worse' and the 'better'. It gradually creates the conditions (we are not permitted by Kant to say the habit) upon which acts of true morality are expected to supervene. These conditions are called, collectively, culture. The 'discipline' of culture (best represented in the process of education or *Bildung*) is again mediate between skill (which produces antagonisms and inequalities) and pure respect for the Idea of the law as translated phenomenally into the institutions of civil order. All political society depends for coherence upon its own immanent perquisites of order, on the protection from moral anarchy which it affords its members. To the extent that man has mastered himself through belonging to a rule-making society, that system carries the Idea of external freedom forward in history. Of course Kant wished this community to be as little arbitrary as possible: 'enlightenment of the masses is the public instruction of the people in its duties and rights *vis-à-vis* the state to which they belong'.[2] But Kant was not willing to sacrifice the precious notion of civil order, *per se*, to any immediate catalogue of public wrongs.[3]

---

[1] *Justice*, p. 71.　　　　　　　　　　　　　　　　[2] 'Old Question', p. 148.

[3] Even though, formally, '. . . only concepts of reason can establish a legal compulsion according to the principles of freedom' ('Perpetual Peace', p. 211), Kant encourages us to look at all civil order as fundamentally reasonable.

—the demand for a perfect justice and the liberal form of 'legalism'—perplexingly. Here Rousseau was more consistent—and less liberal.

The structure and spirit of legality

The material of humanity must fit the proportions of the Idea: 'a long internal working of each political body toward the education of its citizens is required'.[1] 'Whoever throws off [the fetters of tutelage] makes only an uncertain leap over the narrowest ditch because he is not accustomed to that kind of free motion.'[2] The effect is, then, to 'historicize' the notion of natural law by attributing to it an ideal but not an ontological status. Leonard Krieger puts this well: '... natural law is no longer the source of rights and duties [although the moral law implies the obligation to make a nature of freedom], for the law legislated and enforced by the sovereign has replaced it as the union of nature and morality pertinent to the community...[But] both it and the rights of individuals which it prescribes enter into the structure of the sovereign will as its norm and end.'[3] In this interpretation there is a much-noted tendency toward positivism, because existing historical legal systems would seem to furnish the indispensable cultural base for the furtherance of the Idea of a *respublica noumenon*.[4]

'Culture', Kant tells us, '...forces itself to discipline itself',[5] by which, as already indicated, he means that we discipline ourselves and each other in the measure that we grasp and follow the 'guiding thread' of the moral Idea. There follows that most famous of passages:

Man is an animal which, if it lives among others of its kind, requires a master...who will break his will and force him to obey a will that is universally valid, under which each can be free. But whence does he get this master? Only from the human race. But then the master is himself an animal, and needs a master...The highest master should be just in himself, and yet a man.[6]

Kant does not really solve this problem. Instead, he suggests three approaches to it. These suggestions might be called 'natural

---

[1] 'Idea', p. 21. [2] 'What is Enlightenment?' p. 4.
[3] Leonard Krieger, 'Kant and the Crisis of Natural Law', *Journal of the History of Ideas* (Apr.–July 1965), pp. 208–9.
[4] According to Norberto Bobbio ('Deux arguments contre le Droit naturel', *Archives de philosophie politique*, III (1959), p. 177), Kant is a legal positivist, because in para. 41 of *Justice* he states: 'A juridical state of affairs is a relationship among human beings that involves the condition under which alone every man is able to enjoy his right... called public legal justice.'
[5] 'Idea', p. 17. [6] *Ibid.*

legalism', 'rational legalism', and 'ethico-teleological legalism'. In the first image, the organization of a legal system is held to be analogous to the physical laws of action and reaction.[1] The problem of the state is thus made technical, with emphasis placed on the concepts of the understanding. Kant intends this notion only as a guide; but it is well to note that it is also a model of distributive equality and a paradigm of the ethical commonwealth. This is the 'squaring of the circle' that had tempted Rousseau.

The second image is concerned with the tripartite division of functions in the 'republic', patently modelled after the operation of reason in the form of the practical syllogism.[2] The sovereign legislature is the *Wille*, which prescribes the law in the form of an unconditional imperative; the executive agent is the *Willkür*, which transforms law into act by the framing of maxims; the judicial ingredient is the moral conscience, which causes satisfaction to be the result and not the motive of virtuous maxims. The problem here with regard to politics is twofold. In the first place, the ideal source of law may be phenomenally fettered or inoperative and the source of action—as we saw in the discussion of revolution—will be unimpeachable. In the second place, there is an ambiguity concerning the role of the judgment. Some precisions are necessary on this point.

Judgment, by which Kant means the subsumption of particular case under general rule, is the cornerstone of all aspects of the 'critical' philosophy. 'Judgment', as Jaspers writes, 'is the act in which we gain a valid awareness of being...'[3] In judging we derive or fail to derive our technical and pragmatic imperatives from the categorical imperative. Political judgment, in Kant's legal sense, is of course *ex post facto*. The courts are our resource when we are injured, or the resource of civil power where there are crimes. Such is the essence of constitutionalism. But where there is rulership or magistracy, there is an immediate judgment accompanying the

---

[1] 'Perpetual Peace', p. 112.

[2] *Justice*, p. 78. Here, Ernst Cassirer's remark is apposite (*Philosophy of the Enlightenment*, p. 238): 'Just as the mind is capable of constructing the realm of quantity and number entirely from within itself by virtue of its "innate ideas", so it has the same constructive ability in the field of law. Here too the intellect can and should begin with fundamental norms, which it creates from within itself...'

[3] Jaspers, *Kant*, p. 95.

executive act as well as a posterior public judgment. The *Willkür* judges in choosing its maxim. Thus the mere mechanics of 'republicanism' cannot exhaust the question of civil justice; public law requires also that its agents be ethical.

This condition suggests the third image, where the state is seen as teleologically guided by the 'end of nature' evoked in the *Critique of Judgment*. The ethico-teleological formula implies not a specific political constellation but a 'spirit', a 'way of thinking': 'the spirit... entails the obligation of the constituted authority to make the type of government conform to this Idea [of the 'republic'] and, accordingly, to change the government gradually and continually, if it cannot be done at one time, so that it will effectively agree with [the legitimate constitution]'.[1] Republicanism is spirit as well as form.

The third image responds to the *problema morale* discussed in the essay on 'Perpetual Peace'. It allows for phenomenal limitations of the republican ideal. If according to the 'formal principle of his will' one should demand nothing less than a popular and co-legislative government, 'to rule autocratically and yet to govern in a republican way, that is, in the spirit of republicanism and on an analogy with it—that is what makes a nation satisfied with its constitution'.[2] De Vleeschauwer has described the *Rechtslehre* as a systematization of the political philosophy of Frederick the Great.[3] That is, at best, a half-truth. One also detects in Kant traits of Whiggishness, of 1789, and of the Encyclopedist predisposition for a central, powerful and reasonable authority. 'The mode of government' (this should be related to the 'manner of governing' of the *Conflict of the Faculties*), he writes, '...is incomparably more important to the people than the form of sovereignty'.[4] By this, he means the 'spirit' of republicanism as against that of despotism. Kant has, in fact, slurred over the mechanics of republican sovereignty by attributing it sometimes to the united legislative will of the people, sometimes to a monarch *qua* 'legislative chief of the state'.[5]

---

[1] *Justice*, p. 112.
[2] 'Old Question', p. 146 n. Cf. 'Perpetual Peace', p. 96: '...it is at least possible for [monarchy and aristocracy] to assume a mode of government conforming to the spirit of a representative system...'
[3] De Vleeschauwer, *Development*, p. 178.
[4] 'Perpetual Peace', p. 97; 'Old Question', p. 147.   [5] *Justice*, pp. 82, 86.

The 'spirit' or 'manner' of governing is decisive in Kantian politics because it relates the phenomenal character of the legal order to both its baleful anthropological material and to the transcendental moral obligation. Following this mediation of anthropology and ethics through legality, the task will be to defend the moral personality against the tangible historical needs of education to freedom under the aegis of discipline and coercion.

B. TUTELAGE AND HISTORY

'Each man', says Kant, 'is by nature bad and becomes good only to the extent that he is subject to a power that obliges him to be good. But he has the capacity to become progressively better without coercion if the dispositions for good within him are progressively developed.'[1] We are back once again with the anthropological Kant, looking at the sphere of 'humanity' in view of its goals and capacities. Just as the child must go to school, so history is a continuing education for the successive generations of mankind.

Kant's age was suffused with this notion. The powerful analogical contrast was between man as a wild and lawless juvenile and man *diplômé* through culture and reason. On a cosmic, almost mystical level, Lessing's pamphlet on the *Education of the Human Race*, with its Joachimite three-stage rhythm, had traced the rationalization of religion, concluding with a famous paean ostensibly close to the formulas of Kantianism but in spirit less prudent: 'It will come, it will surely come, the time of perfection, when man—the more convinced his understanding feels of an ever better future—will not, however, have to borrow from his future, motives for his actions...'[2] In a practical though no less visionary sense, the model-school experiments of Basedow and others were beginning to attract intellectual attention and princely patronage in Germany; Kant gives a nod of approval to the eccentric founder of the 'Philantropium' in his *Pädagogik*.[3]

---

[1] *Reflex. Moralphil. G.S.* XIX, no. 6906, p. 202.
[2] Lessing, *Education of the Human Race* (trans. J. D. Haney, New York, 1908), para. 85, p. 55.
[3] Cf. Henry Brunschwig, *Crise de l'Etat prussien*, pp. 28–9. For Basedow, see A. Pinloche, *La réforme de l'éducation en Allemagne au XVIIIe siècle : Basedow et le philanthropisme* (Paris, 1889).

Of course, this mania for education is shared between the common-sense French Enlightenment and the more visionary German idealism. Locke's *Some Thoughts on Education* launches the movement, whose pedagogical way-stations are, especially, La Chalotais and Rousseau. But the Germans are the ones who integrate tutelary ideals into the philosophy of history, a cosmic vision of a progressively acculturated and improved humanity. To the very great degree that *Emile* and the *Nouvelle Héloïse* were influential in this development, we may speak of the German palingenesis of Rousseau.

Emile, it will be recalled, announced a 'negative education', a curriculum for limiting needs and desires, a problematic mediation of the demands of humanity and citizenship, and a sharp curtailment of the speculative intellect in favour of 'useful knowledge'. It was a protest against history rather than a vision of historical fulfilment. Moreover, the onto-phylogenetic parallel that is suggested pivoted on the encomium of youth or youthful values and a suspicion of crabbed old age. The essential restraints were to be fixed at the time of puberty, which corresponded in the history of peoples to a 'société naissante'. These perceptions were closely related to Rousseau's choice of the biological cycle as a model of socio-political development.

We will expect a quite different solution within the Kantian premises of teleological evolution despite his esteem for Rousseau. Though both men agree that evil is connected with man's propensity to exercise his lower form of liberty (*freie Willkür*), Kant sees this evil also as 'radical', not created in history but, as it were, created speculatively with life. The Rousseauian problem is to inject morality into nature by promoting it uncontaminated, avoiding the 'gouffre' of civilization; the Kantian problem is to civilize a wild creature who 'needs a master' so that he may later moralize himself. The goals and methods are at variance.[1]

Kant's vision of education is loosely correlative to his remarks on the 'discipline of culture' in the 'Critique of Teleological Judgment'. Man appears on the earth in a state of wild freedom:

---

[1] Of course, one might plausibly argue that the Kantian *Zucht* is far less repressive psychologically than Rousseau's 'discipline of withdrawal', if the latter is taken literally.

'Savagery is the independence from laws. Discipline subjects man to the laws of humanity and commences to make him feel the compulsion of the laws.'[1] More categorically Kant tells us: 'Discipline or *Zucht* changes animality into humanity (*Menschheit*).'[2] Furthermore (*contra* Rousseau), discipline must be inaugurated very early in life so that the human potential may thenceforth be exploited in freedom and reason; the young child must be submitted to rules.[3] Discipline is, to be sure, not an end but an instrument of freedom. Corresponding to *Zucht*, there is *Unterweisung* (instruction) which is the positive part of education, the transmittal of culture after the preparatory conditions have been achieved. However, 'the lack of discipline is a worse evil than the failing of culture, for the latter can still be remedied later, while one will then no longer be able to root out savagery...'[4] Above all, compulsion is necessary. How does this promote freedom? 'I shall accustom my pupil to suffer a constraint on his freedom, and I shall at the same time direct him to his own good use of it.'[5] The formal correlation between pedagogy and human history is completed by the following observation: 'How long should education last? Until the time when nature has determined man to guide himself.'[6] That is also the moment of enlightenment, 'man's departure from his self-incurred tutelage'.[7]

The pupil, like the human race, is guided by an Idea. Truth overcomes his obstacles; 'the Idea of an education, which develops all the talents nature has placed in man, is completely truthful'.[8] Properly disciplined, then cultivated, children should frame their actions not only for the present here-and-now but for the cosmopolitan future.[9] The notion that true freedom alone is won through the conditioning of discipline will be one of the *leitmotivs* of the German nineteenth century, although frequently not with Kant's restraints and high-mindedness.

The correlation of the *Pädagogik* with both the Idea of a morally guided history and the concrete political problems of Kant's time and situation is arresting. That same animal who 'needs a master' is also the one who 'needs an education'.[10] In both cases, the

---

[1] *Pädagogik, G.S.* IX, 442.   [2] *Ibid.* p. 441.   [3] *Ibid.* p. 442.   [4] *Ibid.* p. 445.
[5] *Ibid*, p. 453.   [6] *Ibid.*   [7] 'What is Enlightenment?' p. 4.
[8] *Pädagogik, G.S.* IX, 444.   [9] *Ibid.* p. 447.
[10] *Reflex. Anthrop. G.S.* XV, no. 1423, p. 621.

master must be another man; and the trust, in both cases, is great and equally severe. Ultimately, both the tutelary and political problems of *quis custodiet* must be solved by the preceptor and the moral politician who have 'changed their way of thinking' or 'undergone the interior revolution' and are guided by the Idea, obliged by their moral disposition to bring the 'ends of nature' to pass. The agent of authority must be one who can wield both effectively and morally considerable powers of coercion. The quasi-divine figure, materialized in Rousseau's tutor and legislator images, is brought down to earth by Kant and, so to speak, constitutionalized. In phenomenal history, therefore, a criterion of maturity is erected, enabling one to distinguish between the minority and majority of a people in respect to their political freedom. The essential is that progress be continually realized.

Since the guideline is the Idea and the judgment of its approximation, the custodial problem is also deflected away from the single centre of 'rulership' (*Beherrschung*) toward the 'manner' or 'spirit' of governing and into the ranks of the academic and literary intelligentsia. 'Publicity' becomes the test of progress and enlightenment, and this means not confused public discourse but rather 'the use which a person makes of [his reason] as a scholar before the reading public'.[1] This is a privilege which Kant grants to philosophers, but denies to the clergy and other parts of the official bureaucracy. 'That kings should philosophize or philosophers become kings is not to be expected,' Kant declares. 'But kings or king-like peoples which rule themselves under laws of equality should not suffer the class of philosophers to disappear or be silent, but should let them speak openly. This is indispensable to the enlightenment of the business of government...'[2] What Kant is suggesting has roots in the cultural confidence of the European 'republic of scholars' and their conviction of leading the way to unprejudiced and practical reform. The Encyclopedists and physiocrats, too, had wished for a collaboration between sovereignty and intellect. But from the German idealist perspective the notion assumes greater depth. For these philosophers are not mere technicians of welfare and happiness,

[1] 'What is Enlightenment?' p. 5.
[2] 'Perpetual Peace', p. 116.

173

but the guardians of the Idea that *ought to* prevail in history.[1] This marks a significant distinction between the ideals of Enlightenment 'technocracy', and the idealist formulation of a 'tutelary state' which provides its citizens with scaffolding for a sterner morality than that of the liberal harmony of self-interest.[2]

Despite the tutelary predispositions of the Kantian theory of politics, the conditions of coercion are limited by the ethical law unexceptionably, at least in a formal manner. We do *not* have a duty to subject men to education. But a man *does* have the duty to become educated. However, since there can be no civilization or restraint on violence without positive legal obligation, man not only has a duty to enter a political commonwealth but may be compelled to do so. The essential is that although men can be physically coerced, 'another person...cannot compel me to *have an end*'.[3] The purpose of both the state and the school is to prepare men for self-mastery, for the autonomous proposal of ends, which is the essence of ethical possibility. In one of Kant's most affecting passages, he writes: '...the human being is...but a trifle. But for the sovereigns of his own species also to consider and treat him as such...that is no trifle, but a subversion of the ultimate purpose of creation itself.'[4]

C. PHILOSOPHICAL COMMUNICATION

If philosophy, like the Idea, is to 'help...from afar', the problem of its transmission to humanity becomes an outstanding issue. If, moreover, the essence of that philosophy is an ethics which challenges at every turn the predispositions of human nature, the situation is aggravated. Rousseau had placed himself in declared rebellion against the recondite structures of philosophical argument. 'The study of the universe should raise man to his creator,' he had

---

[1] Kant's restraint in this area should be underscored. If it is essentially the philosophical judgment, with the categorical imperative as its major premise, that provides for the validation of political acts, this means that the philosopher, through public liberty of expression, is performing a judicial function, not that he should arrogate to himself powers of execution. This observation may be profitably compared with the remarks on p. 168 above.

[2] Although the 'tutelary' ideal has distinct Caesarian overtones, it still opposes a certain egalitarianism expressed through the bourgeois value of 'talents' to the aristocratic-romantic notion of 'genius'. See Gueroult, *Doctrine de la Science*, I, 17.

[3] *Virtue*, p. 38. [4] 'Old Question', p. 148.

insisted, 'but all it raises is the level of human vanity.'[1] But Rousseau had also said that thanks to the conscience 'we are able to be men without being scholars'.[2]

That insight, with the seat of morality carefully purged of all sensuous connection and restored to the purview of reason, nourishes Kant's conviction that philosophy need not surrender its liaison with the average man. 'I have no fear with respect to this treatise,' Kant writes, in introducing his second *Critique*, 'of the reproach that I wish to introduce a new language, since the kind of thinking it deals with is very close to the popular way of thinking.'[3] If every man knows the moral law *a priori*, then a universally grasped system of ethics should be plausible. But Kant had already run into extraordinary difficulties in making the *Critique of Pure Reason* fathomable even to the intellectual class. This had led him to issue the simpler *Prolegomena*, and, more importantly, had dictated his choice to proceed with the elaboration of a system of ethics rather than prolonging 'criticism' into a 'metaphysics of nature'.[4] His doubts, though, are still pronounced as he confronts the *Foundations of the Metaphysics of Morals* (1785), which is an analytic prologue to the *Critique of Practical Reason*. This work is laced with second thoughts about the popular presentation of an ethics of duty by a man who hoped to join impeccable method to Rousseauian communicability. 'No doubt,' he writes, 'common men do not conceive [moral knowledge] in such an abstract and universal form, yet they always have it really before their eyes and use it as the standard of their decision.'[5] However, 'wisdom. . .has need of science, not in order to learn from it, but to secure for its precepts admission and permanence'.[6] Finally we learn that 'it is quite absurd to try to be popular in the first inquiry, on which the soundness of the principles depends'.[7]

Needless to say, Kant was never 'popular'. Hegel said truly that it was with Kant that the rupture between philosophy and ordinary intelligent discourse was made.[8] Schiller might in vain

---

[1] *Observations, O.C.* III, 41.   [2] *Emile*, IV, 354.   [3] *C. Prac. R.* pp. 10–11.
[4] De Vleeschauwer, *Development*, pp. 93–6, 115.   [5] *Foundations*, p. 21.
[6] *Ibid.* p. 22.   [7] *Ibid.* p. 27.
[8] *Lectures on the History of Philosophy* (3 vols., trans. E. S. Haldane and F. H. Simpson, London, 1892–96), III, 505.

announce that 'only philosophers disagree concerning those ideas which predominate in the practical part of the Kantian system, but I am confident of showing that mankind has never done so';[1] he was, in fact, unlike Kant, a gifted philosophical vulgarizer. Kant's own doubts continued to invade the *Metaphysics of Morals*: 'to have [a metaphysics of morals] is itself a duty. Moreover, every man has such a metaphysics within himself, although commonly only in an obscure way'.[2] Finally, the *Doctrine of Virtue* tells us that man has 'a duty to diminish his ignorance by education and to correct his errors'.[3] Kant, with the best of intentions, has travelled far from Rousseau. Wisdom remains in need of science.

The problem just described is of fundamental importance to idealism. Historically, it provokes great tension between the *is* and the *ought*; pedagogically, an unrivalled awareness of the great gulf between the cultured and uncultured classes, emphasizing the paramountcy of the educational experience. Politically, there is the hint that if legal and social life are to be ordered according to the Idea, the tutelary role of government, correctly apprehended, will take priority over incautious experimentation. It will also have a connection with forthcoming reappraisals of religion: if indeed the great mass of men cannot raise themselves to a 'religion within the limits of reason alone' but must subsist with the superstitious shadow of the truth, then that shadow may itself have substance in the work of the world: even Kant had written in the *Critique of Judgment* of the popular usefulness 'for us' of theological as opposed to ethical proofs.[4] But this will also become a criterion for setting the learned apart from the masses. The ultimate cry will be Fichte's 'Leben ist ganz eigentlich Nicht-Philosophieren; Philosophieren ist ganz eigentlich Nicht-Leben'.[5] Finally, we border on the charged question of *cosmopolis* (which was always the fatherland of the intellectual elite) versus *nation* (the home of common men): if the intelligentsia was to recapture its connection with common humanity, it would have to be in terms of the latter.

---

[1] F. Schiller, *Aesthetic Education*, in J. Weiss (tr.), *The Aesthetic Letters*, 1st letter, p. 2.
[2] *Justice*, 'Introduction to the Metaphysics of Morals', p. 16.   [3] *Virtue*, p. 46.
[4] *Judgment* ('Teleological'), para. 90, pp. 396–7.
[5] *Rückerinnerungen, Antworten, Fragen, S.W.* v, 343.

D. A SUMMARY: HISTORY AND CONSCIOUSNESS

Rousseau set his 'chimera' against 'prejudice' but could not conceive of an historical rationale for it. Kant now removes it from the pattern of regret and past-orientedness by postulating a 'plan' of history whose terminals are obscure but whose necessary meaning changes every transaction of event. That history itself is a 'dialectic' (resolved only by a doctrine of ethics) whose every future moment is open to freedom but whose ponderous past echoes with the impure acts of an undisciplined humanity. 'Rationalized' as pure practical reason, the chimera is also distributed in germ throughout the whole socialization process, redeeming time in terms of the timeless. Law and culture bestride the passage between the real and desired worlds, emphasizing that the flesh is to be mastered and not discarded. Those mediating Ideas also emphasize the gradual but decisive domesticating role of civilization. In some senses, the end does justify the means in Kant, but the end must always include the treatment of others as ends. This outcome, formally unassailable, assumes more problematic dimensions when mortal flesh is empowered by distant goals. Ideally, respect should keep men from laying unlawful hands on each other. But the inchoate respect of an evolving legal system and the 'discipline of culture' might have other results. Philosophy guards the egg from which the Idea is to be hatched and cackles when enemies draw near; in actuality, however, philosophy, like right, peace and freedom, is itself an Idea.

Kant immanentized reason in his ethical doctrine and futurized it in his teleological history. The problem for subsequent German idealism would be to clarify history as an expansion of (transcendental) freedom while shunning the anthropologism of the Enlightenment. Where reason is immanent and associated with freedom, and social institutions are regarded as historical warrants of the injection of reason into the world, then somehow mind as well as society must be seen to have a (rational) history. This is a mediation which it did not occur to Kant to perform.

Kant did, however, include a curiously suggestive chapter at the end of his first *Critique* called 'The History of Pure Reason'. At the head of that chapter stands this tantalizing first sentence:

The teleology of practical reason

'This title stands here only in order to indicate one remaining division of the system, which future workers must complete.'[1] Kant was not of course enjoining his epigones to historicize a metaphysics grounded on its exemption from time. He does not suggest that philosophical understanding has evolved in some determinable sequence parallel to the phenomenology of the consciousness. What Kant apparently wishes to show is the poverty of previous philosophical solutions and the proof that 'the *critical* path alone remains open'. But the fruit of this reflection will not be a perfection of 'criticism' but rather an interpretation of the world as a genetic history of reason. Philosophy as 'queen of the sciences' and guardian of the Idea will be gradually equated with its own philosophical history.

---

[1] *C.P.R.* A852 = B880, p. 666. On Kant and the development of modern historiography, see Wilhelm Dilthey, *Die Jugendgeschichte Hegels*, in *Gesammelte Schriften* (12 vols., Leipzig, 1921–36), IV, 61 f.

PART FOUR

J. G. FICHTE: THE CHIMERA DOGMATIZED

FICHTE:
INTRODUCTION AND TENDENCIES

A. FICHTE AND ROUSSEAU

'I would show you,' Fichte told his public audience in the course of his fifth lecture on 'The Vocation of the Scholar' in 1794, 'by the example of one of the greatest men of our own age, *what you ought not to be*.'[1] The great man is Rousseau. Fichte's intellectual generation had been marked by the maelstrom of *Sturm und Drang* and intoxication with Rousseau's rebellion against the courtly values of his time. Still an obscure *Hauslehrer*, Fichte had scrawled out, on 24 July 1788, a therapeutic document called 'Random Thoughts on a Sleepless Night', setting forth his intention to describe, in the style of Montesquieu's *Persian Letters*, a perfectly corrupt society dwelling at the South Pole, through which he could heap scorn on all the gallantry, vanity, artificiality and injustice of his own age.[2] This hyperserious young man, born into poverty but elevated to later renown through the good fortune of receiving an advanced education, had detested the Wielandesque *Aufklärung* to his very corpuscles and worshipped Jean-Jacques, who was also *peuple*.[3] In the meantime, however, two decisive happenings intervened: Paris had risen to declare the Rights of Man, and Kant had shown in what sense the human will could be free. Mankind was once again on the march. Now, scarcely five years after his 'sleepless night', Fichte, already gaining notoriety as a radical for his presumed authorship of two pro-Revolutionary pamphlets and as a philosopher of stature for his pursuit of the Kantian method in his *Versuch*

---

[1] *The Vocation of the Scholar*, in William Smith (trans.), *The Popular Works of Johann Gottlieb Fichte* (2 vols., London, 1889), I, 205.

[2] For description and analysis of the 'Zufällige Gedanken', see Xavier Léon, *Fichte et son temps* (3 vols., Paris, 1922–7), pp. 62–4; Ernst Bergmann, *Fichte der Erzieher* (2nd ed., Leipzig, 1928), p. 30.

[3] Born to a poor but enterprising family of ribbon-weavers in Rammenau, Saxony, in 1762, Fichte attracted the attention of the local *grand seigneur*, Baron von Miltitz, with his precocity. The Baron's benefaction enabled him to enter the famous Schulpforta of Leipzig at the age of 13. At 18 he became a student of theology at the University of Jena.

Fichte : introduction and tendencies

zu einer Kritik aller Offenbarung (1792), just rewarded—through Goethe's intercession—with the chair of philosophy at Jena, bode his time until the regular Easter opening of courses by inaugurating his first of many extramural lecture series.[1] At such a prime moment it seemed fitting to put the idealist straight collar on the Genevan poet of sensibility.

This lecture, one of the truly interesting pieces of Rousseau criticism, gives us, compressed, the clash of pre- and post-Revolutionary Romanticism, of two cultures, two personalities. Like Kant (but with a muscularity that scarcely permits their comparison), Fichte was resolved to break open the anti-historical blockhouse in which Jean-Jacques had taken refuge. 'Through the will', he would presently write, 'and only through the will is the future embraced in the present; through the will alone is the conception of the future, as such, made possible, and the will not only embraces but also determines the future.'[2] Of course, if Fichte criticized Rousseau, he also was, in 1794, his follower. What Rousseau had shown to be the rights of man were also reason's rights; and 'the question of right is in no way decided before the tribunal of history'.[3]

---

[1] In 1793 Fichte wrote and published anonymously the Zurückförderung der Denkfreiheit (directed against the censorship regulations of Frederick William II of Prussia) and the Beiträge zur Berichtigung der Urtheile des Publikums über die Französische Revolution (a polemical and philosophical defence of the French Revolution based on arguments of abstract right and transcendental freedom against the Burkean school of August-Wilhelm Rehberg). The authorship shortly became general knowledge. When Fichte was invited in the following year to the chair of philosophy at Jena, he was required to give the authorities assurance that he would not continue the vocation of political pamphleteer. The Versuch zu einer Kritik aller Offenbarung (Critique of all Revelation) was his first serious philosophical work, written under the influence of Kant, and admired by Kant, who forwarded it to his publisher. Since (without Fichte's consent) it appeared anonymously in 1792 at a moment when Kant's own treatment of religion was expected, it was first thought to be of Kant's authorship. The identification of the real author brought immediate fame to Fichte.

[2] Grundlage des Naturrechts, translated by A. E. Kroeger as The Science of Rights (London, 1889), pp. 167–8. Found in Vol. III of the Sämmtliche Werke of Fichte, edited by his son I. H. Fichte (8 vols., Berlin, 1845–6).

[3] Beiträge, S.W. VI, 58. See also p. 71, where Fichte notes that with the French Revolution Rousseau's doctrines had become empirically as well as theoretically true. However, Rousseau himself had been too gentle with the empiricists: 'that was his mistake'. In his late period, Fichte severely modified his 'naturrechtlich' conception. In the Staatslehre of 1813, S.W. IV, 436, Rousseau's social contract is described as 'empirically and arbitrarily fabricated...a pondering over speculative tasks haphazardly without speculative principles'. 'No wonder', Fichte continues, 'that, proceeding from such maxims, [the French Revolution] turned sour.' For Fichte's

This is not the quarrel: empirical historical 'rights' never had a more dedicated opponent than Fichte. But the problem is, on the one hand, to correlate right with the teleological 'plan' of history, to bring the just city down from mid-air, and, on the other, to demolish the backward-looking pattern of *past–memory–regret* in favour of the progress of a freedom 'always posited in the future'.[1]

The defence of learning falls within these boundaries. Fichte chides Rousseau for making the same species of error that the latter had attributed to Hobbes. Rousseau, he explains, has attacked the advance of civilization and, in particular, the mission of the scholar. But he himself was cultivated and he too tried to promote the interests of humanity: thus, 'his actions stand in opposition to his principles'.[2] Rousseau actually wished to have his cake and eat it too: the peace of the state of nature and the moral perceptivity attained only through culture. He committed this error through his disappointment and revulsion at the state of the world; and because 'his knowledge [had] the faults common to all knowledge founded on mere undeveloped feeling...'[3] he saw only *corrupted* scholars, but did not perceive the Idea of the scholar. Allow Rousseau his solitude, his peace, his evasion; what then? Undoubtedly he thought it necessary for 'reflection on his destiny and his duties, thereby to ennoble himself and his fellow-men'. But here, precisely, was the contradiction: 'He thus insensibly transplanted himself and society into this State of Nature, *with all that cultivation which they could only acquire by coming out of the State of Nature.*'[4]

---

[1] *Science of Rights*, p. 77. The motor of this progress in the Fichtean philosophy consists in the disparity between the ego, considered as a finite mind and agent and as the total activity and capacity of the mind as proponent of a moral universe. The function which draws the two conceptions of the ego together is the imagination, morally regarded: 'This relation of the ego with itself and within the ego, since it posits itself simultaneously as finite and as infinite—a relation that furthermore consists of a contradiction with itself and, therefore, a reproduction of itself, given that the ego, wishing to assemble the unassemblable now, tries to grasp the infinite in the form of the finite, then repulsed, tries to posit the infinite beyond that form, but in the very same moment seeks once more to grasp it in the finite form—is the power of the imagination.' *Grundlage der gesammten Wissenschaftslehre, S.W.* I, 215.
[2] *Vocation of the Scholar*, p. 196.   [3] *Ibid.* pp. 197–9.   [4] *Ibid.* p. 201.

---

positions in the 1790s, see the careful analysis by Martial Gueroult, 'Nature humaine et état de nature chez Rousseau, Kant et Fichte', *Revue philosophique* (Sept.–Dec. 1941), pp. 382 ff.

Fichte : introduction and tendencies

The Fichtean analysis, if crisp, was far too simple. Rousseau did not confuse nature and human fulfilment in quite this manner; in fact he did premise a new condition higher than nature which would, however, offer man a substantially 'natural' protection. But it matters only that Fichte took Rousseau in the way he did. Given their personalities, this was almost inevitable. Unlike Kant, Fichte did not conjecturally create a 'progressivist' Rousseau whose discourses had swept the ground clear for the pedagogical and legal constructivism of *Emile* and the *Social Contract*, but rather a Rousseau mired passively in the solace of nature. If Rousseau had energy, it was an 'energy rather of suffering than of action...he forgot the power which the human race possesses—*to help itself*'.[1]

Fichte thought that such yielding, fluctuation and despair before the burden of the human task was a betrayal. At the base of his epistemology, he propounds that 'reason is not a thing which *is* and *exists*, but rather a doing—pure, simple doing...reason cannot contemplate itself otherwise than as what it is; hence as a doing'.[2] We are in the Faustian sphere of *im Anfang war die Tat*. Thus Emile's education is all wrong, at least in its 'negative' aspects. The duty of man is to act on nature, rather than to suffer nature to act on him.[3] Emile is evidently not a child who, burning with zeal and decision, will go forth to give battle to the physical obstacles set in the path of the ego, to master them. But Fichte, on the contrary, declared: 'I never act,' speaking for the 'I' of everyman, 'but in me acts the universe.'[4] Fichte himself had not conceived the *Wissenschaftslehre* (his system of philosophy); God or nature acting

---

[1] *Vocation of the Scholar*, p. 204.

[2] *System der Sittenlehre*, translated by A. E. Kroeger as *The Science of Ethics* (London, 1907), p. 61. In *Sämmtliche Werke*, IV. Cf. also *Ethics*, p. 230: 'I am only what I act.'

[3] *Vocation of Man*, in Smith, I (*S.W.* II), p. 435: 'When men shall no longer be divided by selfish purposes...nothing will remain but for them to direct their united strength against the one common enemy which still remains unsubdued—resisting, uncultivated nature.' X. Léon's conjecture that Fichtean nature is spiritualized because it is an imaginative projection of the infraconscious ideal ego (*Fichte et son temps*, I, 512) is far-fetched; nature is the enemy of intelligence. But even nature will meet its match as the world is brought under the sway of reason. Hurricanes, earthquakes, volcanoes are described as 'nothing but the last shivering strokes by which the perfect formation of our globe has yet to be accomplished'. *Vocation of Man*, p. 425.

[4] *Wissenschaftslehre* of 1801, translated by A. E. Kroeger as *New Exposition of the Science of Knowledge* (St. Louis, 1869), p. 124. Hereafter, *Wissenschaftslehre* of 1801. (In *S.W.* II.)

in him had done so.[1] At the same time he confessed the exaltations and the forfeits of self-determination. To be disposed to construct the world on a principle one must first vibrate with that view of life: 'The kind of philosophy one chooses depends on the kind of man that one is...'[2] The fatalist or the pleasure-seeker will choose 'dogmatism'. But the truly free man, the man of the categorical imperative, will choose transcendental idealism. Fundamentally, there are no other alternatives.[3]

Such insights reveal instantly the psychologism of this philosopher —a tense, almost Calvinist feeling of the distance existing between the saved and the damned. This feeling, as Philonenko points out, is intimately connected with Fichte's view of time. Most men, according to Fichte, are intimately bound to the 'time' of dogmatism; they are prisoners of what he will later describe as the 'round dance' —the chronology of natural inclination and, in essence, of theoretical reason. Opposed to this sense of time are those suited for liberty, a time-sequence that creates itself, thrusting the goal of duty and conscience far into the future through positive free acts.[4]

Fichte is a significant fusion of three strains: the future-directedness of post-Revolutionary Europe (assuredly there are Godwins, Destutts and Saint-Simons to rival the spiritual Germans); the climax of the German cultural effort to *be* the 'classicism', the epitome of European excellence; and the tensions provoked by the political backwardness and civil fragmentation of a *Kulturstaat* aspiring to dizzy heights of humanity, purity and soulfulness. In the background of Fichte, indeed, there is a fourth important strain crossing: the harbinger of upward class mobility. If a few of the hot chunks of lava flung up by the French Revolutionary volcano (men like Babeuf) are excepted, Fichte is the prime contemporary instance of social sensitivity conditioned by escape from the peasant ghetto.

By all these counts, Fichte looks to the future. As we shall presently discover, it is a future conditioned more by profession

[1] Fichte's letter to Reinhold, 21 March 1797, in *J. G. Fichtes Leben und literarischer Briefwechsel* (ed. I. H. Fichte, Sulzbach, 1830), II, 255. But Fichte was speaking here loosely, not philosophically; cf. *Wissenschaftslehre* of 1801, p. 134; 'Unless I elevate myself to moral freedom, *I* do not act, but nature acts through me.'
[2] *Erste Einleitung in die Wissenschaftslehre* (1796), *S.W.* I, 434.   [3] *Ibid.* pp. 426 ff.
[4] Cf. Alexis Philonenko, *La liberté humaine dans la philosophie de Fichte* (Paris, 1966), pp. 158, 258.

than by class. The method developed by Kant for rationalizing Rousseau's 'land of chimeras'—that morally-triggered teleology of culture and discipline—will become 'dogmatized' in Fichte's hands. The chiliastic limits will be trespassed. Before us now is the task of watching Fichte's procedures unfold from the message which, in 1794, he cast back upon Rousseau's *temps mort* of regret and indolence:

What Rousseau, under the name of the State of Nature, and these poets under the title of the Golden Age, place *behind* us, lies actually *before* us. (It may be remarked in passing that it is a phenomenon of frequent occurrence, particularly in past ages, that what we *shall become* is pictured as something which we already *have been*; and that what we have to attain is represented as something which we have formerly lost...)[1]

The man of learning is 'the highest, truest man';[2] man has the ultimate cultural task 'to subject all irrational nature to himself, to rule over it unreservedly and according to his own laws'.[3] This reminds us of Henri de Saint-Simon. But there is also here the noumenal, teleological dimension of 'a community pervaded by design', the pole star of a spirituality only obliquely reflected in the technical organization of a world where man's 'eternal perfecting is his vocation'.[4] This idealist input allows us to distinguish very sharply between the French and German branches of nineteenth-century perfectionism.

B. ACTION AND INTELLECT

If Fichte defended the professorial pulpit against Rousseau's indictment of the striving intellect, he was a very particular kind of pedagogue. He launched himself at pupils and public alike with an original mixture of esoteric philosophy and evangelistic rhetoric. As a young man he had written: 'I know the professorial class; I have few new discoveries to make on that score. As for myself, I haven't the slightest inclination to become a scholar by profession. I want not only to think, I want to act...I have only one desire...to act on my surroundings.'[5] Saved from the parsonage, Fichte was destined to be a scholar-actor. He cultivated the grand prophetic style, especially in his 'popular' lectures. His

[1] *Vocation of the Scholar*, pp. 202–3.   [2] *Ibid.* p. 150.   [3] *Ibid.* p. 156.   [4] *Ibid.* p. 163.
[5] Hans Schulz (ed.), *Fichtes Briefwechsel* (2 vols., Leipzig, 1925), I, 61–2.

delivery abounded in those flowery and rolling periods that Carlyle so much admired. Of the Greeks and Romans, he once noted, 'there was much less written and read than among ourselves; while, on the contrary, there was much more spoken, and vocal discourse was much more carefully cultivated'.[1] This corrective of living speech in which Fichte believed had manifold associations with his activism and his urge to blast learning through the fortresses of social distinction.

Probably no savant in Western history ever wrote and spoke more passionately of the divine mission of education and the scholarly calling, the province of the man who 'loves the Idea, not before all else, for he loves nothing else beside it...'[2] At Jena he preached the French cause and dissolved duelling clubs, rose at five in the morning for a canter on horseback, competed with the divine service on Sundays.[3] A small, stocky, bushy-browed man, the child of country artisans, his eyes blazed with javelins of sincerity, ready to fling. His son's biography furnishes the following portrait:

Fichte's words in his lectures sweep along like a storm-cloud that sheds its fire in separate strokes. He does not move, but he uplifts the soul. Reinhold [Fichte's predecessor at Jena, a noted Kantian, who accepted the chair at Kiel in 1793] wanted to make good men; Fichte wants to make great men. His glance is monitory and his gait defiant. Through his philosophy he aims at directing the spirit of the age; he knows its weak side, and thus tackles it from the angle of politics.[4]

The young Fichte surpassed Kant, he amazed the young, he swept all before him. Even in a culture where academic heroism was not considered totally eccentric, he violated the *bonne mesure* of his intellectual colleagues. Erhard (a legal philosopher and connoisseur of the pre-1793 Revolution) wrote to Niethammer (soon to be the editorial collaborator of Fichte and, later, the friend of Hegel) in 1796: 'God forbid that Fichte should be persecuted, or else there

---

[1] *Grundzüge des gegenwärtigen Zeitalters* (in *S.W.* VII), translated as *Characteristics of the Present Age*, in Smith, II, 106–7.
[2] *Das Wesen des Gelehrten* (1805), translated as *The Nature of the Scholar*, in Smith, I, 215.
[3] For Fichte in his Jena cadre, see W. H. Bruford, *Culture and Society in Classical Weimar, 1775–1806* (Cambridge, 1962), pp. 370–7.
[4] *Leben und Briefwechsel*, I, 52.

might very well emerge a Fichtianity a hundred times worse than Christianity.'[1] Indeed, the *Wissenschaftslehre* sometimes bordered on Fichtianity. Nicolai, the high priest of the *Aufklärung*'s Indian summer in Berlin, simply called Fichte 'eine wilde Schweinskeule' (a wild hamhock).[2] Too brilliant and hard-faceted to cultivate enduring friendships, Fichte suffered the enmity of many who knew him only by the reputation of his cold superiority.

Fichte felt both enormous pride and uneasiness in knowing that he had utterly shattered the horizons of a low birth. A good family man, he nonetheless experienced dismay when his unmannered younger brother proposed to descend on him in Jena for an extended visit from the Saxon countryside. 'You do not realize', he wrote, 'how much there is to learn of which you have absolutely no conception. Learning is the easiest part; the question is one of your entire deportment; to learn that takes time and money in proportion to the lack of it.'[3] This same intolerant sensitivity is re-echoed in Fichte's ethics of striving and politics of improvement. It jumps out of the profundities of the *Wissenschaftslehre*: 'evidently', Fichte tells the uncouth who have been unable to rise to the standpoint of the moral life, 'it must not be quite impossible for you as yet to elevate yourselves to Ideas, since God still tolerates you in the system of appearances'.[4] Fichte is very much a Jacobin of the elect. He is also virtually the first Western secular philosopher to lead a bourgeois family life.[5]

Fichte's vituperative, swollen eloquence is sometimes disturbing to modern students. It would not have been so upsetting to cultivated Americans of Fichte's own era—contemporaries of Daniel Webster and William Ellery Channing and, eventually, Transcendentalism—accustomed to the rhetoric of emerging nationhood and the soulful swells of the pulpit.[6] Fichtianity is not embryonic

---

[1] Erhard to Niethammer, 16 June 1796; quoted by X. Léon, *Fichte et son temps*, I, 470.
[2] Bergmann, *Fichte Erzieher*, p. 136.   [3] *Briefwechsel*, I, 385.
[4] *Wissenschaftslehre* of 1801, p. 149.
[5] For a literary psychoanalysis of our subject, see G. Kafka, 'Erlebnis und Theorie in Fichtes Lehre vom Verhältnis der Geschlechter', *Zeitschrift für angewandte Psychologie*, XVI (1920), pp. 1–24. On marriage, cf. *Ethics*, p. 347: 'To remain unmarried without one's fault is a great misfortune; but purposely to remain so is a great guilt.'
[6] Cf. Van Wyck Brooks, *The Flowering of New England, 1815–1865* (New York, 1936), pp. 104 ff. To be sure, Channing was a sweeter soul than Fichte.

Nazism; it is the high metaphysical nineteenth century, pure and simple. There are, however, disturbing features of Fichte's temperament and thought which it would be idle to sweep under the carpet. Fichte himself believed, as we have seen, that temperament primes thought. If he had rested with this relativistic formula, we should have had little more theory from him than from Herder or the Romantics. But Fichte took sides without ambiguity. He believed, first of all, that some philosophical positions were moral and some very much otherwise. And, above all, he believed that mankind, suspect in its natural inclinations, needed to reach the truth through discipline and learning. He carried this conviction far beyond psychology into history, and therein lies the fascination and danger of his message.

C. APROPOS THE 'WISSENSCHAFTSLEHRE'

Fichte's thought is a set of doctrines in evolution. It might seem, once past that great watershed of 1789, that even basic theories cannot wait for refinement until they are exploded by new factors. With Fichte, and even more so with Schelling, an earlier intellectual coherence vanishes. Philosophy itself is caught in the stream of the world, the famous 'spirit of the times', which, as a mood-phrase, Fichte's lectures on history of 1804–5 did so much to popularize,[1] moving Goethe to write in *Faust I*:

> What spirit of the time you call,
> Is but the scholar's spirit, after all,
> In which past times are now reflected.[2]

Thus we shall have to distinguish a number of main Fichtean divisions. As regards the evolution of his theory of knowledge, they are generally described as the 'three moments' of the *Wissenschaftslehre*, those of 1794–8, of 1801 and of 1804, respectively. There is a correlative movement between the pure ethics of duty exposed in the *Sittenlehre* of 1798 and the more religiously deflected moral system of the *Anweisung zum seligen Leben* or 'Doctrine of

---

[1] Cf. Karl Löwith, *From Hegel to Nietzsche* (trans. David E. Green, New York, 1964), pp. 204–5.
[2] *Faust I*, ll. 577–9, p. 109.

Religion' of 1805.[1] Politically, it is common to refer to Fichte's 'Jacobin' (i.e. pro-French) and 'nationalist' periods, bridged by a kind of transition (1804–8).[2] Other terms such as 'cosmopolitanism', 'Machiavellianism', 'democracy' and 'Caesarism' swirl in the background. The aggressive 'liberalism' of 1793, subject to a gradual process of revision and philosophical deepening, verges toward the communitarian socialism of the *Closed Commercial State* of 1800. In like manner, the concept of 'society', paramount at the opening of the Jena period, has apparently ceded to 'statism' by 1801, and to the notion of the popular 'nation' by 1808, only to reach a kind of formal syncretism with the other elements in the last writings of 1811–14. Any assessment of Fichte's consistency often depends on one's degree of sympathy or admiration for the philosopher.

Three general characteristics of Fichte's development require some introductory comment. The first concerns methodology. From the earliest exposition of the *Wissenschaftslehre* in 1794 Fichte intended his entire structure of philosophy (including most affirmatively the 'practical' areas of right, morality and religion) to depend upon his basic and systematic deductions. And Fichte was constantly reformulating the *Wissenschaftslehre* itself, not only in the principal 'three moments', but in a number of further revised presentations for his lectures at the University of Berlin after 1810.[3] Not only did the 'practical' portions of the formal philosophy receive the impact of these changes to the *Wissenschaftslehre*, but the same preoccupations were also reflected, sometimes prefigured, in his popular works. Fichte laboured continually to perfect his system, always within sight of the public and under the blows of his critics. Even for a man of Fichte's enormously concentrated energy and single-mindedness it was impossible to transcribe all aspects of his

---

[1] As against the pure ethics of duty of the *Sittenlehre*, Fichte will write in the *Grundzüge* (publ. 1806) that to the moral man 'the commanding "thou shalt" comes too late...' *Characteristics*, Smith, II, see generally pp. 262–6.

[2] Cf. the treatment in two different chapters by Reinhold Aris, *History of Political Thought in Germany*.

[3] Namely: the *Wissenschaftslehre* and the *Thatsachen des Bewusstseyns* of 1810 (*S.W.* II), and the *Wissenschaftslehre, Transzendentale Logik*, and *Thatsachen des Bewusstseyns* of 1812–13 (in I. H. Fichte, ed., *Nachgelassene Werke*, 3 vols., Bonn, 1834–5, *N.W.*I) as well as later works in 'practical' philosophy.

doctrines coherently before significant expansions in conception had subtly modified the structure of argument.

The reflux of the world's experience upon the philosopher counts for even more. Fichte, as we know, called his philosophy 'the first system of freedom' and discovered its intellectual genesis in the Revolution. Numerous alterations within the range of the *Wissenschaftslehre* are connected to the stormy realities of history and personal life. The politico-cultural fragmentation of Germany and its posture against the animated revolutionary 'nation' across the Rhine materialized the problem of grounding the ideal moral community; this is the question dealt with in the *Sittenlehre* of 1798, with further implications transmitted into the resurgent Platonism and 'organicism' of the Berlin period.[1] Even more tangibly, the lapse of the ideals of the Revolution in France affronted Fichte's early cosmopolitanism and impelled him to project the homeland of Luther and Kant as a utopian human manifold. Finally, the 'atheism controversy' of 1799, which had its origin in the publication of an article 'Über den Grund unseres Glaubens an eine göttliche Weltregierung' of 1798 (where Fichte apparently equated God with a self-willed moral world order, but, as the philosopher well understood, also provided a convenient *cause célèbre* for rallying his conservative opposition), produced new efforts to restate the correlation between thought and being. All this is somehow contingent upon the 'primacy of practical reason'. For acting, according to Fichte, precedes and determines its factual content in the production of consciousness: the *Thathandlung* is prior to the *Thatsache*.[2] Or, put in another fashion, 'my willing is not itself to be a knowing, *but I am to know my willing*'.[3] The pure dynamic of conscious striving finds its empirical correlative in the human effort to change an

---

[1] More than any previous philosopher, Fichte was concerned to establish the philosophical ground of social solidarity—what is today called the question of intersubjectivity. Unlike the realist philosophy of the French Enlightenment, he could not simply assume the existence of multiple individuals with a social propensity based on self-interest. He raised, as Kant had not felt compelled to do before him—a measure of their relative proximity to the Enlightenment—the question of one's moral and social recognition of other beings, still precariously within a 'natural rights' framework.

[2] Cf. *Grundlage, S.W.* I, 91. Also, *Vocation of Man*, p. 421: 'We do not act because we know, but we know because we are called upon to act: the practical reason is the root of all reason.'

[3] *Ethics*, p. 88.

intolerable world, to roll back the factitious or impure. 'To say, I have causality, signifies always: I expand my limits.'[1] The Fichtean world exists to be expanded into. Thus both the *Wissenschaftslehre* and its inventor magnify the concrete tasks of the will, jousting portentously with history and life. 'All the rest—', Fichte once wrote, 'thought, poetry, science—are valuable only to the degree that they keep contact, in some way, with the life from whence they came and to which they aim to return. That is how my philosophy is directed.'[2] Despite the problems of correlating life and transcendental idealism, Fichte has always in mind a philosophy that is never a 'toter Hausrat' but is always working through the 'clear consciousness' of the best men upon a world that is at an epochal point in its turning. This activism is not the least of the resemblances between Fichte and that fellow Promethean and prophet Karl Marx.[3] One must know and experience that world he wishes to change; one must feel its weight in order to move it.

Finally, the German *Goethezeit*, which Fichte contributed to and received from, was somewhat like a brilliant tourney of knights. Above the whole performance, charmed by its spectacular diversity, harmonizing it in his sensitive reactions, was the titan of Weimar. In the background now, not impregnable but already acknowledged as a classic in the line of Leibniz, stood the little old philosopher of Koenigsberg, whose *Critique of Judgment* had just helped to inspire the cultural flowering.[4] And into the arena rode waves of challengers, some mature and reputed, the Schillers, Herders and Jacobis, others burning for plaudits and the crown of posterity, the Fichtes, Schellings, Schleiermachers and hosts of others. The ride and the play of the joust were brief; the moment of mastery was intoxicating; the fall sometimes dizzy. Between 1790 and 1810, amid that clash of cosmic thoughts, that bacchanale of reason 'where not a member is

---

[1] *Ethics*, p. 99. See the interesting remarks of Georges Poulet, *Les métamorphoses du cercle*, pp. 143–6.

[2] *Sonnenklarer Bericht über das Wesen der neuesten Philosophie*, S.W. II, 333–4.

[3] On their relationship, see Marianne Weber, *Fichtes Sozialismus und sein Verhältnis zur Marxschen Doktrin* (Tübingen, 1900).

[4] Hölderlin's letter to his brother of 1 Jan. 1799 is typical: 'Kant is the Moses of our nation, who is leading it out of Egyptian bondage into the free, solitary wilderness of speculation, and is bringing the vitalizing law down from the holy mount.' Cited in R. Kroner, *Von Kant bis Hegel*, I, 3.

sober' recalled for us by Hegel in the *Phenomenology*, the succession of champions was awesome.

D. TRIUMPH AND ECLIPSE

In Fichte's singular career, two nodes stand out: the eruption of the Revolution and the turning of the century. Fichte is the first legitimate intellectual child of the Revolution, the first to do his lasting work entirely on the hither side of that event. But he is also a man whose career divides into periods of ascendancy and eclipse, split by the last year of the old century, when his credit was irreparably damaged by the atheism controversy and by the rising star of his erstwhile disciple Schelling.

The first attribute enabled Fichte to set a tone, to seize the correspondence between the phenomenality of history and the revelation of his own philosophical vision, as if destiny had yoked the two together. He prospered by this union of events and thought as long as intellectual Germany accepted both values. But at the moment that spirituality and fact separated in the German perception of the events in France, Fichte's philosophy of action began to lose its concrete moorings. The students of Jena might still cheer his staunch radicalism and his dazzling manipulations of the *Ich* and the *Nicht-Ich*; the princes, the authorities and even the scholarly republic, were disturbed. More seriously for Fichte's own first philosophical correlation of ideality and life, the French Republic, on the one hand, began to drop hints of impure hegemonic aspirations, while, on the other, the German soul shied back from the moral missions assigned by the *Wissenschaftslehre*. The rest of Fichte's career was to be spent in a passionate search for new correspondences, finally found in a philosophical patriotism that would demand for the future hopes dashed in the past and present. His generally orderly transvaluation was no doubt aided by his hatred of Bonaparte.

The second aspect is more personal. At Jena Fichte was a meteor; the *Wissenschaftslehre* was philosophy brought to its peak of perfection, and philosophy, the masterpiece of that single triplex axiom set at the head of the *Grundlage*, became indeed queen of the

sciences, the geometry of all knowledge.[1] Kant, earlier enshrined
in a holy trinity of Protestant, speculative and revolutionary belief
with Jesus and Luther,[2] had turned out to be a John the Baptist,
even if the old man refused to concede it. The homages were paid.
From Reinhold, the earliest of the post-Kantians to insist that
'criticism' be perfected into a 'system' by deduction from a single
principle, the supplication arrived: 'Alongside your philosophy lie
the ruins of my system... which cost me so much time and pain.'[3]
Fichtianity was in full swing, and its first caliph promised to be
Schelling.

Suddenly after 1798 the public world turned sour. Enemies and
apostates leaped out of ambush. Clericals descended on Fichte's
moral *ordo ordinans*; conservatives noisily flourished his *Beiträge*;
the ghosts of the pre-Kantian *Aufklärung* sniped at his colossal and
presumptuous subjectivism. The ego-philosophy was satirized
by Jean-Paul Richter, by his old friend the Danish poet Baggesen,
in epigrams by Goethe and Schiller.[4] Romanticism, which by its
own confession had drunk deeply at the spring of the *Wissenschaftslehre*, turned the Revolution against itself and against Fichte,
transforming his insights in a reactionary, Catholicizing, obscuran-
tist direction. Kant disclaimed Fichte's absolute idealism as being
neither of the spirit nor of the letter of 'criticism' in a published
statement, whose strong language mortified its victim and prompted
him to reply through the intermediary of Schelling.[5] But Schelling,
too, was not safe, being about to sail aloft under his own power,
not on the wings of the *Wissenschaftslehre*; in his *Letters on Dogmatism and Criticism*, presented in 1798, a year before Kant's
peevish attack on Fichte, he ostensibly mediated Fichtianity and
Spinozism to the advantage of the former, but actually revealed his

[1] Fichte claims for the *Wissenschaftslehre* the uncompromising exactitude of geometry;
cf. *Sonnenklarer Bericht, S.W.* II, 379.
[2] *Beiträge, S.W.* VI, 104–5.
[3] Reinhold to Fichte, 14 Feb. 1797, *Leben und Briefwechsel*, II, 230.
[4] For these developments, see X. Léon, *Fichte et son temps*, I, 436–7; 506–10; and
passim.
[5] Kant's statement of 7 Aug. 1799, published in the *Allgemeine Literaturzeitung*, says,
inter alia: 'I hereby declare that I consider Fichte's *Wissenschaftslehre* a wholly
untenable system...' Here also, Kant called his own work a fully developed system.
Leben und Briefwechsel, II, 161.

future penchant for a 'philosophy of the absolute' that would set Being above Knowing—bitter medicine for his intransigent master, a juvenile Spinozist himself. Within three years Fichte and Schelling began a vindictive exchange, in which neither the exaggerated hurt of the older man nor the cocksureness of the younger is attractive. Amid these difficulties, while Fichte strained to rally academic support in defence of his theist orthodoxy, Prince Karl-August and Goethe in Weimar concluded that it was time to withdraw support from their controversial protégé. The Germany of 1799 was no longer that of 1791. Disingenuously, Fichte was prompted into tendering his resignation from the University of Jena, and it was accepted without protest.

The wheel of fortune at its nadir, Fichte contemplated briefly the offer of his pedagogical services to the French Republic, whose cause he still associated with the good of humanity. Already in 1798 he had been in correspondence with Commissioner Perret and the authorities of Mainz.[1] For some reason that project was stillborn, perhaps because, even in full distress, Fichte remained what he had always been, a visceral and integral German. 'It is dangerous', Fichte wrote in mid-1799 to Reinhold, who was on the verge of defection to Jacobi's 'philosophy of faith', 'to let oneself be turned out of all sorts of places; this is taught by Rousseau's historical example.'[2]

Berlin, 'liberal' once more by Empire standards after the repressive but mercifully brief reign of Frederick William II, gathered in the famous refugee and his family. A second career, so to speak, began. But, in contrast to the first, it was a defensive career. Fichte was no longer the 'Weltschöpfer' of the German philosophical scene. Moreover, the new mood of Romanticism had settled over German culture, with its focal point in the Schlegels (whom Fichte saw frequently in Berlin), and its extensions in the fideism of Jacobi, the *Naturphilosophie* of Schelling, and the religious doctrines of Schleiermacher.[3] Fichte found it necessary both to reorient the

---

[1] C. Perret to Fichte, *Leben und Briefwechsel*, II, 406–7.
[2] Fichte to Reinhold, 22 May 1799, *Briefwechsel*, II, 104.
[3] Fichte's connection with Romanticism is complex. Himself inspired in some respects by the *Sturm und Drang*, he provided the first generation of German Romanticism with some of its critical concepts, notably the idea of the creative and expansive ego.

Wissenschaftslehre to keep 'philosophy' abreast of 'life' and to fortify it against all the assaults of its detractors, of whom Schelling was intellectually the most dangerous. To this end there began a sequence of conversion whereby the ontological ambiguities of the 'first moment' of the *Wissenschaftslehre* were resolved, on the one hand, by the acknowledgment of an absolute that grounds the primary phenomenon of knowledge, and, on the other, by concessions to fideism in the apprehension of that absolute.

Just as Fichte's Jena years opened with the sequence of lectures on the vocation of the scholar, thereby announcing one of his central and persistent themes, the Berlin period is likewise ushered in with a popular publication on 'The Vocation of Man' (1799–1800) that prefigures new trends in his philosophy.[1] In this rather strange, almost mystical work Fichte, placing the discourse at the standpoint of the human adept, leads him through the stages of 'doubt', 'knowledge' and 'faith'. Faith is, after all, the pinnacle of the human moral pyramid, higher than any mere speculative intellect. From the exposition of the first version of the *Wissenschaftslehre* on, it was clear that Fichte both regarded (psychologically) and was compelled to regard (philosophically) the exercise of theoretical reason as a closed circle of demonstration from which escape was possible only by a leap of practical faith justified by the obligation of the moral law. Fichte had, of course, said this before, but he had never put it so decisively: the Jacobian leaven and the 'spirit of the age' had worked their way into the premises of the original ego-

---

[1] See the excellent discussion in Gueroult, *Doctrine de la Science*, I, 361–4. This work, in particular, examines the theodicy problem. Since it seems evident that moral (autonomous) behaviour is infinitely less effective in changing the world than the egoistic clash of interests and that there is no visible connection between morality and progress, it becomes necessary to judge such things from a suprasensible perspective reached only by constancy of faith. These conclusions, which conflict with passages from the *Sittenlehre* of 1798, are quite manifestly the fruit of reflection on bitter intervening experiences.

But unlike the Schlegels and many other European Romantics, Fichte never had a reactionary conversion. Unlike them also, his philosophy never disowned its rationalist roots, never took the turn to pantheosophism. Looked at broadly, most of the intellectuals of Fichte's generation in Germany may be called Romantics. This may be useful as a literary guide, but it does not take us far in politics. Here, it should be understood that transcendental idealism (in its most exacting form) formed a strategic centre that opposed both the dry rationalism of the eighteenth century and the errant emotionalism of the new age. Fichte is at the centre of this tension, and he defines his attitudes toward both schools in the *Grundzüge* lectures of 1804–5.

philosophy. In the *Vocation of Man* we get the full blast of Fichte's pronounced tendency toward psychologism, already scarcely concealed beneath the dry propositions of the practical part of the earliest *Wissenschaftslehre*, especially in the employment of affective categories such as *Sehnen* (longing) and *Streben* (striving) for the ego's projective activity.[1] The human goal was and remained practical knowledge expressed through striving and work in a material world posited as an obstacle. But faith was life. And, as Fichte had written to Reinhold earlier in the year: 'Life can organize only that which proceeds from life; idealism is truly the opposite of life. Its exclusive aim is knowledge for the sake of knowledge, and its practical utility is only mediate, pedagogical in the widest sense of the word.'[2] The *Wissenschaftslehre* does not produce reality, but it is the propaedeutic to all reality, soon to be conceived as the absolute phenomenon.[3] The widest sense of pedagogy is the entire work of the world, and Fichte's ambition is still nothing less than to encompass that sphere systematically.

We should never forget that in the case of Fichte we are dealing with a man of passion—not so explosive as Rousseau, but far from the Augustan sobriety of Kant. For him, philosophy not only highlighted the remarkable split between life and thought, but it also implicated its acolytes. At his midsummer of ambition he flung off these powerful words to Jacobi: 'We began to philosophize out of pride and so we lost our innocence. Now that we have seen our nakedness, we philosophize by necessity in search of our salvation.'[4]

---

[1] The *Vocation of Man* is both one of Fichte's most significant and most poetic pieces. A. Philonenko reminds us correctly of the parallel with Dante's *Divine Comedy*. Fichte's stages of doubt, understanding and faith do seem a deliberate correspondence with the divisions of the Italian masterpiece. We are also made aware here of the important pedagogical parallel between master (Virgil = philosopher) and adept (Dante = student), a paradigm in which the learning process ends when Dante crosses the threshold of Purgatory into Paradise (i.e. from theoretical into practical reason). This theme is one of the most important metaphors of the idealist theory of politics, as there will be occasion to demonstrate. Cf. A. Philonenko, *Liberté humaine*, pp. 96–7, 126, 316.

[2] Fichte to Reinhold, 22 Apr. 1799, *Briefwechsel*, II, 81; cf. also Fichte to Jacobi, same date, pp. 88 f.

[3] Cf. *Wissenschaftslehre* of 1804, *N.W.* II, 291: '[The *Wissenschaftslehre*] is the only route that leads to [absolute knowledge], and therein only...lies its value.' Also, *Thatsachen des Bewusstseyns* (1813), *N.W.* I, 564, where the *Wissenschaftslehre* is described as 'Erscheinungslehre'.

[4] Fichte to Jacobi, 30 Aug. 1795, *Briefwechsel*, I, 502.

Replying to his critics of the atheism quarrel, Fichte wrote: 'I know and feel it with a strength that uplifts my heart—my cause is the good cause, but none of this concerns my person. Should I go under in this struggle, I will simply have come too early, and it will be God's will that I should go under.'[1] But he was no fatalist; he was simply an aggressive prophet who had been pushed on to the defensive. We owe to the patient and thorough research of Xavier Léon the textual proof that from 1800 on virtually all of Fichte's courses and publications, positive and hortatory as they appear, are angry rebuttals to the Romantics, to Schelling, to Bardili, and to other figures and works of the time.[2] Georges Gurvitch even professes to find in Fichte's post-1810 writings passages directed against the *Phenomenology* of Hegel, which had appeared with very little fanfare in 1807.[3] To chart his way through these shoals, Fichte eases off the helm at some moments, then brings his metaphysical vessel hard on course again. He was not willing that the *Wissenschaftslehre* should be scuttled or supplanted, but meant it to be seaworthy for all ages. The same observation must be made for its 'practical' and popular derivatives, even though these, closer to the world of politics, battles and congresses, seem more abruptly and dramatically in flux.

Up to this point I have introduced Fichte as a figure of his age. I have tried to convey the flavour of his philosophical tendencies, and have touched on the evolutionary character of his thought. Aspects of his relationship with Kant will be treated in the next section. We will have to consider what might be called Fichte's superimposing of epistemology on history and the implications of his solution for the nature and purposes of political life. In the words of Georges Vlachos, 'the dynamic projection toward the future is...the idealist transmutation of the rationalist hypothesis of the primitive golden age'.[4] But this process is complex beyond appearance and penetrated by the whole force of the German

---

[1] *Appellation an das Publikum, S.W.* v, p. 196.

[2] Cf. X. Léon, *Fichte et son temps*, II, *passim*.

[3] G. Gurwitsch (Gurvitch), *Fichtes System der konkreten Ethik* (Tübingen, 1924), pp. 63–4.

[4] G. Vlachos, 'Dialectique de la liberté et dépérissement de la contrainte chez Fichte', *Archives de philosophie du droit*, no. 8 (1963), pp. 80–1.

cultural-political dilemma. The two most prominent strains of German thought are, in fact, on a collision course as the century turns: a cosmopolitan idealism of moral endeavour and a frustrated communitarianism charged with overtones of the idealized Greek *polis*. Christianity and the resonances of the French Revolution are the scarcely secondary elements. Fichte's life and writings are a testimony to this clash of values and the predicament of conjugating them. But this is what German thought now aspires to do. Golden age and nature separate here, mythically, ontologically, historically, and it becomes a question of utmost consequence to determine what is 'fitting' for the interminable meantime that lies between the willing and the knowing. A strategy of history is required.

2

METAPHYSICS AND CONSCIOUSNESS

A. PHENOMENOLOGY AND FINALISM

The Fichtean 'strategy of history' will be constructed both along lines of a revised Kantian teleology and as the objectification of a phenomenology of consciousness. The full correlation of world and self does not appear in Fichte's philosophy until he has delivered his popular lectures on the 'Characteristics of the Present Age' (*Grundzüge des gegenwärtigen Zeitalters*) in 1804–5 (published 1806). However, the procedures for this conversion are already sketched out in the 'first moment' of the *Wissenschaftslehre*. In fact, Fichte states explicitly in the *Grundlage*: 'The *Wissenschaftslehre* should be a pragmatic history of the human mind. Up to now we have laboured only to reach this point.'[1] It remains then to make a convincing connection between mind and world.

Which strains of the Rousseauian and Kantian formulations would propel German idealism forward? To reduce our discussion to simple fundamentals, Rousseau had, as we have seen, a more than rudimentary phenomenology, a vivid sense of the adventure of the self in history, but, on the other hand, he had no completed vision of historical process. If he had had that, it would have of necessity been a diabolism, since he was convinced that the poison of social relations outweighed the antitoxin of the untainted man. In contrast, Kant had suggested an immanently directed finalism that disputed both authoritarian providentialism and historical despair, but he had no real phenomenology. If the emphasis on 'practical reason' suggested a future open to the acquisitions of the will, Kant made no attempt to 'phase' this procedure by abstracting from the materials of history itself or to describe any anthropo-historical forms of consciousness. Even the familiar triple-step Joachimite benchmarks, plundered by Turgot, Lessing and others were absent, not to mention the novel and demysticized sequence of Condorcet's ten epochs. The *Critique of Pure Reason* simply *is*, following a pattern

[1] *S.W.* I, 222.

of analytical discourse; it does not unfold. Mind and history are, so to speak, perpetually divided by Kant's philosophical dualism. History transpires in time; man, when he is most himself, surmounts it.

None of these generalizations is, of course, entirely exact. Just as the German idealists found hints in Rousseau of a future trying to burst from the past, so they could also extract from Kant's philosophy clues about the genetic development of consciousness. These had lurked implicity in the 'Idea' and, especially, the 'Conjectural Beginning'. The *Grundzuge* lectures are not therefore an original revelation in the least. They are, especially, a defensive castigation of the new historical theories of the Romantics and of Schelling, and cannot be fully savoured unless the reader has some notion of the latter's *System des transzendentalen Idealismus* (1800) and his *Vorlesungen über die Methode des akademischen Studiums* (1802).[1] Moreover, all these interpretations reflect a renewed turn-of-the-century interest in philosophy of history as such, a vogue inseparable from Germany's profound cultural self-appraisal by Schiller, Novalis and others. At any rate, this work does represent a historical or 'objective' translation of the genetic method of the early *Wissenschaftslehre*, mediated by Fichte's deduction of the moral community in the doctrine of ethics (*Sittenlehre*) of 1798, and still grounded in an essentially Kantian treatment of the teleological problem (i.e. a teleology of the ego, not of the absolute).

B. THE ELIMINATION OF THE 'DING-AN-SICH'

The 'critical' philosophy was elaborated as a means of overcoming, on the one hand, analyses of Hume and Rousseau by saving both the privilege of reason as the supreme organizer of human decision and the reality of moral freedom vested in the individual, and, on the other, of challenging the authoritarian predicates of the 'historical' school, whether its foundations were Humean or Wolffian. But just as the 'innate ideas' of Descartes and Malebranche had been unacceptable to the English empiricists, a similar relic of

---

[1] On the relation of Schelling's theories to the *Grundzüge* as well as the entire intellectual milieu of the lectures, see X. Léon, *Fichte et son temps*, II, 394–463.

Metaphysics and consciousness

Kantian epistemology annoyed Fichte. The element in question was the *Ding-an-sich* or transcendent and (according to Kant) unknowable substrate of the objects of experience. The *Wissenschaftslehre* is structured by the primary task of overcoming this obstacle. The entirety of the sphere called nature is philosophically explained as a pre-conscious imaginative production of the ego or intelligence.[1]

The academic controversy swirling around the defensibility or expendability of the *Ding-an-sich* that raged in Germany in the 1790s drew Fichte swiftly into its vortex.[2] If, as Kant had maintained in the first *Critique*, both nature (the external world) and the transcendental ego (ideal type of the common human intelligence) were equally real or irreducible, then a transcendental or 'critical' philosophy could not be made 'systematic', that is, derivative from a single principle. The philosophical mind, striving for monistic coherence, would have to remain forever unsatisfied. On the other hand, according to Kant, the human consciousness was at least the formal, if not the material, creator of nature; it imposed space and time as well as the categories of the understanding upon a raw, unintelligible chaos of event. Kant had already gone half-way toward establishing the priority of the ego over the thing.

The most telling argument against Kant's solution was also the simplest: if the essences of objects are asserted to exist but are acknowledged to be completely unknowable or inaccessible to the understanding, then there is absolutely no good evidence for saying that they exist at all. In fact, the 'critical' philosophy has no business to assume their existence. However, if the substrate of external reality is made to vanish in this way, then (philosophically speaking) all one is left with is a system of appearances (phenomena) whose origin must be explained in some other fashion. It becomes a question of determining how we represent these detached appearances to ourselves. The results of this inquest led toward the opposed conclusions of scepticism (the impossibility of a logical

---

[1] In other words, it must be so regarded in order to ground the possibility of liberty. To what degree this is a logical assumption and to what degree it might be a psychological inference is unclear. Much of the philosophical underpinning of the Romantic movement depends on the second possibility. See A. Philonenko, *Liberté humaine*, pp. 322–3; but cf. *S.W.* I, 227.

[2] Cf. Léon, *ibid.* I, 216–61; Gueroult, *Doctrine de la Science*, I, 79–145.

theory of representation) or of an idealism which explained the entire possibility and activity of consciousness from the ego. The latter was the Fichtean position.

Whether or not the Kantian *Ding-an-sich* is philosophically tenable, the 'unknowability' of this enduring substrate of objective experience was counter-balanced by its connection with the noumenal sphere of freedom, which, according to Kant, we can 'know' as the moral law. The *Ding-an-sich* carries us into the realm of obligation and rational faith. It is confusing on numerous occasions to find Kant referring to such Ideas as the perfect civil constitution as 'things-in-themselves'. The *Ding-an-sich* would appear to function confusingly as both a static premise of the ontological certainty of nature and as a final cause of practical Ideas such as the just political community. The two notions converge toward God as the ultimate *Ding-an-sich*, the warrant of the natural order and of the possibility of a 'kingdom of ends'.[1]

Seen from another angle, Kant's retention of the epistemological duality of mind and nature tends to harmonize or balance man within the forms of his experience. It enables him to explain himself as determined or determining, to measure the ambivalence of his determinability. Man is seen neither as a pure inhabitant of nature, as, in varying degree, minor philosophies of the French Enlightenment had visualized him, nor as a pure antagonist to nature, as total idealism would suggest; but as a creature caught between his destinies of flesh and mortality and of intelligence and moral aptitude. Kantian dualism strongly implies that although man has a duty to commit himself to the absolute self-mastery of reason, he can never truly become free and whole, because, though he can shape the material of his existence, he can never produce it. If his goal is the perfect freedom of a 'kingdom of ends', his phenomenal possibilities cannot exceed the just but coercive *Rechtstaat* and the discipline of culture and enlightenment. If Kant's vision of a legal commonwealth seems, in one sense, arid compared to his

[1] Regarding Fichte's departure from Kant, cf. *Ethics*, p. 139: 'There is no such thing as nature by itself: my nature and all other nature, posited to explain mine, is merely a peculiar way of regarding myself...On the standpoint of transcendentalism we have no independent twofold at all, but an absolute simple: and where there is no difference it would be absurd to speak of a harmony, or ask for its ground.'

ethics of freedom, it prevents, as I have shown, any chiliastic confusions and reminds us of our human limits.

Fichte, hot-blooded with the philosophy of freedom and the rights of man, saw the *Ding-an-sich* not as a stabilizer between consciousness and the world but as a hostile obstacle to the complete vindication of human autonomy. Already tactical alliances between Kantianism and theology were being effected. Moreover, the rise of 'criticism' had been paralleled in German intellectual circles by a burgeoning interest in Spinoza's pantheism: shortly before his death, in a famous exchange of letters, Lessing had proclaimed his affinity with Spinozism, and it was common knowledge that Goethe drew philosophical inspiration from this source.[1] Spinoza was the 'dogmatist' *par excellence*, whose unitary, cosmic Nature, in which all particularity was contingent, stood at the antipodes of the Intelligence productive of all reality that Fichte was about to propose.[2]

Fichte still held that he was working within the 'spirit' if not the 'letter' of Kant. We know already of the thunderbolt impression made by the *Critique of Practical Reason* on the young adept who travelled from Warsaw to Koenigsberg in 1791 to sit at the feet of the master.[3] To his friend Weisshuhn he wrote: 'Before the *Critique*, there was no other system for me but that of necessity. Now we can once more write the word ethics, which previously had to be scratched from all the dictionaries.'[4] On the other hand, the *Ding-an-sich* was oppressive and the duality of the 'critical' architecture unsatisfying.[5] Others were already seeking the elusive unity Kant refused; Fichte would solve their riddle, or so he thought, in 1793. From this point on, there is a growing divergence from Kant's

---

[1] See Fritz Mautner (ed.), *Jacobis Spinoza Büchlein* (Munich, 1912), reporting Lessing's Spinozism to Moses Mendelssohn. Also, Wilhelm Dilthey, 'Der entwicklungsgeschichtliche Pantheismus nach seinem geschichtlichen Zusammenhang mit den älteren pantheistischen Systemen', *Archiv für Philosophie*, XIII (1900), no. 3, pp. 307-60; no. 4, pp. 445-82.

[2] Cf. *Grundlage*, *S.W.* I, 120.

[3] X. Léon, *Fichte et son temps*, I, pp. 101 f.

[4] *Leben und Briefwechsel*, I, p. 148.

[5] Actually, while rejecting the *Ding-an-sich* as a speculative presupposition. Fichte, in two places, tolerates it as a question of feeling—a hint both of his psychologism and of his theism: cf. *S.W.* I, 29, 280. It would be possible to interpret this departure as a desire to authenticate what Philonenko calls the experience of the 'common consciousness'.

epistemology. Later, Fichte would write: 'In my opinion the *Critique of Pure Reason* is in no way deficient in fundamentals; clearly it has them: but nothing in it is constructed, and the building materials—although already prepared—lie heaped about in a very arbitrary arrangement.'[1]

It is probably no accident that Fichte attributed the *Wissenschafts-lehre* to a visionary intuition connected with the French Revolution. For, in similar fashion, in his deduction of the *Wissenschafts-lehre*, he attributes the stimulation of conscious moral activity to a 'shock' received by the ego as it seeks infra-conscious expansion toward its pure totality.[2] Fichte's constant tendency is to encompass existence as a dialogue or struggle between the pure practical ego (which, in its essence, is 'striving')[3] and the whole set of exterior conditions flung up, as it were, simply to test its mettle. This is far indeed from Kant and the whole mood of the eighteenth century. And the identity of this historical break is not disguised: '...just as that nation [France] is delivering man from his external [material] bondage, my system liberates him from the chains of the *Ding-an-sich*, from everything that affects him from without'.[4]

C. THE DEDUCTION OF CONSCIOUSNESS

A philosophical system, says Fichte, must be reduced to a unitary principle. Compromises, however ingenious, like Kant's, will always have to be further resolved toward determinism or freedom, the either/or of 'dogmatism' and 'idealism'.[5] Kant has shown how it is apodictically certain that man belongs to a system of freedom, but he has not properly demonstrated how that system exists and

---

[1] *Zweite Einleitung, S.W.* I, p. 479 n.
[2] *Grundlage*, pp. 210 f. The 'shock' (*Anstoss*) of the Fichtean deduction of the conscious-ness is one of the critical elements of his entire range of epistemological metaphors. It may properly be compared with spanking breath into the newborn infant, thereby, as Philenenko puts it, causing 'the first cry in the world', *Liberté humaine*, p. 318.
[3] *Ibid.* pp. 261 f.
[4] *Briefwechsel*, I, 449–51.
[5] *Erste Einleitung, S.W.* I, 425–6. The following discussion depends largely on Fichte's arguments from the two 'introductions' he wrote in 1797, with the intent of clarifying in plain language misconceptions that had arisen from the more technical *Grundlage* and *Grundriss*. Fichte spent a considerable portion of his intellectual life re-explaining himself.

has even confused the demonstration. Moral man *is*, and freedom *is* (this is the reality of the matter), but it will be necessary to establish this fact by inassailable philosophical argument, both in order to create a science of knowledge to which all subsidiary disciplines of the intellect can be systematically joined and to exploit the proof of freedom pedagogically in the world so that men may have not only the capacity but the conviction to act rationally. The business of philosophy is to show how the world is possible. Fundamentally, this can be explained either from the premise of the *Ding* (nature, the external world) or of the *Intelligenz* (the rational self, the mind, the immaterial). Both doctrines depend on demonstrations *per hiatum*, but idealism has the immense advantage of furnishing proof of man's freedom and moral vocation, while 'dogmatism' ultimately reduces him to an automaton.

When we look at the world from a common-sense point of view, we are instantly certain of the reality of the physical objects surrounding us as well as of our own physical attributes. We are similarly convinced of a mysterious power of acting upon them in accordance with the sensation of spontaneity, a faculty which we call freedom. Idealism is not concerned to place these common-sense realities in doubt, but they *will* remain dubious so long as philosophy cannot explain such a world. The idealist demonstration will involve the notion that the entire physical world is only contingently real with regard to the original ego.[1]

Since at a conscious level we receive only the awareness of a double world of subject and object and since that world is *ex hypothesi* a condition of *consciousness itself*, the only conceivable way of explaining the original bifurcation of ego and thing, of knowing and being, is at a pre-conscious or infra-conscious level.[2] No man

---

[1] Among Fichte's many statements affirming this principle, cf. *Zweite Einleitung*, p. 455; *Wissenschaftslehre* of 1801, p. 96: '...it is a great error to suppose that transcendental idealism denies the empirical reality of the material world. It only points out in it the forms of knowledge and annihilates it therefore as for-itself-existing and absolute'; *Science of Rights*, p. 41: 'Philosophy must deduce our conviction of the existence of a world.' Consequently, Fichte calls his theory a 'Real-Idealismus' or an 'Ideal-Realismus', *Grundlage*, p. 281. Cf. *Grundlage*, *S.W.* 1, 183: 'no subject, no object; no object, no subject'.

[2] Cf. e.g. *Ethics*, p. 5: 'Knowing and being...are separated only in consciousness, because this separation is a condition of the possibility of all consciousness.'

can directly experience this genesis of the dualism of the 'real', since that experience is not available *for the consciousness*. However, the philosopher can experience it for him through a process of original reflection which Fichte calls 'intellectual intuition'.[1]

Accordingly, in philososophical discourse, the pure ego is originally an identity with itself. A = A is the primordial proposition of epistemology.[2] This stasis is first disrupted by a deduced sequence of infraconscious propositions established by philosophical reflection: (1) the ego posits itself (*sich setzt*); (2) the ego 'opposites' to itself a non-ego (*Nicht-Ich*); (3) both ego and non-ego are posited as 'divisible' (*theilbar*), that is, they mutually restrict each other as a condition of their being posited.[3]

But the status of the Fichtean ego is uncertain: Is it a cosmological or divine ego actually engaged in producing a world? Is it merely one of an indefinite number of human or finite egos metaphorically preparing a range of self-consciousness that is 'for it'? Is it a solipsistic ego producing a world that is 'for it' but incommunicable to any other? Inasmuch as Fichte failed to clarify these issues conclusively in his early philosophy, it is not surprising that he was innocently or wilfully misread by many contemporaries.

This type of problem did not arise in Kant's philosophy. The retention of the controversial but useful *Ding-an-sich* guaranteed an independent existence of nature apart from the ego or intelligence. Consequently, the ontological status and production of that nature were outside the concerns of the *Critique of Pure Reason*. This meant, in the first place, that the deity could be conceived of as a postulated final ground of nature as well as the warrant of the correspondence between nature and a 'kingdom of ends'. It meant also that the idea of a society of persons, whether viewed phenomenally as an agglomeration of particular interests or morally as a community of ends-in-themselves, was not ontologically questionable. But Fichte's desire to account not only for knowing but for the objects of knowing casts the status of the community in doubt. However, as we shall presently remark, in the development of the *Wissenschaftslehre* the teleological striving of the will or practical ego to recapture its primal unity at a conscious and voluntary level of activity will be

---

[1] *Zweite Einleitung*, pp. 463 f.　　[2] *Grundlage*, pp. 92–3.　　[3] *Ibid.* pp. 98, 104, 110.

reduplicated by human socio-historical striving toward a perfect community of persons.

We should also note the portentous ego-grounded opposition, characteristic of all phenomenality and history, between the Fichtean *Ich* and *Nicht-Ich*, which anticipates the famous Hegelian duality of Self and Other and the cosmic theme of alienation in general, as well as representing the more traditional philosophical cleavage between mind and matter or spirit and nature. Metaphysical realism, or what Fichte called 'dogmatism', never questioned a matter-of-fact world in which all human beings were axiomatically divided between their material and spiritual natures. Fichte, however, rejected the ideal possibility of such a separation. When the point of departure is from the ego, this traditional symmetry is disturbed both by the potential of 'otherness' which alien selves may have for the referential 'self' and by the will's essential striving to overcome all forms of alienation.

Finally, we find in these preliminary propositions of the *Grundlage* the first appearance of the famous triple-step 'dialectic' of thesis, antithesis and synthesis so often associated, mostly unduly and incorrectly, with Hegel.[1] The entire *Wissenschaftslehre* is an abstruse prolongation of this triptych. One should remark in passing the parentage of Fichte's procedures with the Kantian antinomies of pure reason and observe that, unlike the dialectic of Hegel's logic, Fichte's sequence of argument follows the methodology of the 'transcendental logic' which he and Kant shared (based on the law of non-contradiction), and is not to be associated with Hegel's 'ontological' revolution, where 'actual' and 'rational' are presumably joined.

Fichte's idealist perspective leads him to redefine the division between theoretical and practical reason, and to insist on the deduction of the consciousness from both perspectives.[2] This leads, respectively, to a 'real' and an 'ideal' sequence of acts correlative to the dualism of cognition and will. The familiar terminology is

---

[1] *Grundriss des Eigenthümlichen der Wissenschaftslehre*, *S.W.* I, 337–8. On Hegel, see especially G. E. Mueller, 'The Legend of "Thesis-Antithesis-Synthesis"', *Journal of the History of Ideas* (June 1958), pp. 411–14.

[2] *Grundlage*, pp. 119–23: theoretical deduction, pp. 123 ff.; practical deduction, pp. 246 ff.

employed. Under the aspect of practical reason, the ego posits the non-ego as limited (*begrenzt*) by itself. In the case of theoretical reason, the ego posits itself as limited by the non-ego.[1] Conclusions about free and determinate causality similar to those of Kant follow. In this sense noumenal and phenomenal spheres may be said to exist for the *Wissenschaftslehre*, but the ontological priority of the 'ideal' is made evident in view of its sole capacity to ground the real conditions of consciousness and life.

The relation between theoretical and practical reason may be expressed as follows. The practical ego is the 'real basis' (*Real-Grund*) of consciousness, even though it gives rise to the 'ideal' series; the theoretical ego is the *Ideal-Grund*, even though it manipulates the 'real'.[2] Without the theoretical activity we could never elevate ourselves to the understanding of our moral vocation. However, the pure practical ego is the goal or final cause of all theorizing. Ultimately, reality is complete self-determination. The non-ego expresses in itself (*an sich*) no reality except the inevitability of its being posited as a field of striving for the ego. In other words, nature is an instrument, but the pure ego is an end-in-itself. This interpretation, as will be easily seen, is certainly in the spirit of Kantianism, but it is underscored by a shifting of the balance toward pure will. In short, Fichte's philosophy is fundamentally an *ethical* idealism. Non-ego exists only for consciousness and for freedom: 'It is only through the means of a resistance [to Non-Ego] that the activity of the ego becomes perceptible and of a duration in time, since, otherwise, it would be beyond all time, which we cannot even think.'[3] In Fichte's terms, we can do all we will to do, but we cannot do it *immediately*.[4] To be sure, nature cannot be absolutely sloughed off, but it ought to be absolutely mastered: 'The world must *become* for me, what my body *is*.'[5]

One anomaly of Fichte's 'doctrine of science' is that it is simultaneously one of the most difficult and intellectualized master-

---

[1] *Ibid.* p. 246. It is to be noted that the theoretical deduction, if insufficient as a philosophical perspective, takes precedence over the practical deduction in Fichte's 'first philosophy', and, in effect, founds the basis of science from which the leap of freedom alone can establish a connection between thought and life.

[2] *Ibid.* pp. 153 f.; *Zweite Einleitung*, pp. 465 f.

[3] *Ethics*, p. 94.   [4] *Ibid.* p. 98.   [5] *Ibid.* p. 241.

pieces of Western abstract thought and one of the expressions of that thought most unambiguously grounded in the value priority of activity over contemplation. 'It is only through the medium of the moral law that I apprehend *myself*,' Fichte writes. 'And if I apprehend myself in that way, I apprehend myself necessarily as self-active; I contain life within myself, and I take it out of myself.'[1] He continued: 'Without self-consciousness there is, in general, no consciousness; but self-consciousness is possible only in the way I have demonstrated: I am only active.' The same dynamism of the ego, which, in practical form, changes the world, also fills the most arcane recesses of the *Wissenschaftslehre*.

How then does one join the philosopher and the existential man? We have already noted Kant's perplexity in reconciling a philosophical exposition of practical reason with the commonplace mechanism of moral action that he intended to justify—in short, the whole grave rupture between philosophy and life to which idealisms are especially susceptible. Fichte carries us still further away from familiar landmarks with his elimination of the *Ding-an-sich*. The 'two worlds' of Kant are, in a sense, reconciled, but at the intangible levels of an infra-conscious metaphor, of the teleology of the moral adept or, what amounts to the same thing, of the high ground of the idealist philosopher, who becomes inferentially a seer and a leader of disciples. 'In order to be able to *think* the moral world, we *contemplate* it in the material world...and this would be easily comprehended if both worlds appeared in all knowledge,' Fichte writes. 'But common experience teaches that this is not so; that, by far, the fewest individuals elevate themselves to pure thinking, and hence to the conception of a moral world, whilst, nevertheless, everyone has the sense of perception of the material world...'[2]

D. PHILOSOPHY AND LIFE

That is precisely the problem. Idealism is 'true', but it proposes a cosmic solution that only the shackles of diligent application can

---

[1] *Zweite Einleitung*, p. 406.   [2] *Wissenschaftslehre* of 1801, p. 128.

cause the man-in-the-street to accept.[1] If man is to gain in morality, he must understand in what sense he is and can be moral, a problem answered by the *Wissenschaftslehre*. Moreover, with Fichte, as with Kant, culture leads to freedom, and culture requires, above all, discipline: 'The individual must...be brought into contact with exemplary men, who would elevate him and teach him how he *ought* to be...There is no other way of culture.'[2] The moral law is universal, but practical reason does not work automatically. Fichte tried energetically to bridge this gap through his many 'popular' writings and lectures, later derided by Hegel as unworthy of a serious philosopher.[3] But even these productions, assuming that they were understood and applied by their audiences, touched only the very few.

In Fichte, the reflection of moral goals (identical with the knowledge and application of the *Wissenschaftslehre*) back upon the conditions of the phenomenal community produces a harsh discrimination in that social order which can be measured only by the moral progress of its individuals. The 'Jacobin' Fichte, like many of the advanced spirits of his time, had particularly bitter words for the entrenched ecclesiastical privilege and *noblesse héréditaire* of Europe; and against these post-feudal survivals he exalted the classical ideal of a nobility of merit, men worthy of humanity and the laurels of the commonwealth.[4] But the all-encompassing reality of the *Wissenschaftslehre* gives this Fichtean 'nobility' a peculiar and dogmatic pedagogical flavour, conveyed in mounting crescendos of fervour in the various sets of 'vocation' lectures and generally throughout his work. Inevitably, above all formal political institutions and activity are enthroned the Book (*Wissenschaftslehre*) and its prophets (the teachers of idealist philosophy). The subjects of the political state are, correspondingly, the pupils of a 'moralizing' commonwealth. But we must employ Fichte's own words to establish this essential connection:

The proper 'philosophemes' of a transcendental theory are, in themselves,

---

[1] Cf. *Grundlage*, p. 175 n: 'The majority of men would be more easily persuaded to take themselves for lumps of lava...than to consider themselves as an ego'.
[2] *Ethics*, p. 215.
[3] Cf. Hegel to Schelling, 3 Jan. 1807, *Briefe von und an Hegel*, I, 131.
[4] Cf. *Beiträge, S.W.* VI, 190 f.

Metaphysics and consciousness

dead and they have no influence whatever, either good or bad, over life, no more than a portrait can live and move. Thus it is completely contrary to the purpose of this philosophy to share itself with men as such. The scholar, as educator and leader of the people, especially as popular teacher, should certainly possess it as a tutelary regulative principle, and only in him will it become really practical.[1]

Beyond politics, the Fichtean community is really a school of moral discipline whose aim is the increasingly broader inculcation of the *Wissenschaftslehre* as a life principle. At the same time, there is a recognition (foreshortened in the *Reden* and, generally, in the later 'chiliastic' writings) that a hierarchy of morality and intellect is destined to endure for a very long time.

Given the conditions of politics, literacy and social cohesion in the German states of Fichte's time, it is not strange to see this devotee of the Revolution agreeing with the national intelligentsia that 'the dignity of liberty should be raised from bottom to top; but liberation without disorder can proceed only from top to bottom'.[2] That was a commonplace; nobody wanted a *dix août* or a Terror. Order was indeed a value, a supreme one, for Fichte, as it had been for Rousseau and Kant: 'The source of all evils in our present states, as they are constituted, is *disorder*, and the impossibility to produce order.'[3] But a pontification of the following sort may astonish: 'The lower classes [*Stände*] have the vocation...to work directly upon irrational nature for the sake of the rational beings, in order to prepare it for the ends of the latter...'[4] This judgment was given in 1798, when Fichte still praised France as the pole star of mankind. With Kant Platonic terms re-enter the Western philososophical vocabulary: with Fichte, there is a fundamental Platonic reorientation of political theory, although this is a Plato stood on his head. The Fichtean philosopher does not return from

---

[1] *Rückerinnerungen, Antworten, Fragen, S.W.* v, 350.
[2] *Beiträge*, p. 44.
[3] *Rights*, p. 386. On this point, Fichte is conspicuously at odds with the *Sturm und Drang* and radical Romanticism.
[4] *Ethics*, p. 375; cf. p. 376: '...the lower classes cannot well fulfill their duty—to raise their professions—unless they are directed by the higher classes; and hence *it is their duty to respect the members of the higher classes*'.

the sunlight to the cave with his truth, but attempts to drag all the prisoners out into the sunlight.[1]

Though the dynamism of Marxian thought recalls Fichte in numerous ways, Marx has mediated the great gulf between 'philosophy' and 'life' by translating the intense frustrations of idealism into the sphere of work and physical deprivation. Here, activity has been dissociated from thought (the premise of the eleventh thesis on Feuerbach), and political violence has supplanted the 'noiseless revolution' of the conscience. The general class will be no longer the educators of the race, but its mass of general sufferers whose common will denies and negates all existing *de facto* interest. Despite elements of intellectual elitism in Marx, this tendency can hardly be denied. And there is also a hint of Rousseau's castigation of the division of labour in Marx, which is antithetical to Fichte's economic and tutelary theories of political life. However, it should be pointed out that 'the withering away of the state', far from being a Marxist eccentricity, is clearly suggested by Fichte.[2]

E. PHENOMENOLOGY AND IDEAL PEDAGOGY

One further intriguing characteristic of the *Wissenschaftslehre* remains to be covered. This is a facet of the theoretical deduction of consciousness in the *Grundlage* and *Grundriss*; and it concerns the relation of the philosopher to the experiential subject. Here we approach the question of philosophy and life from another angle.

According to Fichte the primal separation between subject and object occurs at an infra-conscious level and is consequently not available as a common 'fact of consciousness'. Rather, its necessity must be deduced by the philosopher in 'intellectual intuition'.[3] This suggests, in connection with the genesis of knowledge, a

---

[1] If we consider Plato as a philosopher of memory, the past, and the contemplation of value and Fichte as a philosopher of striving, the future, and the construction of value, we come closer to their inescapable opposition. Philonenko, *Liberté humaine*, p. 73 n., has some good remarks on this.

[2] See ahead, pp. 282–5.

[3] A. Philonenko puts forward strong arguments for rejecting the concept of 'intellectual intuition' as the clue to Fichte's earlier *Wissenschaftslehre* (*Liberté humaine*, pp. 78–9); however, his thesis does not affect its centrality in Fichte's philosophical development taken as a whole.

disparity of phasing between 'real' and 'philosophical' viewpoints. Indeed, Fichte describes this dualism at some length in his *Second Introduction*, where he points out that philosophies failing to incorporate this distinction have no aptitude for connecting philosophical analysis with experience of the common consciousness:

> In the *Wissenschaftslehre* there are two very different series of intellectual (*geistiges*) activity: that of the ego which the philosopher observes and that of the observations of the philosopher. In the opposed philosophies, there is but *one* series of intellection, that of the thoughts of the philosopher: this because its material is not introduced as thinking.[1]

It is the double series, he asserts in the *Grundriss*, which makes a phenomenology of the consciousness possible.[2] Philosophy can now reproduce the history of consciousness-in-itself; both the *res gestae* and the historian are predicated. However, as the *Sittenlehre* tells us: '...I cannot be for myself without being myself, and I am that in the intelligible world only, which has been presented to my eyes by intellectual intuition.'[3] In the *Second Introduction*, while affirming that the ego constructed by the *Wissenschaftslehre* is an abstraction,[4] Fichte attempts to answer how it can be used to explain reality: 'The ego that is self-constructed [i.e. by the philosopher] is none other than one's own. It can intuit the given act of the ego only in itself, and to do this it must accomplish the act.'[5] The philosopher intuits himself. What Fichte means is that, given the insight, any man would construct the *Wissenschaftslehre* for himself and would prove it by his practical or moral action. But we are still left with the notion of a moral hierarchy judged according to the standards of the *Wissenschaftslehre*.

This is not all. Any objectification of the process of the *Wissenschaftslehre* in history will involve a staggered series of intuitions in which the philosophical series always leads and furthers the series

---

[1] *Zweite Einleitung*, p. 454. Cf. also *Grundlage, ibid.* 216: 'In the first case there is only simple reflection on the phenomenon—the reflection of the observer—while in the second case we are in the presence of a reflection upon the reflection—which is the reflection of the philosopher upon that manner of observing.'
[2] *Grundriss*, pp. 331–2. Fichte does not himself employ the word 'phenomenology'.
[3] *Ethics*, p. 94.   [4] *Op. cit. S.W.* I, 515.
[5] *Ibid.* pp. 459–60. See the discussion by X. Léon on form and content, *Fichte et son temps*, I, 380.

of common experience. The connection between philosophy and life is made by the metaphor of leadership and discipleship, until, at the end—the integrity of consciousness (which means also liberation by overcoming of the subject-object duality through the force of 'practicity')—both series are seen to coincide.[1]

This notion can be illustrated by a parallel chart of the stages of consciousness which Jules Vuillemin has drawn from the *Wissenschaftslehre* in his brilliant work on transcendental idealism:[2]

Derivative Reflection (First series of philosophical abstraction)	*Original Reflection* (Second series of the real consciousness)		*Derivative Reflection* (Superior philosophical perspective)
E_1 Determinability–Imagination	Consciousness of production	A_2 Sensation	Intuition
D_1 Substantiality		B_2 Intuition	Understanding
C_1 Causality		C_2 Understanding	Judgment
B_1 Relation			
A_1 Determination	Consciousness of activity	D_2 Judgment	(Reason)
		E_2 Reason	

It is unnecessary to give a full explanation of the chart. Our attention is confined to the two columns on the right which express the procedures I have been describing. Here one can see how the 'derivative reflection' of philosophy begins one leg up on the 'original reflection' that represents the experience of consciousness. By its passage to the standpoint of reason philosophy leads humanity into the ultimate condition of the 'self-determining' and the 'self-determined' where the subject alone determines its own destiny as an object.[3] The stages of this process within the consciousness are expressed by a

---

[1] Cf. A. Philonenko, *Liberté humaine*, pp. 170, 316, 329.
[2] From J. Vuillemin, *L'héritage kantien et la révolution copernicienne* (Paris, 1954), p. 89.
[3] *Grundlage*, p. 244.

familiar hierarchy of (idealist) philosophical labels. If a transfer from phenomenology to history is made, we may expect to see not only a conception of history drawn in terms of creating a new harmony for the original ego but also a history that is to be led by a phalanx of the *Wissenschaftslehre*, by those who 'love the Idea.'[1] The 'pragmatic history of the consciousness' presented by the 'first moment' of the *Wissenschaftslehre* of the Jena period suggested a system of knowledge absolutely self-creating in itself, or at least from the point of view of the scholar, in essence the philosopher, who is 'the highest, truest man'.[2] Amid the dialectic of *Ich* and *Nicht-Ich*, the critical third term of rationalist philosophy—God— had been left out. Fichte wished neither to say that, having discovered the *Wissenschaftslehre*, he was God, nor to claim that each man who raised himself to the moral life was the God of his own experience. He wished only to show that man is unrestrictedly free. Fichte stated his position in the following way: 'God and religion are given only in life: but the philosopher, as such, is not the full, integral man, but in the position of abstraction.' Consequently, 'the philosopher has no God and can have none; he has only a concept (*Begriff*) of the concept or of the Idea of God'.[3] It goes without saying that this 'Begriff' was the *Wissenschaftslehre*. However, under the blows of his critics and beset with certain problems inherent in the *Wissenschaftslehre*, Fichte was led gradually to posit an absolute (a Being in which Knowing itself is annihilated [*vernichtet*]) beyond the absolute knowing of the *Wissenschaftslehre*. Thus, in the presentation of 1804, the 'pragmatic history' was made a phenomenon of the absolute, and this position was repeated in all ulterior presentations. As Vuillemin expresses it: 'The passage from genesis [of consciousness] to facticity [of being], from the *für sich* to the *an sich*, is simply the passage from man to God as the centre and principle of philosophy.'[4] The ego–philosophy of the *Wissenschaftslehre* was not yielded up, but it became progressively shielded by notions of faith and

---

[1] See Emmanuel Hirsch, *Christentum und Geschichte in Fichtes Philosophie* (Tübingen, 1920), p. 45.
[2] *Vocation of the Scholar*, p. 150.
[3] *Rückerinnerungen*, etc. *S.W.* v, 348.
[4] J. Vuillemin, *Héritage kantien*, p. 126. Cf. *Sittenlehre* of 1812, *N.W.* III, 45: 'The ego must appear to itself only as appearance and not as an independent being, for it is not to be its own life, but the life of something external, something other, the concept.'

beatitude.[1] Beyond the grasping for abstract correlation between life and epistemology, Fichte was concerned to give substance to his notion of community by covering it with a metaphysics that had not been inherent in the practical deductions of the 'first moment' of the *Wissenschaftslehre*. Consequently, we must turn our attention to this problem.

[1] Cf. *Way to the Blessed Life*, in Smith, II, 474–5; also *Wissenschaftslehre* of 1804, *N.W.* II, 291. See Gueroult, *Doctrine de la Science*, II, 99–148, *passim*.

3

LEGALITY AND MORALITY

A. IDEALISM, CONTRACTUALISM AND SOCIETY

Fichte's ideal of the truly moral individual depends on the concept of 'sociability'.[1] The progressive deduction of his 'practical series' in the phenomenology of consciousness leads inescapably to the conclusion that no man is moral by himself, but only within a fixed social order which is conducive to the moral life. 'Each one', writes Fichte, '*shall* live in a community, for otherwise he cannot produce harmony with himself, as is absolutely commanded.'[2] However, following the break in history at the French Revolution and the break in philosophy at transcendental idealism, this community will be no longer a 'natural society' in the sense intended by the Enlightenment or its progeny of theorists of the economic natural order and *laissez-faire*.[3] Diderot's hypothesis that the general will of mankind emerged from man's natural capacity for reason in an 'acte pur d'entendement', already forsworn by Rousseau, is now further surpassed by Fichte in a manner that not only denies the automaticity of political relationships, and beyond them the ethical bonds of community, but insists the more imperiously on their necessity. They must be brought into being in the realm of freedom, which is to say, the whole realm of the future open to man's purposive striving.

But the problems of idealism render especially difficult the philosophical grounding of the human community. The implication of the self-enclosed ego and its productions can ostensibly lead in the direction of either theosophism or solipsism. The existential barrier to all effective communication between moral persons would seem to be closed. But again, nothing could have been further from Fichte's intention. He was on the contrary resolute to prove the

---

[1] Cf. X. Léon, *Fichte et son temps*, I, 490.   [2] *Ethics*, p. 247.
[3] After strong intimations of so doing in the *Naturrecht* (*Science of Rights*) of 1796–7, Fichte breaks entirely with the Enlightenment view of natural harmony in the *Closed Commercial State* of 1800.

Idealism, contractualism and society

moral unity of mankind from an entirely immanent perspective.[1]
Somehow, the man who wrote that 'Kant's great discovery is
subjectivity'[2] must be understood as a foe of that subjectivism with
which his enemies taxed him. His own statements are categorical:
'Man is destined to live in society; he has the duty to live there;
he is not an integral man but is in contradiction with himself if he
lives apart.'[3] How, then, can the ego be propounded as a social ego,
as a finite ego-in-general? What is the connection between the
Fichtean 'monad' and 'monadology'?

With Kant there was no question of positing the transcendental
ego as an absolute because it was always ontologically limited by the
thing-in-itself. The possibility of conceding a reality outside the ego
established the existence of persons; at least there was no likely
contradiction between the real status of other individuals and the
reality of the self.[4] With Fichte, on the other hand, there is a primary
paradox between the objective 'Other' opposed to the subjective
'Self' in the consciousness of the finite ego and the notion of a world
of moral persons. On the other hand, if this problem can be breached,
the solution will lead beyond the characteristically 'liberal' restraint-
of-restraints pattern that looms so large in the Kantian view of
legality and politics toward making, in Hegel's phrase, a 'concrete
universal' of the ethical community.

In Fichte's earliest sustained effort to deal with these problems,
the *Beiträge* of 1793, he had not yet worked out the structure or
implications of his philosophical system. Politically, his position
was radical-liberal and contractual, with heavy inputs of the *Social
Contract*. Philosophically, it was Kantian, with the implications of
the 'primacy of practical reason' carried to their most acute pitch.
But, withal, the work is a curious mixture. The liberalism does indeed
set the value of the individual against that of the state, precisely
because the states known to Fichte deny the imperative of moral

[1] Cf. *Vocation of Man*, p. 342: '[The] consciousness of all individuals taken together constitutes the complete consciousness of the universe.'
[2] Fichte to Reinhold, 28 April 1795, *Leben und Briefwechsel*, II, 227.
[3] *Zweite Einleitung*, p. 306.
[4] Kant, *Foundations*, p. 64. Cf. Gueroult, *Doctrine de la Science*, I, 335. Actually, Kant's explanation of intersubjectivity from the 'practical' standpoint may be regarded as unsatisfactory, because the impossibility of knowing the *Ding-an-sich* would seem to jeopardize the moral recognition of other persons through experience.

progress, are 'clocks turning as if everything had been set once and for all'.[1] But, at the same time, the mission of society is not only set against the state, as liberalism would have it, but also in a certain sense against the individual: society is the great matrix in which culture advances and men are improved or improve themselves.[2] Although Fichte refers constantly to the 'progress of culture' and indeed justifies the Revolution as an inevitable consequence of its stagnation, this ideal of the 'experimental knowledge of the human soul' (*Erfahrungsseelenkunde*) is a fundamentally ahistorical and rationalist notion describing a pure opposition of the unjust *is* and the reasonable *ought to be*.[3] History is understood chiefly as the historical conventionalism of the reactionaries. When Fichte writes, '...we never find anything in the history of the world but that which we have put there ourselves', he is opposing prescription with voluntarism.[4] At the same time, he is conscious that history measured by a progress of popular reform is preferable to an anti-history of revolutionary explosion.[5] The degree of tension between these two perspectives resembles Kant's, but must also be tangibly related to the fact that for a radical in 1793 the destruction of combines of privilege seemed much more pressing than the building of new social harmonies.

The second matter is, however, foreshadowed by the development of Kantian ethics in the essay. And in the form it originally takes for Fichte the criterion of history is absolutely pushed aside:

What is the highest purpose of the political association? depends on the solution of this question: What is the purpose of each individual? The answer to this is purely moral and should be based on the moral law, which alone governs man as man and obligates him to a final purpose... once it is allowed that the final purpose of humanity, taken as individuals and in general, should not be determined from the laws of experience, but according to its original form, the historian has no part in it...[6]

The 'original form' is, of course, the law of duty, as expressed in the faculty of will or 'practical reason'. And this, according to Kant, is

---

[1] *Beiträge, S.W.* VI, 216.   [2] *Ibid.* p. 139.   [3] *Ibid.* pp. 63-4.   [4] *Ibid.* p. 39.
[5] Cf. *Denkfreiheit, S.W.* VI, 9.
[6] *Beiträge*, p. 62. However, an ambiguous dissociation. Historical teleology is exchanged for historical empiricism; cf. pp. 91-92, on progress and development.

the intelligible and timeless possession of every man. Since Fichte is still working within the premises of Kantian dualism, it remains possible to regard the conceptual community of moral persons as anterior to any possibility or act of social formation. Thus that community may be regarded as *a priori* and the problem of deducing it does not arise.

Rather, it is the whole range of social and political organization that will be deduced *from* this principle. The political conventionalism of Rousseau is accepted, but it is based on the notion of a moral state of nature. This is no longer an anthropological theory. As Gueroult puts it: 'the *nature of man* designates his essence, and the *state of nature* [implies] the spontaneous and original conformity to that essence...'[1] This both denies the historicity of Kant's view of moral progress as the struggle to overcome radical evil and that of Rousseau's view of man's career as a record of corruption through society. On the other hand, it accepts and freezes Rousseau's notion of 'original goodness', while emphatically adopting Kant's 'primacy of practical reason' and his conception of civil order as the instrument for the protection of original rights founded on the eternal existence of the moral personality.

Fichte is obviously disturbed by Rousseau's suggestion that the act of political association creates moral relationships. 'Would it not be necessary for me to be a moral person in order to conclude a contract?' he asks.[2] Thus, to describe the sphere of priorities he submits a sketch of concentric circles. The outermost and most comprehensive one is labelled 'conscience' (i.e. the absolute moral person); successively inscribed we find the circles of 'natural right', the 'right of contract (in general)', and finally the 'civil contract'.[3] This paradigm is obviously very useful for the defence of the rights of man and the assault on the dynastic state and its reigning ideology of historical prescription. But it is inefficacious for the building of the new order in a world whose morality is exceedingly problematic, and it will be inconsistent with the genetic dispositions of the *Wissenschaftslehre*.

In the development of the practical deduction of the *Wissen-*

---

[1] M. Gueroult, 'Nature humaine et état de nature', p. 380.
[2] *Beiträge*, p. 134. [3] *Ibid.* p. 133.

schaftslehre, Fichte's views on the character of the social order were already changing in a collectivist direction. In the second lecture of the 'Vocation of the Scholar' series of 1794 he had already asserted, more positively than in the *Beiträge*, the social destiny of man, the 'relation of reasonable beings to each other'.[1] He had further said, however, that 'political society is not a part of the absolute purpose of human life. . . but it is, under certain conditions, a possible means toward the formation of a perfect society'.[2] This dichotomy of society and state was to persist throughout Fichte's writings, with the former—conceived with ever greater concreteness—existing as a higher (moral) goal and the latter as a gradually more powerful instrument of social perfectibility. When state and society are thus opposed it does not necessarily mean (as the liberal cliché would have it) that the emphasis on society leads to theories of the 'weak state'. When society takes on the meaning of a tight-knit moral community, as is progressively true in Fichte from at least 1794 on, we may expect the urgency of the end-in-itself to create an instrument-in-itself cut to its own measure. The preliminary and most detailed exploration of this relationship is found in Fichte's two formal practical continuations of the *Wissenschaftslehre*, the *Grundlage des Naturrechts* of 1796–7 and the *System der Sittenlehre* of 1798. They are complementary works that ground Fichte's notion of the moral community and deal *in extenso* with his first complete, and revolutionary, consideration of the problem of legality and morality.

B. THE LEGAL AND MORAL COMMUNITIES

For reasons shortly to be explained, Fichte thought it necessary to deduce the spheres of right and ethics separately, with the deduction of right intentionally anterior to that of morality. This means that our first hypothetical contact with a plural society of individuals will occur in terms of the legal system. In this respect Fichte's 1796 work on natural right occupies a position of absolute centrality in his philosophical endeavour. Its first pages are nothing less than an attempt to deduce the conditions of intersubjectivity, showing

[1] *Vocation of the Scholar*, p. 160.　　　　　　　　[2] *Ibid.* pp. 163–4.

how the object (non-ego) accounted for by the theoretical deduction of the *Wissenschaftslehre* can, indeed must, be regarded as another free subject if the ego itself is to be free. The act of recognition confers upon the consciousness its practical reality.

'[The Ego]', Fichte writes, 'must posit a limit to...its practical activity.'[1] But, viewed practically, this means not only that the ego feels itself limited by an external world which is a sub-conscious product of its imagination (non-ego), but also by other sources of freedom that restrain it. If I as a free being am to sense my freedom, then another must be free; or, in Fichte's words: 'no free being becomes conscious of itself without at the same time becoming conscious of other similar beings'.[2] We have already noted Fichte's practical principle that there is no consciousness without self-consciousness (*Selbstbewusstseyn*); now we have the consequences of this explicitation. The *Naturrecht* declares: 'Man becomes man only amongst men; and since he can only be man, and would not be at all unless he were man, it follows that *if man is to be at all, there must be men.*'[3]

In the further deduction of the 'Science of Rights', after noting significantly in passing that 'all individuals must be educated to be men; otherwise they would not be men',[4] Fichte goes on to explore the legal implications of the community of individuals. The exposition is fundamentally individualistic ('there can be no *mine* without a *his*'),[5] contractual (Fichte prescribes the need for *three* contracts in the deduction of the state), and descriptive of 'negative' (liberal) freedom. The common supposition of Fichte's passage from a very 'liberal' period in 1796–7 to a very 'socialist' one in 1800 should certainly be moderated by recognizing the systematic role of the various writings to which these interpretations are attached. Fichte's system of law is highly mechanistic and conventional (in a rationalist sense), hence 'liberal', for a very good reason. It expresses the 'technique' of practical reason before the strictly moral aspects of will and personality have been introduced. The ethical system of 1798, rather than registering conceptual changes in the *Wissenschaftslehre*, will rebalance the doctrine and complete it.

[1] *Rights*, p. 42.   [2] *Wissenschaftslehre* of 1801, p. 138.   [3] *Rights*, p. 60.
[4] *Ibid.* p. 61.   [5] *Ibid.* p. 72.

There is a very arresting statement in the *Naturrecht* with regard to the deduction of the community: 'No free being can recognize the other as such, unless both mutually thus recognize each other; and no one can treat the other as a free being, unless both mutually thus treat each other.'[1] Fichte's abstract and perfectly timeless explanation of how legal society is possible does not conclude in a 'struggle for recognition' of which lordship and bondage is the outcome; rather, he proceeds to the contractual state. However, the famous image of Hegel is prefigured in this passage.[2] Another, more Hegelian treatment of the master–slave problem, now historicized, will occur in Fichte's *Grundzüge* lectures of 1804–5.

The *Sittenlehre* repeats and deepens the demonstration of the *Naturrecht*. 'It is a condition of self-consciousness, of egohood (*Ichheit*), to assume an actual rational being outside of myself,' Fichte writes.[3] He emphasizes that the existence of only one other centre of liberty outside the self can be strictly proven by this means, but that it is not excluded that 'there may be many individuals outside of me that influence me'.[4] Here again, in germ, is the Hegelian situation of Self and Other, and an indication of the way that idealism passes back and forth between its essential binary focus and a plural one in its phenomenological proceedings.

After a sequence of demonstrations treating of the dual determinability of free acts according to perspective, Fichte arrives at the important deduction of the moral community:

Each one is to produce absolute harmony with himself in all others outside him, for only on condition of this harmony is he himself free and independent. First of all, therefore, each one *shall* live in a community, for otherwise he cannot produce harmony with himself, as is absolutely commanded. Whoever separates himself from mankind renounces his final end and aim and holds the extension of morality to be utterly indifferent.[5]

Thus, the original ego of the *Wissenschaftslehre* has become a particular ego in the middle of a world of egos, receiving its limita-

---

[1] *Rights*, p. 72.
[2] On the Hegelian genesis of self-consciousness, see my essay 'Notes on Hegel's "Lordship and Bondage" ', *The Review of Metaphysics* (June 1966), pp. 785–91.
[3] *Ethics*, p. 232.   [4] *Ibid.* pp. 232–4.   [5] *Ibid.* p. 247.

tion not only from the inert non-ego of nature but also, at the practical level, from the freedom of others. As a self-conscious person, it cannot take itself for the centre of the world. As Gueroult remarks: 'In its turn the sensible world has to receive a reality that my ego is incapable of producing, at least by itself. . .'[1]

However, this is not all. In the *Sittenlehre* Fichte is interested not solely in producing individuals but in producing them so that they will progressively harmonize according to the principle of the unity of reason. The ethics of duty establishes the dimension of history. Past the 'philosophical' infra-conscious unity, wherever there is self-consciousness, there is also individuality. The noumenal task is to reduce it toward unity, at the same time bringing about the conjunctive inner and outer harmony referred to in the passage above.[2] Whether Fichte conceived of the obligations of moral finality as lying within the world or merely within the soul is a thorny question. In the *Sittenlehre* of 1798 it is best to concede the latter solution, not least because Fichte's imagery of the ideal church or ethical commonwealth so much resembles Kant's argument in *Religion Beyond the Limits of Reason Alone*, which had come out in 1793.[3] Still, one cannot ignore in Fichte's projections a real tangibility that Kant lacks. Regarding his community Fichte declares: 'Each one *shall* have this same end, and it is the duty of each, as sure as he desires to promote universal moral culture, to induce each other one to make this his end.' Ultimately, the solution to that problem will be the scholarly state. Whether the moral unity of man proposed in the *Sittenlehre* is ideal or graspable, it is clear that the progress toward this end can have immense phenomenal repercussions. The chief historical acquisitions (Greek politics, Roman law, St. John's gospel, Luther, Kant, the *Wissenschaftslehre*) can be deciphered. Fichte's later writings will be obsessively involved with translating his earlier thought into act.

---

[1] Gueroult, *Doctrine de la Science*, I, 339.

[2] Cf. Léon, *Fichte et son temps*, I, 510 f.; *Nature of the Scholar*, p. 230: 'Human life has been divided by nature into many parts in order that it may form itself to unity.'

[3] Cf. *Ethics*, p. 248. In his opuscule, also of 1798, the *Ascetik*, Fichte writes specifically: 'Morality is never to be entirely reached; the state constitution [i.e. legality] is capable of fulfilment.' His remarks on mystics shed some light (*Ethics*, pp. 157, 159): 'The final end of all rational being lies necessarily in infinitude. . . The error of the mystics is based on their representing this infinite. . . as an end attainable in time.'

Legality and morality

C. THE IDEALIST INSTRUMENTAL STATE

From what we have already seen of the *Wissenschaftslehre* it is evident that the concentric circles of the *Beiträge* are superseded. This means that the ethical principle of society will have to be built toward, not established *a priori*. It will account for an intensification of the teleological hints already dropped in that early work. Although it would be erroneous to read into Fichte's legal volume, the *Naturrecht*, any but the barest historical overtones, it is permissible in the light of all his later philosophy to regard not only the deduction of the state but historical systems of legal coercion as anterior to the possibility of an ethical community. This idea begins to find expression with the concept of the *Notstaat* (or 'state of necessity') in the *Sittenlehre*, where it is described as 'the first condition of gradual progress to a legal and rational state', the latter being itself a prefiguration of the demise of political coercion.[1] The *Sittenlehre* reflects a historical teleology back on the logical deduction of the *Naturrecht*.

To the adepts of transcendental philosophy in the 1790s it seemed perfectly clear that the rationalist communion between ethics and natural right served only to yoke the aspirations of political liberty to a suffocating paternalism rooted in the alien obligation of civil obedience. This is indeed what Fichte meant when, in the course of his inflammatory pamphlet addressed to Frederick William II on the subject of censorship, he declared: 'No, prince...you should not be *good* to us: you should be *just*.'[2] To have justice it no longer sufficed to cast one's yearning toward the exalted realm of the *jus naturale* if centuries and codes of legal subtlety had pulverized it into *de facto* servitude. What the advanced minds demanded was effective, not ideal, justice, a measure of equality *in situ* and not merely before God. By the same token, the essence of Kantian ethics was man's immanent judgment of himself, excluding the possibility not only of moral coercion by other persons but of all transcendent moral authority whatever. Or, as Fichte puts it, 'although I am subject, I am subject only to

[1] *Ethics*, pp. 251–2.   [2] *Denkfreiheit*, p. 9.

226

my own will'.[1] In this perspective, the difference between the ideas of morality and legality becomes absolutely qualitative, marking the absolute distinction between internality and externality: 'Morality commands categorically; law merely permits...'[2]

Natural right then becomes not a transcendent source of authority from which positive laws are derived according to milieu and circumstance, but rather, a teleological goal for rational civil constitutions. As Fichte puts it in 1796: 'There is no status of original rights for man. Man attains rights only in a community with others... Original rights are, therefore, a pure fiction, but a fiction necessary for the purpose of science.'[3] By 1812, following deep sea-changes in history and in his own thought, Fichte will declare: 'Right is coercive power which, through art, is directed toward a purposive concept [*Zweckbegriff*; i.e. morality]. All right is the right of the state; outside the state there is no right. No one has rights but a citizen.'[4] We are still far from that conclusion, but the way is opened.

In the *Beiträge*, all positive legality depended on the general power to make contracts, contracts depended on natural right, and this latter was posterior to the moral state of nature. The civil contract was, therefore, also a moral contract, provided it was just.[5] This was a completely rationalist perspective which, despite hints of the 'progress of culture', regarded man as a being who, in all times and places, 'carries in the depth of his heart a divine spark that raises him above the animal and makes him the citizen of a world where God is the leading member...'[6] But by 1794 Fichte appeared to share Kant's horror of the pre-historical 'state of nature' and to find in it not the 'essential' man of morality but the savage driven by instinctual impulses of egoism. Morality now became not the origin, but the *Endzweck*, of the state. The *Naturrecht* is Fichte's

---

[1] *Rights*, p. 152; cf. p. 192: 'Each has a claim only to the legality of the other, not to his morality.' [2] *Ibid*. p. 81.
[3] *Ibid*. p. 160. Of course, Fichte bases his system on 'natural rights' but he connects their possibility exclusively with the existence of a lawful community, with 'civic reason'. Throughout his career, the right to be educated receives heavy stress; cf. *Denkfreiheit*, p. 24; 'Each one has the right to receive infinite instruction'; *Aus dem Entwurfe zu einer politischen Schrift* (1813), *S.W.* VII, 581: 'Their right to education is ...their original right.' On the implications of this, see ahead, pp. 269 f.
[4] *Rechtslehre* of 1812, *N.W.* II, 502.   [5] Cf. *Denkfreiheit*, p. 23.   [6] *Ibid*. p. 11.

philosophical demonstration that the conditions of legality are not to be deduced from the moral law, but are intended to subserve and prepare the coming of that law. *Recht* is to be the propaedeutic for *Sittlichkeit*. Since right concerns the external possibilities of persons acting on other persons with the end of liberty, it will be designated as practical philosophy, but its content will in effect be the juridical rules which moral philosophy has prescribed as technical conditions for the edification of the moral community. This was prefigured in Kant, but not in so dissociated a form.[1] Right in this sense neither reduplicates the moral law (because it does not prescribe what *ought to be done*) nor does it resemble natural (physical) law (because it requires the human input of rationality): it simply postulates an order which *ought to be* objectively if a group of persons living together are to act in such a way that no external obstacles are opposed to their exercise of autonomy. The mechanics of lawfulness is thus prior to what was formerly called 'natural law' and is a precondition of its appearance.

Fichte did not, of course, intend by his separation of legality and morality to give law an amoral, let alone an immoral, privilege. He is intercepting the dialectic of reason at a moment when, by virtue of the non-existence of either the moral person or community, the moral question is not yet raised, thereby preceding the human content with a framework of rules.[2] But he is also preparing the political skeleton for the reception of the individual, contrary to the practice of the liberal tradition. Fichte's man will be made for the Sabbath.[3]

There are surely three prime dangers to his method. The first is that, given the teleological dynamism of his philosophy, the method will orient the coerciveness of the state not to the achievement of a tolerable community (the general liberal criterion and 'ideology')

---

[1] See above, pp. 161–2. Gueroult, 'Nature humaine et état de nature', p. 380, goes too far when he writes: 'the doctrine of the *Notstaat*...tends to make right a condition and not a consequence of ethics [this is true], in other words, tends to establish a concept of right completely different from Kant's [this is too strong, because the relation of Kantian public law to transcendental ethics is ambiguous]'.

[2] Cf. X. Léon, *Fichte et son temps*, I, 499.

[3] The logical anteriority of law tends to absolutize it both with respect to ethics and human nature; cf. *Rights*, p. 372: 'It is a very false proposition that law is instituted for the benefit of the governed...Law is, *because* it is; it is absolute; it must be carried out'.

but to the future obligation of a moral one. Plead as he may that 'the state is not a moral, but simply a legal body' in 1796,[1] the basic view of the *Naturrecht*, carried to extremes, cannot but verge on the later proposition that 'right has the task of preparing the moral law on earth'.[2]

In the second place, the Fichtean scheme comes perilously close to saying that the end (which is dubiously within the world, dubiously outside it) justifies the means (which are empirically all too tangible). To be sure, 'there is only a *right* of compulsion, not a *duty* to compel', and moral man is supposed to obey his conscience and suspend the external law unless it is a question of undermining the legal system by that act.[3] To be sure, 'a morally-minded man can never think of bringing men to virtue by compulsory means...nor can morality be compelled through theoretical conviction'.[4] It is, however, 'absolute moral duty to unite with others in a state'.[5] One is 'not allowed to withdraw from [his] country'.[6] And, indeed, 'the duties toward the whole, as the highest and absolutely commanded duties, are to be called *immediate* and *unconditional* duties'.[7] As we have already seen, the lower classes (not necessarily but effectively the poor, for it is a matter of those untouched by the *Wissenschaftslehre*) have a duty to work on 'irrational nature' to accomplish the ends of 'rational beings': a kind of idealist's 'great leap forward'. In this respect, Fichte's *Notstaat* resembles the 'revolutionary state' of Robespierre and Saint-Just: it must last until the advent of reason and morality, just as the latter had to await peace. The French interval, if more violent, was at least shorter.

One may of course argue that Fichte's abstract legal system is 'ideal' and that if it need not accommodate men of good will, it at least requires a cohesive citizenship with a political will and rulers of skill and rectitude. One may say of Fichte, as of Kant, that the restrictiveness of his policy is not oppressive because of the inherent justice of actions it assumes. Fichte, too, attempts to define the 'republic', excluding the extremes of despotism and direct democracy, and he says of the legal constitution, which is 'valid for all time',

---

[1] *Ibid.* p. 368.
[2] *Rechtslehre* of 1812, *N.W.* II, 502; cf. *Sittenlehre* of 1812, *N.W.* III, 92–3.
[3] *Rights*, p. 142.   [4] *Ethics*, pp. 329–31.   [5] *Ibid.* p. 250.
[6] *Ibid.* p. 251.   [7] *Ibid.* pp. 272–3.

that 'infinite modifications [to it] are, of course, possible'.[1] But a criticism of such a defence may be submitted.

If Fichte is describing a *Vernunftstaat* (as one might expect in a sequence of logical deductions), then his polity can have only an ideal significance: it has comparatively little to say to the year 1796. However, there are a variety of hints that this is a *Notstaat* (lengthy concern with systems of coercion, patent allusions to the French Republic, etc.); moreover, the Fichtean procedure is to settle the terms of right before the injection of ethics. If this is a *Vernunftstaat*, it is a most coercive one; if it is a *Notstaat*, Fichte disarms us by providing no information on how the agency of the state will prepare its subjects for morality, a matter to be treated in the *Sittenlehre*.

In short, 'politics' is absent from the *Naturrecht*, as Fichte himself concedes: 'the question, which is the better form of government for any particular state, is not a question for the science of rights to solve, but for the art of politics'.[2] This evasion of the 'forms of government' may have been the better part of discretion in 1796. However, a myriad of political thinkers from Aristotle on, not excluding Kant, had felt this to be within the bounds of their topic. Kant had, to be sure, fallen back primarily on the 'spirit of government' in the *Metaphysics of Morals*, and Fichte does at least evaluate governments *a contrario*. But there is an evasiveness here about formal guarantees that prefigures the *Zwingherr* of the later writings or at least leaves the way open to him.[3]

The deduced state of the *Naturrecht*, is, in fact, an uneasy fluctuation between *Vernunftstaat* and *Notstaat*. However, strategically and historically, it is more the former. This is because 'politics' is seen to be the subject-matter of the compulsory *Notstaat* and a method of preparing its members for legal rationality and, beyond that, for *Sittlichkeit*. Unlike the *Vernunftstaat*, the *Notstaat* is not

---

[1] *Rights*, p. 275.
[2] *Ibid.* pp. 249–50. Aside from excluding unlawful forms of government, Fichte insists that all legitimate states be voluntarily established (by tacit consent; cf. *Ethics*, p. 250, which leaves direct consent to the 'more cultured men') and that they must incorporate a 'checking power' or constitutional body of appeal between people and rulers, named an 'Ephorate' after the rather different Spartan institution. However, in the *Rechtslehre* of 1812, he rejects the Ephorate as too dangerous to contemplate until men are morally improved: *N.W.* II, 633.
[3] Cf. *Staatslehre* of 1813, *S.W.* IV, 436 f.

just logical deduction; it has a historical *raison d'être* connected with improvement and progress. Thus we are not surprised to find Fichte writing that any constitution is just which allows for the movement of progress.[1] How may that progress be interpreted? Obviously by the *Wissenschaftslehre* and its various practical prolongations. Fichte was not, as Vlachos correctly points out, very interested at all in political liberty.[2] But he was riveted to the ideal of moral-philosophical pedagogy. Consequently it is acts (in conformity with the 'doctrine of science') and not the constitutional mechanics or offices that count. How Fichte came to despise those political 'machines' of Enlightenment philosophy![3] Fichte's goal may be stated very simply: state power in the service of the Idea. Scarcely has a methodology been simpler or clearer:

Reason demands, and nature at the same time has made provision,[4] that these state governments shall, in the course of time, approach more and more to the only form of government conformable to reason. Hence the state officials who govern a state, must know the latter form...Plato says: No prince can govern who is not possessed of the ideas; and this is precisely what we say. He must, therefore, necessarily know, firstly, the constitution which he has chosen to administer and the express or tacit compacts on which it rests; secondly, the state constitution, as it ought to be, or the ideal; and thirdly, the way which mankind in general, and particularly his people, must proceed to attain the latter.[5]

In the *Closed Commercial State* of 1800 Fichte distinguishes graphically the real (historical) state, the goal of establishing pure public right (or a *Vernunftstaat*, comparable to the deduction of 1796–7), and the intermediate term of scientific statesmanship which is called 'politics'.[6] Politics, guided by wise rulers, conveys

---

[1] Cf. *Ethics*, p. 252; also, *Characteristics*, p. 172: 'If the purpose of the state be understood...then is the government right and good.'

[2] Georges Vlachos, *Fédéralisme et raison d'Etat dans la pensée internationale de Fichte* (Paris, 1948), p. 63. Cf. *Characteristics*, p. 173: 'Political freedom is, at most, only necessary for one.' [3] Cf. *Addresses to the German Nation*, p. 96.

[4] Nature's 'provision' is even more euphemistic than Kant's 'ruse of nature' because 'there is no such thing as nature by itself' (*Ethics*, p. 139).

[5] *Ibid.* p. 371. This three-step paradigm exposits what Karl Mannheim (*Ideology and Utopia*, p. 123) has called the liberal-democratic utopia. His choice of Fichte as a model is infelicitous because it takes an example which, by its application in the *Closed Commercial State*, is scarcely typical of liberalism.

[6] *Der geschlossene Handelsstaat, S.W.* III, 389–98.

the destiny of the historical state toward the idealist paradigm of legality. In the instance, Fichte was describing a plan whereby the simultaneous closing off of all private commercial exchange with the outside and the scientific allocation of work roles, compensations and general economic justice within could produce a state community both just and prepared for moral greatness. The liberal Prussian finance minister Struensee, to whom it was dedicated and forwarded, did not make the experiment. But Fichte earned the reputation as a founder of state socialism, and the technique of the closed state remained within the orbit of the *Wissenschaftslehre* up to the end. We have only to remark that the *Notstaat* of Fichtean politics, as here described, is both inaugurated for a moral end and exceedingly repressive, a fulfilment of Hegel's attachment of the epithet 'Polizeistaat' to the system of the *Naturrecht*.[1]

The third objection one might pose to the Fichtean separation of legality and morality is simply that the conflict between the *quantum* of morality that *is now* and the system of morality that *is to be* or *ought to be* is never effectively resolved. The first must either suffer the interference of the *Notstaat* or else furnish the energy to coerce others in ways whose morality is dubious; the second probably runs the risk of inspiring fanatics. It is difficult to conceive a 'tolerable politics' between these extremes. The reader will judge for himself whether Fichte's attempted mediation of 'mere negative, formal legality' and man's higher ethical purpose with a popular nationalism proceeding 'from nature or God' was a fruitful solution to the problem.[2]

---

[1] For later observations on the relation of *Notstaat* and *Vernunftstaat*, cf. *Staatslehre*, *S.W.* IV, 236–41, 356–61. Hegel's criticism occurs in the *Differenz des Fichteschen und Schelling'schen Systems* of 1801, *Erste Drückschriften* (ed. G. Lasson, Berlin, 1911), pp. 64 ff.

[2] *Aus dem Entwurfe zu einer politischen Schrift, S.W.* VII, 563.

4

HISTORY AS LOGIC:
THE LOGIC OF HISTORY

A. HISTORY AND CONSCIOUSNESS

The important elements are now in place for an understanding of Fichte's 'logification of history'.[1] From 1794 on, the *Wissenschaftslehre* had developed a phenomenology of consciousness that would be the indispensable model for the notional movement of the Idea in history. The deduction of collective morality of the *Sittenlehre* of 1798, expressing the primacy of the community over its members, was also a precondition for making history as a collective movement intelligible. Now, to these fundamental ingredients must be added the progressively concrete formulation of the two later 'moments' of the *Wissenschaftslehre* (1801, 1804). Hypothetically, the link between time and eternity had been achieved. In the words of the 1801 *Wissenschaftslehre*: '...in all possible time lies hidden the only possible true Being, which, however, has not yet become completely clear to itself...and this Being bears at every moment that degree of clearness which is possible (and hence necessary) from the character of the time passed before it, and the time awaiting it in an infinite future'.[2] As we previously noted, future and infinite are ambiguously identified because they contain, respectively, the potential and actual definitions of the sphere of freedom.

Through the notion of the moral collectivity (cf. '[the] consciousness of all individuals taken together constitutes the complete consciousness of the universe...'),[3] the transmittal of eternity into time is also accompanied by a socialization of time: '...time rolls on in the steadfast course marked out for it from all eternity, and individual effort can neither hasten nor retard its progress. Only the

---

[1] For interesting, somewhat different comments, see G. A. Walz, *Die Staatsidee des Rationalismus und der Romantik und die Staatsphilosophie Fichtes* (Berlin–Grunewald, 1928), pp. 76–8.
[2] *Wissenschaftslehre* of 1801, p. 121. Cf. the discussion by X. Léon, *Fichte et son temps*, III, 221, of the analysis of time in the *Sittenlehre* of 1812.
[3] *Vocation of Man*, p. 342.

co-operation of all, and especially of the indwelling eternal spirit of ages and worlds may promote it'.[1] Time is understood as that time needed for the achievement of the moral community, 'the freedom of mankind in their collective capacity—as a race [*Gattung*]'.[2] Consistent with the premises of transcendental idealism, the production of time remains subjective. But it is collective in the sense that it defines the 'spirit of an age'. Life is not a cosmos of pulsating atoms, but a great mass of energy thrust into time and individuated by its breakdown into stages of collective consciousness:

...to the deeper thought of man, this entire earthly life of the human race, as it now exists, is...a homogeneous mass, projected at once into time, and ever present there, whole and undivided—only as regards *sensuous* appearance spread out into world history. When these homogeneous masses have appeared in time, the general laws by which they are governed may be comprehended...[3]

The correlation between *my* time and *thy* time, a pronounced difficulty for Kantian philosophy, is more resolutely grappled with by Fichte.[4] As a partial consequence of this, while Kant's teleological 'Idea' of history is a conjugation of various 'theses' that explain the progress of humanity toward peace and justice,[5] Fichte's plot of history is phased in ideational categories. His metaphors of history are grounded not in anthropological 'statistics' but in manifestations of *Zeitgeist* that have little to do with the human average but are evidently connected with intersubjective 'prevailing tendencies' understood idealistically.

Several conceptions of history collide in Fichte's writings. The pre-1800 works reveal a conflict between the rationalist relationship of actual and ideal and the teleological implications of a history of the will. The *Beiträge* emphasized the first tendency very clearly with an absolute assertion of right against history, even though the work was also charged with teleological overtones. We could make a similar assertion about the 'actuality–politics–right' triad discussed in the last section, although it is again equally clear that

[1] *Characteristics*, pp. 12–13.   [2] *Ibid.* p. 5.
[3] *Nature of the Scholar*, pp. 226–7. On the subjectivity of time, cf. *Addresses*, p. 113–5.
[4] Regarding Kant, see M. J. Temmer, *Time in Rousseau and Kant*, p. 67.
[5] Cf. 'Idea', in *Kant on History*, p. 16.

the *Vernunftstaat* is a teleological concept. However, on the strength of the description given in the *Closed Commercial State*, all that politics must do, apparently, to mediate between facticity and rationality is to close the frontiers and apportion the work, the produce and the currency.[1] This radical compression of the time-sequence containing the 'political act'—here more strident than anywhere else in Fichte's thought—specifically recalls the rationalist utopias of the pre-Revolutionary period, where the decisive rational act (there associated with 'nature') is a logical act that rebukes temporality.[2] In fact, so long as temporality is associated with habit and prescription, reason must deny its privilege; it is only when reason is seen to have a temporal unfolding of its own that the conception of a *remedial time* becomes possible. In any case, judging by the later writings of Fichte that endorse the economic closing of the state—e.g. the *Grundzüge*, the *Reden*, the *Staatslehre* of 1813— we may regard this scenario as merely one of a number of 'techniques' employed by the compulsory *Notstaat* in its effort to prepare collective morality and effective community. It is not a paradigm of the philosophy of history. As X. Léon correctly observes, the importance of the *Closed Commercial State* is other than historical; its profound meaning is that 'justice demands that morality should be imposed on individuals by force'.[3]

More importantly, Fichte stated in this same work that 'history can and should be nothing other than a genetic reply to the causal question'.[4] This provides effective evidence that, as late as 1800, he had not conceptually united all the conditions for a 'logification of history' or joined the careers of mind and world. The teleological possibilities for a plan of history were, however, already implicit in the temporal practicity of the *Sittenlehre* of 1798.[5]

---

[1] Cf. *Der geschlossene Handelsstaat, S.W.* III, 476.

[2] In his dedication to Struensee, the Prussian Minister of Finance, Fichte defends the project of the closed state as realizable. However, he concedes in a later passage: 'The author is resigned to seeing this project remain a simple school exercise without success in the real world: a link in the chain of the system that he is bit by bit constructing.' *Ibid.* p. 393.

[3] X. Léon, *Fichte et son temps*, II, 99.

[4] *Handelsstaat, S.W.* III, 449. Fichte called his work an 'appendix to the doctrine of right', thus, by reference to the 'mere legality' of 1796–7, stressing its extra-historical flavour.

[5] Cf. *Ethics*, pp. 124–5, 134. On the general distinction between 'causal-functional' and 'immanent-teleological' explanations, see Walz, *Staatsidee*, pp. 97–101.

It should be mentioned in passing that Fichte was a devout opponent of cyclical theories of history, whose mentality he associated with reactionary persons or peoples. In the *Beiträge* he had already drawn a sharp distinction between historical teleology and the 'Kreislauf der Natur'.[1] In the *Reden*, he heaped scorn on the 'Zirkeltanz', castigating those (i.e. foreigners, undisguisedly the French) for whom 'history was finished long ago and has been finished several times already', who 'let eternally-recurring death repeat itself and subside time after time'[2]. The irony is that Fichte's history of the Idea was itself circular. 'Humanity', he declares, rather grandiosely, 'is...essentially one and identical throughout; and is in all its elements destined in the same way lovingly to return to its original and therein to be blessed.'[3]

The new conception which, between the years 1801 and 1804, comes to replace the 'genetic replies to causal questions' is that of the systematic march of the Idea, in its shapes, through the whole of time, exposed in Fichte's *Grundzüge* lectures of 1804–5 and foreshadowed and amplified elsewhere. It involves a five-stage succession of 'epochs', each of them expressing 'the fundamental Idea of a particular Age'. This exists in counterpoint with still another *motif*.

This second pattern is dual, postulating an absolute turning of history or rupture between two fundamental ages designated by Fichte as the 'Alte Welt' and the 'Neue Welt',[4] an imagery clearly borrowed from the Christian idea of the old and new covenants.[5] This distinction is already clearly drawn in the *Grundzüge*, where Fichte mentions 'two principal epochs or ages: the one in which the race exists and lives without as yet having ordered its relations with freedom according to reason; and the other in which this voluntary and reasonable arrangement is brought about'.[6] While Fichte's two images may be superposed without contradiction, they bear somewhat different implications. The five-step vision (of which man is at the mid-point in 1804) projects progress into distant reaches of the future; the dual one hastens and compresses the human acquisition of the *siècle d'or*. Moreover, the pivot of the

---

[1] *Beiträge*, p. 292.   [2] *Addresses to the German Nation*, p. 100.
[3] *Characteristics*, p. 212; cf. also p. 10.   [4] Cf. *Staatslehre*, pp. 497 ff.
[5] Cf. Philonenko, *Liberté humaine*, p. 157: 'As for Hegel, for Fichte time possesses a religious meaning'.   [6] *Characteristics*, p. 6.

first conception lies in a valley of negation, which Fichte calls 'the age of completed sinfulness', while the second has a sharp, positive break, discriminating what Wallner has aptly called the 'theocracy of faith' from the 'theocracy of the understanding'.[1] Obviously, the second scheme is more than casually related to man's situation between the sway of the *Nicht-Ich* and the *Ich*. Its real nodal point is the coming of Christianity; however, it is only in the philosophical and Protestant tradition of Germany, culminating in the *Wissenschaftslehre*, that the 'essence' of Christianity (the true revelation of the supersensible) has become manifest.[2] In the first image, the *Wissenschaftslehre* comprehends the world historically; in the second, it changes it, but obviously only on an ideal plane. Since the second image acquires strategic importance in Fichte's so-called 'chiliastic' writings of 1811–13, while remaining a shadow in the *Grundzüge*, I shall reserve further comment.[3]

B. HISTORY AS SUBJECTIVE SELF-DEVELOPMENT OF THE IDEA

Fichte's *Grundzüge* first explores the question: how is a philosophy of history possible? The response, though in the line of Kant, far exceeds Kant in temerity. To make the 'history' of an age possible, Fichte says, one must first establish that age's Idea and observe its phenomenal revelation.[4] Each Idea is a 'particular epoch of time'; to know these epochs requires a 'comprehension of universal time' or of a 'world-plan, which, in its primitive unity, may be clearly comprehended, and from which may be correctly deduced all the great epochs of human life on earth'.[5] This, then, will be a history *a priori*. Just as earthly life can be deduced from eternal life, so historical time can be deduced from eternal time, Fichte says.

---

[1] Nico Wallner, *Fichte als politischer Denker* (Halle, 1926), p. 256.
[2] *Staatslehre*, p. 534.
[3] E. Hirsch, *Christentum und Geschichte*, and Emil Lask, *Fichtes Idealismus und die Geschichte* (Tübingen, 1914), have written interesting works on Fichte's theory of history, to which I am indebted if not in constant agreement with. Gueroult, *Doctrine de la Science*, and Gurwitsch, *Konkrete Ethik*, are also useful. The subject has hardly been touched in English, though, in one case, rather badly: R. G. Collingwood, *Idea of History*, pp. 106–11.
[4] *Characteristics*, pp. 2–3.   [5] *Ibid.* pp. 3–4.

The formal proof has been given in the *Wissenschaftslehre* and will not be repeated for the popular audience. Thus are phenomenology and history joined: the *Wissenschaftslehre*, as the 'doctrine of science', 'knows' the total historical plan of the Idea. It has far greater 'reality' than Kant's heuristic moral-speculative ordainer.[1] Although more systematic, Fichte is often a good deal less prudent than Kant in his genesis of assumptions. He maintains that a 'plan of history' must be purely *a priori*. The empirical historian is 'a mere collector of facts', an 'annalist', whose discoveries are useful only for illustration.[2] Robbed of its illustrations, history would presumably be identical with the *Wissenschaftslehre*. 'The philosopher employs history only so far as it serves his purpose.'[3] That purpose is to show that 'the end of the life of mankind on earth is this—that in this life they may order all their relations with freedom according to reason'.[4] Fichte is really saying that reason *is* eternally but that freedom *becomes*. Reason is the *an sich*, freedom the *für sich*. Reason is divine; freedom is collectively human. At the end of history, freedom acquires all of reason and makes reason its own. Freedom and knowledge are the same.

The 'metaphor' of this cosmic movement is expressed by the five stages, which are, respectively: (1) 'the state of innocence of the human race'; (2) 'the state of progressive sin', characterized by 'blind faith and unconditional obedience'; (3) 'the state of completed sinfulness', paradoxically also designated as 'the epoch of liberation'; (4) 'the state of progressive justification', where reason is grasped as 'knowledge'; (5) 'the state of completed justification and sanctification', where reason is affirmed as 'art'.[5]

Fichte's 'plan' is quite clearly a secularization of the Christian paradigm of innocence, sin and redemption.[6] The career of thought is encompassed by its religious destiny. Or?—and this is a problem of great moment in German speculation of the *Goethezeit*—is religion not validated only to be superseded by thought?

[1] However, the focus remains subjective; cf. *Addresses to the German Nation*, p. 227:
'. . . providence and the divine plan in creating a race of men. . . exists only to be thought out by men and to be brought by men into the actual world. . .'
[2] *Characteristics*, pp. 154-5.   [3] *Ibid.* p. 156.   [4] *Ibid.* p. 5.   [5] *Ibid.* p. 9.
[6] One should say 'secularization' with some caution, because in the 'third moment' of the *Wissenschaftslehre* the Idea becomes associated with the Johannite Logos. Cf. *ibid.* p. 143. Fichte is a deeply religious man with an arch-humanist philosophy.

The 'spirit of an age' is a collective ideal *ontos*: different ages may criss-cross each other phenomenally; individuals may be in disharmony with the reigning spirit.[1] However, 'science [i.e., the *Wissenschaftslehre*] raises itself above all ages and all times...' It is the core of knowing.

Fichte's intention is to communicate the plan of all ages to his auditors, but especially to dwell on the 'spirit' of the age they are traversing, the third epoch of 'completed sinfulness'. It is fundamentally an age of nay-saying, of negation. But as the age out of which liberation springs, it is also the negation of the negation. We are here anticipating some familiar Hegelian ground. Historically, the third age is the period of empiricism and the Enlightenment.

Fichte has some very harsh words to say about this period, and few good ones. Outside the philosophical framework, we can easily sense the impact of the untracked Revolution, the disruption of Europe, and the bitterness of the atheism controversy and the other polemics. Outside of the *Grundzüge*, we find Fichte writing to Jacobi: 'I believe that I have understood our age as that of the absolute corruption of all ideas. Nevertheless, I am of good cheer; for I know that new life can come only from complete decay.'[2] The incessant targets of Fichte's attack are eudaemonism, materialism, individualism, a whole galaxy of French values, and a whole index of French thoughts and thinkers—Voltaire, especially, and Helvétius, elsewhere described as a 'foreign materialistic and atheistic moralist'.[3] In the third age, 'the natural impulse of self-preservation and personal well-being alone prevails'; '...each individual imagines that he can exist, live, think and act for himself'.[4] It is a 'middle state between humanity and animalism',[5] looking 'only to the immediately and materially *useful*': 'the dominion of attempts to govern degenerate men by means of high-sounding phrases without the aid of firm and inflexible power; or...it hastens in every emergency...to consult the chronicles of the past...and takes from thence the law of its own conduct...'[6] These selected phrases show the range of Fichte's onslaught on

---

[1] *Ibid.* p. 11. [2] Fichte to Jacobi, 31 Mar. 1804, *Briefwechsel*, II, 381–2.
[3] *Ethics*, p. 193; cf. *Characteristics*, p. 30. [4] *Characteristics*, pp. 22–3.
[5] *Ibid.* pp. 28–9. [6] *Ibid.* p. 29.

the Enlightenment. Conservatives and liberals alike reap his scorn; both the miscarried Revolution and its sworn enemies are flayed. What Fichte means is that the Enlightenment had confused progress with materialistic optimism and gadgetry; it had not discovered 'that the heart is at bottom nothing but a base puddle'.[1] But against this he is preaching not the authoritarianism of historical privilege, but the authoritarianism of reason. The Romantics, too, are characteristic of the age. They protest, but imagine 'that to get at the true, we have only to reverse the false, [and] are disposed to place all wisdom in the incomprehensible and the unintelligible'.[2] Nothing but transcendental idealism and its élite pantheon of the past escape. One may profitably—on the psychological plane—compare the scope of Fichte's indictment to Rousseau's earlier castigation of the orthodoxies. But there is comfort in the eternal motion of the idea, its restless search throughout all time to reach an absolute comprehension of freedom. Thus each age, for all its barbarism and turbulence, takes on meaning as part of a dynamic progression.

The first age of 'innocence' is particularly important because of its correlation with the genesis of consciousness in the *Wissenschaftslehre*. Philosophy, Fichte tells us, cannot account for the creation of the human species, any more than the *Wissenschaftslehre* can account for the original ego.[3] But since knowledge exists, we must presuppose a humanity with language as its mode of communication. This postulation evades the 'realist' dilemma of the source of language that so perplexed Rousseau and others, and betrays an indebtedness to Herder, who, in modified form, had accepted the divine origin theory.[4] Now, the question becomes one of identifying the appearance of reason in history. Here Fichte departs very considerably from Rousseau and Kant.'Out of nothing, nothing can arise,' Fichte writes, 'and thus unreason can never become reason.' At no point is he further from Hegelianism and closer to a mythopoeic expression of rationalism. 'Hence,' he

[1] *Characteristics*, p. 31.
[2] *Ibid.* p. 77. Against Schelling, he declared, not without justice: '...mysticism is, and always must be, a *Naturphilosophie*' (p. 130).
[3] *Ibid.* p. 146.
[4] There is a good discussion of Herder's language theory as opposed to Condillac's in Roy Pascal, *The German Sturm und Drang*, pp. 173 f. Fichte's notion of the German *Ursprache* comes chiefly from the Herderian source.

continues, 'in one point of its existence, at least, the human race must have been purely reasonable in its primitive form, without either constraint or freedom.'[1]

Fichte's problem is at bottom the Christian problem of accounting for the translation of perfection (and imperfection) into the phenomenal world structure. His outlook is, however, more Manichaean than Christian. And the method he chooses for dealing with it is akin to the 'derivative reflection' of the philosopher upon the original division of the ego into subject and object beneath the level of consciousness. First the ego must posit itself: '...we are forced to admit the existence of an original normal people, who, by the mere fact of their existence without science or art [theoretical and practical reason], found themselves in a state of perfectly developed reason [to be explained as religious stasis]'.[2]

In the *Wissenschaftslehre* the ego had also to posit a non-ego, reciprocally limiting and limited; the posited ego attained consciousness only by virtue of a shock delivered by the resistance of the non-ego to its expansion. Thus the scenario proceeds: as opposed to the 'normals' a race of 'savages' must be posited, representative of unreason or nature. The dynamism of historical life is a consequence of this collision, just as the phenomenology of consciousness owes its destiny to a similar pattern. The 'savages' are, in effect, the matter on which the 'normals' (form) will work. Taken alone, the 'normals' were completely static and had no history; one day was like the next, and 'religion alone adorned their existence'.[3] The 'normals' incorporated the principle of human destiny, but not the possibility of fulfilling it; the 'savages', on the other hand, furnished the task or the dynamism of history. Ultimately, in historical life, the 'normals', who had the 'absolute culture' of nature, were dispersed among the barbarians and subjugated them. The second age of 'blind faith and unconditional obedience' began. 'In this conflict of culture with barbarism,' Fichte says, 'the germs of all ideas and all science [except religion]...unfolded themselves'.[4] This latter

---

[1] *Characteristics*, p. 147.
[2] *Ibid.* R. Fester, *Rousseau und die deutsche Geschichtsphilosophie* (pp. 133 f.), professes to see a resemblance between Fichte's *Normalvolk* and Rousseau's state of nature. In fact, no two concepts could be more drastically opposed.
[3] *Ibid.* p. 148; cf. also *Staatslehre*, pp. 470, 486.   [4] *Ibid.* p. 149.

comment has probably two significances, conveying both the unfathomability of the creative and eschatological terminals of the Christian cycle (the haven of the religious Odyssey), and the unmistakable tendency of all German philosophy of the period to equate its content with religion.

It scarcely matters that Schelling was first in the field with the quaint idea of the 'normals' and 'savages', and that Fichte probably picked up the hypothesis from his erstwhile follower.[1] The mythology of the Titans and Olympians is in the background. So are all the vast perspectives of the problem of mastery and slavery. But it is important to notice how many important themes of the present, of the future, and of philosophy in general, are met in this brief statement.

In succeeding lectures in the *Grundzüge* Fichte develops the nature and ramifications of the epochs as well as the development of those parallel projections of the Idea, which, as stated here, are in ascending order: art, political science or right, science (*Wissenschaft*) and religion.[2] In the turmoil of the *Goethezeit*, each of the so-called 'higher values' fought for pre-eminence in the persons and theories of Goethe, Schiller, Schelling, Fichte, Schleiermacher, to name but a few apostles. Idealist philosophy sought to comprehend these elements as aspects of the absolute and synthesize them in the pattern of all knowledge. Their correlation with the stages or 'epochs' of historical development is highly problematic, but they are eventually construed as having histories of their own that can be conjoined and further linked both to the phenomenology of consciousness and to idealist history *tout court*.

C. HISTORY AND THE COMPULSORY STATE

In the exposition of the *Grundzüge* Fichte reiterates his views on the state and the moral community in a harsher manner. Any pre-

---

[1] Cf. F. W. J. Schelling, *Vorlesungen über die Methode des akademischen Studiums* (1802), in *Sämmtliche Werke* (Stuttgart and Augsburg, 1854–60), v, 224–5.

[2] *Characteristics*, pp. 62–3. Fichte shifted his catalogues from time to time; cf. *Bestimmung des Gelehrten* (1811), and *Blessed Life*, Smith, II, 448–9. I would suggest that, as for Kant, law is the essential mediating value for Fichte, both establishing the contact between objective reality and the moral person and furnishing the historical matrix in which the 'crooked wood' of humanity is to be straightened by discipline and education.

vious liberalism is gone: that 'the state ought to be almost nothing more than a juridical institution [is] a view which we oppose with deliberate and well-considered determination'.[1] What, then, is the Fichtean state from the vantage point of 1804? For one thing, the *Vernunftstaat* of the past has now been retitled the *absoluter Staat*:

The absolute state is in its form...an artistic institution, intended to direct all individual powers toward the life of the race and to transfuse them therein; and thus to realize and manifest in individual life the general form of the Idea...since the state cannot calculate upon the inward life and the original activity in the minds of men...it follows that this institution must be one of constraint. For those individuals in whom the Idea has assumed a real inward life, and whose wish and desire is nothing else than to offer up their lives for the race, no constraint is necessary and for them it disappears...[The state] is an *artistic* institution...only after it has scientifically penetrated to its complete and perfect purpose in the [fourth] age of reason as knowledge...when the fifth age...has begun.[2]

This is a critical passage where many themes meet. With the disappearance of the chiefly logical superimposition of the moral system expressed in the *Sittenlehre* of 1798 on the structure of 'mere legality' demonstrated in the *Naturrecht* of 1796-7, the destiny of the state has been floated in world history. This temporal objectification of the legal–moral sequence is undoubtedly related to Fichte's own retrenchment from cosmopolitanism toward a clarification of the German mission. But, corresponding to this movement of the forms of the state into time, there is only the linear prospect of 'coercion' (the fourth epoch) to be followed by 'art' (the fifth), nothing of what Hegel was to call 'höhere Sittlichkeit' that could synthesize, tangibly and spiritually, the free and coercive aspects of communal existence, making the Idea a reality in its own time. And, of course, by Fichte's interpretation, a 'fourth epoch' of indefinite duration was fated to descend on the communities of Europe, a 'discipline of culture' with a vengeance, tangibly associated with the growing ideal of German political unity. One might be expected to wait quite a while for the state as 'art' to appear. There are indeed forbidding resemblances between the characteristics of the 'second' and 'fourth'

[1] *Characteristics*, p. 159. [2] *Ibid.* p. 160.

epochs, with the exception, all-important to Fichte, that the earlier age had been based on the authority of fear and superstition whereas the age to come would ground its authority in reason and the fulfilment of the Idea.

This passage shows us that the coercive *Notstaat* of the 'fourth epoch', although based on the ideal of human equality and fraternity, will harshly discriminate between two classes of morality and intelligence. Being free, those 'in whom the Idea has assumed a real inward life' will of course *go* free; the others will be subjected to a discipline that 'penetrates scientifically to its complete and perfect purpose'. In this situation, 'all powers of the individuals' must be appropriated by the state.[1]

In this regard there is a Fichtean tension of aristocratic and democratic values. Fichte had nothing but wrath and contempt for the privileged orders of Church and nobility. In terms germane to his society, he wanted to level the *ancien régime*. This meant essentially an endorsement of 'bourgeois ideology': careers open to talents, abolition of restrictive corporations and feudal 'liberties', approval of a 'nobility of opinion'.[2] Such feelings were shared not only by Kant and most of the German intelligentsia, but by the Girondins, the 'idéologues', Madame de Staël, Benjamin Constant and, on the whole, the 'liberals' of France. But somehow, this obvious statement of fact does not tell the whole story. Fichte's roots were in the people, and, as one knows, he developed a deep strain of populist nationalism, expressed most vituperatively in the *Reden*. Moreover, the very core of the ethics of transcendental idealism was to stress the presumptive equality of the moral person, not just the legal rights of the individual.

Fichte knew well, however, that the world was not moral: chiefly, it was 'sinful', but could be retrieved by the inculcation of 'life in the Idea'. Thus, as needed, the 'formal' ideals of bourgeois legality might have to be sacrificed to the higher purpose. And if the precious bourgeois legality in France quickly tended to degenerate into 'enrichissez-vous', the moral primacy of 'Fichtianity' might

---

[1] *Characteristics*, p. 163.
[2] Cf. *Beiträge*, p. 237: 'Do not tell me that the bourgeois, having entered the highest occupations, will in his turn let himself be ruled by the spirit of caste...'

History and the compulsory state

easily show an opposed tendency to control the spirit of persons on grounds of its own *a priori* spirituality. Ultimately, it meant more to Fichte to be an intellectual than a product of the artisan class of Saxony.

In any case, the Fichtean élite established by these norms will be quite different from those we usually associate with the 'bourgeois revolution'. Fundamentally, it is a heroic aristocracy. This is already prefigured in the *Grundzüge*:

Who has united rude races together, and reduced opposing tribes under the dominion of law?...It was heroes, who had left their age far behind them, giants among surrounding men in material and spiritual power. They subdued to their Idea of what *ought to be* races by whom they were on that account hated and feared...It was an Idea...which inspired them; and it was the unspeakable delight of this Idea which rewarded and indemnified them for all their labours and sacrifices...[1]

Fichte's paean to heroes (among whom Alexander the Great stands out) recalls the penchant of Rousseau, the democrat, for the great founders of peoples, the 'sublime heroes' shadowed by the mists of the past. It also anticipates the mighty figures Hegel will celebrate as the unaware but resolute instruments of the 'List der Vernunft'. However, Hegel believed (at least after the downfall of Napoleon) that the age of heroes had ended.[2] For Fichte, the task of heroes (conquerors, statesmen, artists, religious teachers, scholars) was never-ending or at least not to be ended until history itself should end with the fulfilment of the Idea. In the *Neue Welt*, however, the predominant hero is to be the 'seer' (*Seher*), the adept of the *Wissenschaftslehre* and pathfinder to the boundaries of the 'blessed life', gradually indistinguishable from the *Zwingherr* or *Oberherr*, who will discipline and moralize his people. The Fichtean hero is a blend of Socrates, Caesar and Prometheus.[3] In fact, the hero 'who has

---

[1] *Characteristics*, p. 48. Cf. *Sittenlehre* of 1812, *N.W.* III, 75: 'In them there is spirituality; they are heroes, they are benefactors of the human race.'

[2] Fichte detested Napoleon, not because he was a 'Weltschöpfer', but because he was a vicious and amoral one who rejected the Idea; he 'never understood the teachings of either philosophy or Christianity'. *Staatslehre*, p. 424.

[3] The hero is also connected with the Romantic notion of *genius*, partly promoted by Kant's 'Critique of Aesthetic Judgment'; cf. *Nature of the Scholar*, p. 236: 'Genius is... the effort of the Idea to assume a definite form.'

left his age far behind him' is the embodiment of the paradigm of 'derivative reflection' in the *Wissenschaftslehre*, where the philosophical consciousness precedes existential phenomenology by one stage until, ultimately, both are joined in the realm of reason. Finally, it is of great interest to notice how, in the *Grundzüge*, Fichte launches a frontal attack against Rousseau's anti-teleology of the *Second Discourse*. For Rousseau, historical society was a degenerative sequence ending in mastery and slavery. For Fichte, however, the vocation of man and the teleology of history reverse the terms. Just as the 'golden age' lies ahead, so the plan of the Idea, fleshed out with illustration, establishes the progress of man from the original condition of the absolute inequality of 'normals' and 'savages' through the 'equality of right as right' (which is the acquisition of the French Revolution) to a 'true equality of rights and powers' (presumably the 'absoluter Staat').[1] However, Fichte's end is very different from Rousseau's beginning in nature, which once more emphasizes the tension between a moral community of pure spirit and its phenomenal manifestation. The model is Platonic and integrative, not Rousseauian and distributive: '... equality does not by any means exclude the distinction of classes in society [*Stände*]: that is, the different modes in which human power may be applied...But no class...must be permitted, which is not dedicated to the purpose of the whole...'[2] We find that the teleology of equality still is in the realm of the *Notstaat*. Beyond this mobilization of persons for the sake of the Idea is only beatitude or 'heavenly love', happily penetrating into history at all times and a solace to those who cannot wait for systematic earthly perfection.[3] The elimination of the *Notstaat* is not in politics; is it in time?

However, what humanity (i.e. Europe) really has to conjure with at present is the beginning, not the end, of the *Notstaat*. For that is where this 'Bahnbrecher einer die Geschichte verstehenden Philosophie'[4] places his Berlin auditors. And within three years, in the same city, now French-occupied, he will declare:

At some point within the three years that have gone by since my interpretation of the present age that epoch has come to an end. At some point

---

[1] *Characteristics*, p. 167; cf. *Staatslehre*, p. 508.   [2] *Characteristics*, p. 168.
[3] *Ibid.* p. 190.   [4] F. Medicus, *J. G. Fichte : Dreizehn Vorlesungen* (Berlin, 1905), p. 267.

self-seeking has destroyed itself, because by its own complete development it has lost itself and the independence of that self...It is, therefore,
my duty to acknowledge as past what has ceased to be the present...[1]

We shall now come upon the injection of humanity into the 'state of
progressive justification' by a somewhat different route than that
of the philosophy of history.

[1] *Addresses to the German Nation*, p. 1.

5

COSMIC NATIONALISM

A. NATION AND COSMOPOLIS: INTRODUCTORY

The declamatory cadences of the *Addresses to the German Nation* are surely, in one sense, the slightly grotesque rhetorical pearls of an underdeveloped and emerging nation that is at the same time possessed of a unique and monumental, if overblown, high culture. But Fichte did not invent the terms of the German problem of cosmopolitanism and nationalism. On a strictly cultural level, it simmered in Möser, in Lessing and Herder, even as far back as Leibniz, that paragon of European unity and perpetual peace.[1] The *Sturm und Drang* groped for a national, in some respects 'folkish', culture to oppose to the general European model. Goethe, despite his belonging to culture-at-large, had done much to give the Germans glory and respect. Now, in the waning years of the eighteenth century, philosophers like Kant and Fichte wrested political theory from the hands of the *jurisconsultes* amid general intellectual dissatisfaction with the subservient doctrines of the past. The Germany of their time, it must be remembered, was a hollow, staggering empire-on-paper, in reality a *Kulturstaat* or stateless nation. But it had also a culturally defensive but aspiring intelligentsia of great energy and talent.

Kant travelled too little, lived too early, or saw too broadly to be much touched by these gathering forces. Despite his enormously potent discovery of the ethics of duty and the primacy of practical reason, he was a legitimate man of the eighteenth century and a 'European' in the style of Leibniz. Moreover, the transcendental historical teleology and the purely abstract legal system reinvigorated the traditions of philosophical *Weltbürgertum*. That, too, remained a substantial part of Fichte's legacy.

In 1789, as I have pointed out, the German intellectuals loved

---

[1] See especially, M. Boucher, *Le sentiment national en Allemagne* (Paris, 1947), pp. 7–37; V. Basch, *Les Doctrines politiques des philosophes classiques de l'Allemagne* (Paris, 1927), pp. 19–54; J. E. Spenlé, *La pensée allemande de Luther à Nietzsche* (Paris, 1934), pp. 61–81.

the Revolution, but maintained their distances from French values and the French people. *Ubi bene, ibi patria.* There was, concretely, no German fatherland. A man might love his prince or the province of his birth; the philosophical imagination loved reason more. And reason had come to dwell in France. Even when reason waged international war for the rights of man, there was that spontaneous wave of sympathy which Kant so well reflected. Liberty was not a hegemonic French enterprise. However, when liberty set to dethroning and killing kings, stirring up the masses, pillaging harvests, and finally imprisoning and beheading the generous cosmopolitans of the moderate Girondin ascendancy, it was foreordained that liberty and cosmopolitanism would change sides in Germany.

For most, it was sooner; for Fichte, later. Cast by his self-appointed role on the French side, he was abused by 'establishment' oracles as a 'Jacobin' or a 'democrat'.[1] The *Wissenschaftslehre* was the noumenon of the French Revolution. Unlike Schiller, Herder and others, Fichte's criteria were always much more ethico-political than cultural.

The *Naturrecht* of 1796–7, in its presentation of 'cosmopolitan law', had generally followed Kant's notions of perpetual peace, a league of nations, and the 'law of cosmopolitan hospitality'.[2] There was no reason to believe, on the surface, that Fichte's philosophy would take a different turn. However, superimposed on the 'mere legality' of the *Naturrecht* was that very different vision of the collective moral community achieving itself through time and under a constraint that not only 'hindered hindrances' but mobilized the popular soul for a belief in idealist perfectibility. And behind Fichte's work had always been a particular notion of German values, of the Teutonic resistance to the Roman Empire, of the glitter of the free cities of the Middle Ages, especially of Luther, the popular leader and evangelist for an immanent and truly Christian spirituality— what might be called *Sturm und Drang* or pre-Romantic components.[3] In short, once the French universal mission was denied (a terrible wrench for Fichte because of the circumstances in which the

---

[1] *Gerichtliche Verantwortung gegen die Anklage des Atheismus, S.W.* v, 286.
[2] *Rights*, pp. 475–88.   [3] Cf. *Beiträge*, pp. 129, 238.

Cosmic nationalism

Wissenschaftslehre had been conceived), the materials of transformation were ready to operate. On 3 July 1799, shortly before
arriving in Berlin, Fichte wrote to an acquaintance: '...it has
already become obvious that...the practice on both sides is
completely identical; it even seems that the republican practice is
worse'.[1] The first synthesis of mind and world was collapsing.

B. THE NATION-STATE AS HUMAN COMMUNITY: TRANSITION

In Berlin, all the previsions of Romanticism and embryonic
patriotism swirled about Fichte. He assimilated many of these
influences, even while beating back attacks on the *Wissenschaftslehre*.
He sought communion with his audiences in terms of their experience, hoping to wean them away from their 'completed sinfulness'.
And on the French side, the rhetoric of aggressive nationalism had
mounted from 1794 on: *la nation aux armes, armée populaire,
frontières naturelles*, and all the rest of it. Fichte was deeply impressed
with these developments, not because he loved the French *per se*
or was an unquenchable admirer of the Comité de Salut Public
(or even Babeuf!), as X. Léon dogmatically claims in his otherwise
incomparable study,[2] but because they were dynamic and effective,
the heralds of a new 'spirit of the time'. Fichte was struggling for

---

[1] To Jung, 10 May 1799, *Briefwechsel*, II, 100. However, in his letter of 30 June 1799,
to the same correspondent (p. 130), he can still call Germany 'a foreign land', as indeed
the atheism controversy had seemed to make it, until he was welcomed to Prussia.
Moreover, at practically the same time, he was telling Reinhold that men would no
longer be able to think free thoughts unless the French gained 'the most crushing
preponderance' in Europe. *Leben und Briefwechsel*, II, 259.

[2] Xavier Léon had an intellectual love-affair with Fichte, based on the premise that
Fichte was a complete child of the French Revolution. This devotion occasionally
intrudes on his magnificent history of ideas, *Fichte et son temps*. In particular, Léon
argues that Fichte may very well have been inspired to write the *Closed Commercial
State* by the navigation acts of Barère, put into effect by the Comité de Salut Public in
1793, and by the Babouvist theories of 1796, much reported in the German newspapers
of the time (cf. Léon, II, 101–16). However, it is scarcely likely, even if Fichte remained a champion of the Republic with which he had corresponded for a position,
that he would have noticed Barère's laws or that he would have admired the enemy of
the state, the 'Conspiration des Egaux'. Rather, the seeds of the *Closed Commercial
State* are to be found within Prussian mercantile history itself, as Léon also amply
shows. The most exact treatment of the origin and nature of Fichte's socialism is
Heinrich Rickert, 'Die philosophische Grundlagen von Fichtes Sozialismus', *Logos*,
XI (1922), pp. 149–80, esp. p. 178. I find similarly wishful M. Gueroult's explicit

action and commitment, and against philosophical obsolescence. This is nowhere better indicated than in his entangled relations with Berlin Freemasonry in 1800. Deprived of his university chair and audiences, Fichte hoped to continue his work on the world through this powerful international organization.[1] The consequences of this commitment led him to expose the strategy of Freemasonry as he saw it in a series of 'letters'. Approaching the problem of nationalism and cosmopolitanism in the twelfth of this series, he wrote:

Just as in religion [the Freemason] thinks always of the eternal but directs all his strength to earthly tasks, so in politics he thinks always of the whole, but his special strength goes to his state, his city, his office, his particular place on earth. In his mind patriotism and cosmopolitanism are closely bound, and have a very distinct relationship. Patriotism is his activity, cosmopolitanism is his thought: the former is the phenomenon, the latter the spirit of the phenomenon, the invisible in the visible.[2]

This remained Fichte's philosophical position up to the end. However, the phenomenon came to be ever more powerfully animated by its visibility. It was another triumph of practical over theoretical reason; should we say of 'life' over 'philosophy'?

At bottom, this was the problem of Rousseau, now flung into the future and charged with all the 'perfectible' new creation that the Genevan had inveighed against. For Rousseau, too, *humanité* and the *cité* had been values, contrary ones perhaps, but also yoked by an abiding insistence on simplicity, restriction of scope, and hostility to change. Fichte was not the only German to attempt the patriotic and cosmopolitan conjugation. The Schlegels did it in a very different way.[3] And Joseph Goerres, who travelled from radical cosmopolitanism to national-Catholicism, could write in 1808 to Jacobi: 'we have never lived for ourselves, but always for Europe'.[4]

[1] Cf. X. Léon, *Fichte et son temps*, II, 12–57, for detail.
[2] J. G. Fichte, *Philosophy of Masonry : Letters to Constant* (ed. Roscoe Pound, Seattle, 1945), p. 55.
[3] See Jacques Droz (ed.), *Le Romantisme politique en Allemagne* (Paris, 1963), pp. 70–81.
[4] Letter of 19 Oct. 1808, quoted by M. Boucher, *Sentiment national*, p. 80. Cf. some of Boucher's other texts.

association of the legal theories of the *Naturrecht* with the organization of the French Convention; cf. 'Fichte et la Révolution française', *Revue philosophique* (Sept.–Dec. 1939), pp. 226–320, esp. p. 295.

Increasingly, with the dawn of the new century and its convergence of classical, romantic and idealistic trends, Germany was seen as the ideal microcosm of Europe, the treasury of its most lasting values.[1] It was the syncretism of the 'noble humanity' of antiquity and the profound spirituality of the Christian centuries. Not only had that pregnant and supreme moment in the dialectic of world-history arrived when it was up to the Germans to manifest the Idea by seizing moral and cultural leadership, but a philosophical reflection on all history could show that, from the earliest descriptions of Tacitus, the German race had carried the supreme values of the fullness of time. Few endorsed this image, stark and unmodified. The greatest figure of the age, Goethe, never endorsed it. Moreover, the heat, rhetoric and propaganda of the years 1808–14 led to excesses that can best be attributed to a wartime mentality, to the backwash of the Revolution, now turned on its authors. Other patriotisms (not least, the American) have prospered through grandiose, not always wholesome, convictions of national sanctity. In Fichte's new vision, the relation of an ideal Germany to Europe and to history—to all the values comprehended in those terms—was very much like that of the practical, finite ego to the absolute ego of the *Wissenschaftslehre*. Germany—there was no 'Germany' at the time—*ought to be* the concrete embodiment of *Humanität*. The German experience was the spiritual aspect of the *Menschenbildung* in microcosm.

If this was a nationalism, it was both a nationalism of the future and a nationalism of the 'meanwhile', of the 'fourth epoch', of the *Notstaat*. According to Windelband, it was 'a Germany lying in utopia'.[2] Few will dispute that such was its essence. If an imperialism, it was an imperialism of the spirit, not of the mailed fist: Fichte detested the notion of 'universal monarchy', the spirit of which Napoleon was the contemporary phenomenon.[3] But are spiritual imperialisms themselves more valid?

Yet Fichte's values are of a special sort. They are tied to a historically aggressive notion of obligation. Their superiority is unabashedly

---

[1] Cf. the passage from Schiller's 'Deutsche Grösse', cited above, p. 82.

[2] W. Windelband, *Fichtes Idee des deutschen Staates* (Tübingen, 1921), p. 12.

[3] *Addresses to the German Nation*, pp. 209–10.

ethical. And the dogmatic primacy of their ethical foundation comes to be more and more tangibly related to the historico-ethnic formation of the type of mind that could conceive such thoughts. Furthermore, the dialectic between the special community that produced transcendental idealism and the humanity for which that way of thought is a duty becomes possible only in the context of a philosophy of history that freezes the relation of these terms.

The moral overlay of the *Sittenlehre* abruptly alters the 'liberal' legal picture drawn by the *Naturrecht*. Having answered the question, *how do we obtain a (legitimate) state*, Fichte will now be preoccupied with its power and moral purpose. The teleological relation of *Notstaat* and *Vernunftstaat* is established. And we discover that the logical separation of state *qua* government from the restored atomism of civil society has really been made so as to create a discrete, legitimate instrument for the purpose of moulding its subjects into a moral commonwealth of united will. Already in the *Sittenlehre* the fissure is made between a humanity in general (the focus of moral effort) and a limited political community (as yet without any 'nationalist' overtones) that becomes the model-school of progress.

From this point on, Fichte 'nationalizes' his vision of the community, only to insist on its cosmic relevance the more demandingly. The *Sittenlehre* tells us that mankind has the duty and vocation to converge toward an ever distant point where all shall will the same thing.[1] Elsewhere, this frankly 'ideal' solution takes on a certain worldly flesh: 'It is the vocation of our race to unite itself into one single body, all the parts of which shall be thoroughly known to each other, and all possessed of a similar culture.'[2] Further, we are told that 'the human race is...the only true finite existence'.[3] Such statements appear recurrently during the entire period (1798–1807) when Fichte is engaged in defining and enlarging the prerogatives of the *Notstaat*, culminating in his identification of that necessary form of political life with the 'fourth epoch' of world history. As yet the 'nationalist' apotheosis of the *Reden* has not been reached; but we must bear in mind hints dropped in the Freemasonry letters of 1800 and other writings along the way.

[1] *Ethics*, pp. 266 f.   [2] *Vocation of Man*, p. 429.
[3] *Nature of the Scholar*, p. 223.

In the *Closed Commercial State* of 1800, there is, behind the rabbit-in-the-hat mechanics of Fichte's economic solution, an undisguised movement toward defining a nationalism. We know, in the first place, that the ultimate purpose of the closed state is not economic at all, but moral. But—and it is a large discovery— economic justice is seen as a *prius*. Fichte strongly developed the maxim, foreshadowed in the *Naturrecht*: to each according to his capacities.[1] In 1793 he had demanded for each person willing to work 'nourishing food...adequate clothing...a sound place to live'.[2] In 1796 he had confirmed: 'Precisely as there must be no poor man in a rational state, so also there must be no idler.'[3] By 1800 the conception of the dignity of work is notably enlarged: 'In the [rational] state...no one can make a considerable fortune, but no one either can descend to poverty.'[4] 'Man should work,' he further writes, 'but not like a draught animal that falls asleep beneath its burden.'[5] Finally, the significant 'socialist' conclusion: '...it is the role of the state to give to each one his portion'.[6] The consequence is an absolute division of labour determined by the state, with presumably a small passage left open for the mobility of intellectual 'capacities'.[7] In any case, it is clear that all this economic planning and coerced harmony of interests is intended to subserve the cultivation of the general morality: Fichte's 'natural order' is entirely man-made.[8] 'It is the state alone', Fichte writes, 'that gathers an indeterminate crowd of men into a *closed whole*.'[9] The closed economic system is intended to parallel and complete the closed structures of legality and religion. Can we now imagine a closed communitarian and ethical whole?

In a most Rousseauian passage, Fichte remarks: 'in wishing to be everything and everywhere at home, we have become nothing fitting or integral, and we are nowhere at home'.[10] We remember that in counterpoint to the audacious idea of 'timeless' Germany, there was an acute, defensive sensation of homelessness. But the completely 'closed' state becomes a laboratory for human harmony; it builds a nation and a home: 'Obviously...a closed nation such

---

[1] *Handelsstaat, S.W.* III, 440. [2] *Beiträge, S.W.* VI, 185. [3] *Rights*, p. 294; cf. pp. 291, 295.
[4] *Handelsstaat, S.W.* III, 419.   [5] *Ibid.* pp. 422-3.   [6] *Ibid.* p. 403.
[7] *Ibid.* pp. 420-1.   [8] *Ibid.* pp. 446-7.   [9] *Ibid.* p. 401.   [10] *Ibid.* p. 512.

as this, whose members live only among themselves and scarcely at all with foreigners and which acquires through the measures described, its own way of life, its unique structure and customs, will be a different nation, an absolutely new one.'[1] In this new vision of mankind's moralization, all states will progressively 'close'—the success of the first will determine the actions of the others[2]—and the world will be a conglomeration of similar *polis*-states, each immanently developing its reason. The cosmopolitan ideal will be maintained at the level of state relations by the universal community of scholars (to whom the law of *Weltbürgertum* now exclusively applies),[3] and, most importantly, by the parallel moral vocations of *each* state. Coercion will wane as moral behaviour establishes itself.

Up to this point, the nation has been suggested, not defined. But cosmopolitanism has been made immanent without sacrificing the universal teleology of the *Sittenlehre*. A sharp distinction has been drawn between those who have commerce and contact with the outside (rulers and scholars) and those whose main purpose, in the words of Rousseau, is 'être bon aux gens avec qui on vit'. What is still lacking is the apotheosis of German values.

In the *Grundzüge* these matters are taken up again and further clarified. Here Fichte decisively draws the connection between the smaller whole and the greater whole, completing the echo of the twelfth Masonic letter:

[The State] must regard itself as a completed whole; and as its common purpose is identical with that of the human race, it must regard the aggregate of its citizens as the human race itself...It is therefore the same thing whether we say...that the state directs all individual powers *toward the life of the race*; or...that it directs them *toward its own life as the state*...[4]

The philosopher will debate whether this correlation of teleologies is metaphysical or simply analogical. In any case, no doubt under the impact of the idealization of Greece, a third term has been irretractibly interposed between the polar values of individual and species—an intermediary 'closed whole'.

---

[1] *Ibid.* p. 509.
[2] *Ibid.* This 'automaticity' of example is Fichte's apparent moral equivalent of international agression. Cf. his remarks on national education, *Addresses*, pp. 169–70. It is also a measure of his utopian strain. [3] *Ibid.* p. 506. [4] *Characteristics*, p. 161.

C. THE GERMANIC SPIRIT AND THE FULLNESS OF TIME

Already in 1805 there was a whiff of German disaster in the air; these portents were perceived by Fichte, Schleiermacher and others. Fichte was already preaching, as we know, the abolition of the 'third epoch' through its own self-negation and the emergence of the severe duty and purpose of the 'fourth'. Who was to lead the march? Fichte had cast his lot with Prussia; there can be no serious doubt that he had ceased to look toward the French for the inauguration of moral leadership in the age of the *Notstaat* and the 'Neue Welt'. But what if the state on which the burden of history was to be placed at this moment was not sufficiently powerful? Then, replies Fichte, the state can gradually increase its importance by the 'cultivation of internal strength'.[1] It can, he explains, lure strength (population, talent, etc.) from its neighbours because 'the Christian Europeans...recognize this common Europe as their one true fatherland'.[2] Hence it is expected that the state which best embodies the spirit of progress will command their allegiance. Had this not been so in 1789? In this interesting remark old and new ideals cross and penetrate: the inherent cosmopolitanism of transcendental philosophy tangles with hints of a new Machiavellianism, the mobile *Gelehrtenrepublik* and the cohesive 'closed' *Volksnation* are set at odds, only to be rejoined by historical purpose. At this point Fichte allows himself another significant speculation: 'There is a necessary tendency in every cultivated state to extend itself generally, and to include all men within the unity of its citizenship.'[3] If the allusion is toward the past, toward the cosmopolitan fraternity of the French Legislative Assembly in 1792, the intimation is toward new possibilities, across the threshold of the 'fourth epoch'. Both historically and logically the tension is still very great.

In 1799 Fichte had written: 'I hereby declare with the greatest frankness that there is today no country in Europe where I would prefer to live than Germany.'[4] Now, in the *Grundzüge*, he bids adieu to the past, to that other nation which, after all its promise, has shown its true colours by becoming the plaything of Helvétius and

---

[1] *Characteristics.* p. 228.   [2] *Ibid*, p. 232.   [3] *Ibid.* p. 228.
[4] *Gerichtliche Verantwortung, S.W.* v, 295.

Napoleon: 'The most cultivated state in the European Republic of Nations is in every age without exception the most active and enterprising...[but] a state which feels itself in possession of secure and undisputed superiority easily becomes careless...'[1] The possession of the Idea has passed; the 'fourth epoch' struggles to be born. 'Where then is the fatherland of the truly cultivated Christian European?' Fichte demands:

In general it is Europe;—in particular it is that state in Europe that occupies the highest rank of culture...Let then mere earthborn men, who recognize their fatherland in the soil, the rivers and the mountains, remain citizens of the fallen state,—they retain what they desire, and what constitutes their happiness; the sun-like spirit, irresistibly attracted, will wing its way wherever there is light and liberty.[2]

Thus we see that the almost palpable community of sweat and toil of the *Closed Commercial State*, if not precisely a contradiction to the true vision of a fatherland, was surely no more than a technique on the way to the idealist harmony of souls. This is at the antipodes of Rousseau; we are reminded once again that nature held few charms for Fichte. Again, the absolute division between 'phenomenal' man and 'spiritual' man is emphatically drawn. The spirit awaits Germans and Germany, where 'completed sinfulness' is running its course. But if the Germans are to emerge as the spiritual people *par excellence*, the development of their collective consciousness must be shown to have contained always the seeds of their destiny. As a people 'born without a history',[3] they must have escaped the contamination that has now denied the French their right to lead. Ideally, they must also be the historical people of the 'fullness' of time, the embodiment of the passage of consciousness into *Vernunft*, assuming their vocation at the moment when the Idea has found its literal expression in thought and remains only to be enacted. Finally, as a spiritual race, the Germans alone are equipped to render leadership its due for the period of the compulsory *Notstaat* in the interest of philosophical penetration. Led by the philosophical consciousness which, at the opening of the 'Neue Welt', is still one

---

[1] *Characteristics*, pp. 238–9. On the French philosophical incapacity for greatness, cf. *Staatslehre, S.W.* IV, 422–30; *Entwurf, S.W.* VII, 566–7.
[2] *Characteristics*, p. 240.   [3] *Entwurf*, p. 565.

stage ahead of the people at large, the German mission is to strain purposefully toward that absolute democracy of moral persons which, transcendental and beyond time, is the eternal conquest of time itself.

Shortly after the delivery of the *Grundzüge* and the 'Nature of the Scholar' and 'Blessed Life' lectures, Fichte was given a practical task by the Prussian government: a study of the reorganization of the University of Erlangen, where he was awaiting appointment at the outbreak of the war. The resulting document, important as an expression of Fichte's pedagogical ideals, includes a key passage where he distinguishes between attitudes of 'Atticism' and 'Spartanism'.[1] Here, three images are superimposed: the small 'state' community; the larger, as yet ideal, 'national' community; and, finally, a community of the 'general new-European character'. Fichte opts for 'Atticism', which is a combination of the latter two, a 'comprehensible patriotism...which easily reconciles cosmopolitanism and German national spirit'. The 'Spartan' closed community is no longer adequate as a pedagogical resource. Evidently the mechanics of retrenchment of 1800 have given way to the notion of a community that can mediate between political reality and cosmopolitan ideality. At the level of thought, and in prefiguration of Germany's expanded role in Europe and in history, the earlier quasi-Montagnard community, bent on securing its internal virtue, is opened to culture-bearing Girondin perspectives. It might be said that Fichte enacts in reverse and, to be sure, only in thought, the literal career of the Revolution in France. Yet the ideal of the 'closed' state, now indubitably nationalized, survives in all Fichte's subsequent political formulations, underscored by the declaration of the thirteenth lecture of the *Reden* that political universality is a snare and delusion for the foreseeable future.[2] At bottom, 'Atticism' means for Fichte not a hybrid Europeanism, but the best and purest of the German example. One may wonder whether this Periclean summons did not, in the end, work toward Alcibiadean conclusions. However, at the time of the *Reden*, with the Prussian army broken and the state reduced by two-fifths of its territory, Fichte himself

---

[1] *Ideen über die innere Organisation der Universität Erlangen* (1805–6), *N.W.* III, 284.
[2] *Addresses to the German Nation*, pp. 186–8, 197–200.

was categorical: 'The fight with weapons has ended; there arises now, if we so will it, the new fight of principles, of morals, of character.'[1]

Now the second synthesis of mind and event was broken—unless, as Fichte had said, the 'third epoch' had completely to destroy itself for the new 'spirit of the age' to emerge in all its clarity. But we need not fault his patriotism for the sake of his philosophy: they were now correlative, as they had never precisely been in the 'French' period. The *Wissenschaftslehre* did not need to be 'suspended for the duration'; still this was obviously a time for 'Leben', not 'Philosophieren'. Fichte deepened his emotions by savouring Machiavelli and Tacitus, and by translating parts of Camoẽs's patriotic epic, the *Lusiades*, from the Portuguese.[2]

In 1806 and 1807 he wrote two little 'patriotic dialogues'. The first of these gives his most succinct restatement of the problem of nation, humanity and history. The learned interlocutor, designated as 'B', declares that 'such a thing as cosmopolitanism ["the will that the purpose of life and of man be reached in all humanity"] is really impossible, but that in reality cosmopolitanism must necessarily become patriotism'.[3] The explanation given expresses the entire meaning of the better-known *Reden*:

The patriot desires that humanity's goal be reached first of all in that nation of which he is a member. In our times that goal can be promoted only by science [*Wissenschaft*; i.e. the *Wissenschaftslehre*]. Thus science and its widest possible dissemination in our time must be the immediate goal of humanity, and no other goal can or should be set for it...Only the German can desire this, because only he, through his possession of science and the given capacity of understanding it, can know that this is the immediate goal of humanity. This goal is the only possible patriotic one. Thus only the German can be a patriot. He alone, while serving his nation, can work for humanity as well.

Fichte's war-time writings amount to half-hortatory, half-analytic amplifications of the identity of the Germans as both the *philosophical* and the *historical* people, the flesh and blood on which the *Zeitgeist* and true religio-philosophical lucidity (formally represented by the *Wissenschaftslehre*) converge. But it is not to be imagined that

---

[1] *Ibid.* p. 201. [2] *Leben und Briefwechsel*, I, 525 f.
[3] *Der Patriotismus und sein Gegenteil: Patriotische Dialoge*, I, N.W. III, 228 f.

'history' makes its own decisions, or makes them necessarily when the moment is ripe with possibility. That is man's free task as a moral agent; he *is* history. The tension between the potentiality and the actuality, characteristic of all humanistic and immanent teleologies, is maintained; the 'logification' of history depends on an 'ideal' or 'transcendental' logic. Thus exhortation is very much in order, and Fichte does not shy from it.

To the Prussian soldiers he declares that the war they are engaged in will decide if 'all that humanity has gained since its origin by a thousand sacrifices is to be kept or increased'.[1] Will humanity survive its crisis? If the Roman Empire had been able to subject and destroy the German nation at the time of Augustus and Arminius, human development would have been entirely different and much less noble. Now a greater peril is at hand. 'The decision of this question ultimately falls...to the European state that possesses all the human values actually at stake and is consequently charged with preserving them.'[2] 'If', Fichte muses, 'a German does not establish the government of the world through knowledge...it will be the North American tribes [*sic*] that will do it and put an end to the present state of affairs.'[3]

D. THE 'REDEN': WHAT IS HISTORY? WHAT IS A GERMAN?

Rather than dwelling in detail on Fichte's theory of the German mission as contained in the *Reden*, undoubtedly his most familiar work, it seems enough to characterize it briefly and to focus on two main questions.

With regard to the first point, the *Addresses to the German Nation* are an exaggerative patriotic performance, both stirring and grotesque—no doubt justified somewhat by circumstances—which nevertheless manage to encompass, and encompass systematically,

---

[1] *Anwendung, S.W.* VII, 506. Cf. exhortation, *Addresses to the German Nation, in fine,* pp. 227–8.

[2] *Ibid.* Cf. *Addresses to the German Nation,* p. 225: '...if...the German stock is to be swallowed up in Roman civilization, it were better that it had fallen before the Rome of old than a Rome of today.'

[3] *Patriotische Dialoge,* p. 243; cf. p. 266.

all the major Fichtean themes since 1800. The pedagogical mania, the 'stürmisch' exaltation of the popular spirit of Germany, the praise of the 'profundity' of the national philosophical tradition are there; so, too, is a paean to the purity of the language, its 'imaginability', and of Germans as an *Urvolk* (problematically associated with the *Normalvolk* of the *Grundzüge*). So are the closed commercial state, the reiteration of the new 'fourth epoch' characterized by the *Notstaat* as a source of 'complete regeneration', the assertion that the German mind is the locus of Asiatic (Christian) spirituality, Greek patriotism and European social and institutional evolution. Here the German and Fichtean destinies are colossally joined: 'I am doing [this] solely because no one has done it before me...There must always be one who is first; then let him be the first who can!'[1] What is *sui generis* about the *Reden*, aside from its decibel count, is its assimilation of all the parts of Fichtean practical philosophy within the inferentially highest value of nationhood. Matters of earlier priority —legality, pure ethics, art, science, religion—seem here to be subordinated to the all-consuming matrix of the historical life of a people—a people appointed by destiny.

The first impression is that the *Volk* is Fichte's final and considered answer to the proper organization of human activity. It is true that the concrete substantiality of nationhood—the 'phenomenon' of cosmopolitanism—has surged forward in the Fichtean axiology from 1800 on. It is also true that Fichte gives us little reason to think that older orders of value have not been superseded by an absolute surrender of idealism to history, an absolute suffocation of the 'fullness of time' in a chauvinist's interpretation of the *Geist der Zeit*. Perhaps this is so: the Germany of the *Reden* seems much more palpable than a mere *philosophische Heimat*. That suspicion is seemingly confirmed by Fichte's ardent research in Machiavelli and the terms of his opuscule on the Italian master, where *Staatsräson* and physical power on the international plane join the whole internal apparatus of the *Notstaat* as instruments of verity and progress—conditioned by the very physical principle of survival.[2]

---

[1] *Addresses to the German Nation*, p. 214.
[2] *Über Machiavelli, N.W.* III, 403–53.

But we still have to consider the axiological ambiguities of idealism in general. For the idealist philosopher, each eternal value of the human order entails systematic expression of its philosophical structure in the perspective of that value. Thus, a treatment of law or of religion will encompass other segments of philosophy in a particularly law-oriented or religion-oriented way. The question is one of perspectives on a holistic universe of all knowledge that is very troublesome to grasp in a simultaneous vision. If such a vision is possible, it is usually reduced to a treatment of the bare structure of knowledge, like the *Wissenschaftslehre* or Hegel's *Logik*, and the problem is to match the logical rib-cage with the flesh of a world that is characterized not only by 'practicity' but also by the spatio-temporal dimensions of phenomenality and the manifestations of human activity. Here, the philosopher not only has great difficulty in conveying his central vision, impartial and untilted, to auditors and readers, but also runs the risk of being wilfully misread. This is precisely the question involved in the recurrent debates over Hegel's 'divinization of the state', his correlations of the forms of *Geist*, the relationships within his province of 'absolute knowledge', and so forth. But the problem is no less applicable to Fichte.

In the *Reden* Fichte presents most comprehensively the 'nation' perspective. Thus it is scarcely surprising that the other values, or manifestations of the Idea, are seen from this angle. To compound this difficulty, the *Reden* is an instance of 'popular philosophy' delivered in the emotional circumstances of foreign occupation. In short, it is propaganda. But it is not simply propaganda for German rebirth, it is propaganda for the vision of life according to the *Wissenschaftslehre*, as are all of Fichte's writings from 1794 on. The renewed striving to join 'philosophy' and 'life'—Sisyphean task—is inevitable, and it would be hazardous to say that Fichte had sacrificed philosophy to the nation, when he could dream only of a 'philosophical nation' or, indeed, wisdom to mass sentiment, when that sentiment, too, remained a practical task.

We ask again: what is history? In effect, Fichte tells us that history is what 'ideal' Germans think it to be: a pattern guided by the thread of conviction in moral perfectibility. As against the determinisms and defeatisms of the French, their creed is that man fashions history by creating new things in time.[1] Perilously close at moments to the notion that the Idea is a superhuman stream of energy that drags men along, Fichte always recovers the autonomy of man from the vortex of the absolute and, like Kant, but now within the context of a cosmos that witnesses great, profusive bursts of collective values, symbolic peoples, and heroic actors into historical time, defends the proposition that the human vision creates history.

But how many sea-changes have there been since Kant, who held the individual to be not just the 'accident of the species' but its fundamental prototype? Kant's history was explicitly a tension between the phenomenal (psychological) dispositions of man-in-general and his inextinguishable moral or timeless task. Given the premise that man is to become *man*, the moral primacy follows and phenomenality must paradoxically collaborate in this progress. But Fichte creates contradictions that it is far beyond the power of a theory of knowledge to resolve. The main ones are these:

1. A 'class tension' derived from the harsh separation of 'leaders' and 'followers' or 'tutors' and 'pupils' implicit in the meaning of the *Notstaat* and logically visible ever since the early distinction between the 'original consciousness' and 'derivative reflection' of the *Grundlage*.

2. A 'national tension', now prominent in the terms of the *Patriotic Dialogues* and the *Reden*, which accords to 'Germans', in this instance defined popularly and linguistically as a race, both temporal and eternal pre-eminence over other peoples and *Volksgeister*.

3. A 'historical tension' implied in the paradoxical balancing of the millennial persistence and development of the 'pure' traits of 'Germanness' as against the cosmopolitan and, properly speaking, idealist evolution of the entire culture of the Judaeo-Mediterranean-European sphere.

In terms of the first two perspectives, we find prefigured much of European ideological history for the next hundred and fifty years,

---

[1] *Addresses to the German Nation*, pp. 93–5.

the vast source of debate and battle as to whether the seminal division between community and humanity shall be in terms of 'those who possess the Idea' and those who do not or in terms of 'world-historical' and tributary nations. Whatever concrete historical terms are employed, this represents a struggle between aristocratic or 'value-bearing' elements and servile or unproductive ones. Each instance of this mighty combat has elements peculiar to itself, but the entire unfolding of this problem can be detected within the development of Fichtean thought.

Fichte's 'class tension' is, of course, between ethical 'haves' and 'have-nots'. The predominant vision is that of spiritual 'majors' and 'minors', which we saw prefigured in Kant, cast on both national and world-historical planes. It is a new Sparta, no longer the eight centuries' miracle of stasis and durability, but a dynamic *polis* whose helots are admonished and coerced to lose their chains. Yet, as long as the *Notstaat* lasts, there will be helots impressed beneath the lords-spiritual of the *Wissenschaftslehre*.

With Rousseau this problem could not arise because, while there were ideals, there was no teleological destiny: the vocation of man was to retrench, to succour himself with simple tasks, with simple community, not to expand, not to steal the sacred fire of the gods. With Marx, the vision is yet different: those who are about to possess the Idea, trained in the industrial hells of Lancashire, are not the dutiful pupils of a race of seers, but the ultimate negation and scourge of their pretentious masters. This is partly because Marx has cursed to eternity the fundamental religiosity that Fichte, whatever his personal theological convictions may have been, retained in his paradigm of priesthood and believers. Yet who is to say that the Party did not arise precisely to vindicate Fichte's logic of the *Notstaat* and to cripple Marx's prediction?

The 'national tension' of Fichte is, of course, also 'ideal'. There was no Germany in 1808. And, although ensconced in a free Berlin after 1810 and dean of the faculty at the new university raised by Stein, Hardenberg and Humboldt, Fichte would not outlive the sound of the cannons. For this dynamic moral optimist, it was a fitful moment to speculate *de novo*. But if there *is* no Germany, no philosophical people *de facto*, but only one to be, then the heart's desire is the heart's resource. And this leads to the second important question raised by Fichte: What is a German?

'The Germans', Fichte says, '...as an original people [are] a people that has the right to call itself simply *the* people, in contrast to other branches that have been torn away from it.'[1] Since Fichte's criteria of race are essentially linguistic—and since he has ascribed all manner of virtues to the German *Ursprache*—this is a fairly positive identification.[2] We have here, essentially, the *Muttervolk* of post-classical civilization. Moreover, this is the people that 'understands' and can further deepen true classicism.[3] It was the mission of the nations of neo-Latin language to preserve and disseminate classical learning, but because their hybrid speech was fundamentally out of sorts with their souls, they could not treat it profoundly; they could acquire only *Verstand*.[4] 'True' Christianity was also alien to their Latin ways. On the basis of Fichte's arguments, the 'German' is not an especially elusive specimen.

But then we are confronted by a statement of quite different import:

...whoever believes in spirituality and in the freedom of this spirituality, and who wills the eternal development of this spirituality by freedom, wherever he may have been born and whatever language he speaks, is of our blood; he is one of us and will come over to our side. Whoever believes in stagnation, retrogression, and the round dance of which we spoke, or who sets a dead nature at the helm of the world's government, whereever he may have been born and whatever language he speaks, is non-German and a stranger to us; and it is to be wished that he would separate himself from us completely, and the sooner the better.[5]

Essentially, Fichte's conflict is between the genesis of the nation, cemented by the common experience of (pure) language and its derivative folkways, and the genesis of truth discovered in the growth

---

[1] *Ibid.* p. 92; cf. p. 107.   [2] Cf. *ibid.* pp. 53 ff.   [3] *Ibid.* pp. 74–5.
[4] *Ibid.* pp. 54–5. Fichte's insistence on verbal communication as central to the moral bonds of the community runs throughout his work. Whereas Kantian subjects perhaps reach their most intimate common experience in the aesthetic moment of the beautiful, Fichtean ones are bound by their tongues. This is an important dimension of the distinction between Kant's cosmopolitanism and Fichte's cosmonationalism.
[5] *Ibid.* p. 108; cf. *Entwurf*, p. 573: 'The concept of unity as regards the German people is as yet in no way real, it is a general postulate for the future. But it will not exalt any ethnic or other particularism; it will make the citizen of freedom into something real.'

of the Western consciousness and authenticated by progressive philosophical sophistication. How can the 'Word' mean 'the people of the Word'? The clash is clearly between custom and reason, that perennial problem of human thought since Plato. Either we can decide that Fichte is arguing in a circle (i.e. the 'German' is a believer in transcendental idealism; the transcendental idealist is a 'German'), or else he is defining the German by a double exclusion (one must be a 'German' both of speech and of thought).

Fichte cannot be easily freed from this dilemma. But it is more fruitful to see the collision than to limit the damage. Fichte wanted both the 'aristocratic' cosmopolitanism of the 'thought' world, and the 'democratic' communitarianism of the 'speech' world. The struggle between the visible phenomenon and its inner spirit is not resolved. 'Philosophy' and 'life' remain at odds. Solidarity and diffusion, erudition and simplicity, theoretical and practical reason cannot cohere. Realism, as Fichte reminded the first readers of the *Wissenschaftslehre*, is dual. And we may wonder whether German history—which has been 'kept out of history', pure—is not the 'ideal' sequence set against the 'real' sequence of Christian and Mediterranean Europe, whether German history is not the collective paradigm of the practical ego reaching to grasp the absolute in pure act. It would be tempting to think that Enlightenment values, Napoleonic imperialism, and the French culture in general stand for lower nature, eudaemonism and non-ego, a task—a last task—for German spirituality to overcome. However, as M. Gueroult has effectively shown, that is a far-fetched interpretation, inconsistent with the notion of the common spirituality of all men.[1] Even at the apogee of patriotism, Fichte halts before the conclusion that his opponents are 'objects' and to be so treated. His point is that *they* think themselves and all men to be objects.

Still, not so vaporously behind the philosophical arras lurks the Machiavellian insight, the phenomenalism of statecraft and nation-building. In one of his most aggressive wartime writings, Fichte, in a sentiment as old as Hellas and as modern as the Algerian

---

[1] M. Gueroult, 'Fichte et la Révolution française', p. 307, arguing against the post-World War I thesis of the philosopher Charles Andler; cf. the preface of the latter to *Le pangermanisme philosophique* (Paris, 1917).

revolution, reaches the conclusion that values must be struggled for and not dropped in one's lap: '...in war and by seeing the common and collective struggle through [*durch gemeinschaftliches Durch-kämpfen*] a people becomes a people'.[1] The entry to history is by battle.[2] Moreover, 'the history of a community consists in collective deeds and sufferings...there is still no finally shaped German national character. This lies before us as a future task'.[3] Essentially, this is the Spartan, the Rousseauian, the Montagnard war of defence, the precondition for the purification of the *Heimat* through the procedures of the *Notstaat*. In the *Reden* Fichte specifically disclaims the desire of true Germans to carry to war abroad.[4] History is long, and there is too much to do at home. However, this national introversion means a drawing back from idealist cosmopolitanism toward the limited instrumentalism of the nation-state, later significantly defined as 'a community enveloped by custom [*Sitten*]'.[5]

Nevertheless, the correlation between world history and the German spirit, between *kairos* and *logos*, between time and space, is unambiguously established: 'We are of the opinion that, in regard to time, this is the very time, and that now the race is exactly midway between the two great epochs of its life on earth. But, in regard to space, we believe that it is first of all the Germans who are called on to begin the new era as pioneers and models for the rest of mankind.'[6]

Fichte does not let these thoughts pass without a utopian exercise, the kind of indulgence which Kant's historical prudence forbade. The reader will recall that Fichte's recorded literary career began in 1788 with the 'sleepless night', that sketch of a timeless, rationalist perspective satire, an anti-utopia which, had mood directed otherwise, might as well have been a utopia, style of Diderot's *Voyage de Bougainville*. But how far history has travelled between its past and future identifications. We are now permitted to glimpse 'the republic of the Germans at the beginning of the twenty-second century under its fifth imperial leader [*Reichsvogt*]'. Here, the *Vernunftstaat* or *absoluter Staat* is actualized in all its glory, all historical irration-

[1] *Entwurf*, p. 550.   [2] See Fichte's remarks on a 'just war', *Staatslehre*, pp. 401–15.
[3] *Entwurf*, p. 567.
[4] *Addresses to the German Nation*, pp. 198–200.
[5] *Sittenlehre* of 1812, *N.W.* III, 90.
[6] *Addresses to the German Nation*, p. 40.

ality swallowed up in the ideal of immanent and German humanity.[1] It has taken three hundred years, a modest projection for the anxious Fichte. One further note: the landscapes are charming—almost in the mood of Cobbett. It is the only instance where Fichte seems to have been willing to regard nature as anything but an enemy. Fichte summarizes the whole transformation of the utopian exercise from rationalist to futuristic orientations.

If Fichte's proto-nationalism is shrill at times—cohesive and *gemeinschaftlich*—his aristocracy of the intellect persists undiminished. The end of the *Reden* depicts a joint effort of young, old, scholars, men of commerce, rulers.[2] But, in essence, it is the learned caste, deserting the 'sphere of pure thought' for the 'actual world', bridging the great gulf 'between the idea and the act of introducing it into every separate form of life', who must teach and consummate the republic.[3] Fundamentally, Fichte's is a vested interest. It has not changed since he wrote, over a decade earlier, of the scholar's vocation as 'the most widely extended survey of the actual advancement of the human race in general and the steadfast promotion of that advancement'.[4] But the German scholar-seer-leader has now become the 'phenomenon' of scholarship in general.

---

[1] *Die Republik der Deutschen zu Anfang des 22. Jahrhunderts unter ihrem 5. Reichsvogte*, *S.W.* VII, 538–9. For comment, see Wallner, *Fichte als politischer Denker*, p. 218; Walz, *Staatsidee*, p. 610; Franz Haymann, *Weltbürgertum und Vaterlandsliebe* (Berlin, 1924), pp. 74–5. For an interesting, little-known futuristic utopia from the French side during the First Empire, see Georges Pariset, 'L'utopie de deux Lorrains sous Napoléon Ier', in *Etudes d'histoire révolutionnaire et contemporaine* (Paris, 1929). Some of the resemblances are striking.

[2] *Addresses to the German Nation*, pp. 217 ff. Fichte also addressed 'ancestors' and 'descendants', taking in the fullness of time.

[3] *Ibid.* p. 221.

[4] *Vocation of the Scholar*, p. 188.

6

EDUCATION AND THE FUTURE COMMUNITY

A. IMAGE ONE: THE 'GELEHRTENREPUBLIK'

In 1774 the poet Klopstock, by coincidence a relative of Fichte's wife, published an eccentric work called *Die deutsche Gelehrtenrepublik*.[1] Entirely floated by public subscription, like Pope's translation of Homer had been in England half a century before, it was a commercial declaration of independence for German writers. More importantly, it was also a quaint poetics and politics of the resurgent *Kulturstaat*.[2] Affected by the *Sturm und Drang* current and the wish to break free of French influence, Klopstock takes German culture half way out of the suffocating European 'republic of scholars', where the scarcely invisible dictatorial hand is Voltaire, and builds an imaginary rump parliament of his own. The Gothic corporations, classes, rites, pomps and penalties of this mythical body all amount to a forceful rejection of neo-Latinity. This literary monstrosity well repays careful reading by the student of German politics. Even if the *deutsche Gelehrtenrepublik* is a scholarly community of the spirit, it is, above all, a German republic, nourishing the national flame amid political disunity and princely indifference. In it the acts of high treason are absolutism, contempt for the German language, genius and people, preference for foreign tastes, and courtly flattery. It is conceived as a natural aristocracy, giving little quarter to that passionate but ignorant mob, the *Poebel*. As both 'scholarly' and 'German', it anticipates the dialectic of cosmopolitanism and nationalism. Even Goethe praised this paradigmatic, if clumsy, fantasy; for it touched the nerve of the German intelligentsia's political longing.[3] Germany did not simply catch the fever of the French Revolution in reverse. Germany

---

[1] F. G. Klopstock, *Die deutsche Gelehrtenrepublik* (Hamburg, 1774).
[2] For commentary, M. Boucher, *Sentiment national*, p. 44 f., is excellent. Other early evidence of German cultural nationalism and restiveness: J. G. Zimmerman, *Vom Nationalstolz* (1758); Fr. Karl von Moser, *Von dem deutschen Nationalgeist* (1765).
[3] Goethe, *Poetry and Truth*, II, 64–5.

experienced that fever when it had no state, but only an *esprit centralisant*. The people were not throwing off their chains; the intellectuals, however, were. And, thus, pivoting somewhere between a France that had thrust itself into modernity by political acts and a Republic of Plato where power and wisdom were synchronous, the German masters of idealism fashioned a homeland of culture and spirit out of an ambitious but fragile national rejuvenation. Recognizing this, we are better able to take the measure of Fichte's nationalism and appreciate its peculiarities. For Fichte's own *Gelehrtenrepublik* is a step along the way of actuality from Klopstock's myth, but heavily in its debt. It is a small 'closed' state *qua* ruling intellectual class that betrays these pre-Revolutionary origins, going even behind the vision of the *Wissenschaftslehre*:

In the cultivation of the whole domain of science, and therefore in the constitution of the *Gelehrtenrepublik*, plan, order and system are requisite. From reason as knowledge or the absolute philosophy [i.e. the *Wissenschaftslehre*], the whole domain of science may be completely surveyed, and the office of each individual strictly defined.[1]

Guided by the cosmic grasp of the *Wissenschaftslehre*, the 'scholarly republic' itself will be a kind of *Notstaat*, prevailing until all possible *a priori* knowledge can be certified and its consequences made available for 'art' (fifth epoch).[2]

Thus, in a sense, the *Gelehrtenrepublik* is itself a model for the greater community, for there are evidently degrees of being 'possessed by the Idea'. In fact, however, the scholars are *free vis-à-vis* the world of appearances at large: 'For the republic of scholars there exist no possible symbols, no prescribed direction, no withholding.'[3] By 'symbols', Fichte means the various transitory forms, such as positive religious dogmas, in which the Idea is imperfectly translated to common humanity. Scholars rise above such matters and, in fact, dictate the mutability and reorientation of symbols. The true political import of Fichte's vision lies, then, not in the internal structure of the scholarly world, but in its division from the rest of the citizens of a state. Rigorous selection determines that 'only a few shall devote their lives to science [i.e. wisdom], and by

---

[1] *Characteristics*, p. 117.   [2] *Ibid.*   [3] *Ethics*, p. 263.

Image one : the 'Gelehrtenrepublik'

far the majority to other pursuits [presumably such as the 'closed'
state might assign for the general good]...thus the distinction
between the scholar, or let us say between the learned, and the
unlearned must subsist for a long period'.[1]

Will these scholars then be shut up in their cathedrals of learning,
creating knowledge in an apolitical ivory tower? Assuredly not;
Fichte had especially harsh words for this in the *Reden*.[2] They will
be directing the collective onslaught against nature and moralizing
the people. But if the people at large cannot attain philosophical
wisdom, what have they to fall back on? 'The people', says Fichte,
'must be raised to pure Christianity, such as we have described it
above, as the only medium through which at first Ideas can be
communicated to them.'[3] Fichte himself vacillated throughout his
career over the strategic order of apprehending the Idea; in the
Reden he recommended ethics for the young and religion only for
more mature minds.[4] But the general spirit of Fichte's (and German)
philosophy is consistent: a Christianity of the clarified New Testament, unhindered by bishops, churches and creeds, is the portico to
the cathedral of pure practical knowledge, and indeed the proper
and only access for the majority of men who find themselves outside
the scholarly realm of ideal decision-making. This is an ingenious
and, in some ways, traditional solution to the problem of order.
We might note that the *Grundzüge*, where Fichte argues that purified Christianity makes the Ideas of philosophy more nearly
graspable, anticipates Hegel's *Phenomenology* and antedates it by
one year of publication. In the main, however, Hegel's system is
conceived as a reaction to Fichte, rather than an attempt to press his
conclusions forward.

B. IMAGE TWO: THE MODEL SCHOOL

If the *Gelehrtenrepublik*, in a form derivative from Klopstock, and
of course indirectly from Plato, is one of the critical models for
Fichte's vision of politics, there is a second removed from the realm
of high spirituality and intellectual aristocracy. Related much more

[1] *Characteristics*, p. 115.   [2] *Addresses to the German Nation*, p. 221.
[3] *Characteristics*, p. 115.   [4] *Addresses to the German Nation*, pp. 34-5.

directly to Fichte's 'Jacobinism', his ideal of the cohesive nation, it is also connected with his standard of organic 'Germanness' as set against the cosmopolitan ideal that knows no frontiers. Here, the master is Pestalozzi. The essential paradigm to retain is that the nation is a vast, collective school. In the first image, we saw matters from the perspective of the preceptor and the *idée directrice* of all knowledge; now we see the pupils of a tutelary nation.

Johann Heinrich Pestalozzi himself was the antithesis of the nationalist. With a rather tender humanism that anticipated and affected the nineteenth century, he shared the resurgent bourgeois cosmopolitanism of the eighteenth. He endorsed the French Revolution from the Girondin-cosmopolitan angle. In a famous essay, he deplored the mass violence of the Terror by contrasting it with the 'moral sans-culottism' of the early Christians, who, in their love of freedom, did no violence but suffered it for their faith.[1] Pestalozzi was an eccentric visionary, in the line of Basedow (who had impressed Kant and rather disturbed Goethe),[2] but he was a more resourceful and practical one. He had better fortune with his books and with his model schools: the famous Yverdun attracted attention from all over the continent and unquestionably influenced the philosophy of private education into our own time.

Pestalozzi, too, had digested *Emile*; he, too, stressed the priority of tangible education by observation, plotted the child's course of empirical discovery, and insisted on maternal and familial affection in the learning process. But Pestalozzi recognized that often, especially in poorer families, education in the home was impossible, and that the one-on-one child–tutor relationship was fanciful. In short, he was a pedagogue, not a chimerist. Thus, adopting many applications from Rousseau and discarding others, he expanded the problem of producing 'new men' to the school, and he founded schools for that purpose.[3]

Fichte came early upon Pestalozzi and his theories. The book

---

[1] 'Über Sansculottismus und Christentum', *Pestalozzis Sämmelte Werke* (21 vols., ed. Dejung and Schönebaum, Berlin and Leipzig; Zurich, 1927–64), pp. 263–8.

[2] Cf. note 3, p. 170; also *Poetry and Truth*, II, 156–7.

[3] On Pestalozzi, see Henry Barnard, *Pestalozzi and his Educational System* (New York, 1881); Hans Barth, *Pestalozzis Philosophie der Politik* (Zurich, 1954); and, as concerns Pestalozzi and the French Revolution, A. Stern, *Einfluss*, pp. 45–9.

Image two : the model school

Gertrud und Leonhard was enjoying a wide success. In 1793, through the auspices of his friend the Danish poet, Jens Baggesen, Fichte, winding up his *Hauslehrer* duties and preparing for his career at Jena, met and held several conversations with Pestalozzi.[1] Their exchange of views seems to have produced a harmonious rapprochement of ideas. Although, when in 1808 Fichte carried Pestalozzi's name to his Berlin auditors, he took many exceptions to Pestalozzi's pedagogy (especially its empiricist foundations), he retained a general admiration and a warmth from their encounters.

What Fichte did essentially in the *Reden* was to make the Pestalozzian school—modified by the missions of transcendental idealism—the model for his 'ideal' pedagogical nation. Though the two men differed in method, their major difference is in scope. Pestalozzi was a schoolmaster, but Fichte was the neo–Platonic demiurge of a new political order. Having granted the German potentiality and foreseen the actuality of such a transformation operating in world history, Fichte now felt enabled, in 1808, to demand and receive an obligation, a 'new education' which 'must itself inevitably create the necessity at which it aims'.[2] This is what the first three lectures of the *Reden* are designed to do. In his passion of the moment Fichte oscillates between mission and agents. 'My address', he says, 'is directed especially toward the educated classes in Germany, for I hope that it will be intelligible to them first.'[3] But, he warns, if you do not undertake this responsibility—which amounts, in essence, to a 'true' intellectual stratification of power throughout the 'ideal' nation then 'the present educated classes and their descendants will become the people, while from among the people another more highly educated class will arise'.[4] Torn between his origins and his achievements, Fichte hopes for the latter but is not afraid to threaten the former.

Seen from this angle, the Fichtean community—it is more than a state, because a state is mere 'formality', mere externality; more than a nation, because nations wait in the queue of history for the imposition of a legal and political order; more than both, because it is the

---

[1] On Fichte's contacts with Pestalozzi, see X. Léon, *Fichte et son temps*, I, 211–14; on the assimilation of pedagogical theory, see P. Duproix, *Kant et Fichte*, pp. 150–7.
[2] *Addresses to the German Nation*, p. 18.   [3] *Ibid.* p. 14.   [4] *Ibid.* pp. 14–15.

'phenomenon' and prefiguration of *cosmopolis*—is drawn from two basic models: the Klopstockian heroic aristocracy of intellectual leadership and the Pestalozzian democratic school. Behind it is the shade of Plato; ahead, the prophecy of Marx. And withal, during the indeterminable period of the *Notstaat*, the nation sits at its benches, mastering the lessons of ascent toward a transcendental 'kingdom of ends', while the *Gelehrtenrepublik* governs through its faculty meetings.

C. TOWARD THE PEDAGOGICAL STATE

It now remains to trace this development briefly in Fichte's writings and to establish the connection between scholar and ruler, the Platonic synthesis between knowledge and power.

The reader is by now already familiar with the relation of pedagogy and politics traced through the theories of Rousseau and Kant and with the significance attached to this way of viewing the intellectual and political culture of the period. I have also shown the connection between the epistemological mechanism of the deduction of consciousness through the tension between the 'philosophical' and 'natural' vantage points, which Fichte claimed as his revolutionary contribution to the science of knowledge, and the coercive and educational role of the *Notstaat* in the 'fourth epoch' of world history. Now we can easily discern that both these paradigms are intimately related to the 'master-pupil' image, and that the destination of the individual and the destination of the race are in this respect bound in parallel.

One could infer from Fichte's approach that men, as individuals, are simply to be disciplined and educated until their achievement of self-mastery, and that we have mainly to do with a juvenile and not a political problem. Seen from this angle, it would be possible to say that the ascent of culture is characterized by the transformation of the pupil into a master, his acquisition of a new pupil, and so forth. Like Virgil's Dante, man is thus freed before the gates of Paradise to pursue his own course. But one must not forget that for Fichte most men would sooner regard themselves as 'lumps of lava' than as egos. If self-mastery is imperative, it is also extremely rare in a world malorganized and oriented toward material satisfaction. Therefore, coercive education must be regarded as the essence of the politico-historical process. If the aim is Paradise or 'practical reason', the way is long for persons and for peoples. Thus both education (taken in the widest sense) and philosophical rulership are to be regarded as mediately ethical and so justified. The genesis of the consciousness, the genesis of the world, and the genesis of the moral community are yoked together beneath the prescriptive pedagogy of the Fichtean vision. The Kantian philosopher judges, but the Fichtean philosopher ethicalizes.

The first transposition is from voluntary to forced education and from moral-intellectual cultivation as an individual enterprise to a collective necessity.[1] Kant's hints have ripened into the implications of the tutelary *Notstaat*, which has become, to all practical intent, a *Lehrstaat*. 'No one *is* cultivated,' Fichte wrote pointedly in the *Beiträge*, 'but each one has to cultivate himself.'[2] There is the inevitable Kantian linkage of education to man's teleological destiny: '*Culture*', Fichte writes, 'is the exercise of all faculties in view of absolute liberty.'[3] It is 'the single final goal of man', taken as a physical being.[4]

In the *Beiträge* man's pure moral nature was assumed as prior to his political and social acts; the 'state of nature' and the 'state of grace' were identified. However, this view was a rationalist abstraction which clashed both with the Kantian concept of 'radical evil' (later adapted by Fichte)[5] and with the whole transcendental apparatus of teleological history. Henceforth, original or unsocialized man must be seen as a creature of wilful impulse, a barbarian. In 1794 Fichte brings himself in line with this Kantian conclusion; the pedagogical implications begin to fall in place as well. Since, as the *Naturrecht* will argue, man's *Endzweck* is 'to become a moral being',[6] it then follows that 'all individuals must be educated to be men; otherwise, they would not be men'.[7] Morality is also freedom,

---

[1] This is Duproix's thesis; however, he avoids all the philosophical complexity of the problem.
[2] *Beiträge, S.W.* VI, 90.   [3] *Ibid.* p. 86.
[4] *Ibid.* p. 89. Also, *Vocation of the Scholar*, p. 155. In the years 1790–1 Fichte took extensive notes (preserved in Berlin) on Kant's *Critique of Judgment*; cf. X. Léon, *Fichte et son temps*, III, 295.
[5] *Ethics*, pp. 198–9.   [6] *Rights*, p. 202.   [7] *Ibid.* p. 61.

the 'positive freedom' of transcendental idealism. Although morality in all instances should avoid compulsion, Fichte speaks in 1794 of the duty to diffuse freedom: 'He only is *free* who would make all around him free likewise.'[1] The stage is thus set, by the interlocking of the ideas of scholarship and freedom, for the discernment of history as a vast tutelary enterprise by which the race seizes the Idea. History is essentially a plan established by the 'highest, truest man' or the philosopher, and his task will only be completed when the rational (or moral) is made actual. That is why the world is a school.

From 1798 on, a collective foundation for ethics is created; in gradual steps, leading up to the apotheosis of 1808, it is nationalized as the 'phenomenon' of universality. In the meantime, with the intrusion of the positive state upon all external sectors of the conditioning of morality through the creation of the immanent harmonies of community, the scholar has acquired a preponderate weight in politics. He has become at least the centre of judgment in the *Notstaat*. Politics and pedagogy, *Zwang* and *Erziehung* are approaching a convergence. Moreover, they link the 'closed' state with the rest of the world—until cosmopolis, until utopia. The *Closed Commercial State* says very clearly that 'only the scholar and the higher form of artist [art, too, being a manifestation of the Idea] have need to travel abroad...'[2] The free communication between scholars and artists of all lands is guaranteed.[3]

In view of such an evolution we are not surprised to find Fichte writing, after Jena, that the 'plan of education and the plan of government are identical'.[4] The state is the locus of education and government, of compulsion and spiritual expansion:

Only that state is the true (lawful) one which energetically resolves this contradiction [between coercion and freedom]. The intermediate member is thereupon precisely located: it is the education of all to insight [*Einsicht* is one of Fichte's favourite words in his late writings] derived from law. Only if the coercive state fulfills this condition has it any right to exist... Coercion is itself education—namely, education for insight into [one's] ethical vocation.[5]

---

[1] *Vocation of the Scholar*, p. 167.   [2] *Handelsstaat, S.W.* III, 506.   [3] *Ibid.* p. 513.
[4] *Excurse zur Staatslehre, S.W.* VII, 583; cf. p. 579. Also, *Addresses to the German Nation*, p. 102: 'Only the nation which has first solved in actual practice the problem of educating perfect men will then also solve the problem of the perfect state.'   [5] *Excurse*, p. 575.

The sovereign, or prince, who gathers all coercive power unto himself, has at least one limitation: he cannot hinder education, which is an 'Urrecht'.[1] But education and compulsion are now indissolubly connected. As Fichte will put it in a later passage, compulsion is 'the condition for the bringing forth of insight and the acceptance of discipline'.[2] And we see very clearly from the *Reden* what the method and purpose of this education is to be. Regarding the former, 'the new education must consist essentially in this, that it completely destroys freedom of the will [i.e., arbitrariness, *Willkür*] in the soil which it undertakes to cultivate, and produces on the contrary strict necessity in the decisions of the will, the opposite being impossible'.[3] Fichte's new vision aims at making a habit of reason, thus yoking together the custom which Kantian ethics proscribed and the autonomy which it first defined. Regarding the latter: 'This training...is the training of the pupil's faculty of knowledge, and, of course, not historical training in the actual condition of things, but the higher and philosophical training in the laws which make that actual condition of things inevitable.'[4] We are far from Rousseau's 'negative' teaching of inevitablity.

Insight, discipline, culture...these are Kantian words, and yet we have come a distance from Kant in substance and in tone. The real difference is threefold. In the first place, state and school are no longer an analogy; they have become a symbiosis. In the second place, the element of collective coercion is now as visible as it could be made. Thirdly, the mediating capacity of the nation has been affirmed, fulfilling its mission in all history and in the history of the compulsory 'fourth epoch'. In Fichte's view, this culture-community of a people unites all individuals with bonds stronger than jus-naturalism ever conceived and makes methodical compulsion tolerable as an instrument of the general good and the destiny of mankind.

According to the work, the mood, and the time, Fichte's vision

---

[1] *Entwurf, S.W.* VII, 561. [2] *Staatslehre, S.W.* IV, 440.
[3] *Addresses to the German Nation*, p. 17; cf. p. 18: 'If you want to influence [the pupil] at all, you must do more than merely talk to him; you must fashion (*machen*) him in such a way that he cannot will otherwise than what you wish him to will.'
[4] *Ibid.* p. 21. Moreover (p. 43), 'the education which we have hitherto described is likewise the education for this philosophy'.

of the longevity of the *Notstaat* expands and contracts. We might, however, pay special attention to the Platonism of the *Reden*, where the ideal of a German nation, new-created within the space of a generation, is hypothesized.[1] The parallel, not only with the *Republic*, but with Michel Lepelletier's Montagnard project for French public education, with Saint-Just's *Institutions républicaines*, and other documents of the epoch, is evident. The young people are to be separated from their homes, spared the dwindling but corrosive venom of the 'third epoch'.[2] They will 'form a separate and self-contained community with its organization precisely defined, based on the nature of things and demanded throughout by reason', a miniature *Vernunftstaat*.[3] Thus, just as the Fichtean nation-state is intended as an ideal school writ large, the school is expected to become a state of entirely reasonable beings. Technically, however, they are *Notstaaten* through and through.

D. RULERSHIP

Who shall rule and where shall rulers be found? For a philosopher enjoying the hospitality and employment of a dynastic state, this might be regarded as a touchy subject. But Fichte is now more fearless than he was at Jena. Although the republic is the ideal form, he says in the *Reden*, monarchy has, on the whole, served the Germans well.[4] Yet, prior to the War of Liberation, he sharply reminds Frederick William III that monarchy is expendable unless the monarch truly leads his people and reflects their aspirations.[5]

Fichte's ideal ruler is, however, the scholar, the philosopher-king, the Brahmin of the *Wissenschaftslehre*. A nation of the spirit should be led by the spirit's chief embodiment. After all, was not the

---

[1] On the Platonic connection of Fichte's later writings, see Wallner, *Fichte als politischer Denker*, p. 247.

[2] *Addresses to the German Nation*, p. 28; also, *Nature of the Scholar*, pp. 274–5.

[3] *Addresses to the German Nation*, loc. cit.; also p. 154 ff. Cf. Rousseau's approval of the pedagogical 'little state' he observed in Bern; *Gouvernement de Pologne*, *O.C.* III, 968–9. In *Addresses*, p. 116, Fichte observes: 'Just as the state, in the persons of its adult citizens, is the continued education of the human race, so must the future citizen himself...first be educated up to the point of being susceptible to that higher education.' [4] *Ibid.* pp. 126–7. [5] *Entwurf*, pp. 551–2.

potential of German unity due, not to princes and politicians, but to *Minnesänger*, to Luther, to Leibniz, to Klopstock, to Kant?[1] At the deep core of Fichte's political vision, the magic of the Idea and of the Lutherian *Beruf* dominate.

But does such rulership mean democracy? Not at least during the period of the *Notstaat*, of 'discipline for culture'. Even if 'we want to mould the Germans into a corporate body, which shall be stimulated and animated in all its individual members by the same interest', this has no bearing on political democracy.[2] Now it is recognized that the French Revolution has been a misconceived disgrace. 'Good governments make good majorities,' writes Fichte, expressing a Bismarckian sentiment actually taken from some strophes of Schiller; and not vice-versa.[3] The directorate of Klopstock sits in judgment on the school of Pestalozzi.

In the 1811 series of 'Vocation of the Scholar' lectures Fichte waxes expansive. The 'republic of scholars' has now become the 'inner spirit' of the scholar-directed republic.[4] The scholar is a 'seer' who directly (*unmittelbar*) glimpses the divine, world-creative process; set against the *Seher* is the *Volk*, which receives that vision only as mediated by him. In the 'Alte Welt', seers were prophets and miracle workers; now they are teachers who persuade through *Einsicht*. Again, the fateful dichotomy of the *Notstaat* is drawn. Education will weed out the higher from the lower capacities; it is not simply useful for its own sake, but as an instrument for judging the degrees of 'ideification' among its subjects.[5] The poorer sorts will become the subordinated journeymen of the higher tasks established by the wise. The wise are further discriminated into the pure seers who conceptualize the Idea and bring it into reality and the state officials (*Staatsbeamten*) who are their technical adjutants.[6]

Both Fichte's disposition and the traditional German concept of sovereignty required an absolute ruler. For Fichte this will not be a

---

[1] *Ibid.* p. 572.   [2] *Addresses to the German Nation*, p. 12.
[3] *Rechtslehre* of 1812, *N.W.* II, 634. Schiller wrote, in the first act of *Demetrius*: 'Man soll die Stimmen wägen, und nicht zahlen;/Der Staat muss untergehen, früh oder spät,/Wo Mehrheit siegt und Unverstand entscheidet.'
[4] *Bestimmung des Gelehrten* (1811), *N.W.* III, 160–73, *passim*.
[5] *Ibid.* pp. 184–8.   [6] *Ibid.* p. 175.

hereditary prince, but 'one who stands at the summit of insight regarding his time and his people'.[1] In fact, this *Zwingherr* or *Oberherr*, as Fichte calls him, is nothing but the futurized reincarnation of Rousseau's Legislator. Instead of giving laws and customs, he perfects and embodies them. Instead of forming a people, he is the essence of their value and destiny.

'For him who has knowledge and power,' Fichte writes, 'it is not only a right but a sacred duty, were he alone in the face of all humanity, to coerce men to the rule of law, putting them beneath its yoke by force.'[2] This *Zwingherr* will be 'at one and the same time dictator and preceptor, because in the latter role he cancels what he was in the former'.[3] We are deep within the dangerous German game of negation and dialectic.[4] And we are far from the safety of 'mere' legality, the 'mechanical' French claptrap of Montesquieu and others. Salvation lies in apocalypse, in revelation, in fortuitous necessity; also in messianic longing, the *Streben* and *Sehnen* of the ego toward its goal: 'Some day (*irgend einmal*) one will come and must come who, as the most righteous of his people, is their leader; he will find the means to establish a succession of the best.'[5] The constitutionalism of modern Europe gives way to the majesty of a rediscovered Nocturnal Council; the leader must be chosen in their midst.[6] Even the very notion of legality will depend on this election: 'If a legal sovereign is possible in a nation, it is necessary for that nation to have professors of the people [*Lehrer*], and it is only from their number that one may choose or establish a sovereign.'[7]

With the introduction of the nation to the transcendental philosophical perspective has come the restoration of custom, even tradition; or so it would seem. 'Let our standard of greatness be the old one,' Fichte exclaims at the end of the thirteenth of the *Reden*.[8] But

---

[1] *Entwurf*, p. 565. [2] *Staatslehre*, p. 436. [3] *Ibid.* p. 438.
[4] Caught in the frustrating tension between aspiration and actuality, German cultural thought in this period was heavily preoccupied with the notion of negation and 'nothing'. Not only is it a theme of *Faust I*, but cf. F. Hölderlin's *Hyperion* (*Sämtliche Werke und Briefe*, ed. Zinkernagel, 5 vols., Leipzig, 1914-26, II, 61): 'in the grip of that Nothing which rules over us, who are thoroughly conscious that we are born for Nothing, that we love a Nothing, believe in a Nothing, work ourselves to the bone for Nothing, until we gradually dissolve into Nothing'.
[5] *Rechtslehre* of 1812, p. 635. [6] *Entwurf.* p. 579.
[7] *Staatslehre*, p. 450. [8] *Addresses to the German Nation*, p. 210.

this is actually an illusion. The immanent *Volk* of philosophical history, the people of Christianity and the *Wissenschaftslehre*, has, properly speaking, no *Sitten* except the eternality of the goal of life in reason. Its essence is supersensible and its government is divine. Both must be compelled to unfold by the most sweeping application of the pedagogical art in modern political philosophy. The prize is freedom.

E. EDUCATION AND COERCION

In Kant, one will remember, the 'end of nature' and the 'end of man' were harshly distinguished, the first as a possible phenomenal outcome (involving the mastery of reason, but not the disappearance of the flesh), the second as an intelligible *maximum* or limiting concept. In Fichte the distinction is blurred. This occurs, first of all, because the dialectic of nation and cosmopolis allows the former concept to be associated with the 'end of culture' and the ideal of phenomenal order, while the cosmopolitan goal is frankly divinized or eschatologized. Moreover, the *Vernunftstaat* (or 'state as art') intervenes between the *Notstaat* (or 'state as knowledge') and the sheer intelligibility of the moral world. At the same time, *Recht* (now pure *Staatsrecht*) becomes the necessary precondition for *Sittlichkeit*, while *Zwang* and *Erziehung* (themselves in dialectical relationship) constitute the path to *Freiheit*. In the second place, the emphasis on the compulsive community (intended to root out the facticity in men's lives, overcome obstacles of irrational nature, and create a perfect justice that is the idealist equivalent of Christianity) practically obliges that the *Endzweck* be made visible. Why should men endure the severity and forced harmony of the Fichtean state for immaterial promises, for the sake of an airy ideal? If knowledge is unified and consistent in all its parts and the *Wissenschaftslehre* is a finished 'science of sciences', what we are able to think must also contain the potentiality of its actualization.

Thus, Fichte has raised the chiliastic problem, suggesting a tangible connection between the pure doing and the anticipated results of the ideal act. Rousseau's 'chimera' of fancy and regret is thrust boldly into the teleological schedule of the ages.

The Fichtean state is the *plenum* of what Kant first described as the sphere of culture. It has a consistent destiny throughout the entire course of Fichte's philosophical and historical divagations: to 'wither away' or render itself unnecessary. This is no more plainly stated in the *Beiträge* (1793) or the *Vocation of the Scholar* (1794) than it is in the *Vocation of Man* (1800), the *Reden* (1808), or the *Staatslehre* (1813). In the second of these works, for example, we read that 'life in the state does not belong among the absolute purposes of mankind'; the state is only a 'means to the establishment of a perfect society'.[1] In the *Reden*, Fichte reiterates: '...the State ...is not something which is primary and which exists for its own sake, but is merely the means to the higher purpose of the eternal, regular and continuous development of what is purely human in this nation'.[2] And the *Rechtslehre* of 1812 confirms: 'In its development, liberty has a primary effect: the state, as a principle limiting the will, disappears. It tends, thus, to suppress itself, for its ultimate end is morality. Morality suppresses it.'[3] The *Staatslehre* speaks of a 'falling away of judges, police, and other compulsory power'.[4] Fichte goes well beyond the tangible limits of Kantian speculation, forming a curious bridge between the optimism of certain liberal economists of the nineteenth century and Marxian hints of apocalypse. However, like Marx and unlike the liberals, Fichte's view is dialectical rather than linear; the state does not just slide downhill toward a vanishing point, but asserts itself in a positive and dictatorial manner in order that it may later be extinguished. And, unlike Marx, it is not a proletariat but an aristocratic rule of the wise that makes this possible. Nor does Fichte have in mind a prevailing commercial exchange society or a society of productive labour, but an ideal society of moral persons.

F. FINALITY AND ULTIMACY CONFUSED

If Fichte is constant in forecasting the suppression of the state, he is vacillating regarding the achievement of the ideal moral community. But his thinking shows a steady progression from denial to affirmation, almost correlative to his deflection of the focus from Revolu-

---

[1] *Op. cit. S.W.* VI, 306. [2] *Addresses to the German Nation*, p. 125.
[3] *Op. cit. N.W.* II, 542. [4] *Op. cit. S.W.* IV, 599.

tionary France to the ideal potential of Germany. We are speaking now of the Kantian 'end of man', as opposed to the 'end of nature'. In the *Beiträge* Fichte is categorical that the *Endzweck* can never be fulfilled.[1] And we have seen that as late as the *Sittenlehre* of 1798 he continues to argue the impalpability of perfection.[2] By 1800, however, the tone has changed: 'This is not a goal toward which we have to strive only so as to practice our powers for higher ends, but whose actualization we must forswear: this goal should be, it must become actual, it must at some time be achieved.'[3] The *Grundzüge* sustains this argument.[4] And in the *Thatsachen des Bewusstseyns* of 1810, Fichte speaks of an 'infinite...which it is possible to realize at some point in actual time [*irgend einmal in der wirklichen Zeit*]'.[5]

We know already the conditions for such an achievement. As a first step, for the state to 'wither away' or become a *Vernunftstaat*, all citizens must be virtuous: 'If all its members were virtuous, it would lose completely its character of coercive power and become merely the leader, guide and faithful counsel of the free-willing.'[6] The purely moral community, however, is a universal society of identical or syncretized wills, 'an *Eins*, a single subject'.[7] In Fichte's last writings, this vision is harmonized completely with his own conception of Christianity: 'The kingdom of right that reason demands and the kingdom of heaven on earth promised by Christianity are one and the same thing.'[8] 'Christianity', he declares in the same work, 'is not mere doctrine; it must be brought about in this world that God uniquely and universally rules, as ethical presence [*sittliches Wesen*], through free will and insight.'[9] Fichte's University of Berlin lectures show how completely this identification was announced. However, it is clear that 'as an ethical presence' the God of Fichte is still the ontological ground of the 'absolute content' of the *Wissenschaftslehre*.[10] Transcendental idealism, in turn, is indistinguishable from 'the revelation of this [supersensible] kingdom

---

[1] *Beiträge*, p. 102.   [2] *Ethics*, p. 159.
[3] *Vocation of Man*, p. 436.   [4] *Characteristics*, p. 16.
[5] *Op. cit. N.W.* II, 635.   [5] *Characteristics*, p. 188.   [7] *Vocation of the Scholar*, p. 167.
[8] *Staatslehre*, p. 582.   [9] *Ibid.* p. 579.
[10] Cf. *Addresses to the German Nation*, p. 34: 'Religion is simply knowledge; it makes man quite clear and intelligible to himself...'

[which] is the essence of Christianity...its absolute...purpose for all time'.[1]

Fichte now has another set of symbols for the dialectical struggle between 'thing' and 'intelligence', 'ego' and 'non-ego', normal people and savages, 'old' and 'new' worlds: 'Faith and understanding are the two basic principles of humanity, through whose reciprocity history is propelled.'[2] Faith is the pure principle, but no progress is possible with it alone. Such progress depends 'on the progressive triumph of understanding over faith,' provided that the former 'assumes the content of the latter in the nobler form of clear insight...'[3] History is 'the struggle of faith and understanding and the triumph of the latter over the former'.[4] At the end of the Fichtean *saeculum*, practical reason, having absorbed all irrationality, becomes theoretical reason or the content of the *Wissenschaftslehre*. And this is the kingdom of heaven. In one or another form, it is also the logical destination of an idealist system.

Fichte's immanent, neo-Christian chiliasm is of more than passing interest to students of such ideas. But the main political problem does not really lie in how the 'chimera' of human moral potential itself is to be drawn within the boundaries of time. Fichte, after all, did not lead an army or mobilize a revolution. Despite his urgent emphasis on practical reason, he was at bottom a thorough intellectualist.

The problem lies in the sphere of order, of *Zwang* and *Erziehung*, not of apocalypse. For the tangibility of the chiliastic *telos* serves to legitimize and 'moralize' the procedures of the *Notstaat* and its heroic aristocracy. It matters little whether the goal is perfect communion under God, *Vernunftstaat*, or a spiritual nation of Leibnizes. All these facets of the idealist *lendemains qui chantent* furnish teleological justifications for the 'rule of the best' in deprecation of 'mere legality'. 'Up to now,' Fichte writes, 'the human race has been educated through God and will still for a long time be thus educated, until it wakens within itself and undertakes its own education with freedom and emerging art.'[5] It is the 'long time'

---

[1] *Staatslehre*, p. 534.
[2] *Ibid.* p. 493. See the comments by Wallner, *Fichte als politischer Denker*, p. 252.
[3] *Ibid.*   [4] *Ibid.* p. 495.   [5] *Sittenlehre* of 1812, *N.W.* III, 42.

that disturbs us. If the 'chimera' is intangible and extrahistorical, inner and personal, the *Notstaat* is a cheat. If, on the other hand, it is plausible, *irgend einmal in der Zeit*, then the *Notstaat* is divine, is the incorporation of the Idea, as long as it shall last.[1] Neither perspective endows or creates a tolerable politics in the world of men. But the latter one is less wholesome, for cheats are quickly discovered. In other words, Fichte's dogmatization of the 'chimera' in history, his identification of the future with the infinite, make of the world a task under political conditions that are frankly sub-chimerical.

[1] Cf. Hirsch, *Christentum und Geschichte*, pp. 34–5.

PART FIVE

G. W. F. HEGEL: THE CHIMERA 'CANCELLED AND PRESERVED'

HEGEL DENIES THE POTENCY OF THE FUTURE

A. IDEALIST FORMS OF THE CHIMERA

The preceding fluctuations of the 'chimera' could be called a prolegomenon to Hegel. I do not mean by this that Hegel gives us uniformly satisfactory answers to the eternal questions of man in society or man in his world. But it is clear that with Hegel's consummation of the idealist tradition these problems must henceforth be visualized in new ways.

I propose here to deal with only a few Hegelian dimensions. A selective 'phenomenology' for approaching Hegel has been unfolded —one that has sought to avoid the extremes of historical suffocation in 'facts' and of rigid abstraction in the mere timeless geometry of 'problems'. If, in Hegel's own formula for the phenomenological dialectic, 'the truth is the whole; but the whole is only the essence perfecting itself through its development',[1] then our modest 'phenomenology' captures but a few of the *Gestalten* that Hegel himself so artfully manipulated. But, given that other Hegelian dictum that 'an individual [cannot] overleap his age',[2] there may be some greater excuse than economy for reaching toward Hegel from the world of his immediate predecessors. These men spaded up much of the ground in which Hegel would labour, themselves probing the riddle of the historical consciousness and searching for nodes of order in the stream of time. In the present chapter, then, we shall make an attempt to comprehend the subject-matter as 'the result together with its becoming'.[3]

The metaphor of the 'chimera' has been no less elusive for us than for the philosophers of record because of its uneasy flotation between thought and act, conceivability and possibility, legendary

---

[1] *Preface* to the *Phenomenology of Spirit* (trans. Walter Kaufmann), in Kaufmann, *Hegel* (New York, 1964), p. 390. I have preferred Kaufmann's translation of the Preface to Baillie's.

[2] Preface to the *Philosophy of Right* (ed. and trans. T. M. Knox, Oxford, 1962), p. 11.

[3] *Phenomenology* (K), p. 370.

past and impalpable future, intention and deed, 'désir' and 'pouvoir'.

To say that we are talking of the legal state or of the community of custom or of the ethical commonwealth, of utopia or of eschaton, still does not exhaust the play of meanings, the richness of the idea. All the available mythic, historical and institutional symbols, in the space of community and the time of recorded history, are gathered in to become 'moments' in the total concept. That catalogue cannot be rerun here. But we can ascend to the quasi-infinite reaches of 'humanity' and the *saeculum* for our notion, we can fasten on the 'simulation models' of Rousseau's Clarens, Geneva or Sparta or of Fichte's 'German republic at the beginning of the twenty-second century', or we can dive within the pure pattern of the transcendental ego itself in this quest for unity and order. We are looking for a common denominator of spirituality, well-being and purpose, a new immanent gospel, a 'second nature', a natural law self-imposed, self-creating and self-preserving by contrast to the inviolable mechanics of its physical analogue.[1]

---

[1] 'Second nature', the classical metaphor for custom, becomes translated, within the premises of transcendental idealism, to the always obligatory but never perfectly attained imperative of duty, the *Sollen*. The politicization and spatialization of this moral formula (implying at the same time a return toward the classical ideal) is indicated by Schelling, who writes: 'A second and higher nature must, as it were, be raised above the first, possessing a natural law, but a completely different one from that which rules in visible nature, namely a natural law for the purpose of freedom.' (*Syst. des transz. Idealismus, S.W.* III, 583). For Schelling the 'second nature' was the *Rechtsverfassung*, the legitimate civil constitution. Branching out from Schelling, the Romantics took the second nature to mean the state itself, moreover a state of traditional and irrational *Gemeinschaft*. Hegel associates the idea with *Sittlichkeit*, his legal-moral, traditional-ideal symbiosis; cf. *Die Vernunft in der Geschichte* (ed. J. Hoffmeister, Hamburg, 1955), pp. 115 f.: '*Sittlichkeit* is duty...second nature, as it has been rightly called; for the first nature of man is his immediate animal being.' Cf. also *Philosophy of Right* (ed. and trans. T. M. Knox, Oxford, 1962), Introduction, paragraph 7, p. 20: 'The will is free, so that freedom is both the substance of right and its goal, while the system of right is the realm of freedom made actual, the world of mind brought forth out of itself like a second nature.' Also, *Enzyklopädie*, ed. 1830 (eds. F. Nicolin and O. Pöggeler, Hamburg, 1959), paragraph 250, p. 203. In references to the Knox edition of the *Philosophy of Right*, the designation 'C' means 'continuation' of Hegel's own argument (in his own words); 'A' means 'addition', not in his own words but inserted by his early editor, Gans, on the basis of student notes. Knox has wisely compiled all the 'additions' in the back of his volume. Another rich source is the *Randbemerkungen*, Hegel's marginal notations in his own hand, unfortunately not included by Knox. These are cited from *Grundlinien der Philosophie des Rechts* (ed. J. Hoffmeister, Hamburg, 1955), pp. 301 ff. There is an excellent discussion of the whole problem in Hermann U. Kantorowicz, 'Volksgeist und historische Rechtschule', *Historische Zeitschrift*, CVIII (1912), pp. 295–326, esp. pp. 315–21.

Idealist forms of the chimera

The harmony of nature, with man as participant, which was postulated by the sociological extensions of Newtonianism and under-written by the deist theodicies, is torn apart. It could scarcely hold, given its all too obvious contradiction of the facts and feelings of existence. If not yet defined as an ideology, it was felt as one, nowhere more deeply than by Rousseau. Rousseau laid the burden of the failure on man, not on nature, and he sought speculatively to resolve the gnawing issue by attacking history with 'chimeras' that reformulated the existence of man, models that were, in one way or another, nature-substitutes. In so doing he arrived at extreme conclusions of withdrawal, limitation, and introversion. Civilization was indicted in this despairing attempt to define the arbitrary but fatal corrosion of human social relations.

The development of German idealist metaphysics took an op-posite turn. Nevertheless, it owed much to Rousseau on two prime counts. It absorbed his assault against the deepening *ancien régime* malaise as well as against the 'dogmatic' philosophers' view of natural harmony, and it sought for a universal statement of the possibility of human freedom. Kant's categorical imperative was the pure crystallization of the latter quest. But, paradoxically, whereas Rousseau had sought to reintegrate man and nature by attacking civilization, and consequently history, the speculative German liberation of man from the shackles of authority was directed prima-rily against 'nature' and regarded civilization as the means to a not yet actualized 'morality'. This transmutation placed enormous emphasis upon the 'guiding thread' of history and culture, indeed upon its 'divinity'. But it also created a portentous rift in man's horizon between nature and morality, between the 'determined' and 'free' parts of his existence. The destiny of man was to be as 'free' as possible. And, being by definition a creature of reason (all idealism proceeds from this *a priori*), man was 'free', but he was not free in his world. In terms of *Verstand*, nature was indeed the essence of regularity, *absolut verständlich*; but from the 'free' vista of *Vernunft*, it was, in Fichte's sense, unreasonable because unfree. Hegel would later call it *Ohnmacht*, 'impotence'.[1]

We have seen how the problem of freedom became, paradoxically,

---

[1] Hegel, *Enzyklopädie* (1830), paragraph 250, p. 203.

historicized. Paradoxically, because in the Kantian epistemology the essence of freedom, which is the moral law, is not in time at all, but supratemporal. Nevertheless, it was inevitable for the practical purposes of philosophy that freedom should be shown to erupt into phenomena for purposes of forwarding the Idea of human moral destiny. The transcendental idealists found the medium for this exchange of potency and effect in the will. The 'primacy of practical reason' meant among other things that human freedom had the possibility and obligation of filling up empty time with its values. That, then, was the meaning of history—and all history and its permanences, the domesticating institutions and civilizing works thrown up in its course, became blessed with the sanction of the Idea. Freed from the arbitrary and ruthless coercion of heredity and superstition, idealist man quickly found himself governed by the teleological ordinances of his moral mission. Criteria of 'historical rationality' began to come into view as arbiters of the progress and palpability of the 'chimera'. The standard was created for a philosophically purposive politics in which the alternatives were either chiliastic expectation or, to rest with Kant, the training of 'nature' through *Bildung* and legality to 'culture', from whose pinnacle the starry heaven of an ethical commonwealth might finally be glimpsed. In Fichte, the endless journey and apocalypse touched.

The position of politics and the state was ambiguous in this situation. Both were seen as a means by the transcendental idealists, yet they became metaphysically grounded in the compass of the Idea. Kant foresaw the perpetuity of the fundamentally legal-liberal *Rechtsstaat* as regulator, as sustainer of the 'external conditions of freedom'; Fichte, on the basis of his oft-repeated statements, expected its 'withering away' after a period of enforced culture-building which, but for the incommensurateness of their concrete aftermaths, might be compared with Marx's notion of the 'dictatorship of the proletariat'. But the state and politics as *means* signifies something different from a liberal reduction of state beneath society when seen from the teleological perspective. The state is not simply a conventional matrix into which the 'natural harmony' of society flows, not merely a convenient aggregation of individuals or corporations, but rather the mould in which that harmony is created, taught, enforced and transmitted. If the Idea of the state were to be lost, all would be lost. Correlatively, a 'good' politics is itself not a constitutional mechanics, but rather a spirit of politics in the service of the Idea. As Fichte wrote, 'political liberty is at most necessary for one'. With the historicization of the teleological formula, the notion of 'rational compulsion' based on the analogy of class and school, pupil and teacher becomes manifest. At the same time, also somewhat paradoxically, because of the subjectivist genesis of idealist teleology (concealed but not overcome in Fichte's collectivized ethics), the augurs of history and, in consequence, the inspectors of the correlation between the historical state, the Idea, and the progress of the Idea become the philosophers themselves. They, after all, have generated the goals of history through their deductive, unquestionably moral virtuosity. Rulership is essentially an expertise in *Vernunft*. Thus, as the fulfilment of Idea recedes in expectation, the state increases its potency as a purposive means. But because infinite journeys are scarcely endurable, the chiliastic expectation tends to be remitted into time.

This might be called the 'rhythm' of idealist politics. Its other significant facet is speculative and involves the positioning of political life within the system or architecture of knowledge. Here, I believe, we should not permit ourselves to speak of politics, but only of 'political implications'.

Viewed systematically, the politics of transcendental idealism can be no more than a derivative system of 'political implications' because it is in no sense a code of prudential political techniques dependent on a theory of human nature and because it is, eminently, part of a total project transcending the mere fact of politics.[1] The Idea of the state participates, together with the Ideas of art, morality, religion and knowledge, in the comprehensive Idea which is the absolute reflection of all harmony. This holism leads back to the point just discussed. But it also means that the purely political aspects of idealist philosophy cannot be interpreted *sui generis* without

---

[1] Kant's extreme separation but preservation of both 'anthropology' and 'anthroponomy' represents, paradoxically, a middle ground for approaching politics in terms of the 'raw content' of human nature, since it does not directly threaten the ontological reality of the natural disposition.

likely distortion. Abstracted from their architectural whole, certain political expressions of the Germans (indeed of Rousseau) turn out to be, according to one's choice, liberal, reactionary, totalitarian, often quite maddening to the thoughtful empiricist. This is why the present study has dwelt on epistemology and metaphysics more than some might find palatable. But it is important to understand not only *that* but *how* the Idea both informs and supersedes the political vision. Sociologically, I think it is quite fair to say, as the Young Hegelians began to do, that this exquisitely intellectual transcendence of politics was a reflection of the frustrated ideality of the German *Kulturstaat*.[1] It is, at any rate, not a concomitant of political philosophy in general. Where theories of community and the state begin with a *conception* of man-in-nature rather than from a *concept* (in this case, freedom) whose essence is its own supranatural *telos*, the question of a 'metaphysical state' need not arise. But if human nature is to be regarded as an impure basis for the theory of political life, then only metaphysics can be summoned to destroy 'physics'.

We have witnessed a curious change of relationships between politics and history. History as lived has been sternly rejected as a ground for making the structures of political society legitimate. Rousseau discharges the final cannonade in this sense. But the idealists now proceed to implant another sort of historical control. The bad institutions of the past can only be reformed and perfected in and through history. Logically, this involves giving history a mission and moral purpose. As we have noted, such a doctrine can be made consistent with the freedom of the will only by assigning the power of historical improvement to those far-sighted and ethical beings who are competent to penetrate the secrets of human destiny and 'make history'. Thus acts and events of the present are anchored to moral previsions of the future, just as, for the sake of reigning authority, they were once linked to the accumulated wisdom of the past or, in the case of Rousseau and much eighteenth-century utopianism, to speculative egalitarian beginnings. History is no

[1] On this, see, especially, K. Löwith, *From Hegel to Nietzsche*, pp. 65 ff.; Herbert Marcuse, *Reason and Revolution: Hegel and the Rise of Social Theory* (Boston, 1960), pp. 251 ff.

longer the simple record of the past from which lessons of despair or rules of obedience are drawn, but a total plan of human ascent in which the dark past somehow joins the pregnant future along a 'guiding thread'. The whole meaning of history is thus captured and placed at the service of an ethico-political vision.

This intellectual sea-change was necessarily much influenced by the great upheavals of the period. One consequence of the French Revolution and its shock waves was that the senses of human space and human time entered into new and complex relationships. Nationalism, social solidarity and popular sovereignty probably do not require philosophical explanations. Nevertheless, the idealist vision of history has certain intimate connections with the new organization of political space. For the transcendental freedom of empty time will disrupt the very harmony it sets as a goal if not supplemented by an immanent spatial order of life in common.[1]

The historical problem of nationalism is beyond the scope of this study. But we have already seen the Rousseauian *polis*-size community of escape, equality and reassurance (where nature and custom were ambiguously joined) transformed across the ardent, yet somehow misty, cosmopolitanism of Kant into Fichte's symbiotic solution of the ideal nation-state, with its natural and 'closed' frontiers, its autarky and virtue, that 'phenomenon' of all human spatiality, particularized by being defined as the purest part of the human. We noted the tensions involved in that exercise. Somehow, the closing and intensification of life in space was related to grasping the pure imaginable on the boundaries of time. Once history's goals are set teleologically, then this 'laboratory' of the human experiment—as the empiricists had put it—becomes the theory or logical form of that experiment, the set of results that one is bound to expect. The laboratory aspect is shifted toward the organization of essential space (defined, like the *polis*, as the locus of human order) within the parameters of the time-plan. And the effective manner of organizing this space is authoritative coercion.

[1] Accounting in part for the progressive German reformulations of Rousseau's critical concept of the 'general will', which was itself a metaphorical extension of a theological issue. Regarding the evolution of this problem, see, especially, Hegel's *Philosophy of Right*, paragraph 258C, pp. 156–8.

B. RECONCILIATION

Hegel's quest for an absolute philosophy developed in this milieu of 'political implications'. Of course they in no way exhaust the reach of Hegel's world view. He aspired to be the Aristotle of modern thought and the Proclus of Christian speculation.[1] His deep involvement in the structure of knowledge and the rationale of all historical life—whose qualitative opposition he mediated with his dialectic or logic of the 'real'—reached toward the concrete unity of thought and being, faith and knowledge, action and reflection, life and morality, the eternally true and the eternally present, and, most palpably, the reconciliation of the classical and Christian traditions.[2] Indeed the great drama of Hegel's work lies in the Sophoclean manner in which he conceived these vast confrontations—an aesthetic power felt most deeply in the *Phenomenology*. The excitement in Hegel is not that he presumed to solve the riddle of the universe, but rather that his expressions of unification and resolution—the notions of *Vermittlung* (mediation) and *Versöhnung* (reconciliation, etymologically related to Christ as the appearance of God in time)—bob like corks, seaworthy, but diminutive, upon an ocean of *Trennung* (separation), *Entzweiung* (bifurcation), *Entäusserung* (alienation), and *Zerrissenheit* (dismemberment). Philosophical science itself is that arduous Golgotha which conquers history and redeems the time through the perfect correspondence of thought that has become will and will that has become thought.[3] Thought maintains itself upon the turbulent sea: 'The resolution to philosophize hurls itself pure into thought (thought by itself is a lonely thing), it hurls itself as into a shoreless ocean; all bright colours, all landmarks are swallowed up.' 'The pole star',

---

[1] Cf. Hegel, *The Philosophy of History* (trans. J. Sibree, New York, 1956), p. 272. This edition, being a student-note and editorial pastiche of Hegel's lectures, should be used sparingly and ignored for the solution of critical problems. For Hegel's view of Proclus, see Hegel to Creuzer (draft letter), end of May 1821, where Proclus is described as the 'real turning point, the passage from ancient philosophy to Christianity'. *Briefe von und an Hegel*, II, 266.

[2] Cf. *Lectures on the History of Philosophy* (trans. Haldane and Simpson), I, 29.

[3] This image occurs in the staggering last sentence of the *Glauben und Wissen* (ed. Lasson, *Erste Drückschriften*, Berlin, 1911), *in fine*; and in the Preface to the *Phenomenology* (K), p. 404.

Hegel continues, 'is the star of the spirit carried within.'[1] For all his undoubted emphasis on the collective values of people, state and religion—the *sittlich* and cultural *organon* of world-historical civilizations—Hegel's grasp of reality and existence was no less lonely than Rousseau's; both sought to build the epiphanic point of truth into a cosmos of truth where the ego could have peace, achieving mentally what both thought to have once existed objectively in a sunnier Aegean clime.

Since Kantian-Fichtean transcendental philosophy promised liberty 'für sich' on a real epistemological footing but could propose nothing more reassuring than a coercive teleological mission pointed at the fullness of time, the young Germans following in its path were torn between new wine and old wineskins. Novalis wrote feelingly of the 'two indestructible forces at the heart of humanity':

...on the one hand the devotion to the past, attachment to a historic constitution, love of ancestral monuments and of an old and glorious dynasty, the joy of obedience; on the other hand, the exalted feeling of liberty, the infinite hope of mighty spheres of action, the taste of novelty and youth, familiar bonds among all citizens, pride taken in universally human and valid truths, the savour of individual rights and collective property, and a vigorous civic feeling.[2]

It is to be noted here how the strains of harmony and liberty, memory and anticipation float between the poles. That was one sort of bifurcation which the political and philosophical revolutions had caused in Germany. Schiller expressed a more explicitly philosophical tension: 'If...reason abolishes the state of nature, as she necessarily must, to substitute her own place in it, she risks the physical and actual man for the problematic moral man, the existence of society for a merely possible (though morally necessary) ideal of society.'[3] Cruel dilemmas! Novalis sought to conquer his by imagining a restoration of the old order purified by new ideals, a rosewater

---

[1] 'Rede zum Antritt des philosophischen Lehramtes an der Universität Berlins, Okt. 22, 1818', *Berliner Schriften* (ed. J. Hoffmeister, Hamburg, 1956), p. 20. Cf. letter to Daub, 20 Aug. 1816, where, in referring to his work on the *Logik*, Hegel writes: 'In no other discipline...is one as lonely as in philosophy,' *Briefe*, II, 116.

[2] Novalis, *Christenheit oder Europa*, *G.W.* V, 31–2.

[3] *Letters on the Aesthetic Education of Man* (tr. T. Weiss, Boston, 1845), Third Letter, pp. 8–9.

composition of Catholicism and Fichteanity harmonized by love and art. Schiller, thrusting politics away, saw aesthetic deepening and the cultivation of the *Spieltrieb* as furnishing the access from natural life to the moral society. The surest approach to Hegel is probably through Schiller, who 'humanized' and 'deformalized' Kant in his enormously influential *Letters on the Aesthetic Education of Man* in 1795. If one wishes to look for clues to Hegelian problems, one finds them immediately in such ideas as the following: 'The phenomenon of Grecian humanity was undoubtedly a maximum which could be neither maintained nor surpassed.'[1] 'There was no other method of developing man's manifold dispositions than by placing them in opposition' (a notion which, in Schiller's hands, lies midway between Kant's 'unsocial sociability' and the *Zerissenheit* of the Hegelian 'unhappy consciousness').[2] 'The state...must not dispeople the realm of phenomena, while extending the unseen realm of morals.' '...Totality of character must be found in a people who would be capable and worthy of exchanging the state of necessity for the state of freedom.'[3] Finally, Schiller writes: 'The *Spieltrieb* will aim at abolishing time in time.'[4] This latter notion, with the *Spieltrieb* exchanged for the suspended eternality of absolute thought or self-knowing knowledge, was to become Hegel's specific problem; the others are subsidiary but important ones. Out of the echoing clash of classicism, Christianity, tradition and revolution rises the will to find some calm centre of indifference that could contain, and in containing explain but not obliterate, what Hegel later called 'this pure unrest of life and this absolute differentiation'.[5] Wanted, therefore: a system as total as Spinoza's (the true record of idealism's love–hate relationship with Spinoza remains to be written) that would comprehend both the variegated pluralism of Herder and the Kantian freedom from the side of the subject.

Although Fichte was fond of opposing his own rigour to Spinoza's,

---

[1] *Letters on the Aesthetic Education*, Sixth Letter, p. 25.   [2] *Ibid.* p. 26.
[3] *Ibid.* Fourth Letter, p. 13. This and the foregoing.
[4] *Ibid.* Fourteenth Letter, p. 65. The *Spieltrieb*, mediate between the *Form-* and *Stoff-triebe* (form and content) was Schiller's aesthetic explanation of how man's two natures could be conciliated and modified. Philosophically, it was an extension of the first part of Kant's *Critique of Judgment*. For Hegel's assessment, see *Enzyklopädie* (1830), 'Vorbereitung', paragraph 55, pp. 80–1.
[5] Preface to *Phenomenology* (K), p. 424.

the credit must go to Schelling for undertaking the mission described above. Schelling followed in Schiller's path, making of art an ultimate and supernal value, however, instead of a mediating and human one, which was to abort the fundamental syllogism of transcendental idealism into a prelude to mysticism and Romantic nirvana.[1] Since, despite an intermittently rich suggestiveness, Schelling's thought is manifestly inferior to Hegel's, it is sometimes overlooked that Schelling's *System des transzendentalen Idealismus* (his greatest work) prescribes much of the mission, if not the strategy, that would influence Hegel's own Jena system and, beyond it, his mature works. There were, however, three inadequacies in Schelling. First of all, unlike Fichte and all superior philosophers associated with the rationalist tradition, he was impatient with logic—a true Romantic in this regard. Secondly, he deduced his ideal-realism from an 'absolute identity' in which all differentiation was perfectly epiphenomenal, a night, as Hegel put it, 'where all cows are black'.[2] Finally, despite Schelling's claims for his 'absolute', he never achieved a real unity of system; philosophy he defined as 'the science which has for its subject, subjectively, the absolute harmony of mind with itself; objectively, the return of everything real to a common identity'.[3]

Hegel's response to these three aspects of Schelling provides a useful shorthand for establishing his idea of a philosophical system. In the first instance, he saw clearly by 1801 that the inherent movement of reason would have to be seized in the form of metaphysical logic in order for philosophy to come to grips with all actuality; this is the way his system began at Jena and this is the way it ended in paragraph 577 of the third edition of the *Encyclopedia*, where logic or pure Idea mediates and cements the dialectically opposed spheres of Nature and Spirit; the Hegelian last word.[4] Of logic he wrote: 'The study of this science, the residency and work in this shadow-

---

[1] Cf. *Syst. des transz. Idealismus*, pp. 607 ff.
[2] Preface to *Phenomenology* (K), p. 386. Cf. *Differenz des Fichteschen und Schelling'schen Systems*, in *Erste Drückschriften*, p. 21, where Hegel speaks of the 'Nacht der Totalität'.
[3] Schelling, *Propädeutik der Philosophie* (1804), *S.W.* I, 78.
[4] See the excellent explication of the three concluding syllogisms of the *Encyclopedia* in Reinhart Klemens Maurer, *Hegel und das Ende der Geschichte: Interpretationen zur 'Phänomenologie des Geistes'* (Stuttgart-Berlin-Cologne-Mainz, 1965), pp. 85–6.

kingdom, is the absolute education and discipline of the consciousness.'[1]

As regards the second point, Hegel knew that the oppositions of life had to be mediated and reconciled, that they could not simply be dismissed with *a priori* allegations of contingency and impurity: spirit acquires no richness by regarding its itinerary in the world only as a path to the absolute; that path, as past, 'reduced to abbreviations and to the simple determinations of thought', is both means and end of the absolute.[2] 'The truth of science [i.e. philosophy, *Wissenschaft*]', Hegel wrote while in Jena, 'is a peaceful light that illuminates and rejoices everything.'[3] But, in contrast to Schelling's neo-Platonism, that peace and light can be won only through struggle and darkness, through the dynamic unity of opposites achieved by the tortuous supremacy of reason in its 'conscious certainty that it is all reality'.[4]

In the third case—here in opposition to all his idealist predecessors—Hegel unceasingly argued that there are not two ways of looking at things, that freedom requires unity of thought and method and is found only in thought. The only philosophical question we may ask about something is: 'Is it true *an und für sich*?'[5] This means: can mind hold an object fast as the essence of its own activity, as itself, as justified by the same claims that mind makes for itself in the world as reason or as philosophical consciousness in general? Or, in the familiar formula of the *Phenomenology*, can 'substance' and 'subject' unite by an immanent dynamic to authenticate and moralize—these words are synonymous for Hegel—a situation rendering it both true and 'world-historical' and the one because of the other?[6] Hegel's basic logical tool, the *Begriff*, 'is at the same time immobile work of art and history of the world',[7] the absolute spirit

---

[1] Introduction to *Logik, Sämtliche Werke* (ed. H. Glockner, 26 vols., Stuttgart, 1927–40), iv, 57.
[2] Preface to *Phenomenology* (K), p. 404.
[3] 'Jena Aphorisms', *Dokumente zu Hegels Entwicklung* (ed. J. Hoffmeister, Stuttgart, 1936), p. 358.
[4] *Phenomenology of Mind* (trans. J. Baillie, London, 1949), p. 273.
[5] *Philosophy of History*, p. 371.
[6] Cf. Pref. *Phenomenology* (K), p. 388: '...everything depends on this, that we comprehend and express the true not as substance but just as much as subject'.
[7] *Jenenser Realphilosophie*, II (1805–6) (ed. J. Hoffmeister, Leipzig, 1931), 273.

that knows itself and is at peace and the restless objective spirit that wills, fashions the world, and perishes. 'The history of mind is its own act. Mind is only what it does, and its act is to make itself the object of its own consciousness.'[1] On the other hand, 'that the true is actual only as system, or that the substance is essentially subject, is expressed in the conception which speaks of the absolute as spirit'.[2] Mind is what it does, but all deeds are 'real' in the mind. This means that Schelling's 'absolute harmony of mind with itself' is viewed by Hegel as an identity with the plural manifold of its indispensable (*wirklich*) experience, not as an exchange of subjective and objective points of view upon the world. All of Hegel's philosophy is a working out of the principle he declared in 1801: Truth is the identity of identity and non-identity.[3] In other words, 'moments' of the truth abide in the negative, the *Nicht-Ich*, if one pleases, and are brought to concretion or actuality through the movements of opposition that the spirit encounters. In the mind that grasps this reality, they are both cancelled and preserved as the truth, made 'subject' and 'substance' in the concrete unity of being and knowing: 'Moments of mind [in true knowledge]...no longer involve the opposition between being and knowing; they remain within the un-divided simplicity of the knowing function; they are truth in the form of truth, and their diversity is merely diversity of the content of truth.'[4] Marx, while accepting Hegel's logical procedures, saw very clearly that in terms of the world, of actual life, this mentalized 'diversity of the content of truth' might be the deception or 'ideology' of an inadequate world-historical perspective.

C. HEGEL AGAINST TRANSCENDENTAL IDEALISM

We have now enough of the character of Hegel's system to return the problem to its environment. Hegel, as is well known, fell out with Schelling because of certain references to the latter's shallow-

---

[1] *Philosophy of Right*, paragraph 343, p. 216.
[2] Preface to *Phenomenology* (K), p. 396.
[3] *Differenz*, p. 113. Cf. 'Fragment: Love and Religion', in *Hegels theologische Jugend-schriften* (ed. Herman Nohl, Tübingen, 1907), p. 377: 'We cannot posit the Ideal out-side ourselves, or it would be an object—[but] not in ourselves alone, or it would not be an ideal.' Also, *ibid.* p. 348.
[4] Preface to *Phenomenology* (K), p. 414.

ness. However, Hegel did not so much disown Schelling's quest for unity as the inadequacy of his procedures for dealing with the problem. But if Schelling, not to mention Jacobi and the Romantics in general, was inconsequent and increasingly sectarian, the dangerous enemy was to be found elsewhere. Precisely because of their philosophical rigour and the implications of that rigour for actuality, Kant and Fichte were the sources of a really dangerous *Schwärmerei*. This was a compliment to their importance. Hegel's quest for unity may be substantially regarded as an attempt to rejoin the whole universe that his predecessors had set asunder. The reasons for this were both philosophical and highly practical, but all these reasons were united by an overpowering wish to master the contradictions of the world and be spiritually at home in it, to challenge disharmony with the sheer virtuosity of mental effort and recapture, now at a 'mediated' rather than a simple and direct level, the mythical integrity of classical Hellenism.[1] If Greece, as Hegel once said, was the 'paradise of the human spirit',[2] a paradise which, as Hegel, Goethe and Schiller knew, could never return, then the task for philosophical science was to endure its 'Golgotha' and be resurrected in the higher, if drabber, costume of subject–substance. Eden would have to be exchanged for Heaven. Among other things, the *Phenomenology* is Hegel's passionate swan-song to 'substantial' antiquity and his acceptance of the fate of consciousness in the crucible of history. It is not too much to say that at the last he has a certain wistful revenge when the Christian 'beauty of holiness' furnishes the truth of its content to philosophy and is swallowed up in the perpetual Aristotelian *Genuss* of self-knowing spirit. And yet only Christianity and the mystery of the Incarnation have made it possible to think the principle of philosophical history at all.[3]

The at times bitter and always complicated opposition of Hegel to his two great idealist compatriots is often misunderstood, and this misunderstanding has led to mistakes. A hundred and fifty years of

---

[1] Essentially, in Hegel's terminology, the distinction between 'immediate' (*unmittelbar*) and 'mediated' (*vermittelt*) is that between 'felt' and 'thought'. The Athenian was unreflectively at one with his entire cosmos; the modern European must intellectualize and justify it.

[2] 'Rede zum Gymnasial-Schuljahres-Abschluss, Sept. 29, 1809', *Nürnberger Schriften* (ed. J. Hoffmeister, Leipzig, 1938), p. 309.

[3] See Karl Löwith, *Meaning in History* (Chicago, 1949), chapter on Hegel.

hindsight foreshortens the view on this problem and encourages many simply to combine these philosophers as 'German idealists', to insist on their general unity of approach, and to see their systems as correlative and sequential. Usually, in this view, Hegel is charged with being the most presumptuous, obscure and 'menacing' of the three, not least of all because of his theory of the state. These assertions contain a modicum of truth. Even the conscientious reader of Hegel will find some of his doctrines, like, for example, that of criminal punishment, disturbing, and no one will deny his pretentiousness and obscurity.[1] Yet intellectual and historical honesty may well produce another conclusion. If Hegel can be viewed amid the problems of his time and not in the light of repercussions that he would have disowned, it is possible, indeed useful, to regard his work as an intelligent defence against Kantian–Fichtean tendencies that could scarcely form the basis for a tolerable political community. No single slant on Hegel is the truth *about* Hegel. But it seems clear that the 'political implications' of Hegel's philosophy represent a profound rejection of the real dangers of transcendental idealism and that Hegel, in terms of his time and philosophical tradition, recognized those dangers with consummate insight. This is not to relieve Hegelian politics of its own perils nor even to insist that, *in toto*, Hegel's views are preferable to those of Kant and Fichte.

The first task, then, is to define the scope of Hegel's philosophical reaction. In so doing, we must dispel the powerful magic of generalizations such as the following: 'Hegel became a Kantian the moment he understood the revolution brought about by Kant's Critical Philosophy; and he remained a Kantian throughout his life, no matter how much he disputed many of Kant's doctrines and even his fundamental position.'[2] Of course, both by proximity and by a common concern with common problems, Hegel is closer to Kant than, say, to Descartes. Certainly both (although in substantially different ways) are 'idealists'. Certainly the young Hegel

---

[1] Kant's *lex talionis* is, however, equally disturbing, and for similar reasons. Both legal systems, in this respect, are derivative from the ancient principle of expiation, or the restoration of cosmic balance through symmetrical payment for a crime.

[2] Richard Kroner, introduction to *Friedrich Hegel on Christianity: Early Theological Writings* (tr. T. M. Knox, New York, 1961), pp. 4–5. T. M. Knox makes fundamentally the same point in his essay, 'Hegel's Attitude to Kant's Ethics', *Kant-Studien*, XLIX (1957), pp. 70–81.

fell heavily under Kant's sway. Indeed, he never ceased to admire Kant's innovative power. In the *Encyclopedia* he complimented 'criticism' for establishing the cardinal rule of philosophy: 'one must know the instrument before he can undertake the work'.[1] He continuously raised transcendental idealism to a high place, whether in the form of *Moralität* or of the highest and truest form of 'subjective freedom', and he posed the Nature–Spirit–Idea syllogism of Kantianism immediately before his own in that asceptic mental apocalypse at the end of the *Encyclopedia*. But there is another side.[2]

To understand that side, we must recall that Hegel's entire philosophical method was never simply to oppose or reject but to encompass. This notion, proceeding from Kant's own struggle with the antinomies and Fichte's dialectical method of the *Grundlage*, was to become singularly his own. Within this procedure, however, the panoramic argument that Hegel waged with Kant and Fichte from 1797 to the end of his life is often strident.

According to Hegel's view there are two chief antagonists to true philosophical self-awareness. The one is the general principle of transcendence, a 'beyond', wherever it may be located, that presents itself to consciousness as 'otherness' (*Anderssein*).[3] The other is the intellectual feeling of being a stranger in the world, of not being 'at home', as Hegel so often puts it. In fact, these problems are absolutely identical. Hegel's own highly intellectualistic system is intended to absorb this cardinal dualism within knowledge. 'I am at home in the world', he writes, 'when I know it, still more so when I have understood it.'[4] The word here for 'understand' is *begreifen*: Hegel means, by his terminology, to have seized a thing conceptually, asserting the basic proposition that 'spirit is the only reality'. In another

---

[1] *Enzyklopädie* (1830), paragraph 10, p. 43.

[2] Cf. *ibid*. 'Vorbereitung', paragraph 60, p. 85: 'The principle of the autonomy of reason, its absolute independence unto itself, is from now on to be regarded as the universal principle of philosophy as well as one of the prejudices of the time'; for the 'Kantian' syllogism, see paragraph 576, p. 462.

[3] Of course, Hegel's absolute rejection of transcendence is not only central to his rejection of transcendental idealism but also to his radical departure from Christian orthodoxy. Despite his protestations (cf. *Berliner Schriften*, pp. 572–5) Hegel was no Christian in a normal sense. On this point, see Jean Hyppolite, *Genèse et Structure de la Phénoménologie de l'Esprit de Hegel* (2 vols., Paris, 1946), I, 525.

[4] *Philosophy of Right*, paragraph 42A, p. 226.

instance, he speaks of true philosophical science as 'einheimisch', i.e. native and indigenous unto itself.[1]

Hegel viewed the problem of reconciliation with the object as the rationalization of the human function in maximum conditions of freedom, and as intimately connected to the question of the proper training of the human capacities (*Bildung*). In so doing he rejected both the Kantian separation of technical and moral practicity and the anti-intellectualism of Rousseau.[2] We know from previous chapters that Kant and Fichte also saw transcendence as *the* problem. It was connected in their view with arbitrary ecclesiastical and political authority, 'dogmatism' and specious determinism. Kant attacked and destroyed transcendent metaphysics in the *Critique of Pure Reason*. Fichte, however, believed that its vestige still lurked in the *Ding-an-sich*; whereupon he attempted to eliminate that 'otherness' by deducing the *Nicht-Ich* from the pure ego at an infra-conscious level. For Hegel, however, these solutions were untenable, because they maintained the existent world divided between actuality and pure possibility, postulating a 'longing for a beyond and a future... a longing which, however, can never be united with its eternal object'.[3] Knowing and being were eternally separate, creating a whole unbearable historical tension. Objects, for Hegel, were not simply physical constraints but the entire world of 'otherness' presented to the consciousness; even Fichte's 'unending shock [*Anstoss*]' was an appearance of the *Ding-an-sich*.[4] 'Whether a thing is called an alien impact, or an empirical entity, or sensibility, or the "thing-in-itself", it remains a principle precisely the same, viz. something external and foreign to that unity.'[5] The 'infinite progress' of Kant and the early Fichte is nothing more than the 'Other' in its most sophisticated form, the 'never-ending *Sollen*'.[6] In short, with their 'bad infinity', the straight-line infinity that is also the unproductive negation of the finite,[7] Kant and Fichte are

---

[1] 'Rede zum Antritt', *Berliner Schriften*, p. 17.
[2] Cf. *Philosophy of Right*, paragraph 136C, p. 81.
[3] *Glauben und Wissen*, p. 309.
[4] *Enzyklopädie* (1830), paragraph 415C, p. 345.
[5] *Phenomenology* (B), p. 280. Cf. Nohl, *Jugendschriften*, p. 374, re Fichte, 'Practical unity posits itself by the total suppression of its opposite.'
[6] *Enzyklopädie* (1830), 'Vorbereitung', paragraph 60, p. 83; *Philosophy of History*, p. 90.
[7] *Enzyklopädie* (1830), paragraph 94, p. 112; *Philosophy of Right*, paragraph 79C, p. 61.

really guilty of *Verstand*, defined as 'an activity of subjective thinking applied to some matter externally'.[1] *Vernunft*, 'the conscious certainty of being all reality', becomes spirit or *Geist*, 'when...[it is] *consciously* aware of itself as its own world, and of the world as itself'. Further, '*Geist* is consciousness in general', which is to say, in Hegel's terms, that which is spiritual and eternal in all individuals mediated by the active but unified Idea of spirit-in-itself.[2] Kant and Fichte have achieved only 'abstract' universality; Hegel's solution is allegedly 'concrete'. The *Phenomenology* is the voyage toward the concrete through the imperishable but incomplete *Gestalten* of the past; at its termination 'the moments of the spirit...no longer fall apart into the opposition of being and knowledge, but abide in the simplicity of knowledge...'[3] No longer then does 'the limited *Verstand* revel in its triumph over *Vernunft*, which is the absolute identity of the highest Idea and absolute reality...'[4]

D. POLITICAL FEEDBACK

All of this is completely pertinent to Hegel's estimation of the politics of transcendental idealism. If 'dogmatic' transcendence imposed an authority upon men and cemented it through habit and 'positivity', in opposing fashion Kant and Fichte appeared to recommend the irresistible coercion of the *Jenseits*, the *Endzweck* and the tutelary predispositions of the ever-receding Idea. It is generally to Kant that Hegel attributes the most exquisite form of immanent moral coercion, that of the natural self by its infinite master, reason;[5] but in Fichte's philosophy he senses the implacable premonition of physical coercion for the sake of the Idea, an absolute separation of rulers and ruled and of the subjects themselves into putatively 'free beings of reason' and 'modifiable materials...mere things to be handled'.[6] It is frequently said that the little-read *Differenz* is a mediation between the philosophies of Fichte and

---

[1] *Philosophy of Right*, paragraph 31C, p. 34.
[2] *Phenomenology* (B), pp. 457, 459.
[3] Preface to *Phenomenology* (K), p. 414.
[4] The reference is to Kant; *Glauben und Wissen*, p. 252.
[5] Cf. 'The Spirit of Christianity and its Fate', in Knox (trans.), *Early Theological Writings*, p. 211.
[6] *Differenz*, p. 64.

Schelling. So it may be; but it also wields a very heavy cudgel against Fichteanity and its moral-legal implications. Fichte's *Notstaat* is compared with a police state where the authorities must know 'where each citizen is at every hour of the day and what he is feeling'.[1] 'If the community of rational beings should really be a limiting of true freedom,' Hegel comments, 'it would then be the highest tyranny *an und für sich*.'[2] The rather remarkable thing is that virtually all of Hegel's extended comments on Fichte (here and in later writings) appear to be based on his interpretation of the 'first moment' of the *Wissenschaftslehre*, on the quasi-liberal *Doctrine of Right* of 1796, and on the *Sittenlehre* of 1798. We know that Hegel read (and disapproved of) the *Grundzüge* and that he knew the *Reden*, but we can only infer his reactions.[3] At any rate, he had a remarkably clear view of the Fichtean evolution, encompassed by the *Closed Commercial State* and the chiliastic Berlin lectures, and found this anticipation abhorrent.

Hegel's distaste for Fichte is, of course, compounded of many factors, not all of them totally speculative. For one thing, Hegel hated 'popular philosophy' and preaching.[4] But, more pertinently, he charged Fichte both with being *naturrechtlich* and with driving morality and legality apart, a combination of notions intelligible only in the German philosophical tradition, especially in view of its appreciation of the Greek *polis*.

The German understanding of the French Revolution is absolutely critical in connection with Hegel's attitude toward Kant and Fichte, for his reaction to both revolution and transcendental philosophy is of entire consistency. In both manifestations freedom appeared in the world—a fitful and admirable occurrence—but this

---

[1] *Differenz*, p. 67.

[2] *Ibid.* p. 65. For further analysis, see Günter Rohrmoser, 'Hegels Lehre vom Staat und das Problem der Freiheit in der modernen Gesellschaft', *Der Staat*, III, 4 (1964), esp. p. 395.

[3] Cf. Hegel to Schelling, 3 Jan. 1807, *Briefe*, I, 131; to Creuzer, 28 June 1808, I, 235. See the comment of Jean Wahl, *Le malheur de la conscience dans la philosophie de Hegel* (Paris, 1951), p. 61: '...certain expressions of Hegel would suggest that the Fichtean consciousness and the Jewish consciousness [i.e. with regard to transcendence] are one and the same consciousness, ruled by a perpetually ideal *ought* and by a "synthesis of domination..."' Fichte would not have appreciated the parallel.

[4] Cf. Preface to *Phenomenology* (K), p. 450: '...philosophy should again be made a serious pursuit'; also, *Dokumente*, 'Jena Aphorisms', p. 371.

was, alas, the 'leere Freiheit' of *Verstand*. Hegel does not appear to have made this correlation fully until his later period; in fact the *Phenomenology* implies that Revolution and Terror are logical outgrowths of the *Aufklärung*, whereas the higher principle of Kantian–Fichtean *Moralität* reposes above it as a kind of neo-Stoic *Zerissenheit*. Neither is it possible to equate the Fichtean 'tyranny' of the *Differenz* with Robespierre and the 'absolute negativity' of death, where heads are cleaved like cabbages.[1] In this regard the earlier Hegel was undoubtedly more sound, at least more historical. However, by the Berlin period, with Revolution and Empire belonging to the *temps révolus*, Hegel linked these phenomena.[2] What had been granted to the Germans by Kant in the form of 'tranquil theory' had been enacted in France through deeds and destruction.[3] Hegel's praise of the day when men sought to put into practice the idea that ' "nous" governed the world'[4] is tinged with a certain irony that those who would justify Hegel through his supposed fidelity to the Revolution, usually French writers, fail to perceive. Unmistakably clear, however, is Hegel's searing comment on 'the prodigious spectacle of the overthrow of the constitution of a great actual state and its complete reconstruction *ab initio* on the basis of pure thought alone...[an] experiment [that] ended in the maximum of frightfulness and terror', where the names of both Rousseau and Fichte are invoked.[5] In *Philosophy of Right*, paragraph 5C, again implicating Kant and Fichte (see paragraph 6C), he charges that the freedom of *Verstand*, so long as it remains purely theoretical, leads to a 'Hindu fanaticism of pure contemplation', whereas in practice 'it takes shape in religion and politics alike as the fanaticism of destruction—the destruction of the whole subsisting social order...'[6] Such is the consequence of the transcendental infinite of 'unrestricted possibility'.

Certain ironies should be recalled here. In the first place, Rousseau appears to have been no lover of revolutions. In the second

[1] *Phenomenology* (B), pp. 605–8.
[2] Cf. *History of Philosophy* (trans. Haldane-Simpson), III, 426: 'Kant's philosophy is the Enlightenment reduced to method.'
[3] *Philosophy of History*, p. 443.　　　　　　　　　　　　　　　[4] *Ibid.* p. 447.
[5] *Philosophy of Right*, paragraph 258C, p. 157. On the levelling effect of the Revolution, see *Jenenser Realphilosophie*, II, 260, marginal note.
[6] *Ibid* . 'Introduction', p. 22.

place, whatever philosophical extrapolations may be drawn, Kant believed in tutelage and discipline, at most the 'Revolution nach oben', and his relationship to the state of Frederick II, who was his employer, is not without resemblance to Hegel's own position *vis-à-vis* Frederick William III. In the third place, Fichte, in terms not so distant from Hegel's, came to chastise the French Revolution as *verständlich*, *willkürlich* and *empirisch*. But the greatest irony is this: that Hegel, the architect of the abolition of transcendence, which had been associated by all the philosophy of the eighteenth century with despotism and *arbitraire*, deduced his way into a position that can be described with some justice as an encouragement to political quiescence.

E. IDEOCENTRISM

It is impossible to weigh the balance of temperamental and purely speculative components in Hegel's astonishing constructions. But his entire approach precluded any sympathy with Fichte's 'philosophy to fit the man' slogan. Hegel's philosophy was at once a mighty triumph and a submission. Every area of his enterprise is tinctured with this combat. The volcanic intellect that could write a passage such as the following: 'I am the struggle [between the poles of infinity and finitude], for this struggle is a conflict defined not by the indifference of the two sides in their distinction, but by their being bound together in one entity. I am not one of the fighters locked in battle, but both, and I am the struggle itself. I am fire and water...'[1] could appear to his friend Hölderlin as 'ein ruhiger Verstandesmensch'.[2] Subject to hypochondria, loneliness and constant disappointment, Hegel developed a personality of implosive composure and produced a system to match. But it was a system raised on paradoxes of both irony and tragedy, an aesthetic system, intended to justify the ways of time to the eternal. It was also an intellectualistic system to match Descartes': the motto of Hegelianism is that 'man is not free when he is not thinking'.[3]

---

[1] *Vorlesungen über die Philosophie der Religion*, S.W. (Glockner), xv, 80.
[2] Quoted from J. Glenn Gray, *Hegel's Hellenic Ideal*, p. 35.
[3] *Philosophy of History*, p. 439.

Neither is man entirely free until he has made the world his own in thought. The contradictions of life are 'gripped' and held in this immortal vice. Only in this context can we make sense of the tendentious statements about the identity of the actual and the rational, the insistence that 'what is universally valid is also universally effective'.[1] The Hegelian theodicy is in the mind. Whatever allegations Hegelianism makes about the dialectical reciprocity of world and self, practicity tends to be swallowed up in a theoretical reason that is no longer cut to the measure of Kant's 'science' but to the fit of all existence. *Erfahrung* is no longer an ordering of empirical materials. Thought surmounts and compresses all moments that lie within its grasp. The owl of Minerva flies at dusk, to be sure, like Plato with the Hellenic *polis*, Proclus with the tradition of classical philosophy, and Hegel himself with the intellectual comprehension of the Christian *saeculum*. But thought is also Christ rising from the depths of negation: '. . . when the power of unity disappears from men's lives. . . then the need for philosophy arises'.[2] The Estates of Württemburg should vanish, because their time is past.[3] 'Once the realm of thought is revolutionized,' Hegel wrote to Niethammer, 'reality cannot hold out.'[4] Hegel sought amid his changing times for a reciprocal conception of thought as will and will as thought, and attempted to locate this in the harmony of mind or spirit.

The point deserves some elaboration. The critical notion of transcendental idealism was the 'primacy of practical reason' and its critical tool was the will that universalizes itself. In this perspective, mind mediates between nature and the Idea, shaping the former in view of the latter. This is the proposition that Hegel reverses, not on behalf of nature, but in favour of the mediation of the Idea itself. The consequence is that the sphere of will (*Wille*), which is

---

[1] *Phenomenology* (B), p. 289. As is well known, the young Hegel searched in Life, Religion, Love for an absolute principle of philosophy before settling on his particularly intellectualized—yet, in overtones, mystical—conception of Geist. See A. Koyré 'Hegel à Iéna', *Revue d'histoire et de philosophie religieuses* (1935), pp. 429–31.

[2] *Differenz*, p. 14.

[3] Cf. 'On the Recent Domestic Affairs of Wurtemberg', in *Hegel's Political Writings*, p. 244; *Philosophy of Right*, 'Introduction', paragraph 3C, p. 17; *Schriften zur Politik und Rechtsphilosophie* (ed. G. Lasson, Leipzig, 1913), p. 199.

[4] To Niethammer, 28 Oct. 1808, *Briefe*, I, 253.

labelled 'objective spirit' and concerns society, the state, law, ethics
and world history, is surmounted by an 'absolute spirit' that 'knows
itself *an und für sich*'.[1] That is the ultimate manifestation of the Idea
fleshed out, according to Hegel's constant principle: 'Das Wesen
muss erscheinen.' In Kantianism the spirit extended itself toward the
Idea by means of *Wille* or 'pure practical reason'. In Hegelianism
the Idea is not just immanently produced but immanently grasped
by the spirit at all actual (*wirklich*) moments of its journey. Thought
fulfils the concept (*Begriff*), producing the concrete unity of its
moments, and only thereby exalting will to a universal. This is
specified in Hegel's discussion of the evolution of consciousness-
in-general in the difficult but important Introduction to the *Philosophy of Right*:

...it is in the will that the intrinsic finitude of intelligence has its beginning; and it is only by raising itself to become thought again, and endow-
ing its aims with immanent universality, that the will cancels the difference
of form and content and makes itself the objective, infinite will. Thus they
[i.e. Kant and Fichte] understand little of the nature of thinking and willing who suppose that while, in willing as such, man is infinite, in thinking
he, or even reason itself, is restricted. In so far as thinking and willing
are still distinguished, the opposite is rather the truth, and will is thinking
reason resolving itself to finitude.[2]

If this has a peculiar intellectualizing effect on all life, individual
and collective, by comprehending the 'sheer restlessness' of volition
within the evolution and result of what has been thought, it has also
the paradoxical effect of making the *epigones* of thought 'at home'
with their conclusions and curbing their temptation to become the
stern moral shepherds of the practical world, bent, *à la* Fichte, on
the prophetical coercion of souls for the sake of the Idea. For Hegel's
is an Idea which, constructed of its necessary moments, can bear to
live with them. The past becomes not simply a path to eternity but
a path *of* eternity. Since, in the highest form of knowledge (the
philosophical), thought absorbs will by willing itself as knowledge,
the philosopher is no less exalted than before, but he is detached

[1] Cf. *Enzyklopädie* (1830), paragraph 469, p. 379: '...as will spirit enters actuality, as
knowledge it forms the basis for the universality of the concept'.
[2] *Philosophy of Right*, paragraph 13C, p. 26.

from the struggles of a world that he has already explained. Only by losing its prescriptiveness can philosophy become explanatory in the highest sense. This is not only wisdom; it is the pure pleasure, the Sovereign Good. And this is why Hegel terminates the great summary of his philosophical system with the following words of Aristotle:

And thinking in itself deals with that which is best in itself, and that which is thinking in the fullest sense with that which is best in the fullest sense. And thought thinks on itself because it shares the nature of the object of thought; for it becomes an object of thought in coming into contact with and thinking its objects, so that thought and object of thought are the same...[1]

Absolute knowing resolves the Kantian dichotomy because it is also the ultimate of 'practical reason'. Still in Aristotle's words, 'it is active when it possesses [its] object. Therefore the possession rather than the receptivity is the divine element which thought seems to contain, and the act of contemplation is what is most pleasant and best'. The 'freest man' is therefore, unavoidably, he who thinks the most comprehensively. That is what Hegelian freedom must mean in the last analysis. But since it is not given to all men to be philosophers of the absolute, we must then ask what freedom must mean for man in general, whether the *Bildung* and *Zucht* of the philosophically oriented state carry him toward the Idea or whether there is yet another option. This is a vital question too often over-looked and sometimes mis-stated in analyses of the Hegelian theory of politics. In the following chapter I shall try to pursue this investigation.

---

[1] Aristotle, *Metaphysics*, XII, 7. Cited in *Enzyklopädie* (1830), p. 463. I owe the rendering of the Greek to G. E. Müller's interpretive translation of the *Encyclopedia of Philosophy by Hegel* (New York, 1959), p. 287.

2

A POLITICAL CONTEXT

In quest of the 'political implications' of the Hegelian system I propose to deal in five major categories with the working out of the position generally described in the last section. Although these categories are illustrative rather than exhaustive, each continues and completes a major theme introduced in connection with the thought of Rousseau, Kant and Fichte. This treatment should provide a sense of the tradition, highlight certain distinctions within it, and suggest the flavour of Hegel's approach to political problems.

A. TIME AND HISTORY

To understand Hegel's much-argued view of history, his theory of time must be understood. That, too, is not an easy problem. As Koyré writes: '...Hegel's philosophy, in its deepest intuitions, seems to have been a philosophy of time. And, consequently, a humanistic philosophy. And this, despite the effort to join time to eternity, or more exactly thanks to the Boehmian notion of non-temporal evolution to introduce time within eternity and eternity within time.'[1] Koyré's important essay inspired Kojève's influential *Introduction à la lecture de Hegel*, which argued, on the basis of the *Phenomenology*, along Feuerbachian 'anthropological' lines that Hegel was a Promethean atheist who brought history to a close by understanding and suppressing it with his *Phenomenology* and *Logic*, and the chiliastic termination of the master–slave dialectic.[2] Kojève's formula may be expressed thus: Work and Struggle = Freedom = Time = History = Transience = Nothing = Man. In overcoming time, man supersedes his humanity, terminates his history, and

---

[1] A. Koyré, 'Hegel à Iéna', p. 435. The reference to Boehme derives from the criticism of Feuerbach (cf. *S.W.*, ed. Bolin and Jodl, Stuttgart, 1959, II, 194–5) as does the entire Koyré–Kojève line of interpretation.

[2] See Alexandre Kojève, *Introduction à la lecture de Hegel* (ed. Raymond Queneau, Paris, 1947), a recapitulation of Kojève's courses on the *Phenomenology* given at the Sorbonne in the years 1933–39, which exerted a powerful influence on Sartre, Merleau-Ponty and on the French academic interpretation of Hegel in general.

abolishes a freedom inseparable from progress and effort. He makes himself a utopian.[1] Koyré extracts a marginal note from Hegel's Jena lectures of 1803–4 that says: 'Geist ist Zeit.'[2] Thus the absolute conquest of spirit is equally the conquest of time and humanity. On this frail reed the splendid theory rests.

It is better, however, to make one's own examination of Hegel's texts. And it is of greatest importance in approaching these texts to recall the grounds for Hegel's thundering disapproval of *der unendliche Progress* and 'bad infinity'.[3] If one is to reject the theory of time that leads either to 'Hindu mysticism' or 'the fanaticism of destruction' and yet retain an evolutionary dialectic of consciousness and history, then the alternatives are either to propose a chiliasm such as Kojève suggests (and toward which Fichte, on other grounds, was tempted) or to eternalize the present by the necessary activity of the free spirit, that is, to make each present, in so far as it is 'actual', an expression of the constituent concepts necessarily retained in the mind as the substance of culture, reason and freedom. The latter is Hegel's path: 'In the free will, the truly infinite becomes actual and present; the free will itself is this Idea whose nature it is to be present here and now.'[4] Elsewhere he writes that 'the ideality of the finite is the leading principle of philosophy'.[5] This means that the finite (the effects of will, the events and creations of the past) becomes 'real' only through the mediation of that thought by which it is 'cancelled and preserved' (i.e. eternalized).

Now Hegel does say that time is negativity; it is the analogue of dying and perishing: 'it is not *in* time that everything originates and passes away; time itself is this evolution, this originating and perishing'.[6] But *Geist* is not *Zeit*, because *Geist* exceeds the mere measure of man and is the unifying spirit that links him with the objective movement of the eternal:

Only the natural is subjected to time, in so far as it is finite; but the true, the Idea, the *Geist*, is *eternal.*—The concept of eternality must not,

---

[1] Hegel would surely judge Kojève's interpretation as utopian and a case of 'unmittelbares abstraktes Fürsichsein'. Cf. *Phenomenology* (B), pp. 374–82, esp. p. 382.

[2] Koyré, p. 449.

[3] *Enzyklopädie* (1830), paragraph 94, p. 112.

[4] *Philosophy of Right*, paragraph 22C, p. 30.

[5] *Enzyklopädie* (1830), paragraph 95, p. 114.   [6] *Ibid.* paragraph 257C, p. 210.

Time and history

however, be taken negatively as the abstraction from time so that it would exist outside of it, especially not in the sense that eternity would come *after* time: that would make eternity into a future, a moment of time.[1]

Kant had said substantially the same thing as this in his resolute attack against chiliasm, but he had extracted eternity from time by making time a human form of apperception. Hegel's perspective of the mediated absolute renders eternity incomprehensible apart from the conditions of its appearance. The eternal is what is thought: 'Thought is itself the last, the deepest, the aftermost; it is completely itself. But thought also has an appearance.' Essentially the difference is between Kant's speculative Stoicism and Hegel's speculative Christianity.

For Hegel, as we have seen, Kantianism ends in *Verstand* or an irrepressible transcendence, further defined as 'the thought of an eternal opposed to the temporal, an infinite and unlimited thing opposed to the finite and limited'.[2] As a consequence, 'the world is torn into two separate parts—a realm of the present and a realm of the beyond'.[3] To the interior *Trennung* or 'unhappy consciousness' of Kantianism is added the divisive *Notstaat* of Fichtean 'bad infinity'. The symbol of *Verstand* is the straight line, but that of *Vernunft* (reason according to the 'concept') is the circle whose end is a perpetual beginning.[4] The circle is to be understood neither as the cycle of nature (nature, after all, regarded teleologically, proceeds to its goal by the shortest means) nor as a recurrent cycle of history based on the same principle (as the ancients had understood it), but as the metaphorical motion of reality itself in its appearance as *Geist*, a comprehending rather than a confrontation of the objects of knowledge. 'The way of spirit is mediation, the *Umweg* (detour).'[5] This represents the deepening of knowledge turning back into itself in ever greater awareness around its fixed point of *now*, the 'rose in the cross of the present'.

[1] *Enzyklopädie* (1830), paragraph 257C, p. 210.
[2] *Einleitung in die Geschichte der Philosophie* (ed. J. Hoffmeister, Hamburg, 1959), p. 120.
[3] 'Rede zum Antritt', *Berliner Schriften*, p. 11.
[4] *Ibid.* p. 9. Cf. Preface to *Phenomenology* (K), p. 388: 'The true is its own becoming, the circle that presupposes its end as its aim and thus has it for its beginning.'
[5] *Einl. Geschichte Phil.* p. 62. Cf. *ibid.* p. 65, where development is described as 'Arbeit ... Tätigkeit... Umbilden.'

Just as there are 'bad' and 'true' infinities, there are bad and true 'nows'. The 'now' of *Verstand* is the finite present, fixed abstractly between past and future and ever swallowed up in nothingness.[1] Hegel says that this 'now' produces the subjective representations of fear and hope; and we are reminded immediately of Rousseau. But 'what is absolutely present or eternal is time itself as the unity of present, future and past'.[2] In this sense, it can be said that 'the present is the highest': it mediates time and eternity.[3] The true 'now' is the actuality of true eternality.

If, as subjects of time, things perish, time is also the redeemer of its own destruction, being, as Kant puts it, the 'internal sense' where the essential moments of truth may be gathered in the mind. In this vision, space separates but time rejoins, making a perpetual communion of reality, a *Geisterwelt* which is neither forsaken, because 'the wealth of its previous existence is...still present to consciousness in memory',[4] nor 'beyond'. This present perfect is also represented in knowledge by the congruence of philosophy with its development; as Hegel writes: '...we must not regard the history of philosophy as dealing with the past, even though it is history'.[5] The Hegelian 'kingdom of ends' is a kingdom of reason's venerability, in which consciousness spiritualizes and comprehends its objects and knows itself through them. 'Such an end is pronounced to be the highest end attainable by man.'[6]

This remarkable formulation not only allows Hegel to crystallize and possess antiquity as an eternal moment but to base the title of that possession squarely on the central Christian mysteries of Incarnation, Crucifixion and Resurrection, thus effecting the passage from metaphysics to history by a 'speculative' route, a route superior to logical analogy. The philosophies of *Verstand* are, in Hegel's view, Mosaic, intellectual theisms without the presence of Christ.

The form of the absolute, which is beauty, was the discovery of

---

[1] *Enzyklopädie* (1830), paragraph 259, pp. 210–11.
[2] *Jenenser Realphilosophie*, II, 10.
[3] *Lectures on the History of Philosophy* (Haldane-Simpson), III, 547.
[4] Preface to *Phenomenology* (K), p. 382.
[5] *Lectures on the History of Philosophy* (Haldane-Simpson), I, 38.
[6] *Ibid.* I, 106.

the Greeks: 'he who has never known the works of the ancients has lived without knowing what beauty is'.[1] However, its content, truth and freedom, is Christian; and history is to be construed as the working out of truth and freedom. Therefore, Christianity may itself be described as 'the goal and the starting point of history'.[2] Löwith asserts correctly that Hegel's is the last great philosophy of Christian history, though one may doubt that it is a Christian philosophy of history.[3] For Hegel the 'science' of history is unthinkable outside of Christian forms and an immanently transformed version of the Christian notion of the 'fullness of time'.[4] Kroner comments aptly that the *Aufhebung* of Christianity by philosophical science, that is, of 'faith' by 'knowledge', is a good deal less amazing than Hegel's prior assertion of an absolute claim for this religion.[5] However, Christianity provides the substance of Hegel's two critical notions—*Versöhnung* and 'Das Wesen muss erscheinen'—and becomes the fundamental speculative matrix for his dialectic of the present and the eternal. Although working in the same tradition and claiming the licence of Christianity in the development of their ethical teleology, Kant and Fichte encountered the mystery of Christ as a hurdle. Socrates or Epictetus might have sufficed. But for Hegel this aspect is of critical importance.

Philosophy or *Wissenschaft* mediates the form and the content of truth, creating an absolute 'concept', which is also the fulfilment or concrete universality of the Idea, the necessity of free thought.[6] The eternal is made of both the sum and the components. Hegel juxtaposes these two ideas harshly in his lectures on the history of philosophy. 'We must not regard the history of philosophy as dealing with the past, even though it is history,' he says.[7] At the same time, he grants himself a *verständlich* metaphor: 'A long time is undoubtedly required by spirit in working out philosophy...like the

---

[1] *Nürnberger Schriften*, p. 309.
[2] *Philosophy of History*, p. 319.
[3] Cf. Karl Löwith, 'Hegels Aufhebung der christlichen Religion', *Hegel-Studien*, I (1962), p. 235.
[4] This is because history itself is 'mind [i.e. spirit] clothing itself with the form of events', *Philosophy of Right*, paragraph 346, p. 217.
[5] Cf. Richard Kroner, 'System und Geschichte bei Hegel', *Logos*, xx (1930), pp. 243–58.
[6] *Enzyklopädie* (1830), paragraph 572, p. 450.
[7] *History of Philosophy* (tr. Haldane-Simpson), I, 38.

immensity of space spoken of in astronomy.'[1] Again, the resolution must be found in the mind that can grasp the unity of eternality and development: 'In order to find a system in the history of philosophy, one must already have an insight into the system of philosophy. Thus it is the job of the teacher, who has this already, to demonstrate a systematization or logical development in the history of philosophy.'[2] This is the image of that curious circle of *Vernunft*, which must somehow be broken into; we see immediately that behind the famous Hegelian question of system *vs.* history lies the further question of *Bildung*.

It was Dilthey who first broadcast 'the contradiction between the historical consciousness of the relativity of each historical actuality and the metaphysical need for a last conclusive word and an absolute value'.[3] This became a question of perennial importance and mystery for a positivistic age in which Hegel's sense of Christianity had virtually disappeared. A wealth of literature accompanies the subject and the subsidiary matter of the 'end of history'.[4] It is an enormously complex problem, charged with all the conflicting values of the intellectual breakdown of the nineteenth and twentieth centuries, and it obviously cannot be settled here. It is possible, however, to make some reference to Hegel's position as unclouded by later developments.

History, for Hegel, is of two sorts—I am not referring here to the distinctions that he makes in the introduction to his lectures on the philosophy of history[5]—which are often confused and indeed easily become confused in the light of Hegel's presentation. The one is the history of the absolute, which deals not with a past but with an eternal present. The other is 'world history', which deals with the essential patterns and matrices in which the absolute

---

[1] *History of Philosophy*, I, p. 36. Cf. *Philosophy of Right*, paragraph 62C, p. 51: 'It is about a millenium and a half since the freedom of personality began through the spread of Christianity... This may serve to show the length of time that mind requires for progress in self-consciousness.'

[2] *Einl. Geschichte Phil.* p. 139.

[3] Wilhelm Dilthey, *Die Jugendgeschichte Hegels*, in *Gesammelte Schriften*, IV, 187.

[4] Besides Koyré and Kojève, *opera citata*, see also Kroner, 'System und Geschichte'; Maurer, *Hegel und das Ende der Geschichte*; and M. Rubenstein, 'Die logischen Grundlagen des Hegelschen Systems und das Ende der Geschichte', *Kant-Studien*, XI, I (15 Feb. 1906), pp. 40–108.

[5] For these, see *Die Vernunft in der Geschichte*, pp. 4 ff.

appears (as the highest and unifying component of 'objective spirit').[1] The confusion lies in the fact that these types of history are conjugated with each other, with logic or the 'development of the concept', with the normative psychology of human experience (the fact that so much distressed Haym),[2] with the central myth of Christianity, and, not least, with a richness of empirical interpretation. This latter indebtedness is, in fact, critical to understanding Hegel: it is the way one 'breaks into' the closed circle of knowledge, and it distinguishes Hegel's method of history from the deductively organized speculations of Kant and Fichte. However, empirical history has nothing to do with any 'grasp' of history; it only furnishes an access. Hegel curtly dismisses historical positivism as 'eine Geschichte, die zugleich keine Geschichte ist'.[3] In sum, Hegel's procedures are an extensive sequence of dynamic analogies held together, for better or worse, by the cement of a logic fit for reality.

Despite the conflicting citations which scholars hurl about, I see little question that, on the plane of the history of the absolute, Hegel spoke of the conceptual 'end of history', not simply in the tautological sense of the eternality of the absolute but of the comprehension of the absolute together with its moments, the 'identity' with the 'non-identity'.[4] This is the point toward which his whole philosophy tended. Nor was he content to express it in perfectly abstract terms. 'The Christian world', he wrote, 'is the world of completion; the grand principle of being is realized, consequently the end of days is fully come.'[5] Even though this declaration is made with reference to *Weltgeschichte*, we can take it to mean that the

---

[1] These two notions of history are correlates of the two basic notions of Hegelian time: the homogeneous continuity of time (necessary for the unfolding of the manifold of the Idea), and the contemporaneity of time (guaranteeing the logical existence of the social whole at a given moment of historical actuality). For a brilliant discussion of these concepts and their relation, see Louis Althusser, *Lire le Capital* (2 vols., Paris, 1966), II, 38–43.

[2] Cf. R. Haym, *Hegel und seine Zeit* (Reprint: Hildesheim, 1962), p. 241: '...etwas Anderes ist die Geschichte und etwas Anderes ist die Psychologie'.

[3] *Einl. Geschichte Phil.* p. 133. See also, *Phenomenology* (B), *in fine*, p. 808.

[4] The reason why, contrary to Kojève, Hegel does not 'equal God' is that God is the 'identity' which must be mediated with 'non-identity' or 'restless diversity' (the world) in order to become reality. Because 'das Wesen muss erscheinen', Hegel's God is not 'real', but is yet, paradoxically, the form of all reality.

[5] *Philosophy of History*, p. 342.

process of history as such, interpreted in the Christian sense, has brought mind or spirit to a point where the 'Sichwissen des Geistes' has become possible. The product and not the milieu is being judged. The superiority of the present (Hegelian) consciousness over the past—i.e. all recorded history thought in Christian terms—is this achievement of a platform of judgment, philosophy's conquest of 'the goal...that it might be able to relinquish the name of love of knowledge and be actual knowledge'.[1] If that is not true, if it can be 'overjudged', then the whole logic of Hegelian historical comprehension falls apart. This is made explicit in Hegel's important letter to the Hamburg hat-manufacturer Duboc, in 1822. Speaking of truth, he wrote: '...I think it dwells in every authentic consciousness, in all religions and in all philosophies, but...our present point of view has been to understand its development.'[2] That is a claim of utmost simplicity, yet of utmost presumption. It takes on depth when we recognize that Christ is the *an sich*, Hegel the *für sich* for the completed development of historical understanding. And once history is 'begriffen', system becomes possible, and vice-versa.

The greater problem arises with regard to 'world history' itself. Let us not even debate whether Hegel anticipated a fundamental continuity to empirical history: the point seems too obvious. The 'restlessness of life' is contained but not destroyed: that is what 'Vermittlung' means. What we are concerned with is to determine whether the 'principles' of world history are not themselves consummated by the philosophical grasp of the 'fullness of time'. Here, I think, Hegel is indecisive, for both speculative and strategic reasons. Speculatively, there is the problem of mediating between the absolute or 'eternally present' values of art, religion and philosophy and the restless spiritual turmoil of historical states and institutions. This seems like apples and oranges. Hegel settles the matter by saying that world history is the tribunal of its successive acts.[3] That notion has been attacked by many who ignore that there is a religio-philosophical consciousness judging world history. It is the

---

[1] Preface to *Phenomenology* (K), p. 372.
[2] Letter to Duboc, 30 July 1822, *Briefe*, II, 329.
[3] *Philosophy of Right*, paragraph 341, p. 216. Cf. John F. Kennedy's inaugural address of 20 Jan. 1961: 'With a good conscience our only sure reward, with history the final judge of our deeds...'

latter judgment which, both historically and 'eternally', injects its values into the course of civilizations. If this were not so, Hegel—whether one likes his concept of freedom or not—could never describe history as the working out of the problem of freedom. The Idea of world history, then, is consummated in so far as it accepts and actualizes the truth that philosophy has comprehended. However, set against this notion is the rather jarring dialectic between a Christianity that has furnished the possibility of historical consciousness and a philosophy that has made it eternal.

This still does not settle the problem of a phenomenal time-lag, and here Hegel is notoriously obscure. Sometimes 'the spirit...is at work giving itself a new form'—*via* philosophy;[1] sometimes it is engaged in painting 'grey on grey'. It seems to rotate around actuality. Or sometimes, it would seem, spirit and its works are in congruence: 'It is of the nature of truth to prevail when its time has come.'[2] In most of Hegel's political writings—especially the earlier ones—the spirit is represented as the manifestation of the concrete or *sittlich* life of a people. Did Descartes and Bacon anticipate a new age? Did Plato close one? Was Hegel 'abreast of his age'? I do not think we can easily answer these questions in Hegelian terms, and must thereby forfeit the whole matter of priority in history. Hegel did not anticipate the problem of the Marxists, with their structure and superstructure. What we can say is that the Idea of a historical community or institution is the extrojective essence of the meaning that philosophy reads into the entire cultural complex.[3] This is what Hegel believed Plato had done in the *Republic* and that he himself had achieved in the *Philosophy of Right*. It is the *Begriff* that makes the actual rational. The point is of critical importance when we oppose Hegel's 'extrojective' approach to the 'projective' technique of the transcendental idealists. It is at the core of the difference between their 'futurism' and Hegel's own 'present-orientedness'.

Finally, we must acknowledge that Hegel shared with his contemporaries a common appreciation of the European and German traditions, however much he disliked the *unendliche Aufgabe*. In his

---

[1] Preface to *Phenomenology* (K), p. 380.   [2] *Ibid.* p. 456.
[3] This is the essential significance of the 'contemporaneity of time'. Cf. L. Althusser, *Capital*, II, 39–40.

historical conception, through the medium of his immanent version of Christian providentialism, he attempted to wed *logos* and *kairos* by remaining a man of his culture and by thrusting out 'bad infinity'.[1] His rejection of cosmopolitanism in favour of 'Weltgeschichte' can be seen partially in this light. Like Fichte, he praised Luther, and saw 'the pure inwardness of the German nation' as 'the proper soil for the emancipation of spirit'.[2] But this meant, too, paradoxically, that the Germans were the very apotheosis of the 'unhappy consciousness', a sensation Fichte may have felt but never expressed.[3] Again, like Fichte, Hegel perceived in the Romanic nations 'a disharmony', based not on language but rather on the tense contradiction between politics and religion, a critical category for him since his early so-called theological essays.[4] There is the same ambiguity in Hegel between Germany and the principle of 'Germanness' that we find elsewhere. On the whole, Europe is a 'Germanic' culture with a final world-historical mission, but Germany is evidently its purest part.[5] However, the Idea of the Hegelian state has no necessary connection with Germany but is the philosophical theory of all modern government in general. It was Schiller, not Hegel, who said that it belonged to the Germans to 'reap the harvest of time as a whole'.[6] And it would not be difficult to compile an anthology of praise for other parts of European civilization from Hegel's writings.

Beyond its important and difficult ramifications, the Hegelian interpretation of time and history has a concrete function in the philosophical disputes of his day: to rationalize—while touching all points of the speculative compass—the response to the coercive and divisive implications of transcendental idealism, and thus to achieve a harmony, a 'being at home', that would be also a triumph of thought over all thinking. As we turn to the Hegelian state, this should be carefully borne in mind.

---

[1] On *logos* (timeless truth) and *kairos* (the vital moment of fulfilment), see Paul Tillich 'Ideologie und Utopie', *Die Gesellschaft*, x, 6 (Oct. 1929), pp. 348–55.

[2] *Philosophy of History*, pp. 416–20.

[3] Koyré, 'Hegel à Iéna', comments acutely, p. 430: 'Religion is salvation; but only for happy peoples...And Hegel belonged to an unhappy one.'

[4] *Philosophy of History*, p. 421.

[5] *History of Philosophy* (trans. Haldane-Simpson), I, 101, 105.

[6] See above, p. 82.

A political context

B. 'VERNUNFTSTAAT' VERSUS 'VERSTANDESSTAAT'

For the most part, it is misleading to attach 'isms' to Hegel. However, to the extent that such labels apply, this much can be said. Serious philosophy—the creative deployment of systematic intellectual power—is scarcely conservative. In political theory, the real conservatives—Burke, de Maistre, Haller—are pseudo-philosophers.[1] Nothing, indeed, is in its way more radical than Hegel's notion of reason. Still, it is true from a certain number of angles— emphasis on order, defence of functional inequality, respect for the power of tradition, antagonism to the demands of the 'never-ending ought-to-be'—that Hegel is a conservative. He and Aristotle are the most conservative of the first-class philosophers, and Hegel felt this kinship intensely. In the line of Aristotle, Hegel's philosophy of the state is a most serious attempt to conquer the discrepancy of 'chimera' and 'prejudice' by the sheer power of reason.

Hegel's political philosophy—especially his conceptions of the state and of war—has been picked to pieces by generations of scholars. This is not the place to repeat the operation.[2] There are, however, some positions which the essay seeks to avoid. In the first place, it is an error to judge Hegel's political theory in terms of either the vanished *polis* or the nascent *industria*. Secondly, it is misleading to excise Hegel's politics from his total metaphysical construction, as a recent writer has invited us to do.[3] Thirdly, while one may welcome scholarly attempts to deliver Hegel's political philosophy from a long accumulation of crude misunderstanding, it is advisable to resist the temptation to read Hegel with too much liberal or progressivist indulgence.[4] Finally, it is likely, contrary to

[1] See Karl Mannheim's fundamental work 'Das konservative Denken', *Archiv für Sozialwissenschaft und Sozialpolitik*, Feb. 1927 (pp. 68–142) and April 1927 (pp. 470–95) for a general sociology of political conservatism and, *inter alia*, an attempt to isolate what in Hegel is conservative and what is not. See especially, the explanation of why Hegel's 'system' is not the truly conservative component of his thought (p. 87 n). This is a much more delicate operation than the same author's passages on Hegel in *Ideology and Utopia*, e.g. pp. 60–7.

[2] Despite 'statist' proclivities shared with his brilliant mentor Friedrich Meinecke, Franz Rosenzweig, *Hegel und der Staat* (2 vols., Munich and Berlin, 1920), remains the surest and most thorough guide to Hegel's political development.

[3] Notably Z. A. Pelczynski, in his lengthy, and in many ways creditable, introduction to T. M. Knox (trans.), *Hegel's Political Writings* (Oxford, 1964), p. 136.

[4] Notably: Eric Weil, *Hegel et l'Etat* (Paris, 1950); and Weil's student Eugène Fleischmann, *La philosophie politique de Hegel* (Paris, 1964).

Hegel's own view, that his Idea of the state functioned as the intellectual solution to an important section of his vast problem rather than as the unerring description of any concrete forms that the philosopher remembered, knew or anticipated.

The last point deserves special comment. Fundamentally, three sets of issues are involved. The first has to do with the teleological development of the political community in history. The second concerns the Idea of the state as analogue to other parts of the Hegelian system. The third matter concerns the state's particular role in the system.

The general outlines of the first question are very obvious. Man is a socio-political being. In all the historical distance between Periclean antiquity and the Napoleonic present man has been living in a condition of psychological disharmony whose deepest causes are those analysed by Rousseau: a fracture between the notions of individualism and citizenship, and between the demands of the other-worldly religious consciousness and the public consciousness. Of course, for Hegel these were aspects of the same problem. If we can distinguish Hegel's 'taste' from his belief in historical necessity, it is then possible to say that all politics between the collapse of the *polis* and the time when it became possible to 'think' the modern state in its profundity has been a record of antagonistic or disembodied forms of community. If, on the other hand, we restore the teleological dimension, we perceive the 'justice' of what has happened. With the Greeks, 'the divine in its form and objectivity has immediately a double nature [i.e., individuality and civic cohesion: Hegel almost invariably idealizes Periclean Athens], and its life is the absolute unity of this nature'.[1] But this society of 'Schönheit' and 'Kunstwerk' cannot be maintained;[2] its 'concrete substance' must be mediated: 'Reason must pass out of and leave this happy condition. For only implicitly (*an sich*) and immediately (*unmittelbar*) is the life of a free nation the real objective ethical order.'[3] The 'tragedy of *Sittlichkeit*' is the tragedy of

---

[1] *Schriften zur Politik und Rechtsphilosophie*, p. 384.
[2] Cf. *Jenenser Realphilosophie*, II, 251.
[3] *Phenomenology* (B), p. 378. The tension is very great here. As Hegel puts it, one cannot be sure whether 'spirit has broken away [from its destiny], or...not yet attained it: for both can be said with equal truth'.

'critical reason' as against 'felt reason', already explicit in one way in *Antigone* and later, in another, in the trial of Socrates. From the felicity of 'substantiality' ('so *sind* sie—so *leben* sie')[1] the Western consciousness must endure its historical *saeculum* of 'alienation' or 'bifurcation'. However, this is the charge of freedom. The Greeks knew only that 'some are free' and they furthermore lacked 'conscience' and 'conviction'.[2] Only the deepening of the Christian message and the circuitous working out of Christian history could supply these ingredients. Much of the *Phenomenology* is a record of this painful voyage.

Now it is essential to remember that for Hegel the Greek harmony represented *lebendiges Leben*, the fullness of life. He had also decided —at least by 1805—that such a paradise could never return.[3] Indeed, several years earlier—for example, in the unfinished essay on the German constitution—he had resolved to compose thought with actuality, and he believed that he glimpsed the means of the breakthrough—through the creative assimilation of vanished objects by the mind. But Greek thought had presumably developed from the matrix of 'beautiful life', producing those 'golden apples in silver bowls' that adorned Hegel's true altar of devotion.[4] Hegel would essay the opposite procedure—whatever he may have argued—by imposing thought upon life, partly, and in part paradoxically, to save life from the tyrannical premises of *Verstand*. This compelled him to seek whatever 'substantiality' he could find beneath the frothing surface of a Europe churned up by Enlightenment, Revolution and vicarious fluctuation between doubt and hope, continuity and disorder. Quite naturally this meant a regression toward the kind of traditionalism that the transcendental idealists had forsworn, but it was not an abdication to Burkean–Rehbergian 'empiricism'.[5] Against the categories of conventionalism

[1] *Phil. Rechts Randbemerkungen*, paragraph 147, p. 414. [2] *Ibid.*
[3] Cf. marginal note in *Jenenser Realphilosophie*, II, 251. [4] *Nürnberger Schriften*, p. 310.
[5] For a balanced (but somewhat abstract) judgment, using the polarities of Rousseau and Burke as standards of reason and custom, see Jean-François Suter, 'Tradition et révolution', *Hegel-Studien*, I (1962), pp. 307–26. A clearer idea of Hegel's sense of tradition may be gained, not by comparing him with Burke, but with Pascal: 'Man is ignorant at birth; but he learns continually as he goes along; for he benefits not only from his own experience, but also from that of his forerunners because he keeps fast in his memory his acquired knowledge and because that of the ancients is always

and rationalism, Hegel devised a historical rationalism. It differed from the Kantian–Fichtean solution in that its development was not to be constantly menaced by the power of its goal and that, without chiliastic overtones, the goal was foreshortened into the very rhythm of development. Hegel first attempted the working out of this problem by opposing an 'absolute' method to the 'empirical' and 'reflective' ones in his early essay 'On the Scientific Treatment of Natural Right'.

In that article and in the *System der Sittlichkeit* of 1802 Hegel seemingly toyed with the idea of thrusting the *polis*-ideal bodily into the modern world.[1] We cannot underestimate his passion for that solution—an intellectual passion redolent with *Hauslehrer* frustrations—but it is advisable to give closer attention to the Jena system of 1805–6, where, for the first time, Hegel's political philosophy is set down in a form that will remain remarkably unchanged despite all subsequent changes in the politics of Europe: here is the relinquishment of the *polis*, the introduction of modern *Sittlichkeit*, the rationalization of constitutional monarchy, world history and most of the rest.[2]

The solution that emerges is the following. Modern Europe is becoming 'repolitized', in the sense that arbitrary rule, superstition and mystification are at an end. But participation in the *res publica* can no longer be simple, direct, 'felt'; it must be mediated through the complex organs of modern society, through 'thought'. The 'will' of the political community, authentic in the sovereign prince for the purposes of an act, is distributed confusingly throughout the valves and capillaries of the society. Hegel's descriptions here have little to do with any *polis*. However, Hegel's formal structure (account taken for the critical injection of 'subjectivity' into modern life) is

---

[1] On Hegel's cultivation of the Greek ideal in his Frankfurt period, see especially, Rosenzweig, *Hegel und der Staat*, I, 63–100; Johannes Hoffmeister, *Hölderlin und Hegel in Frankfurt* (Tübingen, 1931).

[2] Hegel's position regarding the armature of the modern state appears to fluctuate gradually from his earlier Napoleonic leaning (which, in terms of Germany, it must be remembered, meant constitutionalism)—institutionalized regime, new bureaucracy and nobility—toward the vision of a traditional but rationalized Prussia. For his ideas at mid-stream and later, see F. Rosenzweig, *Hegel und der Staat*, I, 218–21; II, 66–8.

---

present to him in the books they have handed down.' *Pensées et opuscules* (ed. H. Brunschvicg, Paris, 1912), p. 79.

very *polis*-like, consciously reminiscent of the rational harmonies of classes and functions in the *Republic*.[1] One can see immediately why this is so: (1) all *lebendiges Leben* is somehow comprehended within the theory of the state instead of just the 'mere legality' of the natural right tradition; (2) Hegel's theory is, in the widest sense, an explanation of social functions rather than of constitutional offices; (3) there is an explicit correlation between the microcosm of consciousness and the macrocosm of 'objective spirit' (cf. the passage of *Vernunft* to *Geist* in the *Phenomenology*: 'the Ego that is "we", a plurality of Ego, and "we" that is a single Ego')[2] that is lacking in the political theory of the Enlightenment, interpreted as an antinomy in Rousseau, and still underdeveloped in Kant and Fichte, not least because of their breach between morality and legality.

In Hegel's treatment of absolute spirit, it will be recalled, the 'form' is beauty and the 'content' is truth, as expressed, respectively, by the Hellenic and Christian ideals. His construction of the Idea of the state follows somewhat the same pattern. Formally, the state comprehends, enables, satisfies; it is the vessel of the *gemeines Leben*, the materialization of *Volksgeist*.[3] But in content (related to the subjectivist principles of Christian freedom and the liberal individualism of bourgeois 'civil society', *bürgerliche Gesell-*

---

[1] On these relations, see the fascinating study by Michael B. Foster, *The Political Philosophies of Plato and Hegel* (Oxford, 1935).

[2] Foreshadowed in *Phenomenology* (B), p. 227; authenticated p. 455 f. Hegel's immanently developed theory of inter-subjectivity and community is a critical hinge of his whole political system. It depends on the notion that 'strangeness' or 'otherness' is interior to the person as well as external, that the ego 'recognizes' itself in other persons and that the phenomena of 'Self' and 'Other' are not restricted by the proportions of physical bodies. See ahead, in general, my discussion of mastery and slavery, pp. 333 ff. It is interesting to compare Hegel's position here with Kant's dialectic of the individual and the race (above, pp. 117 ff.). The critical hurdle of the passage from 'I' to the 'we' is of course death perceived as a *telos* but also as a form of otherness. Cf. *Phenomenology* (B), pp. 470–1: '...death is the fulfilment and highest task which the individual as such undertakes on his behalf. But so far as he is essentially a particular individual, it is an accident that his death was connected directly with his labour for the universal whole, and was the outcome of his toil...' Of course, Hegel's 'universal whole' is the concrete *sittlich* community, not the projective cultural *plenum* of mankind.

[3] On the concept of *Volksgeist* (Hegel seems to have been the first to use this precise term) and its relation to Montesquieu's *esprit général*, see Kantorowicz, *op. cit.*; and J. Hyppolite, *Etudes sur Marx et Hegel* (Paris, 1955), p. 21.

schaft) it betrays that very 'restlessness of life' that history records. The completion of this 'Begriff' is, as elsewhere, in the unifying matrix of philosophical comprehension, of 'concrete' and 'pure' thought, of subject-substance. The state is, in effect, the mediated 'einheimisch' community, rendered habitable by thought. The Greeks 'felt' their state; it goes without saying that the Germans must think theirs. The tension is between an absolutely demanding teleology that sanctifies the secular development of the political community in history and the tacit acknowledgment that the whole history of the Christian consciousness has been tendentiously anti-political and therefore anti-human.

But can the mind really re-order life and make it *lebendig*? Evidently only the philosophical consciousness can do so. Who is the philosopher, and how may the others feel 'at home'? This can now be seen as the truly central question of Hegelian politics. I shall attempt to give a satisfactory answer in the last portion of this chapter.

The previous argument has explored one correlation between the Idea of the state and the general notion of 'concrete universality' in Hegel's system. When Hegel says that a concept is 'divine' or is a 'concrete universal', we must understand him as saying that it is something man cannot do without if he is to fulfil his humanity, a 'situation' that he cannot be abstracted from. The state is pre-eminently a concept of this kind.[1] Hegel also calls the state a 'temple of human freedom'.[2] This means both that the state is the comprehensive essence of all life lived in common and that it is the spiritual organ that creates the conditions of peace (through the bureaucratic moderation of the factional clashes of civil society and the insurance of the national defence) in which the higher life can put down roots, in which alone, in fact, the state can be thought as such. We grasp Hegel's formulation of the state only when we take both roles into account. The idea is nowhere better expressed than in the address delivered upon his installation in the chair of philosophy at Berlin in 1818. After a description of the turmoil of the

---

[1] Franz Grégoire, *Etudes hégéliennes : Les points capitaux du système* (Louvain and Paris, 1958), has some sober remarks about this, pp. 235 f.
[2] *Philosophy of History*, p. 335.

'Vernunftstaat' versus 'Verstandesstaat'

imperial wars where 'the inner life of the spirit could win no peace', he continues with an image familiar from other writings: 'the world spirit, so entirely occupied in actuality [i.e. war, politics], torn by external event, was obliged to turn inward upon itself and to dwell upon itself and take pleasure in its native habitat [*eigentümlichen Heimat*]. Now,' he goes on, 'since this stream of actuality is broken and the German nation in general has preserved its nationality, the basis of all fullness of life [*lebendigen Lebens*], the time has come, within the state under the regimen of the actual world, for the free realm of thought to blossom forth independently...'[1]

It is important to recall that Hegel's predecessor in this chair (it had remained vacant since 1814) had been Fichte, and that it is customary in such circumstances to comment, however obliquely, on the tradition. This is exactly what Hegel does, setting his own political ideal of tranquillity and the independence of speculation against the 'practicity' and coerciveness of the *Notstaat* that had been engulfed in the patriotic strains of the *Reden*. For Hegel, patriotism is not the furiously inspired drive to bring the *Sollen* into actuality. It is, rather, an 'assured conviction with truth as its basis...a volition which has become habitual...a product of the institutions subsisting in the state...'[2] Hegel shared with Bentham an antipathy to the 'sacrifices for future generations' argument.

Hegel is also indirectly opposing Schiller's solution of mediation-through-art as fundamentally impracticable. Schiller had written: 'Should we look for [the restoration of human totality] from the state? That is impossible, since the state as at present constituted has induced the evil, and the state which reason presents to itself as an Idea, instead of being able to found this improved humanity, must first be founded thereon itself.'[3] To Hegel this smacked of *coterie* and was a *verständlich* denial of the 'substantiality' of culture. The state qua culture that produces the thought of itself in the image of freedom possesses already the pervasive essentiality of that freedom. How has it then induced evil? 'The culminating form of... subjectivity', Hegel writes, '...can be nothing except what was

[1] 'Rede zum Antritt', *Berliner Schriften*, p. 3.
[2] *Philosophy of Right*, paragraph 268, p. 163.
[3] Schiller, *Aesthetic Education*, Seventh Letter, p. 29.

implicitly present already in its preceding forms...it knows the objective ethical principles, but fails in self-forgetfulness and self-renunciation to immerse itself in their seriousness and to base action upon them.'[1] We pluck knowledge of the truth from our medium of actuality, and in this sense 'my being convinced *is* something supremely trivial if I cannot *know* the truth'.[2] So much for Kant's categorical imperative that has no other milieu but its own moral point of concentration. But one might argue that Hegel himself bends community to the purposes of the mind and then announces their reciprocity.

The community–mind–culture symbiosis, frequently called *Volksgeist*, recalls the synthetic tenacity of Hegel's system. However, the distinction between *Wirklichkeit* and *Wahrheit*, actuality and truth, that subsists up to the very borders of the absolute[3] suggests the special nature of the state: 'The state is the spirit of actuality.'[4] It is, in the highest sense, *Leben*. It is, in fact, as the introduction to the *Philosophy of Right* makes quite clear, *Wille* or pure practical reason itself. It is the matrix where 'everything legal, moral and religious is concentrated'.[5] As such, it is 'objective spirit', objectively and concretely valid, but still perishable without the 'absolute' interpretation that philosophy provides. We might also say that it is the highest and most rational form of 'positivity', because within the state 'the realm of fact has discarded its barbarity and unrighteous caprice, while the realm of truth has abandoned the world of beyond and its arbitrary force'.[6] As life succours thought, the state succours the apprehension of the true. But within the state, life must be tolerable, liveable; only in such a connection can it be said that 'the state knows its aims'.[7]

Where Hegel is most eloquent about the state and its correlative inspiration of *Sittlichkeit*, he has two things strategically in the front of his mind. One is the historical transgression of institutionalized religion against the rational harmony of public order, against

---

[1] *Philosophy of Right*, paragraph 140C, p. 102. [2] *Ibid.* pp. 100–1.
[3] *Wirklichkeit* is associated with the Aristotelian *energeia*; *Wahrheit* is the goal of speculative philosophy. See Martin Heidegger, 'Hegel und die Griechen', in *Die Gegenwart der Griechen im neueren Denken* (Tübingen, 1960), pp. 53–4.
[4] *Jenenser Realphilosophie*, II, 270. [5] 'Rede zum Antritt', *Berliner Schriften*, p. 5.
[6] *Philosophy of Right*, paragraph 360, p. 222. [7] *Ibid.* paragraph 270C, p. 171.

the *Gemeinwesen*. One may indeed say that Hegel deals religion a double blow by subordinating its worldly power to the civil community and its spiritual claim to the superiority of philosophy. However, this is a tendency he shared—in a complex way—with all modern philosophies. More relevant to us is the other form of attack, which is against *Verstand*.

Verstand, according to Hegel, puts the legal state at the service of 'bad infinity', implying a 'reasonable' but apparently endless coercion. Hegel agreed with Fichte that the *Zwangstaaten* of the past (corresponding to Fichte's 'second epoch') had been necessary forms of compulsion in the path to freedom: 'Through tyranny the immediate alienation of the actual, individual will is achieved—this education to obedience. Through this education to obedience ...tyranny becomes superfluous and the rule of law enters.'[1] But Hegel was unwilling to concede that this coercive *Bildung* (now at the service of the infinite) should be re-enacted in modern Europe. In like manner, Kant's morality is pilloried: his principles of action 'make the standpoint of ethical life [*Sittlichkeit*] completely impossible, in fact they explicitly nullify and spurn it'.[2] These are not criticisms discovered in Hegel's 'old age' but arguments consistently made from 1800 on. The Kantian–Fichtean 'legal' state is an 'abstract universal', a framework of rules, not a living ethical structure. The Kantian–Fichtean 'moral' person is a contentless and disembodied will, arbitrary whenever it seeks a content. Finally, neither is the state a living community nor the person a whole individual. And such a state can only do damage to the person in its pursuit of the ideal.

The Hegelian answer to this *contretemps* is *Sittlichkeit*, 'die Idee als *wirkliches* Leben'.[3] This is not the Greek *Sittlichkeit* of the earlier essays, but rather 'the identity of the good with the subjective will, an identity which therefore is concrete and the truth of them both'.[4] It appears to be a consent in necessity dictated effortlessly through custom—now a custom of freedom. Speculatively, it is a complex juncture of the conditioning of law, morality and religion.

[1] *Jenenser Realphilosophie*, ii, 247.
[2] *Philosophy of Right*, 'Introduction', paragraph 33, p. 36.
[3] *Phil. Rechts Randbemerkungen*, paragraph 141, p. 411.
[4] *Philosophy of Right*, paragraph 141, p. 103.

Since it includes all the 'moments' of human socio-political intercourse in both their harmony and their independence, it would seem at least to return the Idea of freedom to the present and to moderate the practical-intellectual imperative of coercion for humanity's sake. But anyone familiar with the history of 1805, 1817 or 1821 must recognize that Hegel's complex philosophical theorization of the post-Revolutionary state was one part wish, one part polemic, one part systemic consistency, and one part shrewd—extremely shrewd—empirical analysis. It is especially the rigour and brilliance of the last aspect that stimulates modern interest in Hegel and justifies claims of his foresight—whether it be in predicting industrial tensions, the Weberian rational bureaucracy, the conservative constitutional state of Bismarck, or the twentieth-century welfare state. That facet must not be denied: Hegel's genius had much to teach sociologists, empirical investigators and statesmen. Neither can we overlook the *wish*—which he shared, generally, with all the German intelligentsia of his day. Nor should we ignore the systemic aspect, though, as Hegel commented metaphorically, this involved the philosopher in a virtually shoreless ocean of thought. What I have tried to stress here, however, is the polemical side—what Hegel, especially Hegel as philosopher, was *against*.

Voltaire's irksomely Gallic *boutade*, 'Voulez-vous avoir de bonnes lois?—Brûlez les vôtres et faites-en de nouvelles,' was far from Hegel's way of thinking. He read all too much of this attitude into both transcendental idealism and the French Revolution. Tocqueville has shown us the continuity of the latter, while, as we have seen, the teleological history of Kant and Fichte, too, required its 'guiding thread'. But Hegel saw also that the past might become a pittance weighed against deceitful promises of the future.

It emerges very clearly that, from the moment his notion of organic—and, the point is critical, happy—antiquity carried him away from Kant in 1797 (the date of 'The Spirit of Christianity and its Fate'), he could not stomach the political and psychological implications of transcendental idealism. Virtually at the moment when Fichte cleaved legality and morality asunder—ostensibly to save the *justum* from the blemished *honestum* of his time—Hegel foresaw how this separation could do damage to the integrity of the individual and the peace of the community.[1] But his harmonization of all practical reason in the state provides an answer that cannot be regarded as an adequation of the 'actual' and the 'rational'. It was a species of logico-historical mystification, pertinent to the way a general consciousness-in-being regards itself as a synthesis of what it knows. For all its marvellous intricacy and solid revelation, Hegel's is a *Gedankenstaat*. Yet if the idealist position was not to be abandoned, this was the most profound reply to philosopher-teachers who would drive their wards toward the turrets of an invisible but beckoning just city. In this sense, a conservative defence of freedom was plausible.

C. MASTERY AND SLAVERY

Many brilliant and influential Hegel commentators have been struck, philosophically and poetically, by the symbolic power of the master–slave image throughout most of his corpus of philosophical writings.[2] Most fully developed in the *Phenomenology*, this tableau is also covered more tersely in the *Philosophische Propädeutik* (1808–16) and the *Encyclopedia* (editions 1817, 1827, 1830, and, post-humously, 1840–5), essayed in rudimentary form in both series of Jena lectures on the philosophy of spirit (1803–4 and 1805–6), alluded to in the *Grundlinien der Philosophie des Rechts* (1821), and foreshadowed in the so-called early theological essays. Mastery and slavery is the most 'humanized', the most 'anthropological' form of *Trennung* in Hegel's entire picture gallery of dualisms.

Despite the fact that mastery–slavery is a species of the genus *Trennung*, and not vice-versa as enthusiasts like Kojève have suggested, the frequent appearance and palpability of the image make it a useful device for locating Hegel's doctrinal positions. Elsewhere, at greater length, I have tried to show that it is not simply concerned with the primal fact of social confrontation but also with primal ego

---

[1] See, especially, *Philosophy of Right*, paragraph 141A, p. 259.
[2] It is sometimes said that Hegel's meaning is distorted by allowing the connotations of slavery to subsist with the terms 'Herrschaft' and 'Knechtschaft'. However, Hegel attaches no profound significances of nuance to the synonyms 'slavery', 'bondage' and 'servitude', but uses them quite interchangeably.

tension and the mediate pattern of ego–world relationships.[1] For present purposes, some old words must be repeated and new ones added.

The tripartite meaning of this critical image in Hegel's deduction of *Selbstbewusstsein* may be expressed as follows: On the overtly social plane there are, at a given point in history, slaves and masters. This is the foundation of the necessary but unfree pseudo-community of force, as against the free community of right, also alluded to on one occasion by Hegel as the 'right of heroes'.[2] In the interior of consciousness, each man possesses faculties of slavery and mastery in his own regard that he struggles to bring into harmony—aspects of the otherness of spirit that are not mere instances of physical curtailment. In turn, the social and personal oppositions are mediated by man's capacity to enslave others and be enslaved by them according to both the moral and physical determinants of the 'situation'. In brief, man remits the tensions of his being upon the world of fellow beings and is himself changed in the process. This relationship furnishes the bridge between psychology and history.

The 'struggle for recognition' (*Kampf des Anerkennens*) *motif* which precedes and produces the result of lordship and bondage is a dual deduction of consciousness 'für sich' (or self-awareness) and of society. It is the premonition of both the free spirit of man and of the condition of rational intersubjectivity—a moment of emergence for soul and state from the biological rhythm of nature.[3] The confrontation of course reminds us of Fichte's legal deduction of self-consciousness. But we do not proceed from here to the necessity of an objective legality, which is the logic of the 'natural rights' argument.[4] Rather we are launched into the immensity of a *Men-*

---

[1] 'Notes on Hegel's "Lordship and Bondage"', *The Review of Metaphysics* (June 1966), pp. 780–802.

[2] Cf. *Philosophy of Right*, paragraph 93C, p. 78; paragraph 349, p. 219.

[3] However, only a premonition; see note 2, p. 327, above. The struggle for recognition has important Biblical resonances, secularized in Hegel's hands. Cf. Jacob's struggle with the angel (Genesis xxxii. 24–8): 'Let me go and I will bless thee'. Jacob's antagonist delivers a blessing, conferring on him the name of Israel; in Hegel both the antagonists are of human proportion, and the loser receives his life for his servitude.

[4] The kind of freedom resulting from this formula of legal recognition is mentioned in passing by Hegel under the heading of 'abstract right'. Cf. *Philosophy of Right*, paragraph 48C, p. 44: 'To be free from the point of view of others is identical to being free in my determinate existence.'

schenbildung which is both psychological and historical, transacted 'phenomenologically' upon an exemplary or ideal type of ego. If the Self and the Other of this primeval confrontation are, evidently, men, they are also principles that dwell within each man. Logic, psychological self-awareness, maturation and history are joined in this image.

In the *Phenomenology* Hegel writes:

The conception of this its unity [i.e., of *Selbstbewusstsein*, 'self consciousness' or 'self-awareness'] in its duplication, of infinitude realizing itself in self-consciousness, has many sides to it and encloses within it elements of varied significance. Thus its moments must on the one hand be strictly kept apart in detailed distinctiveness, and, on the other, in this distinction must, at the same time, also be taken as not distinguished, or must always be accepted and understood in their opposite sense...[1]

Hegel is evidently encouraging us to draw the plenitude of association from the Self–Other confrontation. Thus, although it is difficult to convey Hegelian meanings by static formulations: Self = Other; Self = Self+Other; Self (Other)< >Other (Self); and Self+Other in Self = Self+Other in Other, etc. A following discussion expands the idea:

This process of self-consciousness in relation to another self-consciousness has...been represented as the action of one alone. But this action on the part of the one has itself the double significance of being at once its own action and the action of that other as well...The action has then a *double entente* not only in the sense that it is an act done to itself as well as to the other, but also in the sense that the act *simpliciter* is the act of the one as well as of the other regardless of their distinction.[2]

The awakening of opposed faculties in the ego (the subject-object relationship in all its breadth) proposed by the fact of society is the principle on which self-consciousness would seem to depend, and vice-versa. Hegel's formulation here establishes the mediating link between consciousness and society, serving somewhat the same purpose as the analogous device of the *homo economicus*.[3] Hence-

---

[1] *Phenomenology* (B), p. 229.
[2] *Ibid.* p. 230. Cf. also *Philosophische Propädeutik*, Glockner, III, 108.
[3] Cf. his reference to Robinson and Friday, *Propädeutik*, p. 110.

forth, the problem of history (freedom) will be the problem of consciousness. They will be inseparable in their development.

Much more could be said about the meaning of this confrontation, the ensuing struggle, and its resolution in the dialectic of mastery and slavery. But the particular point of interest here is the continuity between inner and outer, psychological and historical, moral and legal. If we recognize that 'mastery and slavery' contains all these developments, we need not be greatly disturbed by Hegel's leaps between the social and the solitary in his delineation of the various forms of 'otherness'. We will also be in a position to grasp his position *vis-à-vis* transcendental idealism more surely.

Not only for Hegel, but for his great predecessors and his age as a whole, mastery and slavery was a multi-dimensional problem. We saw this already in Rousseau's profound research into the warring sides of the human personality which the shock of social relations had induced. 'He who is a master cannot be free,' he had written.[1] Rousseau attempted to conjugate equality, autonomy and inevitability. From Hegel's perspective, the problem was not only vast but paradoxical. The paradox was this. Antiquity, which had sanctioned the institution of slavery, had nevertheless shown intense awareness of the dilemma of man's enslavement of himself. By contrast, the Enlightenment progressively attacked social bondage as abusive and immoral, while scratching only at the surface of its spiritual dimensions. Self-liberation could only be partial in a community of alien and particular wills. The revival of antiquity, in substance as well as form by Rousseau on the one hand and the idealists on the other—even when the battle of ancients and moderns had been seemingly won by the latter—is in part a response to this perplexity.

Then there was the problem of history. The Enlightenment had furnished a sense of momentum; it had not restored the conviction of harmony. Both the mind and the social order were implicated. If society was in process, then the mind could not be explored statically as the rationalists had taught. Hegel attempts to mediate these elements, by recognizing that mind has a history of its own, a

[1] *Lettres écrites de la Montagne, O.C.* III, 841–2; *Contrat social,* I, i, *ibid.* p. 351; *Emile,* v, 515.

sequence of pitfalls and half-truths which, however, constitute its necessary *Bildung*. The tensions that propel social history are translated to the development of the ego.

Kant and Fichte had attempted to resolve both these problems, but in an unsatisfactory manner. They had managed only to devise more sophisticated systems of mastery and slavery. The only difference between the Shaman of Siberia, the Pope, the Puritan and Kant's subject following the commandment of duty, Hegel had noted in 1797, was that the latter 'having his master within, is by that token his own slave...'[1] Hegel may also have noticed a very striking image from Fichte's *Beiträge* borrowed from the French poet and historiographer Marmontel:

From our birth, [reason] invited us to a long and terrible duel where liberty and slavery were at stake. If you are stronger [Fichte is addressing the arbitrary conventionalism of the Church and nobility], he told us, I will be your slave. I will be a very useful servant for you; but I will also be a restless servant, and as soon as there is some slack in my yoke, I will defeat my master and conqueror...I will profit by my right of conquest to seek your total destruction.[2]

When Hegel formulated his mature system, he was, as we know, not an unqualified admirer of the French Revolution or of the corresponding 'bad infinity' of abstract reason. The new 'right of conquest' had no more appeal than the old. Hegel did not care much for the aphorism 'man is an animal that needs a master', whether it be his own higher self or some outside power. This much must be acknowledged, even if the *amor fati* of state and *Sittlichkeit* did not solve the problem. In a passage bitterly critical of Fichte's *Sittenlehre*, he wrote: 'To be one's own lord and servant certainly seems to improve on the condition in which man is the servant of a stranger.' But, he goes on, '...a subjective lordship and bondage, a personal subjugation of one's nature...becomes much more unnatural than the relation in natural right whereby the possessor of power and command appears as another, external being'.[3] To

---

[1] Nohl (ed.), *Jugendschriften*, pp. 265–6.
[2] Fichte, *Beiträge*, *S.W.* VI, 87. Cf. especially Aristotle, *Politics* (1255b) I, 5 (ed. and trans. Sir Ernest Barker, New York, 1962), pp. 16–17: 'The part and the whole, like the body and the soul, have an identical interest; and the slave is a part of the master, in the sense of being a living but separate part of his body...'   [3] *Differenz*, p. 70.

establish and authenticate the indubitably free part of the human being Kant and Fichte had split the personality. And this accounted for a new 'tyranny', an antagonism of inner and outer toward whose dissolution Hegel directed his philosophical skill.

Without judging the success of Hegel's attempt to break down the barrier between inner and outer, we can easily see its pertinence to the related oppositions of will and fate, morality and legality, 'für sich' and 'an sich'. It is also a clue to penetrating the complex procedures by which consciousness and history are reconciled—an achievement that is necessary if man is to feel 'at home'. Three further issues are, I think, important in this line of interpretation.

The first concerns the dialectical reciprocity of the master and slave images. Kojève writes: 'The Slave alone is able to transcend the World as it is (in thrall to the Master) and not perish. The Slave alone is able to transform the World of his own making where he will be free.'[1] But this is a wilful misreading of Hegel's whole philosophical method—which is just as clear in the *Phenomenology* as in his later works. It is also to take one tableau as the synoptic clue to a whole philosophy.

Rather, remembering the free play of inner and outer, we might read the sequence as follows. The 'master' who emerges from the struggle for recognition can be identified with the primitive notion of control or decision. Hegel tells us specifically that this act of victory is the birth of freedom.[2] Man is the only creature willing to stake its life for a spiritual good. This is, so to speak, the first creative act of the human personality: the 'slave' will invent history, but only after the 'master' has made humanity possible. In this master–slave situation, however, there is neither education, nor progress, nor history—only the repetitive fulfilment of the master's wants. In this impasse, the master-principle—courage, decisiveness, idealism—is seen to become a new form of desire (*Begierde*).[3] Higher development can come only from the slave-principle, which has been transformed through the experience of subjection and terror into

---

[1] Kojève, *op. cit.* p. 34.
[2] *Enzyklopädie* (1817), Glockner, VI, paragraph 355, p. 254. Comparable, perhaps, to Rousseau's observation that the child's first impulse is to tyrannize?
[3] Kojève, *Lecture de Hegel*, is absolutely correct; cf. p. 52.

Mastery and slavery

the activities of labour, conservation and memory: the conditions of the human advance.[1]

This is history, but it is not the content of history. In fact history shortly surpasses the crude condition of bondage for more subtle forms of alienation: 'This false, comparatively primitive phenomenon of slavery is one which befalls mind when mind is only at the level of consciousness [i.e. 'aware' but not 'self-aware']. The dialectic of the concept and of the purely immediate consciousness of freedom brings about at that point the fight for recognition and the relationship of master and slave.'[2] Thus, both principles implanted in the (model) consciousness at this point will be equally vital in the progress of the spirit toward its destiny. The idea of fate is much involved with their capacity to interact; the correlation of freedom and fate depends on their mediated unity, which Hegel of course finds in the 'gebildeter Staat'.[3] Hegel did not grant the career of the world to the slave, for he knew as well as Hobbes that 'it is the one universal [principle of] self-consciousness—not to want to be a slave, but a master'.[4] Nor did he ever cease to praise the masterly virtue (involved in a complex manner with his defence of war): 'To risk one's life is better than merely fearing death.'[5] Hegel's delicate balance is dramatically underscored by subsequent European thought on the subject of slaves and masters: if Marx developed one side of the dichotomy, Nietzsche seized upon the other.[6]

---

[1] Among Hegel's range of historical associations for this image, we must, in the first instance, think of Eastern despotism, promoted to a typology by Montesquieu, elaborated as the dawn of history in Fichte's *Grundzüge*. But we cannot ignore the problem of the Greek *polis*, and especially of the social conditions of slavery attendant upon the Roman conquest of Hellas. I have personally no doubt that Hegel, Hölderlin and many others related their menial and often ungracious *Hauslehrer* experiences in the German upper bourgeois families to the impressment of Greek intellectuals to Roman families of a similar sort. The analogy certainly deserves further study. Hegel of course saw slavery as the stumbling block of the 'beautiful antiquity' that he cherished. In *Philosophy of History*, p. 254, he represents slavery as the necessary condition of an 'aesthetic democracy'. Democracy and slavery became inalterably associated in Hegel's mind.   [2] *Philosophy of Right*, paragraph 57C, p. 48.

[3] *Phil. Rechts Randbemerkungen*, paragraph 3, p. 303.   [4] *Ibid.* paragraph 57, p. 336.

[5] *Philosophy of Right*, paragraph 328A, p. 212. Cf. Letter to Zellmann, 23 Jan. 1807, *Briefe*, I, no. 85, where he attributes the force of the French explosion into Europe to the fact that they have 'put aside the fear of death'.

[6] The struggle for recognition and its outcome in mastery and slavery, with its brilliant imagery of hostility and suspicion, may also be regarded as a paradigmatic exposure of the genesis and possibility of ideology. See K. Mannheim, *Ideology and Utopia*, p. 61.

The second observation concerns the historico-philosophical genesis of lordship and bondage. Fichte, one will remember, apparently indebted to Schelling and the Schlegels, had postulated the 'normals' and 'savages' as an *a priori* of history.[1] This idea reflected a natural and absolute inequality (nervously recalled later by the image of the *Urvolk* in the *Addresses to the German Nation*) which it was the purpose of history to overcome through its sequence of epochs. Hegel is not prepared to believe that reason and unreason could be 'immediately' placed in history in this fashion. Very likely he regarded the notion as a foundation for a theory of tyranny. At any rate, he declared its utter unacceptability.[2] Reason was not a natural principle in Hegel's anthropology, any more than it was for Rousseau: it must 'appear'. Fichte's historical deduction was in contradiction with his social deduction.[3] Since Hegel believes that the phenomena of mastery and slavery result necessarily from struggles of awareness and recognition within the ego and not from the absolute opposition of racial principles embodied in discrete historical individuals, he is defending a doctrine of original equality curiously denied by Fichte.

Of course, contrary to Fichte, Hegel was not concerned to derive a historical teleology proceeding from greater to lesser inequality. Against equality (which he regarded as chimerical) he set the absolute value of liberty, an essentially ideocentric liberty that is most commonly challenged by writers in other philosophical traditions. Hegel in fact believed that the progressive complexity of modern political life dictated an increase in functional inequality, and that this condition was consonant with the increase of liberty, given the premises of the Hegelian state.[4] Even if one is sceptical of Hegel's position it must be said that circumstances on an empirical level have not disproved him, and we may have some sympathy for his

---

[1] See above, pp. 241–2.
[2] *Die Vernunft in der Geschichte*, p. 31.
[3] The latter was essentially the same as Hegel's ('Es ist ein Selbstbewusstsein für ein Selbstbewusstsein'), but without any historical dimension and in the 'atomic' sense of individual legality that Hegel found insufficient for purposes of grounding the ethical community. For Hegel, the notion of subject-substance supplants the merely abstract determination of 'Fürsichsein' with an intersubjective will.
[4] *Philosophy of Right*, paragraph 49, p. 44; also paragraph 185 and C, pp. 123–4; and paragraph 200, p. 130

judgment that the Fichtean teleology would make political life unbearable.

The third point is connected with the preceding. It relates to the strategic position of servitude in history. Contrary to Rousseau and like his compatriots, Hegel placed great emphasis on discipline and subjection as character-builders. History and consciousness are indissoluble, as are political and pedagogical power. And 'slavery', Hegel writes, 'is something historical'.[1] He describes the condition of the servant as 'a necessary moment in the education [*Bildung*] of every man'. 'No man', he adds, 'can, without this will-breaking discipline, become free and worthy to command.' As for nations, 'bondage and tyranny are necessary things in the history of peoples'.[2] As the appropriate fate of their time, lordship and bondage are not to be regarded as conditions of moral guilt: 'It cannot be a question of guilt on the part of this or that individual that there are slaves... or that there are masters.'[3] It is the fault of the will of all. But there is not to be, there need not now be, any Fichtean 'fourth epoch', parallel to the superstitious repression of the past but now in the service of 'insight' and 'understanding'. The chimera of 'bad infinity' is a mirage, a despotism. Legality must not chasten, education must not compel for the sake of a 'Jenseits' morality; all facets of *Bildung* must collaborate in the revelation of the truth-bearing present where 'all are free'. On the Kantian–Fichtean topmost step to the plateau of wisdom lurks also the last enemy.

D. 'BILDUNG'

Although it may not be precisely accurate to impute the method of Hegel's *Phenomenology* to a reading of Rousseau's *Emile* and to say,

---

[1] *Phil. Rechts Randbemerkungen*, paragraph 57, p. 336.

[2] *Enzyklopädie* (1840–5), 'System der Philosophie', Glockner, x, paragraph 435A, p. 288. Cf. Aristotle, *Politics* (1277b), III, 4, p. 105: '...you cannot be a ruler unless you have first been ruled'.

[3] *Phil. Rechts Randbemerkungen*, *loc. cit.* Cf. *Philosophy of Right*, paragraph 57A, p. 239. The strong parallel between pedagogy and political coercion is asserted in *ibid.* paragraph 93C, p. 67: 'Coercion by a schoolmaster, or coercion of savages and brutes, seems at first sight to be an initial act of coercion, not a second...But the merely natural will is implicitly a force against the implicit Idea of freedom which must be protected against such an uncivilized will and made to prevail in it.'

with M. Jean Hyppolite, that Hegel 'found in this work a first history of the natural consciousness raising itself to freedom by way of personal and specially formative experiences', there are piquant resemblances between the two books.[1] Both are pedagogical dialogues between master and pupil (distinguished—sometimes ambiguously—by the Hegelian 'für uns' and 'für es', respectively): both are model representations of what man needs to know, through the help of others, if he is to be free. Hegel conceived his first major —and, in the opinion of many, best—work as an introduction to philosophy, that is, an education for the 'naive' natural consciousness that would make sense out of the tangled assault of *Erfahrung*— the whole experience of culture. The *Phenomenology* is his profound, vigorous testament to the comprehensiveness of *Bildung*—a word that means not only education, but maturation, fulfilment, joy, suffering, a drenching in the stream of time and an emergence to the plateau of judgment. This occult, fascinating treatise is Hegel's wordy but never boring paradigm for the acquisition of all worthwhile knowledge. 'This becoming of science in general or knowledge is what the phenomenology of the spirit represents...it...has to work its way through a long journey.'[2] However, the spirit never moves in a straight line; it circles its prey: 'Der Weg des Geistes ist die Vermittlung, der Umweg.'[3]

In another sense, this is not *Emile* at all. *Emile* is a controlled experiment in naturalism that cuts history dead. Thus, the *Phenomenology* is a spiritual triumph over but not against history. At its end, history (properly viewed) mediates between truth and experience. 'Paradise', Hegel says elsewhere, 'is a park, where only brutes, not men, can remain.'[4] He has no longing for that park; he desires a spiritual centre of peace, where the mysterious circle of self-knowing knowledge turns in its endless course. The *Phenomenology* is designed to thrust the adept into that paradoxical cycle of restlessness and content where 'this phase of spirit begins all over again its formative development, apparently starting solely from itself, yet at the same time it commences at a higher level'.[5] We

[1] Hyppolite, *Genèse et structure*, I, 16.
[2] Preface to *Phenomenology* (K), p. 400.
[3] *Einl. Geschichte Phil.* p. 62.
[4] *Philosophy of History*, p. 321.
[5] *Phenomenology* (B), p. 808.

know of R. Haym's complaint about Hegel's confusion of history and psychology, and we have explored the Hegelian meaning of history. Psychology was for Hegel essentially a series of attitudes or postures related to the process of education.[1] The main problem of the *Phenomenology* is not history, but *Bildung*. Such education is the breach into knowledge—into system—where, it seems, one can start 'solely from himself', fulfilling the unbroken circle of the pursuit of wisdom. Hyppolite comments sensitively that the end of this phenomenological process means the disappearance of the philosopher in a knowledge that is now objective, no longer directed.[2] And with the vanishing of the 'für uns', the 'für es' or 'natural consciousness' vanishes as well into the universe of wisdom; they become the partners in that wisdom, Virgil-and-Dante-like, and no longer fill the roles of master and apprentice, which is the pedagogical paradigm for lord and servant, for conqueror and slave. According to the metaphor, knowledge then *is*. Only now is it possible to have a system that *is*, not simply 'für uns' but 'an und für sich'. By this definition, Fichte's *Wissenschaftslehre* is a 'phenomenology'. The difficulty there is that master and pupil, pure ego and finite ego, 'intellectual intuition' and experience of the consciousness, can never make up their difference in the terms of *Verstand* and 'bad infinity'. 'System' can never be achieved, and perpetual coerciveness is the result. The entire consequences of this fact are remitted upon the secular world of politics, the state and the questions of duty and rulership.

Seen from another angle, we might say that Hegel's solution is a mediation between the proposals of Rousseau and Lessing. Rousseau wanted to trace out an education whereby Emile might feel at home in the world; this, too, was Hegel's aim. Lessing desired a procedure whereby knowledge would supplant fideism; so did Hegel. Lessing had said that revelation was to history as education was to the indi-

---

[1] Cf. *Phenomenology* (B), p. 331: '*Psychology* contains the collection of laws in virtue of which the mind takes up different attitudes towards the different forms of its reality given and presented to it in a condition of otherness.'

[2] Hyppolite, *Genèse et structure*, I, 14–15. The motive is from Christianity, and may be directly from St. Paul; cf. Galatians iii. 24–6: 'Wherefore the law was our schoolmaster to bring us unto Christ, that we might be justified by faith. But after that faith is come, we are no longer under a schoolmaster. For ye are all the children of God by faith in Christ Jesus.'

vidual: both were necessary shortcuts to the truth. But Fichte himself had declared that the scholar was one who tested the veracity of all things with his own intelligence. By 1806 Hegel felt that he had both seized the rational method of truth and achieved—through mental torture—the secret of 'being at home'.[1] He must have felt vindicated when a disciple described the *Phenomenology* as 'the key to that new gospel which Lessing prophesied'.[2]

Hegel's *Bildung* moves back toward Rousseau in the phenomenological sense; he is not afraid of experience, for experience must be correlated in the Idea, not sacrificed to it. But one great difference is that Hegel regards antiquity not as a substitute for lost nature but as a 'paradise of the spirit'. Hegel is for Athens, as Rousseau was for Sparta.[3] Antiquity (even *Sittlichkeit*) is not anti-intellectual for Hegel, but rather the ripe germ of all intellectual cultivation.[4] Through the study of antiquity, Hegel told his students in Nuremberg, 'we reconcile ourselves with it and thereby find ourselves again in it, but the self which we then find is the one which accords with the tone and universal essence of the mind'.[5] With such an attitude, it is little wonder that the *Phenomenology* dwells at such length on Greek problems and that the Eleatics, Plato and Aristotle comprise about a third of the lectures on the history of philosophy. Hegel makes every conscious effort to adapt what is relevant of the classical ideal in his notions of curriculum and education for modern citizenship.[6]

It should certainly be no secret that if the essential paradigm of history is Christian for Hegel, the fundamental base of culture and education is classical. In the *Phenomenology* this penchant is wrung out to agonizing length; in the following passage it is foreshortened:

[1] Cf. Karl Rosenkranz, *Hegels Leben* (Berlin, 1844), p. 381: '[Hegel] gradually got used to the notion that for speculative education salvation could indeed only be found within his philosophy.'

[2] Windischmann to Hegel, 27 Apr. 1810, *Briefe*, I, 307.

[3] German 'classicism' was resolutely anti-Sparta. As prime documents, see Schiller's *Die Gesetzgebung des Lykurgus und Solon*, *S.W.* VII, 70–106, and Hegel's own remarks in the *Philosophy of History*, pp. 258–65.

[4] Rather, it is the concentrated, unselfconscious (in the English sense of the word), *sittlich* intellect, joining brilliant individuality and civic coherence.

[5] *Nürnberger Schriften*, p. 312.

[6] See, especially, Löwith, *From Hegel to Nietzsche*, pp. 290–4.

...education [*Bildung*] is the absolute transition from an ethical substantiality which is immediate and natural [i.e. Greek *Sittlichkeit*] to
the one which is intellectual and so both infinitely subjective and lofty
enough to have attained universality of form [i.e. the Christian mediation
of the classical content]...It is through this educational struggle that the
subjective will itself attain objectivity within, an objectivity in which
alone it is for its part capable and worthy of being the actuality of the
Idea.[1]

The murky paragraph says a great deal. It says that antiquity is
priceless. It also says that since Christianity has been the conqueror,
it must redeem the truth of antiquity by restoring 'substantiality'
as a value, recovering it in the 'subjective' *Selbstbewusstsein*. And
thus *Bildung* strives toward thought and system, picking up the
essential, kicking over the material traces:[2] 'Formal *Bildung* through
philosophy is the study of formal thought in general...In philosophy, I confess, one departs from the plane of looking at things [*des
Anschauens*], its world is in thought; hearing and sight must be put
behind one.'[3] In Hegel it is not simply a question of arguing
political, legal and moral matters according to the forms of philosophical discourse, but of placing them within a matrix where
thought swallows all. Thought revenges history and asserts eternal
life; yet thought is one with history and can rescue the beautiful
perishings only in an ideal form.

At first glance there is not much to distinguish between Hegel's
notion of education and that of the transcendental idealists. 'Man is
what he should be, through education, through discipline,' Hegel
declares.[4] 'Man must form himself...[he] is free...only through
education.'[5] Finally: 'Education is the negation of natural inclina-

---

[1] *Philosophy of Right*, paragraph 187, pp. 125–6. It is to be noted that *Bildung* is a facet
of 'civil society'.
[2] It is also markedly a descent into the whole negative aspect of historical movement.
Hegel knew that 'the formative process [*Bildung*] of moulding self-consciousness'
involved rebellion. Here he is describing the *ancien régime*: 'This type of spiritual
[better: intellectual] life is the absolute and universal inversion of reality and thought,
their entire estrangement the one from the other; it is pure culture.' See the whole
discussion, *Phenomenology* (B), pp. 540–2.
[3] 'Rede zum Antritt', *Berliner Schriften*, p. 18.
[4] *Vorlesungen über die Philosophie der Weltgeschichte* (ed. Lasson, 4 vols., Leipzig, 1944),
I, 5).
[5] *Phil. Rechts Randbemerkungen*, paragraph 57, pp. 336–8.

tion [*Weise*].'[1] This sounds entirely like Kant. Indeed, in drawing distinctions in Hegel's attitude, one must not disguise the considerable body of tradition and approach he shared with his forerunners. The difference is that Hegel scorned the infinite human experiment, the sacrifice of any present for a future. Referring to the 'right of heroes' or great men, he wrote: '[Their] power is not despotism, but tyranny...yet, it is necessary and just.' However, in Hegelian Europe the 'right of heroes' is now understood as ended. If tyranny was necessary for the creation of the community through 'education to obedience', it 'has now become superfluous and the rule of law has entered'.[2] To be sure, he recognized that children needed to be educated, that administrators needed to be trained, that the grasp of philosophy and culture was not born with the pupil.[3] Both with nations and with individuals he recognized the necessity for arduous preparation, and he was in that regard certainly an élitist—at the antipodes of Rousseau. He ridiculed the Gascon 'who would not go into the water until he could swim'.[4] Thus he designed the *Phenomenology* as a practical 'swimming lesson'. Here, he thought, philosopher and pupil enter the common ocean of the mind and emerge as intellectual peers. If this equality of the intellect sounds exclusive and forced—inaccessible to the toiling millions— Hegel at least, by virtue of his political philosophy, recognized their place and worth in the 'situation' and rejected any *Notstaat* or model school that would 'force them to be free' on behalf of an infinite endeavour or any promised plunge of infinity into life as lived.

'Education', Hegel is reported to have said, 'is the art of making men ethical.'[5] If it is the propaedeutic to wisdom, it is also the preparation for community, the assimiliation of the highest freedom and the justest fate. For if 'the educated man...develops an inner life and wills that he himself shall be in everything he does', such a

---

[1] *Einl. Geschichte Phil.* p. 151.
[2] *Jenenser Realphilosophie*, II, 246–7.
[3] Cf. *Philosophy of Right*, paragraph 174C, p. 117: '...the right of the parents over the wishes of their children is determined by the object in view—discipline and education'. Also *ibid.*, paragraph 239, p. 148: 'In its character as a universal family, civil society has the right and duty of supervising education inasmuch as education bears on a child's capacity to become a member of society.'
[4] *Religion*, Glockner, XV, 70.
[5] *Philosophy of Right*, paragraph 151A, p. 260.

man may be understood, *prima facie*, as one 'who without the obtrusion of personal idiosyncrasy can do what others do'.[1] This symbiosis of custom and inventiveness is the answer to the absolute division of the *Notstaat*. Growing up in a community is itself the 'phenomenology' for this standpoint of shared participation.[2] And in that life, as in thought, the infinite pedagogy implied by Fichte is dissolved in the circle of citizenship.

The problem of *Bildung* is, of course, an aspect of the problem of authority. At the beginning of the Enlightenment Locke's great contribution to political thought had been to disentangle the skeins of obligation and authority that had been woven together organically in earlier theory. Despite its many confusions, the *Second Treatise* is at least clear on the distinction between parental authority and political authority. The question of tutelary authority, which is the third type, has not really arisen, because the commonwealth is presumed to consist of mature (and rational) members. Lockean rationalism is untroubled by the idea of a historical development which would link tutelary authority with political authority metaphorically. However, that is precisely the connection that German transcendental idealism aims at.

In our period of concern the political aspects of parental authority are fairly well disposed of. In one of Rousseau's significant passages the tutor declares that he is Emile's real parent. Hegel himself connects the clash of familial with political authority not with the Christian sphere of royal right but with the classical dilemma of Antigone.

The tutor takes the place of the parent, then; can he also take the place of the political ruler? That is the solution at which Fichte seems to arrive, working as we have seen from premises that lie very deep in his integral philosophical method. 'Bad infinity' suggests a constant and coercive rulership.

---

[1] *Philosophy of Right*, paragraph 107A, p. 248; paragraph 187A, p. 268. Education is, in fact, fundamental to Hegel's notion of the free community; cf. *ibid.*, paragraph 209, p. 134: 'It is a part of education, of thinking as the consciousness of the single in the form of universality, that the ego comes to be apprehended as a universal person in which all are identical.'

[2] Hegel says, for example, that in the *Stand* (professional estate) 'one cultivates [*bildet*] his consciousness'. *Jenenser Realphilosophie*, II, 253.

Hegel combatted this conclusion first on the front of knowledge, but second on the front of politics. That connection is not simply holistic; it depends practically, as we have seen, on the notion that knowledge can flourish only in conditions where the state provides peace and security. Thus the familiar Hegelian triad of 'family', 'civil society' and 'state'—comprehended by the device of *Aufhebung* —is also a comment on the relationship of the three types of authority. *Bildung*, as we know, together with the coercive and disciplinary organs of the corporation and the police, lies within the second category. Parental authority and tutelary authority persist, but only beneath the judgment of a political authority that resolves and surpasses their claims, a sphere in which 'all are free'. That is the fundamental Hegelian solution to the problem of authority.

It comes therefore as no surprise that, given the Hegelian premises, the thesis could be destroyed only by denying the claims that Hegel made for the state as a final matrix of judgment and freedom. This is what Marx attempted in his early manuscript, the *Critique of the Philosophy of Right* (1843). Using Feuerbach's 'transformative method', he presented the state as the predicate of the bourgeois civil society, rather than vice-versa as Hegel had proposed.[1] This insight had heavy consequences both for the development of historical materialism and for the theory of ideology. But that is a matter beyond the scope of the present inquiry.

E. PHILOSOPHY AND LIFE

The problem of life is purpose, order, fullness —*lebendiges Leben*; the problem of philosophy is justification through comprehension— the *Sichwissens des Geistes*. Life actualizes; thought eternalizes: they do this to each other. The state is the amniotic protection for this exchange. Where the political community is impotent, fragmented or 'accidental' to its role, thought retreats to subjectivity and life is cleaved into private wish and public act, into 'chimera' and 'prejudice'.

[1] See Shlomo Avineri, 'The Hegelian Origins of Marx's Political Thought', *The Review of Metaphysics* (Sept. 1967), pp. 33–56.

How is a philosophical politics of life possible? Assuredly, one may claim, with Hegel, that when the persistently real Idea of the state is grasped in thought, revealing not utopia but destiny, the thinker is at home in his world. Yet, despite all intellectual rigour in justifying the state and its purpose, in making it a 'concrete universal', a 'second nature', men must still live in it. And they may not see it from the standpoint of wisdom. They may protest that it is not 'for them', that it is not the vehicle of the freedom of all, that it is defective in the Idea. Even if the state is good and just, 'ethical', might men not fail to understand why this is so? If the mass of men are not philosophers, is there then some *deuteros prous* that reconciles the factions of civil society, making life worthwhile and furthering the peace of the community?

Hegel, unlike Fichte, did not have much confidence in teaching philosophy to the masses: 'Philosophy, according to its nature, is something esoteric, being neither made for the mob nor capable of being prepared for the mob.' It must 'recognize that the people might possibly elevate themselves to it; but it must not lower itself to the people'.[1]

Philosophy, however, has a brilliant second. Hegel's earliest thoughts on the subject of community had turned to religion, which, in harmony with custom, art and life itself, had formed the cement of the 'substantial' Hellenic culture. At that time he had heaped scorn on Christianity, the universal and joyless religion that belonged to no one: 'Christianity has emptied Valhalla, felled the sacred groves, extirpated the national imagery as a shameful superstition...'[2] Germany had 'no religious imagery', and, correspondingly 'no political imagery'. Rosenkranz reports a fragment from 1798 where Hegel speculates on the emergence of a new religion (Novalis's wish, also) fit for a 'free people', in which 'the infinite pain and the whole burden of antagonism' could be overcome.[3] However, as we know, in the *Glauben und Wissen* of 1802, 'the juxtaposition of faith and knowledge...[had] been removed into philosophy itself'.

Nevertheless, Christianity had furnished Hegel with the paradigm

---

[1] *Erste Drückschriften*, pp. 126–7.
[2] 'Positivität', Nohl (ed.), *Jugendschriften*, p. 215.
[3] Rosenkranz, *Hegels Leben*, p. 141.

of history, which was also the mediation of spirit and world.[1] With particular reference to religion, he would later write: 'The spiritual is the absolute unity of the spiritual and the natural.'[2] Unlike the transcendental idealists, Hegel continued to believe that true religion must be truly natural as well as *moralisch*. It must be concrete and *sittlich*: where there are bad religions there will be bad governments.[3] Religion could not divorce itself speculatively from common life as the Enlightenment had insisted, and as Kant had gone to particular pains to show in his book on religion.[4] Despite and perhaps because of his early writings, Hegel had a respect for collective 'faith' in a manner that his predecessors would have taken exception to.[5]

And yet we have seen that Hegel dealt religion a double blow by surrendering its 'positivity' to the civil power and its absolute claims to the philosophical power. He had associated both processes with history. In the latter case, the *Phenomenology* is categorical: 'The content of religion...expresses earlier in time than science what spirit is; but this science alone is the perfect form in which spirit truly knows itself.'[6] In the case of the former, the extended passage on church–state relations in the *Philosophy of Right*, which deserves careful study, affirms that 'religion of a genuine kind...recognizes the state and upholds it'.[7] The toleration of the state in religious matters varies directly with its power, which has been an affair of historical development.

The resolution to this paradox is, I think, that Hegel, supremely respectful of the 'muscle' of religious conviction, wanted to 'borrow' its energy for the realms of both public life and speculative thought. Thus, both his notions of the state and of *sagesse* (*Wissen*) resemble

---

[1] Walter Kaufmann's *Hegel*, a long overdue but slightly overdone 'humanization' of Hegel in English, suffers from the defect of treating Hegel's religious attitudes with a glibness that makes him seem almost a member of Baron d'Holbach's circle. A second defect in this commendable work is its unconvincing dismissal of the problem of the 'end of history', a consequence of its treatment of the religious question.

[2] *Religion*, Glockner, xv, 218–19.

[3] *Ibid.* p. 257. Cf. *Philosophy of History*, p. 51.

[4] *Religion Within the Limits of Reason Alone*, p. 32.

[5] Cf. on the early community of Christian love and friendship, 'Positivität', Nohl, *Jugendschriften*, p. 179.

[6] *Phenomenology* (B), p. 808; *Philosophy of Right*, paragraph 270C, pp. 172–3.

[7] *Ibid.* p. 168. The same thought is expressed more vividly in *Jenenser Realphilosophie*, II, 270. 'The state is the spirit of actuality...the church is the spirit knowing itself in universal form, the absolute inner assurance of the state.'

Rousseau's earlier answers to correlative problems, albeit in a way that seems complex and 'modern' compared to the Genevan's wistful reflections on civil religion, the benevolence of the Gospel, and the like. Moreover, Hegel had a system for reconciling diversity and unity, subjective and concrete apprehensions, man and state.

At any rate, in both these senses, the 'moment' of religion is, as Hegel puts it, 'preserved' as well as 'cancelled', and it indeed appears, almost surreptitiously, as a unifying bond between the *Sittlichkeit* of the state and the eternality of wisdom. In suppressing religion as a formal element of 'objective spirit'—that is, in removing the Church from the political order—Hegel preserves it as a source of insight—though not the most comprehensive one—for judging the clatter of states through world history. What Marx later castigated and respected as the 'opium of the people' has been consecrated.

We have little difficulty in establishing the point if we refer to two major but little-known Hegelian documents. The first is his letter to the hat-maker Duboc, where, in as simple language as possible, he tried to convey the import of his philosophical system. The second is his Berlin inaugural address. In the letter he writes: 'I can exempt myself from saying that for mankind in general truth is primarily revealed in the form of religion, enlivened and enriched by one's experience of himself and of life; for seizing it in the form of a thought...knowing it through thought...is a different need.'[1] In the Berlin speech (which is a paean to the study of philosophy) we may read: 'Religion is the way in which men generally achieve the consciousness of their being [*Wesen*].'[2] However, 'in it the essences of nature and of their spirit are in opposition'. Further, here repeating the argument of the *Phenomenology*:

Feeling (*Gefühl*) remains the chief form in religion...Thus God is... represented (*vorgestellt*)...as an activity from without, as an event, in the manner and relationships of finite things...in time and space, another time, another space, another actuality.[3]

For philosophers, this situation is untenable. *Vernunft* can counte-

---

[1] Letter to Duboc, 30 July 1822, *Briefe*, II, 326.
[2] 'Rede zum Antritt', *Berliner Schriften*, p. 13.
[3] *Ibid.* p. 14.

nance no transcendent object. Even the class of religious teachers, for all its accomplishments, is now 'more or less in oblivion'.[1] However, as equivalent with the content of truth, religion is still a 'representation' of harmony. And one can very well imagine Hegel, imbued with his ideals of *Volksleben* and the cohesion of the concrete state, saying with Faust as he remarked the worshipful faces on Easter morning:

> They celebrate the resurrection of the Lord
> For they themselves are resurrected.[2]

In the last analysis, Hegel's real grasp of political community is a kind of *polis–ecclesia* symbiosis that regulates and comprehends the variety and tensions of the post-Revolutionary state structure. It is a novel conception that parries both subjectivism and the irrational *Gemeinschaft*, doing conscious homage to both the classical ideal and the 'spirit of the time'. It is the solution to a problem that the interior development of philosophy had arranged, and cannot really be understood without that entire background, just as it depends also on the history through which it evolved. But, above all, it should be seen for our purposes as a resolute counterattack on the philosophy of infinite goals, where, in political life, the goalmasters are all too apt to sponsor a repressive enlightenment and where, in moral life, the subject is torn between his own worth and wretchedness.

By every intellectual art Hegel brings us to a 'present' that some have called a communion, others an abdication. We return, often if piecemeal, to his mood and insights, even if we are persuaded that Hegel's world reconciled in thought was itself a 'chimera', and may well have been a 'prejudice'.

---

[1] 'Rede zum Antritt', *Berliner Schriften*, p. 13.   [2] Goethe, *Faust I*, ll. 921–2, p. 133.

PART SIX

EPILOGUE: THE FUTURE UNREDEEMED

EPILOGUE: THE FUTURE UNREDEEMED

No reader should be tempted to view this extended voyage as some forced arrival at Hegelian moorings. The relationship of the world of knowledge and the world of politics has many other moments of valid or useful definition. The English-speaking person is conditioned neither by his culture nor by his intellectual experiences to grasp the problems of politics in this fashion. And there is an ongoing tradition of later continental thought—in which the present author reserves special places for Marx and the movement of 'phenomenology' begun by Husserl—that both disrupts and renews the relevance of Hegel.

Engels felt that Hegelianism could be exploded only 'from within'. This is precisely what the radical or 'young' Hegelians attempted to do, one of the most interesting efforts in the political sphere being Marx's *Critique of the Philosophy of Right* (1843). We are more apt to feel that German idealism was an otherworldly curiosity all along, that Hegel had always been successfully combatted 'from without', usually in the name of science, precision, objectivity or positivistic validation. Why, then, can it be argued that Hegel and the currents of thought treated in this essay are still significant to our controversies? Is it because they are spiritual and esoteric, not accepting the blank cheque of 'science' but demanding some new kind of coin for their transactions? Is it because their original focus upon the recognition of persons in a community reminds us of much that psychology has subsequently discovered and that models of nation-building now take into account? Is it because of our dark fascination with the tragedy of Europe and our restless search for every plausible 'why'? Or is it because we are still fretful about the dialectical problem of freedom *in* history and freedom *from* history? One suspects that all these themes are relevant. Thus this study may also be relevant.

The purpose has not been to resuscitate old views. Still, I have hoped that this essay would be not merely an antiquarian exercise, but also a small revelation of the background of persisting issues.

In the interest of analytical rigour I have avoided making too many forward glances. What I have tried to do is spadework. Perhaps it can link up with other researches stretching further toward our own times. Since the Western tradition of political thought paused but did not expire at this point, summation and distillation is a never-ending procedure.

This study, then, does not stop with Hegel because Hegel claimed to complete the method for the apprehension of the historical world. It does stop here, though, because of a certain inescapable periodicity which judicious selection must impose on a range of historical and philosophical problems. Perhaps the real stoppage at this point is the barrier of the factory, the locomotive and the steamboat, the vanishing of the European wilderness, and the portentous arrival of the democratic age. Hegel and Goethe both sensed this rupture in the last years of their lives. As the student knows, Hegel's 'book' did not accomplish history; it could not reproduce or enclose the circulations of that errant zephyr. Kant understood this hindrance better than Hegel. The Hegelian 'still point of the turning world' is soon ruptured, because the human mind cannot quiet itself but remains eternally split between some kind of *Jenseits* and its longing to feel 'at home' in the destiny in which it is cast. Yet Hegel's great achievement is a monumental summation and a fundamental statement of the problem of knowledge and judgment.

The schools of thought he engendered in his wake practised his method not for resolution but for dissolution. His method of speculation—and I am persuaded that Hegel knew this—could not possibly have produced quiescence. Hegel wished to confine the longing and restlessness of mind and will to the turning circle of their vast possibilities. But the 'naive consciousness' and the 'philosophical consciousness' could not be so easily yoked in a fixed planetary orbit. History could not concede to any such logical control.

Essentially Hegel's weakness lay in two realms. He was perhaps unaware of their connection. The first weakness lay in his overt and daring conjugation of history and reason, in the claims he made for his secular providence of the will that had become mind, the mind that had become will. Whatever history is, it is obviously not reason, no matter how reasonable the mind that perceives it, even if that mind is a creature of history. History is probably closer to Herder's variety of forms than to any idealist union of life and divinity created or imposed by the conceptual apparatus. The second Hegelian weakness is his continued assertion of the European cultural claim. This depended on the religio-political synthesis that I described in the last chapter: the philosophical comprehension of all the dramatic moments of the Europocentric destiny within an ever renewing and deepening system of speculation. Within little more than a decade the religious pattern had been attacked by Strauss, Feuerbach and Bauer and the political pattern by Ruge and Marx. Their criticism exploded the cultural homogeneity of Europe by discovering masters and slaves where Hegel had thought to close the problem. Coercive transcendence, soon to be remitted to other continents, remained.

The whole challenge to the Hegelian synthesis really amounted to a fundamental denial of the centrality of Europe and an opening toward the new assertion of a global, truly anthropological man. *Comment peut-on être Persan?* This man was ultimately a creature that no figure of the Enlightenment—except possibly Rousseau or Buffon, in glimpses—had ever really conceived, except for satirical or heuristic purposes. Marx is very much implicated in this development, despite his own historical and cultural biases. The theme of that mutation, however, cannot be pursued here.

It remains, then, to furnish some afterthoughts.

I would hope that the much cogitated but often misunderstood link between the cultures on opposite sides of the Rhine, especially between Rousseau and the German idealists, has been clarified through a continuous focus on their basic sense of historical destiny and its political and pedagogical ramifications. Sociologically, we perceive a contrast in terms of confidence, or rising expectations, or spirituality, or daring. Philosophically, there is a deep clash between methods and the search for a method.

Secondly, we have, I think, a deeper appreciation of the differences of the 'futurism' of the French and of the Germans. Although this distinction could be pursued in many directions, one brief illustration may be particularly pertinent. Why should Marx and Ruge, on the heels of Hegel, turn to flamboyant atheism, while

Saint-Simon was acknowledging the need for a 'new Christianity'? Was it not because German philosophy had swallowed religion while the French Enlightenment expelled it? The one was oppressed by an undigested dumpling, a *Jenseits*, while the other staggered on an empty stomach.

In the third place, the traditional identification of German philosophy as the 'ideal replication' of the materially enacted consequences of the French Revolution may require deeper examination. Probably there is more truth than error in this parallel: at least Hegel, Heine, Von Stein, Marx, Engels and others subscribed to its validity. Possibly, however, it is too appealingly simple. Kant did not simply decapitate God the way Robespierre decapitated the King, as the poet Carducci would have it. Research continues today in the documents and writings left by proponents of the ideology of the French Revolution in Germany, especially in the South. Yet I cannot escape the feeling that contemporaneous German so-called *Staatslehre* had very pronounced indigenous roots. The Revolution challenged and forced modifications in German political doctrine, but it did not ultimately control that development—even in Kant and Fichte. What the Revolution really did in Germany was to pose the question of the utopia of the future in tense competition with the prevailing Greek literary ideal. That had lasting repercussions in German political thought, and provided the *raison d'être* for Hegel's attempted mediation on behalf of the present. The point is not that Germany 'lagged' behind France and thus went for phantoms rather than results, but that it quite self-consciously opposed its 'spirituality' to the physical and political prowess of its neighbour. Even Fichte's *Addresses* are no exception to this form of response.

The last point is most interesting and promising. It regards the vast correlation we have witnessed between the images of the school and the state, between pedagogical and political strategies, with the end of creating, respectively, the man fit to be a culture-bearing citizen and the citizen capable of promoting the destiny of the culture-bearing state. There is every reason to believe that this is one of prevailing images of Western politics and that in the context of German idealism it took a peculiar and distinctive form. Indebted to Rousseau but, on the whole, quite contrary to the way that he had pictured the problem, the German tutelary ideal became a metaphor of the onslaught on nature rather than of the sense of belonging in it. The notion of a natural order is utterly overthrown, and the elitism of the philosophical consciousness enters with a vengeance.

Not only does this theme help to define the distances between German idealism and the French Enlightenment and between both and Rousseau, but it remains a fruitful line of inquiry for nineteenth-century political studies. With regard to that remarkable age of widening literacy and instruction, there has been a deplorable gap between research in educational theory and in political theory. To interpret Marx from this angle might, for example, lead to some solid revelations and results of great interest.

At the end I am left with the feeling that Rousseau may be the most relevant of our four thinkers. This may seem a sequential *volte-face*, and I shall try to justify my opinion briefly. Rousseau positioned man against history, in one sense, and, in still another, he placed man in a history he could not summon or command. That much connects him with current moods and problems. His sensitive communication of the experience of human disruption touches a world where millions have felt disrupted in the two centuries since he put down his pen. We are no longer optimists, even in the Kantian sense: the diversity of the world and the enormity of our acts have oxidized the apodictic moral law. The roughshod upward crusade of Fichte is not ours. Neither is the turbulent but sovereign security of Hegel. We look around in the fascinating junkyard of our artifacts and we try to find ourselves. For this task Rousseau is an eminent companion.

Rousseau did not solve problems, but he transmitted some of the most important ones across the debris of history, in works that we read for insight more than for system. He did not possess formal philosophical equipment, although he intellectualized basic notions far more than he cared to admit. He was frankly a neurotic, but he was also a sociological neurotic of the most productive kind. His ideology is so subtle and, in operational terms, contradictory that it has founded no party, especially no *internationale*. Unlike Burke, he preferred 'chimeras' to 'prejudices'; unlike the idealists he despaired of their realization, even in an ethical time beyond sensual time.

The ruler can learn from Rousseau that his legitimacy is at best precarious. The subject can learn that he owns by right a modest portion of the judgment that makes all rulers nervous and that he owes a modicum of respect to his fellows, who participate equally in the judgment. The democrat can find here the substantial psychological basis for his principles. If democracy becomes a merely passive reflex—a parody of what Constant would later call 'modern liberty'—Rousseau is on hand to berate. If cosmic Whiggery ('modernization', development, etc.) carries us away, he is there to warn. Rousseau directs us neither toward Hobbesian fatality nor toward the hypocrisy of secular sainthood, but he does focus in a profoundly original way on the problem of how men act, usually less than well, and how they cause each other to suffer in the social order. All this is to say that in an age of change, an age of enormous complacency and enormous claims, Rousseau may have been the greatest realist of all.

BIBLIOGRAPHY

BIBLIOGRAPHY

A. CONTEMPORARY (PRE-1830) SOURCES

d'Alembert, Jean le Rond. *Œuvres* (5 vols., Paris, 1821–2).
—— *Preliminary Discourse to the Encyclopedia* (trans. R. N. Schwab, New York, 1963).
Bossuet, Jacques Bénigne. *Discours sur l'histoire universelle* (2 vols., Paris, 1823).
Burke, Edmund. *Reflections on the French Revolution* (London, 1955).
Condillac, Etienne Bonnot de. *Traité des sensations: Première partie* (Paris, 1893).
Condorcet, Marie Jean Antoine Nicolas Caritat de. *Œuvres complètes* (21 vols., Paris, 1804).
Descartes, René. *Discours de la Méthode* (ed. E. Gilson, Paris, 1947).
Diderot, Denis. *Œuvres complètes* (ed. J. Assézat and M. Tourneux, 20 vols., Paris, 1875–7).
Droz, Jacques (ed.). *Le romantisme politique en Allemagne* (Paris, 1963).
Eckermann, J. P. *Gespräche mit Goethe* (Wiesbaden, 1955).
Encyclopédie ou Dictionnaire raisonné des arts, des sciences et des métiers (17 vols., Paris, 1751–65).
Fichte, Immanuel Hermann. *J. G. Fichtes Leben und literarischer Briefwechsel* (2 vols., Sulzbach, 1830).
Fichte, Johann Gottlieb. *Nachgelassene Werke* (ed. I. H. Fichte, 3 vols., Bonn, 1834–5).
—— *Sämmtliche Werke* (ed. I. H. Fichte, 8 vols., Berlin, 1845–6).
—— *Addresses to the German Nation* (ed. G. A. Kelly, New York, 1968).
—— *New Exposition of the Science of Knowledge* (trans. A. E. Kroeger, St. Louis, 1869).
—— *Philosophy of Masonry: Letters to Constant* (ed. Roscoe Pound, Seattle, 1945).
—— *The Popular Writings of Johann Gottlieb Fichte* (trans. William Smith, 2 vols., London, 1889).
—— *The Science of Ethics* (trans. A. E. Kroeger, London, 1907).
—— *The Science of Rights* (trans. A. E. Kroeger, London, 1889).
—— *Fichtes Briefwechsel* (ed. H. Schulz, 2 vols., Leipzig, 1925).
Fontenelle, Bernard le Bovier de. *Œuvres* (11 vols., Paris, 1766).
Goethe, Johann Wolfgang von. *Faust* (Part II abridged, trans. Walter Kaufmann, New York, 1963).

363

Bibliography

—— *Gespräche mit Goethe.* See J. P. Eckermann.

—— *Poetry and Truth* (trans. Minna Steele Smith, 2 vols., London, 1908).

Hegel, Georg Wilhelm Friedrich. *Sämtliche Werke* (ed. H. Glockner, 26 vols., Stuttgart, 1927–40).

—— *Berliner Schriften* (ed. J. Hoffmeister, Hamburg, 1956).

—— *Briefe von und an Hegel* (ed. J. Hoffmeister, 4 vols., Hamburg, 1952).

—— *Dokumente zu Hegels Entwicklung* (ed. J. Hoffmeister, Stuttgart, 1936).

—— *Einleitung in die Geschichte der Philosophie* (ed. J. Hoffmeister, Hamburg, 1959).

—— *Enzyklopädie der philosophischen Wissenschaften* (1830 edition, ed. F. Nicolin and O. Pöggeler, Hamburg, 1959).

—— *Erste Drückschriften* (ed. G. Lasson, Berlin, 1911).

—— *Grundlinien der Philosophie des Rechts* (ed. J. Hoffmeister, Hamburg, 1955).

—— *Jenenser Realphilosophie: 1805–6* (ed. J. Hoffmeister, Leipzig, 1931).

—— *Logik* (ed. G. Lasson, 2 vols., Hamburg, 1948).

—— *Nürnberger Schriften* (ed. J. Hoffmeister, Leipzig, 1938).

—— *Die Phänomenologie des Geistes* (ed. J. Hoffmeister, Hamburg, 1952).

—— *Schriften zur Politik und Rechtsphilosophie* (ed. G. Lasson, Leipzig, 1913).

—— *Theologische Jugendschriften* (ed. H. Nohl, Tübingen, 1907).

—— *Die Vernunft in der Geschichte* (ed. J. Hoffmeister, Hamburg, 1955).

—— *Vorlesungen über die Philosophie der Weltgeschichte* (ed. G. Lasson, 4 vols., Leipzig, 1944).

—— *Friedrich Hegel on Christianity: Early Theological Writings* (ed. T. M. Knox, introd. Richard Kroner, New York, 1961).

—— *Lectures on the History of Philosophy* (trans. E. S. Haldane and F. H. Simpson, 3 vols., London, 1892–6).

—— *The Phenomenology of Mind* (trans. J. Baillie, London, 1949).

—— *The Philosophy of History* (trans. J. Sibree, New York, 1956).

—— *The Philosophy of Right* (ed. and trans. T. M. Knox, Oxford, 1962).

—— *Political Writings* (trans. T. M. Knox, introductory essay by Z. A. Pelczynski, Oxford, 1964).

Helvétius, Claude-Adrien. *De l'Esprit* (Paris, 1845).

Herder, Johann Gottfried von. *Sämmtliche Werke* (ed. B. Suphan, 33 vols., Berlin, 1877–1913).

—— *Ideen zur Philosophie der Geschichte der Menschheit* (2 vols., Leipzig, 1828).

Bibliography

Hölderlin, Friedrich. *Sämtliche Werke und Briefe* (ed. Zinkernagel, 5 vols., Leipzig, 1914–26).

Hume, David. *Moral and Political Philosophy* (ed. Henry Aiken, New York, 1948).

Kant, Immanuel. *Gesammelte Schriften* (24 vols., Berlin, 1902–64).
—— *Critique of Judgment* (trans. J. H. Bernard, London, 1931).
—— *Critique of Practical Reason* (ed. and trans. L. W. Beck, New York, 1956).
—— *Critique of Pure Reason* (trans. N. Kemp Smith, New York, 1963).
—— *The Doctrine of Virtue* (ed. and trans. M. J. Gregor, New York, 1964).
—— *Fundamental Principles of the Metaphysics of Morals* (trans. Thomas K. Abbott, New York, 1949).
—— *Kant on History* (ed. L. W. Beck, New York, 1963).
—— *The Metaphysical Elements of Justice* (trans. John Ladd, New York, 1965).
—— *The Philosophy of Kant* (ed. C. J. Friedrich, New York, 1949).
—— *Religion Within the Limits of Reason Alone* (ed. T. M. Greene and H. H. Hudson, New York, 1960).

Klopstock, Friedrich Gottlieb. *Die deutsche Gelehrtenrepublik* (Hamburg, 1774).

La Bruyère, Jean de. *Les Caractères* (2 vols., Paris, 1871).

Lessing, Gotthold Ephraim. *Education of the Human Race* (trans. J. D. Haney, New York, 1908).

Locke, John. *An Essay Concerning Human Understanding* (ed. A. Campbell Fraser, 2 vols., New York, 1959).

Mautner, Fritz (ed.). *Jacobis Spinoza Büchlein* (Munich, 1912).

Mercier, Sébastien. *De J.-J. Rousseau considéré comme l'un des premiers auteurs de la Révolution* (2 vols., Paris, 1791).

Montaigne, Michel de. *Essays* (trans. E. J. Trechmann, New York, 1946).

Montesquieu, Charles-Louis Secondat de. *Œuvres complètes*, vol. 1 (ed. R. Caillois, Paris, 1949).
—— *De l'Esprit des lois* (ed. G. Truc, 2 vols., Paris, 1956).
—— *Lettres persanes* (ed. G. Truc, Paris, 1946).

Mounier, J.-J. *De l'influence attribuée aux philosophes, aux francs-maçons et aux illuminés sur la Révolution française* (Paris, 1822).

Mueller, G. E. (ed.). *Encyclopedia of Philosophy by Hegel* (New York, 1959).

Novalis (Friedrich von Hardenberg). *Gesammelte Werke* (ed. C. Seelig, 5 vols., Herrliberg–Zurich, 1943).

Bibliography

Oelsner, Karl Engelbert. *Charles Engelbert Oelsner: Notice biographique, accompagnée de fragments de ses mémoires rélatifs à l'histoire de la Révolution française* (ed. A. Stern, Paris, 1905).

Pascal, Blaise. *Pensées et opuscules* (ed. L. Brunschvicg, Paris, 1912).

Pestalozzi, Heinrich. *Sämmelte Werke* (ed. Dejung and Schönebaum, 21 vols., Berlin and Leipzig; Zurich, 1927–64).

Rehberg, August-Wilhelm. *Untersuchungen über die französische Revolution* (2 vols., Hanover and Osnabrück, 1793).

Robespierre, Maximilien. 'Le Défenseur de la Constitution', *Œuvres Complètes*, IV (Société des Etudes robespierristes, Nancy, 1939).

—— 'Lettres à ses commetans', *Œuvres complètes*, V (Société des Etudes robespierristes, Nancy, 1961).

Rousseau, Jean-Jacques. *Œuvres complètes* (ed. B. Gagnebin and M. Raymond, 3 vols., Paris, 1959–64).

—— *Œuvres de Jean-Jacques Rousseau* (ed. Didier, 17 vols., Paris, 1834).

—— *Emile ou de l'éducation* (ed. F. and P. Richard, Paris, 1961).

—— *The Political Writings of Jean-Jacques Rousseau* (ed. C. E. Vaughan, 2 vols., New York, 1962).

—— *Corréspondance générale de Jean-Jacques Rousseau* (ed. T. Dufour, 21 vols., Paris, 1924–32).

St.-Just, Louis Antoine Léon de. *Œuvres* (ed. J. Gratien, Paris, 1946).

St.-Pierre, Charles Irénée Castel de. *Nouveau plan de gouvernement des Etats souverains* (Rotterdam, 1738).

Schelling, Friedrich Wilhelm Joseph von. *Sämmtliche Werke* (14 vols., Stuttgart and Augsburg, 1856–61).

—— *The Ages of the World* (trans. F. Bolman, New York, 1942).

—— *Of Human Freedom* (trans. and intr. James Guttmann, Chicago, 1936).

Schiller, Johann Cristoph Friedrich von. *Sämtliche Werke* (ed. C. Höfer, 22 vols., Munich and Leipzig; Berlin, n.d.).

—— *Schillers Persönlichkeit* (ed. Hecker and Petersen, 3 vols., Weimar, 1904–8).

—— *The Aesthetic Letters, Essays, and the Philosophical Letters* (trans. J. Weiss, Boston, 1845).

Schleiermacher, Friedrich. *On Religion* (New York, 1958).

Staël, Anne-Louise Germaine de. *Considérations sur la Révolution française* (2 vols., Paris, 1862).

—— *De l'Allemagne* (Paris, 1871).

Voltaire, François-Marie Arouet de. *Œuvres complètes* (52 vols., Paris, 1877–82).

Bibliography

B. SECONDARY SOURCES (BOOKS)

Althusser, Louis, *et al. Lire le Capital* (2 vols., Paris, 1966).

Anderson, E. N. *Nationalism and the Cultural Crisis in Prussia, 1806–15* (New York, 1939).

Aris, Reinhold. *History of Political Thought in Germany, from 1789 to 1815* (London, 1936).

Aron, Raymond. *La théorie de l'histoire dans l'Allemagne contemporaine* (Paris, 1938).

Asveld, Paul. *La pensée religieuse du jeune Hegel: Liberté et aliénation* (Louvain and Paris, 1953).

Aulard, Auguste. *L'éloquence parlementaire pendant la Révolution française: Les orateurs de la Législative et de la Convention* (2 vols., Paris, 1885).

Bach, Roman Ludwig. *Die Entwicklung der französischen Geschichtsauffassung im XVIII. Jahrhundert* (Bruchsal, 1933).

Baldwin, James Mark (ed.). *Dictionary of Philosophy and Psychology* (2 vols., New York, 1940).

Barnard, Henry. *Pestalozzi and his Educational System* (New York, 1881).

Barth, Hans. *Pestalozzis Philosophie der Politik* (Zurich, 1954).

Barzun, Jacques. *The French Race* (New York, 1932).

Basch, Victor. *Les doctrines politiques des philosophes classiques de l'Allemagne* (Paris, 1927).

Beck, Louis White. *A Commentary on Kant's Critique of Practical Reason* (Chicago, 1963).

Bergmann, Ernst. *J. G. Fichte der Erzieher* (2nd ed., Leipzig, 1928).

Berlin, Isaiah. *Historical Inevitability* (London, 1954).

Borries, Kurt. *Kant als Politiker* (Leipzig, 1928).

Boucher, Maurice. *La Révolution de 1789 vue par les écrivains allemands, ses contemporains* (Paris, 1954).

—— *Le sentiment national en Allemagne* (Paris, 1947).

Bourke, Vernon J. *Will in Western Thought* (New York, 1964).

Braune, F. *Edmund Burke in Deutschland* (Heidelberg, 1917).

Bréhier, Emile. *Histoire de la Philosophie*, vol. II, 3 of *La philosophie moderne* (Paris, 1932).

Bruford, W. H. *Culture and Society in Classical Weimar, 1775–1806* (Cambridge, 1962).

—— *Germany in the Eighteenth Century: The Social Background of the Literary Revival* (Cambridge, 1965).

Bruno, Antonino. *Illuminismo e romanticismo in Rousseau e Hegel* (Bari, 1953).

Bibliography

Brunschwig, Henry. *La crise de l'Etat prussien à la fin du XVIIIe siècle* (Paris, 1947).

Buber, Martin. *Paths in Utopia* (London, 1949).

Burdeau, Georges. *Traité de Science Politique, V: L'Etat libéral et les techniques politiques de la démocratie gouvernée* (Paris, 1953).

Bury, J. B. *The Idea of Progress* (London, 1920).

Butler, E. M. *The Tyranny of Greece over Germany* (Cambridge, 1935).

Cairns, Huntington. *Legal Philosophy from Plato to Hegel* (Baltimore, 1949).

Carré de Malberg, Raymond. *Contributions à la théorie générale de l'Etat* (2 vols., Paris, 1920–2).

Cassirer, Ernst. *Kants Leben und Lehre* (Berlin, 1921).

—— *The Myth of the State* (New Haven, 1946).

—— *The Philosophy of the Enlightenment* (trans. F. C. A. Koeller and J. P. Pettegrove, Boston, 1964).

—— *The Question of Jean-Jacques Rousseau* (trans., intro. Peter Gay, Bloomington, 1963).

—— *Rousseau, Kant, Goethe* (Princeton, 1947).

Champion, Edme. *J.-J. Rousseau et la Révolution française* (Paris, 1909).

Chappelle, Albert. *Hegel et la religion* (Paris, 1963).

Chinard, Gilbert. *L'Amérique et le rêve exotique dans la littérature française au XVIIe et au XVIIIe siècle* (Paris, 1934).

Cobban, Alfred. *Rousseau and the Modern State* (London, 1934).

Cohn, Norman. *The Pursuit of the Millenium* (New York, 1961).

Collingwood, R. G. *The Idea of History* (Oxford, 1946).

Composto, Renato. *La quarta critica kantiana* (Palermo, 1954).

Copleston, Frederick, S.J. *A History of Philosophy*, vol. VII, Part One: *Fichte to Hegel* (New York, 1963).

Croce, Benedetto. *History as the Story of Liberty* (trans. Sylvia Sprigge, London, 1941).

—— Hartmann, N. *et al. Etudes sur Hegel* (special number of *Revue de métaphysique et de morale*, Paris, 1931).

Delbos, Victor. *De Kant aux postkantiens* (Paris, 1940).

—— *La philosophie pratique de Kant* (Paris, 1905).

Delvaille, Jules. *Essai sur l'histoire de l'idée de progrès* (Paris, 1910).

Derathé, Robert. *Jean-Jacques Rousseau et la science politique de son temps* (Paris, 1950).

—— *Le rationalisme de J.-J. Rousseau* (Paris, 1948).

Deregibus, Arturo. *Il problema morale in Jean-Jacques Rousseau e la validità dell'interpretazione kantiana* (Turin, 1957).

Bibliography

Dilthey, Wilhelm. *Die Jugendgeschichte Hegels*. In *Gesammelte Schriften*, IV (Leipzig and Berlin, 1921).

Doren, Alfred. *Wünschräume und Wünschzeiten* (Leipzig, 1924–5).

Droz, Jacques. *L'Allemagne et la Révolution française* (Paris, 1949).

Dunan, Marcel. *L'Allemagne de la Révolution et de l'Empire* (Cours de Sorbonne, Paris, n.d.).

Duncan, A. R. *Practical Reason and Morality* (Edinburgh, 1957).

Duproix, Paul. *Kant et Fichte et le problème de l'éducation* (Geneva, 1895).

Durkheim, Emile. *Montesquieu and Rousseau: Forerunners of Sociology* (Ann Arbor, 1965).

Duveau, Georges. *Sociologie de l'Utopie* (Paris, 1961).

Engelbrecht, H. C. *Johann Gottlieb Fichte* (New York, 1933).

Faguet, Emile. *La politique comparée de Montesquieu, de Voltaire et de Rousseau* (Paris, 1883).

Fester, Richard. *Rousseau und die deutsche Geschichtsphilosophie* (Stuttgart, 1890).

Fetscher, Iring. *Rousseaus politische Philosophie* (Neuwied, 1960).

Findlay, J. N. *Hegel: A Re-examination* (New York, 1962).

Fleischmann, Eugène. *La philosophie politique de Hegel* (Paris, 1964).

Flint, Robert. *The Philosophy of History in France and Germany* (London, 1874).

Foster, Michael B. *The Political Philosophies of Plato and Hegel* (Oxford, 1935).

Fraisse, Paul. *The Psychology of Time* (trans. Jennifer Leith, New York, 1963).

Freyer, Hans. *Die politische Insel* (Leipzig, 1936).

Friedrich, Carl J. *Inevitable Peace* (Cambridge, Mass., 1948).

—— (ed.). *Nomos II: Community* (New York, 1959).

Gay, Peter. *The Enlightenment: An Interpretation* (New York, 1966).

—— *The Party of Humanity* (New York, 1964).

Giese, Gerhardt. *Hegels Staatsidee und der Begriff der Staatserziehung* (Halle, 1926).

Godechot, Jacques. *La contre-révolution, 1789–1804* (Paris, 1961).

Goetz-Bernstein, H. A. *La politique extérieure de Brissot et des Girondins* (Paris, 1912).

Gooch, George P. *Germany and the French Revolution* (London, New York, 1920).

Gray, J. Glenn. *Hegel's Hellenic Ideal* (New York, 1941).

Grégoire, Franz. *Etudes hégéliennes: les points capitaux du système* (Louvain and Paris, 1958).

Bibliography

Groethuysen, Bernard. *J.-J. Rousseau* (Paris, 1949).
—— *Philosophie de la Révolution française* (Paris, 1956).
Gueroult, Martial. *L'évolution et la structure de la Doctrine de la Science chez Fichte* (2 vols., Paris, 1930).
Gurvitch, Georges (Georg Gurwitsch). *Fichtes System der Konkreten Ethik* (Tübingen, 1924).
—— *L'Idée de droit social* (Paris, 1932).
—— *The Spectrum of Social Time* (Dordrecht, 1964).
Haering, Theodor. *Hegel, sein Wollen und sein Werk* (2 vols., Leipzig and Berlin, 1929–38).
Hatfield, Henry. *Aesthetic Paganism in German Literature* (Cambridge, Mass., 1964).
Havet, Jacques. *Kant et le problème du temps* (Paris, 1947).
Hayes, Carleton J. H. *The Historical Evolution of Modern Nationalism* (New York, 1931).
Haym, Rudolf. *Hegel und seine Zeit* (1857; photo-reprint Hildesheim, 1962).
Haymann, Franz. *Weltbürgertum und Vaterlandsliebe in der Staatslehre Rousseaus und Fichtes* (Berlin, 1924).
Hazard, Paul. *La crise de la conscience européenne, 1680–1715* (Paris, 1961).
Hendel, Charles William. *Jean-Jacques Rousseau, Moralist* (2 vols., London and New York, 1934).
Hirsch, Emanuel. *Christentum und Geschichte in Fichtes Philosophie* (Tübingen, 1920).
Hobhouse, Leonard T. *The Metaphysical Theory of the State : A Criticism* (London, 1960).
Hobsbawm, E. J. *The Age of Revolution, 1789–1848* (New York, 1964).
Hoffmeister, Johannes. *Hölderlin und Hegel in Frankfurt* (Tübingen, 1931).
Hubert, René. *Rousseau et l'Encyclopédie* (Paris, 1928).
—— *Les sciences sociales dans l'Encyclopédie* (Paris, 1923).
Hyppolite, Jean. *Etudes sur Marx et Hegel* (Paris, 1955).
—— *Genèse et structure de la Phénoménologie de l'Esprit de Hegel* (2 vols., Paris, 1946).
Jaspers, Karl. *Kant* (ed. H. Arendt, New York, 1962).
Jean-Jacques Rousseau et son œuvre (Symposium, Paris, 1964).
Jouvenel, Bertrand de. *Sovereignty : An Inquiry into the Political Good* (trans. J. F. Huntington, Chicago, 1957).
Kateb, George. *Utopia and its Enemies* (New York, 1963).
Kaufmann, Walter A. *Hegel* (New York, 1965).

Bibliography

Kesting, Hanno. *Geschichtsphilosophie und Weltbürgerkrieg* (Heidelberg, 1959).

Kojève, Alexandre. *Introduction à la lecture de Hegel* (ed. Raymond Queneau, Paris, 1947).

Korff, H. A. *Humanismus und Romantik* (Leipzig, 1924).

Kroner, Richard. *Von Kant bis Hegel* (2 vols. in 1, Tübingen, 1961).

Kuhn, Hans Wolfgang. *Der Apokalyptiker und die Politik: Studien zur Staatsphilosophie des Novalis* (Freiburg, 1961).

Lacherrière, René de. *Etudes sur la théorie démocratique* (Paris, 1963).

Lanson, Gustave. *Histoire de la littérature française* (Paris, 1895).

Lask, Emil. *Fichtes Idealismus und die Geschichte* (Tübingen, 1914).

Lavelle, Louis. *Du temps et de l'éternité* (Paris, 1945).

Lefebvre, Georges. *Etudes sur la Révolution française* (Paris, 1963).

—— *The French Revolution from its Origins to 1793* (trans. E. M. Evanson, New York, 1962).

LeFlamanc, Auguste. *Les utopies pré-révolutionnaires* (Paris, 1934).

Léon, Xavier. *Fichte et son temps* (3 vols., Paris, 1922–7).

—— *La philosophie de Fichte* (Paris, 1902).

Leroy, Maxime. *Histoire des idées sociales en France;* vol. 1: *De Montesquieu à Robespierre* (Paris, 1946).

Lévi, Anthony. *French Moralists* (Oxford, 1964).

Löwenstein, Julius. *Hegels Staatsidee: Ihr Doppelgesicht und ihr Einfluss im XIX. Jahrhundert* (Berlin, 1927).

Löwith, Karl. *From Hegel to Nietzsche* (trans. David E. Green, New York, 1964).

—— *Meaning in History* (Chicago, 1949).

Lübke, Hermann (ed.). *Die Hegelsche Recht* (Stuttgart–Bad Cannstatt, 1962).

Maier, Josef. *On Hegel's Critique of Kant* (New York, 1939).

Mannheim, Karl. *Ideology and Utopia* (New York, 1936).

Manuel, Frank E. *The New World of Henri Saint-Simon* (Cambridge, Mass., 1956).

—— *Shapes of Philosophical History* (Stanford, 1965).

Marcuse, Herbert. *Reason and Revolution* (2nd ed., Boston, 1960).

Margenau, Henry. *Ethics and Science* (Princeton, 1964).

Mathiez, Albert. *Girondins et Montagnards* (Paris, 1921).

—— *La révolution française et les étrangers* (Paris, 1918).

Maurer, Reinhard Klemens. *Hegel und das Ende der Geschichte* (Stuttgart, 1965).

Meinecke, Friedrich. *Die Entstehung des Historismus* (2 vols., Munich and Berlin, 1936).

371

Bibliography

Meinecke, Friedrich. *Weltbürgertum und Nationalstaat* (Munich and Berlin, 1919).

Meinhold, Peter. *Rousseaus Geschichtsphilosophie* (Tübingen, 1936).

Metzger, Wolfgang, *Gesellschaft, Recht und Staat in der Ethik des deutschen Idealismus* (Heidelberg, 1917).

Meyerhoff, Hans (ed.). *The Philosophy of History in our Time* (New York, 1959).

Meynier, Albert. *Jean-Jacques Rousseau révolutionnaire* (Paris, 1912).

Michon, Georges. *Robespierre et la guerre révolutionnaire, 1791–2* (Paris, 1937).

Montgomery, Marshall. *Friedrich Hölderlin and the German Neo-Hellenic Movement* (London, 1923).

Mornet, Daniel. *Les origines intellectuelles de la Révolution française* (5th ed., Paris, 1954).

Mucchiélli, Roger. *Le mythe de la cité idéale* (Paris, 1960).

Münch, Fritz. *Erlebnis und Geltung: eine systematische Untersuchung zur Transzendentalphilosophie als Weltanschauung. Kant-Studien*, Ergänzungsheft No. 30 (1913).

Mumford, Lewis. *The City in History* (New York, 1951).

—— *et al.* 'Special Number: Utopia', *Daedalus*, Spring 1965.

Mure, G. R. G. *The Philosophy of Hegel* (London, 1965).

—— *A Study of Hegel's Logic* (Oxford, 1950).

Negley, Glenn and Patrick, J. Max (eds.). *The Quest for Utopia* (New York, 1962).

Nicolin, Friedhelm. *Hegels Bildungstheorie* (Bonn, 1955).

Palmer, R. R. *Twelve Who Ruled* (Princeton, 1941).

Parker, Harold T. *The Cult of Antiquity and the French Revolution* (Chicago, 1937).

Pascal, Roy. *The German Sturm und Drang* (Manchester, 1953).

Paulsen, Friedrich. *Geschichte des gelehrten Unterrichts auf den deutschen Schulen und Universitäten* (2 vols., Leipzig, 1896–7).

Pepper, Stephen C. *World Hypotheses: A Study in Evidence* (Berkeley and Los Angeles, 1957).

Philonenko, Alexis. *La liberté humaine dans la philosophie de Fichte* (Paris, 1966).

Pieper, Josef. *The End of Time* (trans. Michael Bullock, London, 1954).

Pinloche, A. *La Réforme de l'Education en Allemagne au dix-huitième siècle : Basedow et le philanthropisme* (Paris, 1889).

Polak, F. L. *The Image of the Future*, vol. 1: *The Promised Land, Source of Living Culture* (New York and Leyden, 1961).

Bibliography

Poulet, Georges. *Etudes sur le temps humain* (Paris, 1949).

—— *Les métamorphoses du cercle* (Paris, 1961).

Proust, Jacques. *Diderot et l'Encyclopédie* (Paris, 1962).

Ravier, André. *L'éducation de l'Homme nouveau* (2 vols., Lyons, 1941).

Rehm, W. *Griechentum und Goethezeit* (Bern, 1952).

Reidt, Konrad. *Das Nationale und das Übernationale bei Fichte unter besonderen Berücksichtigen seiner Pädagogik* (Giessen, 1926).

Reynaud, L. *Histoire générale de l'influence Française en Allemagne* (Paris, 1915).

Rodman, John R. *The Rational State: Hegel's Political Philosophy in the Context of its Time* (Harvard University Ph.D. thesis, September 1958).

Rosenkranz, Karl. *Georg Wilhelm Friedrich Hegels Leben* (1844; photo-reprint, Darmstadt, 1963).

Rosenzweig, Franz. *Hegel und der Staat* (Munich–Berlin, 1920).

Rouché, Max. *La philosophie de l'histoire de Herder* (Paris, 1940).

Rudé, George. *Revolutionary Europe, 1783–1815* (New York, 1964).

Ruyer, Raymond. *L'utopie et les utopies* (Paris, 1950).

Sacheli, C. A. *Rousseau* (Messina, 1942).

Schargo, Nellie Noémie. *History in the Encyclopedia* (New York, 1947).

Schinz, Albert. *Etat présent des travaux sur Jean-Jacques Rousseau* (New York and Paris, 1941).

——*La pensée de Jean-Jacques Rousseau* (Paris, 1929).

Sénelier, Jean. *Bibliographie générale des œuvres de J.-J. Rousseau* (Paris, 1949).

Seznec, Jean. *Essais sur Diderot et l'Antiquité* (Oxford, 1957).

Shklar, Judith N. *After Utopia: The Decline of Political Faith* (Princeton, 1957).

—— (ed.). *Political Theory and Ideology* (New York, 1966).

Sieben, E. *Die Idee des Kleinstaats bei den Denkern des XVIII. Jahrhunderts* (Basel, 1920).

Simon, Walter M. *The Failure of the Prussian Reform Movement* (Ithaca, 1955).

Smith, D. W. *Helvétius: A Study in Persecution* (Oxford, 1965).

Soboul, Albert. *Précis d'histoire de la Révolution française* (Paris, 1962).

—— *Les sans-culottes parisiens en l'an II* (Paris, 1962).

Sorokin, Pitirim A. *Sociocultural Causality, Space, Time* (Durham, 1943).

Spenlé, J. E. *La pensée allemande de Luther à Nietzsche* (Paris, 1934).

Spink, John Stephenson. *Jean-Jacques Rousseau et Genève* (Paris, 1934).

Stadelmann, Rudolf. *Der historische Sinn bei Herder* (Tübingen, 1925).

Starobinski, Jean. *Jean-Jacques Rousseau: la transparence et l'obstacle* (Paris, 1958).

Stein, Lorenz von. *History of the Social Movement in France* (ed., trans. Kaethe Mengelberg, Totowa, N.J., 1964).

Stern, Alfred. *Die Einfluss der französischen Revolution auf das deutsche Geistesleben* (Stuttgart and Berlin, 1928).

—— *Philosophy of History and the Problem of Values* ('s Gravenhage, 1962).

Strauss, Leo. *Natural Right and History* (Chicago and London, 1953).

Sydenham, M. J. *The Girondins* (London, 1961).

Sydow, Eckart von. *Der Gedanke des Ideal-Reichs in der idealistischen Philosophie von Kant bis Hegel in Zusammenhange der geschichtsphilosophischen Entwicklung* (Leipzig, 1914).

Taggart, Frederick J. (ed.). *The Idea of Progress* (Berkeley and Los Angeles, 1949).

Talmon, J. L. *The Origins of Totalitarian Democracy* (New York, 1961).

—— *Political Messianism: The Romantic Phase* (London, 1960).

Temmer, Mark J. *Time in Rousseau and Kant* (Geneva and Paris, 1958).

Troeltsch, Ernst. *Der Historismus und seine Probleme* (Tübingen, 1922).

Tuveson, Ernest Lee. *Millennium and Utopia* (Berkeley, 1949).

Utopies à la Renaissance, Les (collection), (Paris and Brussels, 1963).

Vlachos, Georges. *Fédéralisme et raison d'Etat dans la pensée internationale de Fichte* (Paris, 1948).

—— *La pensée politique de Kant* (Paris, 1962).

De Vleeschauwer, Herman-J. *The Development of Kantian Thought* (trans. A. R. C. Duncan, London, 1962).

Vorländer, Karl. *Immanuel Kants Leben* (2 vols., Leipzig, 1921).

—— *Kant, Fichte, Hegel und der Sozialismus* (Berlin, 1920).

Vossler, Otto. *Rousseaus Freiheitslehre* (Göttingen, 1963).

Vuillemin, Jules. *L'héritage kantien et la Révolution copernicienne* (Paris, 1954).

Vyverberg, Henry. *Historical Pessimism in the French Enlightenment* (Cambridge, Mass., 1958).

Wahl, Jean. *Le malheur de la conscience dans la philosophie de Hegel* (Paris, 1951).

Wallner, Nico. *Fichte als politischer Denker* (Halle, 1926).

Walz, Gustav Adolf. *Die Staatsidee des Rationalismus und der Romantik und die Staatsphilosophie Fichtes* (Berlin–Grunewald, 1928).

Weber, Marianne. *Fichtes Sozialismus und sein Verhältnis zur Marxschen Doktrin* (Tübingen, 1900).

Bibliography

Weil, Eric. *Hegel et l'Etat* (Paris, 1950).
—— *Problèmes kantiens* (Paris, 1963).
Wells, G. A. *Herder and After* (The Hague, 1959).
Wichmann, Otto. *Platon und Kant* (Berlin, 1920).
Willey, Basil. *The Eighteenth Century Tradition* (London, 1950).
Windelband, Wilhelm. *Fichtes Idee des deutschen Staates* (Tübingen, 1921).

C. SECONDARY SOURCES (ARTICLES)

Adam, Antoine. 'Rousseau et Diderot', *Revue des sciences humaines* (January–March 1949), 21–34.
Avineri, Shlomo. 'The Hegelian Origins of Marx's Political Thought', *The Review of Metaphysics* (September 1967), 33–56.
Beck, Lewis White. 'Deux concepts kantiens du vouloir', *Annales de philosophie politique*, IV (1962), 119–37.
Benrubi, I. 'Rousseau et le mouvement philosophique et pédagogique en Allemagne', *Annales de la Société Jean-Jacques Rousseau*, VIII (1912), 99–130.
Bobbio, Norberto. 'Deux arguments contre le droit naturel', *Annales de philosophie politique*, III (1959), 175–90.
Chevallier, J.-J. 'J.-J. Rousseau ou l'absolutisme de la volonté générale', *Revue française de science politique* (January–March 1953), 5–30.
Child, Arthur. 'Five Conceptions of History', *Ethics* (October 1957), 28–38.
Chinard, Gilbert. 'Montesquieu's Historical Pessimism', in *Studies in the History of Culture* (Menasha, Wis., 1942).
Choulguine, Alexandre. 'Les origines de l'esprit national moderne et J.-J. Rousseau', *Annales de la société Jean-Jacques Rousseau*, XXVI (1937), 7–283.
Dautry, Jean. 'La politique de Robespierre en 1792', *Annales historiques de la Révolution française* (April–June 1956), 113–38.
Delobel, Georges. 'Fichte et la Révolution française', *Annales révolutionnaires*, IV (1911), 299–320.
Dilthey, Wilhelm. 'Der entwicklungsgeschichtliche Pantheismus nach seinem geschichtlichen Zusammenhang mit den älteren pantheistischen Systemen', *Archiv für Philosophie*, XIII (1900), 3 (307–60); 4 (445–82).
—— 'Fragmente aus Wilhelm Diltheys Hegelwerk. Mitgeteilt von H. Nohl', *Hegel-Studien*, I (1962), 103–34.

Bibliography

Duguit, Léon. 'Jean-Jacques Rousseau, Kant et Hegel', *Revue du droit public et de la Science politique en France et à l'étranger* (April–June 1918), 173–211; (July–September 1918), 325–77.

Durkheim, Emile. 'Le contrat social de Rousseau', *Revue de métaphysique et de morale* (January–February 1918), 1–23; (March–April 1918), 129–61.

d'Entrèves, Alexandre P. 'Le droit naturel', *Annales de philosophie politique*, III (1959), 147–57.

Fabre, Jean. 'Réalité et utopie', *Annales de la société Jean-Jacques Rousseau*, XXXV (1959–62), 181–221.

Fackenheim, Emil L. 'Kant's Concept of History', *Kant-Studien*, XLVIII (1957), 381–98.

Fessard, Georges. 'Deux interprètes de la Phénoménologie de Hegel', *Etudes* (1947), 368–73.

Fetscher, Iring. 'Probleme der Hegelinterpretation', *Philosophische Rundschau* (1954–5), 204–16.

―― 'Rousseau's Concept of Freedom in the Light of his Philosophy of History', *Nomos IV: Liberty* (New York, 1962), 29–56.

Gay, Peter. 'Carl Becker's Heavenly City', *Political Science Quarterly* (June 1957), 182–99.

Gossman, Lionel. 'Time and History in Rousseau', *Studies on Voltaire and the Eighteenth Century* (ed. T. Besterman), XXX (1964), 311–50.

Gouhier, Henri. 'Ce que le vicaire doit à Descartes', *Annales de la société Jean-Jacques Rousseau*, XXXV (1959–62), 139–60.

―― 'Nature et histoire dans la pensée de Jean-Jacques Rousseau', *Annales de la société Jean-Jacques Rousseau*, XXIII (1953–5), 7–48.

Gueroult, Martial. 'Fichte et la Révolution française', *Revue philosophique* (September–December 1939), 226–320.

―― 'Fichte et Xavier Léon', *Revue philosophique* (April–June 1946), 170–207.

―― 'Nature humaine et état de nature chez Rousseau, Kant et Fichte', *Revue philosophique* (September–December 1941), 379–97.

Gurvitch, Georges (Gurwitsch). 'Kant und Fichte als Rousseau-Interpreten', *Kant-Studien*, XXVII (1929), 138–64.

Hassner, Pierre. 'Les concepts de guerre et de paix chez Kant', *Revue française de science politique* (September 1961), 642–70.

Haymann, Franz. 'La loi naturelle dans la philosophie politique de J.-J. Rousseau', *Annales de la société Jean-Jacques Rousseau*, XXX (1943–45), 65–110.

Bibliography

Heidegger, Martin. 'Hegel und die Griechen', in *Die Gegenwart der Griechen im neueren Denken* (Tübingen, 1960), 43–58.

Hiebel, F. 'The Modern View of Hellas and German Romanticism', *Germanic Review* (Fall 1954), 31–9.

Hirsch, Emanuel. 'Rousseaus Geschichtsphilosophie', in *Rechtsidee und Staatsgedanke: Beiträge zur Rechtsphilosophie und zur politischen Ideengeschichte* (ed. K. Larenz, Berlin, 1930), 223–42.

Höffding, Harald. 'Rousseaus Einfluss auf die definitive Form der Kantischen Ethik', *Kant-Studien*, II (1898), 11–21.

Hoffmann, Stanley. 'Rousseau on War and Peace', *American Political Science Review* (June 1963), 317–33.

Hook, Sidney. 'Hegel Rehabilitated?' *Encounter* (January 1965), 53–8.

Hubert, René. 'Essai sur l'histoire de l'idée de progrès', *Revue d'Histoire de la Philosophie et d'Histoire générale* (15 October 1934), 289–305; (15 January 1935), 1–32.

—— 'La notion du devenir historique dans la philosophie de Montesquieu', *Revue de métaphysique et de morale* (October 1939), 587–610.

Hyppolite, Jean. 'La signification de la Révolution française dans la 'Phénoménologie' de Hegel', *Revue philosophique* (December 1939), 399–426.

—— 'Les travaux de jeunesse de Hegel d'après les ouvrages récents', *Revue de métaphysique et de morale* (July 1935), 399–426; (October 1935), 549–77.

Jankélévitch, S. 'Du rôle des idées dans l'évolution des sociétés', *Revue philosophique* (September 1908), 256–80.

Jimack, P. D. 'Rousseau and the Primacy of Self', *Studies on Voltaire and the Eighteenth Century* (ed. T. Besterman), XXXII (1965), 73–90.

Jouvenel, Bertrand de. 'Essai sur la politique de Rousseau', introd. to *Du Contrat Social* (Geneva, 1947), 15–160.

—— 'L'Idée de Droit naturel', *Annales de philosophie politique*, III (1959), 159–74.

Kafka, Gustav. 'Erlebnis und Theorie in Fichtes Lehre vom Verhältnis der Geschlechten', *Zeitschrift für angewandte Psychologie*, XVI (1920), 1–24.

Kantorowicz, Hermann U. 'Volksgeist und historische Rechtsschule', *Historische Zeitschrift*, CVIII (1912), 295–326.

Kaufmann, Walter A. 'The Hegel Myth and its Method', *Philosophical Review* (October 1951), 459–86.

Kelly, George Armstrong. 'Notes on Hegel's "Lordship and Bondage",' *The Review of Metaphysics* (June 1966), 780–802.

Knox, T. M. 'Hegel's Attitude to Kant's Ethics', *Kant-Studien*, XLIX (1957), 70–81.

Koyré, A. 'Hegel à Iéna', *Revue d'histoire et de philosophie religieuses* (September–October 1935), 420–58.

—— 'Note sur la langue et la terminologie hégéliennes', *Revue philosophique* (November–December 1931), 409–39.

Krieger, Leonard. 'Kant and the Crisis of Natural Law', *Journal of the History of Ideas* (April–June 1965), 191–210.

Kroner, Richard. 'System und Geschichte bei Hegel', *Logos*, XX (1931), 243–58.

Lacherrière, René de. 'J.-J. Rousseau: Interprétation et permanence', *Revue du droit public et de la science politique* (1961), 469–531.

Lanson, Gustave. 'L'unité de la pensée de Rousseau', *Annales de la société Jean-Jacques Rousseau*, VIII (1912), 1–31.

Lapassade, G. 'L'œuvre de J.-J. Rousseau: Structure et unité', *Revue de métaphysique et de morale* (July–December 1956), 386–402.

Larenz, Karl. 'Staat und Religion bei Hegel', in *Rechtsidee und Staatsgedanke: Beiträge zur Rechtsphilosophie und zur politischen Ideengeschichte* (Berlin, 1930), 243–63.

Leeuw, G. van der. 'Primordial Time and Final Time', in *Papers from the Eranos Yearbook*, III (ed. Joseph Campbell, New York, 1957), 324–50.

Léon, Paul-L. 'L'idée de la volonté générale et ses antécédents historiques', *Archives de philosophie du droit et de sociologie juridique* (1936), 148–200.

Lévy-Bruhl, L. 'The Cartesian Spirit and History', in *Philosophy and History: The Ernst Cassirer Festschrift* (ed. R. Klibansky and H. J. Paton, New York, 1963), 191–6.

Löwith, Karl. 'Hegels Aufhebung der christlichen Religion', *Hegel-Studien*, I (1962), 193–236.

Lovejoy, Albert O. 'The Supposed Primitivism of Rousseau's Discourse on Inequality', in *Essays in the History of Ideas* (New York, 1960), 14–37.

——'Herder and the Enlightenment', in *Ibid.* 166–82.

Lübke, H. 'Philosophiegeschichte als Philosophie: Zu Kants Philosophiegeschichtsphilosophie', in *Einsichten: G. Krüger Festschrift* (Frankfurt a/M, 1962), 204–29.

Mannheim, Karl. 'Das konservative Denken', *Archiv für Sozialwissenschaft und Sozialpolitik* (February 1927), 68–142; (April 1927), 470–95.

Marcuse, Herbert. 'Aus Wahrheitsproblem der soziologischen Methode', *Die Gesellschaft*, X (October 1929), 356–69.

Bibliography

Marx, Karl. 'Critique of the Hegelian Dialectic and Philosophy as a Whole', in *The Economic and Philosophical Manuscripts of 1844* (ed. D. J. Struik, New York, 1964), 170–93.

—— 'Zur Kritik der Hegelschen Rechtsphilosophie', in Karl Marx–Friedrich Engels, *Werke* (39 vols., Berlin, 1957–67), I, 201–333.

Mathiez, Albert. 'Les philosophes et le pouvoir au milieu du XVIIIe siècle', *Annales historiques de la Révolution française* (May–June 1936), 193–203.

McNeil, Gordon H. 'The Anti-Revolutionary Rousseau', *American Historical Review*, LVIII (1953), 808–23.

Morel, Jean. 'Recherches sur les sources du Discours de l'Inégalité', *Annales de la société Jean-Jacques Rousseau*, V (1909), 119–98.

Mornet, Daniel. 'L'influence de J.-J. Rousseau au XVIIIe siècle', *Annales de la société Jean-Jacques Rousseau*, VIII (1912), 33–67.

Mueller, G. E. 'The Legend of "Thesis-Antithesis-Synthesis"', *Journal of the History of Ideas* (June 1958), 411–14.

Muntéano, Basil. 'La solitude de Rousseau', *Annales de la société Jean-Jacques Rousseau*, XXXI (1946–9), 79–169.

Nicolas, Jean. 'Une lettre inédite de Jean-Jacques Rousseau', *Annales historiques de la Révolution française* (October–December 1962), 385–96.

Pappas, John N. 'Berthier's Journal de Trévoux and the Philosophes', *Studies in Voltaire and the Eighteenth Century*, III (Geneva, 1957).

Pariset, Georges. 'L'utopie de deux Lorrains sous Napoléon Ier', in *Etudes d'histoire révolutionnaire et contemporaine* (Paris, 1929), 241–59.

Plessner, Helmuth. 'On the Relation of Time to Death', in *Papers from the Eranos Yearbook*, III (ed. Joseph Campbell, New York, 1957), 233–63.

Pöggeler, Otto. 'Zur Deutung der Phänomenologie des Geistes', *Hegel-Studien*, I (1962), 225–94.

Polin, Raymond. 'Les relations du peuple avec ceux qui le gouvernent dans la politique de Kant', *Annales de philosophie politique*, IV (1962), 163–87.

Proust, Jacques. 'La contribution de Diderot à l'Encyclopédie et les théories du droit naturel', *Annales historiques de la Révolution française* (July–September 1963), 257–86.

Rickert, Heinrich. 'Die philosophischen Grundlagen von Fichtes Sozialismus', *Logos*, XI (1922), 149–80.

Rohrmoser, Günter. 'Hegels Lehre vom Staat und das Problem der

Bibliography

Freiheit in der modernen Gesellschaft', *Der Staat*, IV (1964), 391–404.

Rubenstein, M. 'Die logischen Grundlagen des Hegelschen Systems und das Ende der Geschichte', *Kant-Studien*, XI (1906), 40–108.

Ruyer, Raymond. 'Les limites du progrès humain', *Revue de métaphysique et de morale* (October–December 1958), 412–23.

Ruyssen, Théodore. 'La philosophie de l'histoire selon Kant', *Annales de philosophie politique*, IV (1962), 33–51.

Schnur, R. 'Weltfriedensidee und Weltbürgerkrieg', *Der Staat*, II (1963), 297–317.

Schrecker, Paul. 'Kant et la Révolution française', *Revue philosophique* (September–December 1939), 394–425.

Shklar, Judith N. 'Rousseau's Images of Authority', *American Political Science Review* (December 1964), 919–32.

—— 'Rousseau's Two Models: Sparta and the Age of Gold', *Political Science Quarterly* (March 1966), 25–51.

Sichirollo, Livio. 'Hegel und die griechische Welt: Nachleben der Antike und Entstehung der "Philosophie der Weltgeschichte"', *Hegel-Studien*, II (1963), 263–84.

Silber, John R. 'Kant's Conception of the Highest Good as Immanent and Transcendent', *Philosophical Review* (October 1959), 469–92.

Soboul, Albert. 'Classes populaires et Rousseauisme sous la Révolution', *Annales historiques de la Révolution française* (October–December 1962), 421–38.

—— 'Un manuscrit oublié de Saint-Just', *Annales historiques de la Révolution française* (October–December 1951), 323–59.

Stromberg, R. N. 'History in the Eighteenth Century', *Journal of the History of Ideas* (April 1951), 295–304.

Suter, Jean-François. 'Tradition et révolution', *Hegel-Studien*, I (1962), 307–26.

Tillich, Paul. 'Ideologie und Utopie', *Die Gesellschaft*, X (October 1929), 348–55.

Trevor-Roper, Hugh. 'The Historical Philosophy of the Enlightenment', in T. Bestermann (ed.), *Studies on Voltaire and the Eighteenth Century*, XXVII (Geneva, 1963), 1667–87.

Tubach, Frederic C. 'Perfectibilité: der zweite Diskurs Rousseaus und die deutsche Aufklärung', *Etudes germaniques* (April–June 1960), 144–51.

Vlachos, Georges. 'Dialectique de la liberté et dépérissement de la contrainte chez Fichte', *Archives de philosophie du droit*, VIII (1963), 75–114.

Bibliography

Vlachos, Georges. 'Le droit, la morale et l'expérience dans les écrits révolutionnaires de Fichte', *Archives de philosophie du droit*, VII (1962), 211–45.

Wagar, W. Warren. 'Modern Views of the Origins of the Idea of Progress', *Journal of the History of Ideas* (January–March 1967), 55–70.

Wahl, Jean. 'La bipolarité de Rousseau', *Annales de la société Jean-Jacques Rousseau*, XXXIII (1953–55), 49–55.

Walzer, Michael. 'On the Role of Symbolism in Political Thought', *Political Science Quarterly* (June 1967), 191–204.

INDEX

Index

Mendelssohn, Moses, 131
Mill, John Stuart, 35 n.
Mirabeau, Victor de Riquetti de, 94
Möser, Justus, 79, 248
Mommsen, Theodor, 80
Montagne, 70, 72, 85, 86, 258, 267
Montaigne, Michel de, 28, 37 n.
Mornet, Daniel, 69
Montesquieu, Charles-Louis Secondat de, 35 n., 61, 80–1, 137, 181, 280, 339 n.
Moser, Karl von, 84
Müller, Johannes von, 79
Mumford, Lewis, 39

nature: deduction of nature, 207–9, 223; Enlightenment view, 1; 'end of nature', 142–3, 283; human nature, 2, 7, 38, 51, 81, 108–9, 134–5, 324–5; natural development, 47–9, 55–6, 62, 92–5, 334, 345–6; natural law and right, 52, 54, 159–62, 221–2; nature and evil, 40–1, 54, 111, 291; nature and history, 25–7, 42–3, 58–60, 70–1, 121–2; nature and morality, 60, 89, 91, 100, 113, 132, 171–2, 291, 297, 350; nature and 'unsocial sociability', 121, 134, 152; nature as model, 11, 14, 64, 67–8, 164, 235, 297; nature ordered by man, 139–41, 254; 'second nature', 11–12, 54, 100, 112, 121, 133, 144, 170, 186, 216, 243, 290, 349; 'state of nature', 12, 93, 182, 186, 227, 241, 297; 'voice of nature', 51
Newton, Isaac, 31, 97, 98, 114, 144, 291
Nicolai, Friedrich, 188
Nicholas of Cusa, 29
Niethammer, Friedrich Immanuel, 187, 310
Nietzsche, Friedrich, 152, 339
Novalis (Friedrich von Hardenberg), 1, 201, 297, 349

Oelsner, Karl Engelbert, 86

Paine, Thomas, 85
Peace of Basel, 77, 147, 148
Perret, Commissioner, 195
Pestalozzi, Johann Heinrich, 272–4, 279
phenomenology, 18, 21, 29, 123–4, 214–16, 224, 233, 241, 313–14, 335–8, 342–3
Philonenko, Alexis, 185
Plato, 130–1, 134, 212–13, 270, 278, 321, 344

Pliny, 81
Plutarch, 28, 61
Pope, Alexander, 86
Proclus, 296, 310

Rayneval, Gérard de, 76
Rehberg, August-Wilhelm, 87, 182 n.
Reinhard, Karl Friedrich, 85
Reinhold, Karl Leonard, 187, 194, 195, 197
Richter, Jean-Paul, 194
Robespierre, Maximilien, 69–70, 86, 229
Roman law, 165, 225
Romanticism, 26, 37, 68, 83, 189, 194, 195–6 n., 201, 240, 250
Rosenkranz, Karl, 349
Rousseau, Jean-Jacques: analogies of the state, 11, 14–15, 33–4, 45; anti-teleological, 28, 43; and Corsica, 58–60; Emile, interpretation of, 47–51; and epigones, 69; epistemological position, 33–4, 44, 46–7; and Fichte, see Fichte; freedom and historical pessimism, 25–7, 63; function in this study, 2, 8, 14–16; and Germany, 13, 75–6, 78, 291, 294; and Hegel, see Hegel; history and self-certainty, 32–3, 38–9; and intellectual arrogance, 13, 30–1, 40; and Kant, see Kant; knowledge and corruption, 29–31; legal community, 53–6; man and citizen, 47–9; methodological individualism, 34–5; moral analysis, 35–8, 44–5, 53–4, 336; order, 64–8; and Pestalozzi, 272; and 'phenomenology', 28–9, 359–60; and reason, 36–7, 65, 340; relationship with Switzerland and France, 8–9; and religion, 31, 40; sense of history, 20, 39–40, 50, 64, 71–2, 246, 359–60; truth and existence, 37–8, 56, 65–6; virtue and custom, 58–61
Ruge, Arnold, 357

Saint-Just, Louis Antoine Léon de, 70, 229, 278
St Justin Martyr, 31
Saint-Pierre, Charles Irénée Castel de, 40
Saint-Simon, Henri de, 185, 186, 358
Savigny, Karl Friedrich von, 88
Schelling, Friedrich Wilhelm Joseph von, 83, 164, 189, 192, 194–5, 196, 198, 201, 242, 299–302, 307, 340
Schiller, Johann Cristoph Friedrich von, 50 n., 68–9, 76, 78, 81–2, 84, 85, 87, 192, 194, 201, 242, 249, 297–9, 302, 322, 329

Index

TEXTS

LIBERTY, EQUALITY, FRATERNITY, *by James Fitzjames Stephen.* Edited, with an introduction and notes, by *R. J. White*

VLADIMIR AKIMOV ON THE DILEMMAS OF RUSSIAN MARXISM 1895–1903. An English edition of 'A Short History of the Social Democratic Movement in Russia' and 'The Second Congress of the Russian Social Democratic Labour Party', with an introduction and notes by *Jonathan Frankel*

TWO ENGLISH REPUBLICAN TRACTS. PLATO REDIVIVUS, *by Henry Neville and* AN ESSAY UPON THE CONSTITUTION OF THE ROMAN GOVERNMENT, *by Walter Moyle,* edited with an introduction and notes by *Caroline Robbins*

J. G. HERDER ON SOCIAL AND POLITICAL CULTURE, translated, edited and with an Introduction by *F. M. Barnard*

STUDIES

1867: DISRAELI, GLADSTONE AND REVOLUTION. THE PASSING OF THE SECOND REFORM BILL, *by Maurice Cowling*

THE CONSCIENCE OF THE STATE IN NORTH AMERICA, *by E. R. Norman*

THE SOCIAL AND POLITICAL THOUGHT OF KARL MARX, *by Shlomo Avineri*

MEN AND CITIZENS. A STUDY OF ROUSSEAU'S SOCIAL THEORY, *by Judith N. Shklar*